The Many Sides of
History

The Many Sides of History

Readings in the Western Heritage

VOLUME I

The Ancient World to Early Modern Europe

EDITED BY

Steven Ozment

HARVARD UNIVERSITY

Frank M. Turner

YALE UNIVERSITY

MACMILLAN PUBLISHING COMPANY
NEW YORK

Copyright © 1987, Macmillan Publishing Company,
a division of Macmillan, Inc.

PRINTED IN THE UNITED STATES OF AMERICA

All rights reserved. No part of this book may be reproduced or transmitted in any form or by any means, electronic or mechanical, including photocopying, recording, or any information storage and retrieval system, without permission in writing from the Publisher.

Macmillan Publishing Company
866 Third Avenue, New York, New York 10022

LIBRARY OF CONGRESS CATALOGING-IN-PUBLICATION DATA

The many sides of history.

Contents: v. 1. The ancient world to early modern Europe—v. 2. The seventeenth century to the present.
 1. Europe—History. I. Ozment, Steven E.
II. Turner, Frank M. (Frank Miller), 1944-
D20.M316 1987   940   86-16379
    ISBN 0-02-390300-7 (v. 1)
    ISBN 0-02-390310-4 (v. 2)

Printing: 1 2 3 4 5 6 7   Year: 7 8 9 0 1 2 3

ISBN 0-02-390300-7

Preface

In recent years many new dimensions have been added to our understanding of the European past. Historians have begun to probe one novel area of research after another. Groups of people previously virtually neglected have now found a place in the historical record. Areas of human activity once ignored or spurned by historians now find themselves the subject of intense investigation. At the same time many of the more traditional fields of historical writing have continued to attract distinguished researchers and to arouse ongoing curiosity.

This collection of essays in recent European historical writing presents a selection of excellent work across the spectrum of contemporary research. No existing anthology has attempted to represent the pluralism and variety of such writing. It is that pluralism—the many sides of contemporary historical research—that this reader seeks to make available to teachers and students. However it may be used—whether as supplementary reading in introductory European survey courses or in courses on historical method—its editors hope that both students and instructors will come to admire the sheer variety of contemporary historical writing and to realize that the complexity of the past necessarily invites investigation along numerous different paths of interest and methodology.

The editors would like to thank Eric Carlson and Eva Milofsky for their assistance in preparing the selections.

S. O.

F. M. T.

Contents

INTRODUCTION
 The Changing Agenda of Historical Study *1*

PART ONE
The Ancient World

THORKILD JACOBSON
 The Mesopotamian View of the World *11*
M. I. FINLEY
 Was Greek Civilization Based on Slave Labor? *34*
WAYNE A. MEEKS
 Who Were the First Christians? *51*
RAMSAY MacMULLEN
 The Vitality of Roman Paganism *69*

PART TWO
The Middle Ages

FRANCIS OAKLEY
 A Vision of Medieval Politics *83*
BARBARA H. ROSENWEIN AND LESTER K. LITTLE
 The Social Meaning of Monks and Friars *100*
SUZANNE WEMPLE
 Monogamous Marriage Among the Franks *121*
SHULAMITH SHAHAR
 Townswomen *134*
DAVID HERLIHY
 Medieval Children *155*

PART THREE
The Late Middle Ages and Renaissance

EDWARD MUIR
 Art, Pageantry, and Politics in Renaissance Venice *177*
JEREMY COHEN
 The Friars and the Jews *187*
SCOTT H. HENDRIX
 The Quest for the True Church *203*

WILLIAM J. COURTENAY
 The Black Death and English Higher Education *220*
WILLIAM J. BOUWSMA
 The Image of Man in Renaissance Culture *236*

PART FOUR
The Age of Reformation

ROBERT M. KINGDON
 Was the Reformation a Revolution? The Example of Geneva *257*
R. W. SCRIBNER
 Print and Propaganda in the German Reformation *278*
J. J. SCARISBRICK
 The Reign of Henry VIII *300*
JANE DEMPSEY DOUGLASS
 Women and the Reformation *318*

PART FIVE
Early Modern Europe

DONALD R. KELLEY
 Religious Warfare in France *339*
EDWARD GRANT
 Copernicus and the Scientific Revolution *356*
CHRISTINA LARNER
 Who Were the Witches? The Scottish Witch Hunt *369*
KEITH WRIGHTSON
 English Family Life *383*

Introduction: The Changing Agenda of Historical Study

The study of history has undergone an upheaval over the last two decades, as new ways of doing history have successfully challenged the older ways. The changes tell us something not only about historians and their craft, but also about our society at large. Although not so rapid nor so total as in other fields, the changes in my own field of specialization, the Renaissance and Reformation, are representative of the larger picture.

When I began graduate studies in 1964 my teachers (I will call them the "old historians") shared certain common assumptions about historical study. They stressed, first of all, the importance of historical context, by which they meant the study of an age within its own milieu. Few had an overriding desire to relate the past immediately to the present. One rather studied the past to learn about the past, to appreciate its otherness, its distance, its uniqueness, regardless of any immediate relevance it might have to modern society. Historical study was supposed to give one perspective and a sense of precedent.

One's main goal was to become contemporaneous with one's subjects. This was believed to be a relatively uncomplicated achievement. Historians simply immersed themselves in primary sources, reading widely and reflecting profoundly on the writings of the men and women of the Renaissance and Reformation. In this undertaking no one thought about borrowing models and categories from modern anthropology, psychology, or sociology. Had such borrowing been suggested, my teachers would have viewed it as likely to becloud the historian's vision, driving a wedge between historians and their sources and predisposing them to a "modernized," unhistorical reading of the past.

The historian studied seminal figures and historically engaged individuals and groups, people whose role in and contribution to society were clear and memorable. Why study people who played no definable and lasting role in the shaping of society's culture, laws, and institutions, whether for good or for ill? Just "being there" was not sufficient qualification for an object of historical study; sheer numbers did not add up to historical importance. The study of history was the study of change and achievement.

Ideas, beliefs, and values were the motor of history. My teachers in 1964 were, above all, proponents of intellectual, cultural, and religious history; they were qualitative rather than quantitative historians. This did not mean that they were romantic idealists who dwelt on what ought to be rather than what actually happened in the past. They simply believed that people regularly sacrifice their best material self-interests to abstractions and superstitions, being easily inspired or misled by doctrines and slogans that do little to improve their earthly lot and, indeed, may do much to harm it. Nothing seemed clearer to my teachers than the power of intellectual and spiritual forces in history; the key to behavior lay in the heart and mind as much as in the stomach.

The surgical tool of the historian was language, for language alone permitted the historian to become contemporary with the past. To read and think in the language of the past—that, above all, defined a historian. For my teachers, however, language meant first and foremost Latin, the tongue of the learned. The main objects of historical study were the writings of the learned or the powerful.

The great scholarly sin for my student generation was failure to appreciate the past for itself. One was not supposed to ask the past questions it did not ask itself; one did not pose modern problems to pre-modern people. To have done so would have been not only rude but, much worse, as the French historian Lucien Febvre pointed out, psychologically anachronistic, the imputation of the emotional make-up of one age to another. Cultures were rather discrete; they had lives of their own; the past did not "live" in the modern world; the people of the past could not fairly be asked to feel and act like modern people.

Already in the 1960s, what is known as the "new history" had taken hold across the historical spectrum. In 1962 two straws in the wind foreshadowed the changes in historical study for scholars of the Renaissance and Reformation. One was a small book by a German church historian named Bernd Moeller. Entitled *Imperial Cities and the Reformation*, this book decried the narrow preoccupations of German Reformation scholarship—too much theology, too much Martin Luther, too little attention paid to larger social and political forces. Moeller caused a stir by explaining the success of the Lutheran Reformation in nontheological terms and by minimizing the role played by great men. While he did not deny the importance of religious belief, he deemed it secondary to urban social and political experience in bringing about the Reformation. People turned Protestant, he argued, because they perceived Protestant teaching to be an ally of their traditional civic freedoms and their desire for independence from the overlordship of princes and prelates. In this interpretation, a crude sociology began to displace theology and religion in the explanation of the Reformation.

In the same year that Moeller criticized Reformation historians for narrowness, the first paperback edition of another trend-setting book appeared: Erik Erikson's psycho-historical study, *Young Man Luther* (original, 1958). Erikson, a Harvard psychologist, portrayed Luther as a gifted young man with a "delayed identity crisis." Here was an interpretation of the great reformer that stressed his common humanity, not his theological genius. A national best-seller, it gave psychology a firm place in the canon of modern historical scholarship and laid the foundation for an indigenous American study of collective mentality and behavior.

Whereas Moeller focused on common social and political experience, Erikson looked to common psychological development to find the decisive clues to individual and group behavior. In both cases, shared structures and shared institutions—society, politics, and family life broadly and dynamically conceived—became the key contexts for historical analysis. Historians now focused on factors larger than individual life, subtle demographic and economic forces that unconsciously influenced behavior. What individuals consciously think and do became secondary to what such larger forces do to them above and beyond their will and in the aggregate.

The focus in all fields of historical study has progressively shifted away from the thoughts and deeds of particular individuals to the behavior of the masses over centuries. This development has been led by French historians whose scholarly medium is the journal *Annales*. The things that people have in common, their collective culture and behavior, have become more interesting to historians than the things that distinguish and set them apart, their individual achievements.

The many have replaced the few. Statistics are now "hard" data; the self-interpretation of contemporaries, their own reflections on their times in tracts and chronicles, diaries and letters, sermons and books, seem by comparison "soft"—too unrepresentative, too subjective, too given to individual bias.

Like the old historians, the new historians share common assumptions and values. They are deeply influenced by modern anthropology, psychology, and sociology, whose models and theories routinely order their data. Historians may not always agree with such models and theories, but they find in them a new scientific basis for historical inquiry.

New historians are particularly devoted to popular or vernacular culture—the study of the masses, the simple folk. They read Latin, the language of elites, when it gives them access to "the people," the general public. The new history wants to tell its story from the ground up, not from the eagle perch of society's elite. It wants to be "total" history, at home on the farm as well as in the city, conversant with ordinary people as well as with intellectuals.

New kinds of texts have come into the foreground with the new history, and this is perhaps its most original achievement. Group activities like riots and processions are now key "documents" of popular consciousness. What did the masses hold dear? What moved the general public? One must read their actions to find out, as it is only here that they have left their mark. There is accordingly keen interest in carnival, when the world is turned upside down, and in social rituals designed to enforce local moral codes, like *charivari*, boisterous demonstrations that reaffirm the expected social roles of men and women in peasant society. The records of the Inquisition have also become popular among modern historians because of their seeming ability to convey the thoughts and feelings of the common people. Recent studies of village heresy, sexual mores, the world-views of simple folk, and witch hunts purport, in varying degrees, to have tapped into the "voice of the common man" through Inquisitorial records. Insofar as such records convey the reflections of contemporaries on their behavior, studies based on them are also bringing identifiable individuals and ideas back into the mainstream of historical study, albeit at the opposite end of the social spectrum studied by the old historians.

New historians consider a high level of objectivity and neutrality on the part of the historian near impossible and not really very important. Subjectivity and self-interest are recognized as inevitable in all historical writing. Historians such as Leopold von Ranke, who believed the past could be reconstructed "as it really was," are today likely to be ridiculed. The historian's irrepressible modernity is deemed an asset by some, as it ensures that the writing of history will not be antiquarian but engaged and relevant to the present.

New historians unabashedly modernize the past, that is, they test modern social theories and political agendas, especially in the burgeoning new fields of women's and family history. Pre-modern people are routinely asked modern questions and required to take a stand on modern issues. Recent biographies of Martin Luther express less interest in him as a late medieval monk and theologian than as an alleged anti-Semite, sexist, and exponent of political absolutism. Anorexia is discovered among female religious; nunneries turn into refuges from paternalism and misogyny; saints' lives provide windows to domestic behavior and reigning social values; high infant mortality rates become a proof of "low affection" between parents and children; successful urban religious reform movements and unsuccessful rural peasant revolts illustrate the truths of Marxism.

There is interest in the exposé of learned and powerful elites. Studies of civic myths and rituals in Europe's great cities reveal the way rulers shrewdly maintained their power and reinforced their control over their subjects. The sexual lives of saints reveal their all-too-common humanity and explain their political and religious choices. A striking new genre, witchcraft studies — an area of remarkable scholarly interest over the last two decades — portrays society's elite as the true villains of the witchhunts, more superstitious, cruel, and obsessed with demonological beliefs than were the masses of ordinary people, for whom belief in magic and the occult often proved to be a constructive social force within local villages. In the new history, the brightest and the best often appear also to be morally the sickest. There is a corresponding tendency to revalue the uneducated and politically disenfranchised. The careful reader can find in recent studies of popular culture a reemergence of Jacob Burckhardt's secular, a-Christian, protomodern "Renaissance man," not among learned Italian humanists, but among simple craftsmen and peasants.

If a shortcoming of the old history was narrowness, excess seems to be a problem of the new. If the old history paid too little attention to the full range of historical experience, the new has seemed all too confident about history's most important features. Bernd Moeller, who can take some credit for the new directions in historical study, has recently denounced present trends in Renaissance and Reformation history as "sociologism." By this he means a new historical myopia, one-sidedly sociopolitical rather than theological and intellectual, but in the end no less distorting of the variety of historical experience. Lawrence Stone, Princeton historian and strong advocate of the new historical directions, has also recently lamented their susceptibility to distortion.

Perhaps one should neither credit nor blame historians too much for the way they record the past. Powerful forces have been at work shaping perceptions and values for us all over the last two decades. The cultural egalitarianism that pervades historical study today also pervades the universities and society as a whole. We have democratized both the profession and the subject matter of history to unprecedented degrees. This has brought about enormously more variety in personnel and topics, and freer play has also been given the historian's imagination. History today is more fun than it used to be. But the rapid broadening of historical study has also created more history that treats the past as a guinea pig for present-day theories and a soap box for modern ideologies.

It is remarkable that over the past fifteen years the number of history majors in American universities has dropped by 58 per cent. Although historical study has become more entertaining and relevant to modern interests, many seem not to consider it vital to the life of an educated person. To be fair, it must be pointed out that the problems that exist for historical study exist also for the humanities generally within the modern university. The numbers of English and literature majors have fallen by an equally great amount (60 per cent) over the last fifteen years. What we seem to be in danger of losing is consensus on what constitutes an educated person. In the absence of such consensus and such standards, we run the risk of a laissez-faire system of liberal arts education that is increasingly focused on vocational success and security rather than broad learning. Agreed-upon intellectual standards and a clear common purpose are obviously as much a problem for society at large as for the modern historian; the historian's study is not so far from the public forum.

If one asks about the future course of historical study, one can identify forces at work attempting to restore a lost balance. The old history deserved much of the criticism it has received and it has profited from it. The history of culture, ideas, and politics will not again be written in quite the same way. Thanks to the new history, such works are now broader and richer. But the new history also has something to learn from the old, both in style and in substance, and that process is just beginning. The recently noted, and in some circles lamented, "revival of narrative" is only one straw in the wind. The new history must take account of the interests of the old as the old has been forced to take account of the interests of the new, for both have something to learn from each other. Their common ground must be the fact that history has many interrelated sides; both old and new historians have written about things that are real. We need to understand the few as well as the many, ideals as well as trends, the short term as well as the long, letters as well as numbers, religious experience as well as social experience, ideas as well as bullion.

The selections in this reader represent the many sides of history. A conscious effort has been made not to focus only on the trendy genres, which capture interest today but may be forgotten tomorrow. There are examples of intellectual and religious history, historiography, biography, and political narrative, as well as numerous selections from the newer fields of family history, women's studies, and popular culture. The hoped-for result is a balanced presentation of the different dimensions of historical reality and the variety of ways in which the story of history is told.

Because the writing of good history is not a recent invention, three generations of historians appear in the selections. Sights were set on substantial pieces of scholarship that will be as true to their subject and as interesting to the reader in fifty years as they are today. The selections are somewhat longer and also more challenging than those of a traditional history reader. Times have changed in the American classroom; "dumbing down" has gone out of style. Teachers and students want books they can read with respect. The meatier selections in this reader allow students to gain detailed knowledge of a particular subject and seriously engage in the process of historical reflection and analysis. The intention has been both to inform readers about the past and to give them a sense of what it means to write history.

A few selections may be described as experimental. Most are interdisciplinary, employing methods from more than one discipline and attempting to bridge two or more fields of study. A number are written by traditional historians who have consciously "retooled" under the influence of the new history. A few selections are, unapologetically, rigorous old-fashioned history. The most interesting selections may be those where the concerns of old and new historians converge in what may be described as an emerging "hybrid" history, part old, part new.

An eighth-century B.C. alabaster relief of Gilgamesh, the godlike hero of an ancient Sumerian epic poem. *Art Resource, NY*

PART ONE

The Ancient World

Western civilization began in the river valleys of the Tigris and Euphrates in Mesopotamia (the land "between the rivers") and the Nile in Egypt. By around 3000 B.C. organized urban life existed along the banks of these great rivers. From it sprang the diverse politics and rich cultures of the ancient Near East and the major Western religions of Judaism, Christianity, and Islam. Penetrating western Europe through the trade routes, Near Eastern cultures and religions also influenced Greek and Roman philosophy.

It is a truism of history that geography is destiny; climate and environment shape the characters of civilizations. The people of ancient Mesopotamia, the first Western civilization, lived at the mercy of Nature, which was far harsher in the valley of the Tigris-Euphrates than along the Nile. Thorkild Jacobsen discovers in Mesopotamian beliefs about the cosmos a people's long struggle with their geography.

The creation and maintenance of a complex civilization was an enormous undertaking in ancient times. It required many minds and hands, not all of them free. Slavery was a pervasive feature of ancient civilization, although its exact nature and dimensions cannot easily be measured. M. I. Finley estimates the extent of Greek dependence on captured slaves for physical and economic well-being.

No event stands out more prominently in late antiquity than the success of Christianity in the Roman empire. Why did Christianity win so many hearts and minds? Wayne A. Meeks raises a prior question: whose hearts and minds did Christianity win? By identifying the kinds of people who readily became Christian, the historian discovers a social as well as a religious dimension in the triumph of Christianity. The motives behind conversion appear to have been several and complex.

Christianity did not, however, eradicate all other ancient philosophies and religions. Pagan beliefs and practices not only survived Christianity, but flourished down to modern times. The ability of Christians and pagans to coexist and of Christian doctrine and pagan philosophy to blend are remarkable facts of Western civilization and the subjects of Ramsay MacMullen's essay.

The Mesopotamian View of the World

THORKILD JACOBSEN

Unlike the ancient Egyptians, the Mesopotamian people did not attach great significance to physical things and worldly achievements. For them, what was lasting and important in life was such only because of its connection with a transcendent spiritual realm, whose power and influence were believed to pervade all reality.

World views reflect a people's experience with two inescapable forces in their lives: nature and culture. For ancient Mesopotamians, nature was hostile and their culture a primitive democracy rife with potential conflict. Whereas Egyptian geography placed the Egyptian people within a fairly secure and predictable environment, Mesopotamian civilization developed within a harsh and ever-changing one. Nature constantly interrupted human plans and inflicted physical hardship through flood and famine. People came to believe that the power to do one's will lay in a world beyond the temporal; the cosmos above controlled the world below.

Cosmic order existed only because the gods agreed to it. The many powerful competing forces in the universe acknowledged one another's sphere of influence. In so believing, Mesopotamians portrayed the universe on the model of their own political experience. The power of their own government and the order within their own society had resulted from the voluntary integration of many conflicting smaller wills into one large will—the State, whose laws were deemed to be as immutable as those of nature and unquestionably obeyed.

Mesopotamians not only designed the universe after their own historical experience, they also believed that a real connection existed between cosmic forces and physical reality. The gods took a direct and abiding interest in the physical world, every part of which was believed to be alive with a spirit, personality, and will of its own. In the Mesopotamian world-view, every person and thing became a sentient part of an immense cosmic-temporal commonwealth.

Reprinted with the permission of the University of Chicago Press from *The Intellectual Adventure of Ancient Man*, Henri and Henriette Antonia Frankfort, eds. Copyright © 1947 by the University of Chicago.

Influence of Environment in Egypt and Mesopotamia

In passing from ancient Egypt to ancient Mesopotamia, we are leaving a civilization whose enduring monuments still stand, "proud pyramids of stone proclaiming man's sense of sovereign power in his triumph over material forces." We are moving on to a civilization whose monuments perished, whose cities—in the words of the prophet—"have become heaps." There is scant reminder of ancient grandeur in the low gray mounds which represent Mesopotamia's past.

It is altogether fitting that this should be so. It suits the basic moods of the two civilizations. Were the Egyptian to come back today, he would undoubtedly take heart from the endurance of his pyramids, for he accorded to man and to man's tangible achievements more basic significance than most civilizations have been willing to do. Were the Mesopotamian to return, he could hardly feel deeply disturbed that *his* works have crumbled, for he always knew, and knew deeply, that as for "mere man—his days are numbered; whatever he may do, he is but wind." To him the center and meaning of existence always lay beyond man and his achievements, beyond tangible things, in intangible powers ruling the universe.

How the Egyptian and the Mesopotamian civilizations came to acquire these very different moods—one trusting, the other distrusting, man's power and ultimate significance—is not an easy question. The "mood" of a civilization is the outcome of processes so intricate and so complex as to defy precise analysis. We shall therefore merely point to a single factor which would seem to have played a considerable role—the factor of environment.... Egyptian civilization arose in a compact country where village lay reassuringly close to village, the whole ringed around and isolated by protecting mountain barriers. Over this sheltered world passed every day a dependable, never failing sun, calling Egypt back to life and activity after the darkness of night; here arose every year the trusty Nile to fertilize and revivify the Egyptian soil. It is almost as though Nature had deliberately restrained herself, as though she had set this secure valley apart so that man could disport himself unhindered.

It is small wonder that a great civilization arising on such a scene should be filled with a sense of its own power, should be deeply impressed with its own—with human—accomplishments. The attitude of early Egypt [has been described] as "a frontier spirit of visible accomplishments, of the first success in a new line. There was a youthful and self-reliant arrogance, because there had been no setbacks. Man was enough in himself. The gods? Yes, they were off there somewhere, and they had made this good world, to be sure; but the world was good because man was himself master, without need for the constant support of the gods."

The experience of Nature which gave rise to this mood found direct expression in the Egyptian notion of the cosmos. The Egyptian cosmos was eminently reliable and comforting. It had "reassuring periodicity; its structural framework and mechanics permitted the reiteration of life through the rebirth of life-giving elements."

Mesopotamian civilization grew up in an environment which was signally different. We find there, of course, the same great cosmic rhythms—the change of the seasons, the unwavering sweep of sun, moon, and stars—but we also find an element of force and violence which was lacking in Egypt. The Tigris and the Euphrates are not like the Nile; they may rise unpredictably and fitfully, breaking man's dikes and submerging his crops. There are scorching winds which smother man in dust, threaten to suffocate him; there are torrential rains which turn all firm ground into a sea of mud and rob man of his freedom of movement: all travel bogs down. Here, in Mesopotamia, Nature stays not her hand; in her full might she cuts across and overrides man's will, makes him feel to the full how slightly he matters.

The mood of Mesopotamian civilization reflects this. Man is not tempted to overrate himself when he contemplates powers in nature such as the thunderstorm and the yearly flood. Of the thunderstorm the Mesopotamian said that its "dreadful flares of light cover the land like a cloth." The impression which the flood made on him may be gathered from the following description:

> The rampant flood which no man can oppose,
> Which shakes the heavens and causes earth to tremble,
> In an appaling blanket folds mother and child,
> Beats down the canebrake's full luxuriant greenery,
> And drowns the harvest in its time of ripeness.
>
> Rising waters, grievous to eyes of man,
> All-powerful flood, which forces the embankments
> And mows mighty *mesu*-trees,
> (Frenzied) storm, tearing all things in massed confusion
> With it (in hurtling speed).

Standing amidst such powers, man sees how weak he is, realizes with dread that he is caught in an interplay of giant forces. His mood becomes tense; his own lack of power makes him acutely aware of tragic potentialities.

The experience of Nature which produced this mood found direct expression in the Mesopotamian's notion of the cosmos in which he lived. He was in no way blind to the great rhythms of the cosmos; he saw the cosmos as order, not as anarchy. But to him that order was not nearly so safe and reassuring as it was to the Egyptian. Through and under it he sensed a multitude of powerful individual wills, potentially divergent, potentially conflicting, fraught with a possibility of anarchy. He confronted in Nature gigantic and wilful individual powers.

To the Mesopotamian, accordingly, cosmic *order* did not appear as something given; rather it became something achieved—achieved through a continual integration of the many individual cosmic wills, each so powerful, so frightening. His understanding of the cosmos tended therefore to express itself in terms of integration of wills, that is, in terms of social orders such as the family, the community, and, most particularly, the state. To put it succinctly, he saw the cosmic order as an order of wills—as a state.

In presenting this view here, we shall discuss first the period in which it may be assumed to have originated. We shall then take up the question of what the Mesopotamian saw in the phenomena of the world around him in order to show how it could be possible for him to apply an order from the social sphere, the state, to the basically different world of Nature. Lastly, we shall discuss that order in detail and comment on those forces which played the most prominent part in it.

Date of the Mesopotamian View of the World

The Mesopotamian's understanding of the universe in which he lived seems to have found its characteristic form at about the time when Mesopotamian civilization as a whole took shape, that is, in the Proto-literate period, around the middle of the fourth millennium B.C.

Thousands of years had already passed since man first entered the valley of the Two Rivers, and one prehistoric culture had followed another—all basically alike, none signally different from what one might have found elsewhere in the world. During those millenniums agriculture was the chief means of support. Tools were fashioned from stone, rarely from copper. Villages, made up of patriarchal families, seem to have been the typical form of settlement. The most conspicuous change from one such culture to another, surely not a very profound one, seems to have been in the way pottery was made and decorated.

But with the advent of the Proto-literate period the picture changes. Overnight, as it were, Mesopotamian civilization crystallizes. The fundamental pattern, the controlling framework within which Mesopotamia is to live its life, formulate its deepest questions, evaluate itself and evaluate the universe, for ages to come, flashes into being, complete in all its main features.

In the economic sphere appeared *planned large-scale irrigation by means of canals*, a form which forever after was to be characteristic of Mesopotamian agriculture. Concurrent with this and closely interrelated with it was a spectacular increase in population. The old villages expanded into cities; new settlements were founded throughout the country. And, as village grew into city, the political pattern of the new civilization emerged—*Primitive Democracy*. In the new city-state ultimate political power rested with a general assembly of all adult freemen. Normally the everyday affairs of the community were guided by a council of elders; but in times of crisis, for instance, when war threatened, the general assembly could confer absolute powers on one of its members and proclaim him king. Such kingship was an office held for a limited term; and, as the assembly could confer it, so it could also revoke it when a crisis was past.

The centralization of authority which this new political pattern made possible may have been responsible, along with other factors, for the emergence of a truly *monumental architecture* in Mesopotamia. Imposing temples now began to rise in the plain, often built on gigantic artificial mountains of sun-dried bricks, the famous *ziqqurats*. Works of such imposing proportions clearly presuppose a high degree of organization and direction in the community which achieved them.

As these things were happening in the economic and social fields, new peaks of achievement were attained in the more spiritual fields of endeavor. *Writing* was invented, at first serving to facilitate the ever more complicated accounting which had become necessary with the expansion of city and temple economy. Eventually it was to become the vehicle of a most significant literature. Moreover, Mesopotamia produced *art* worthy of the name; and the works of these early artists compare very well with the best of later periods.

In economics, in politics, and in the arts Mesopotamia thus found at this early stage its guiding forms, created set ways in which to deal with the universe in its various aspects as they confronted man. It would not be surprising, therefore, to find that the view taken of the universe as a whole should likewise have clarified and taken form at that time. That this actually happened is indicated by the world view itself. As we have already mentioned, Mesopotamian civilization interpreted the universe as a state. However, the basis of interpretation was not the state that existed in historic times but the state as it had been before history—a Primitive Democracy. We have therefore the right to assume that the idea of a cosmic state crystallized very early, when Primitive Democracy was the prevalent type of state—indeed, with Mesopotamian civilization itself.

The Mesopotamian Attitude Toward the Phenomena of Nature

Assuming, then, that the Mesopotamian view of the universe was as old as Mesopotamian civilization itself, we must next ask how it could be at all possible to take such a view. Certainly for us it has no meaning whatever to speak of the universe as a state—of stones and stars, winds and waters, as citizens and as members of legislative assemblies. Our universe is made up largely of things, of dead matter with neither life nor will. This leads us to the question of what the Mesopotamian saw in the phenomena which surrounded him, the world in which he lived.

The reader will remember that the world appears to primitive man neither inanimate nor empty but redundant with life. It has been said of primitive man that "any phenomenon may at any time face him not as 'It' but as 'Thou.' In this confrontation 'Thou' reveals individuality, qualities, will." Out of the repeated experience of the "I-Thou" relationship a fairly consistent personalistic view may develop. Objects and phenomena in man's environment become personified in varying degrees. They are somehow alive; they have wills of their own; each is a definite personality. We then have what the late Andrew Lang disapprovingly described as "that inextricable confusion in which men, beasts, plants, stones, stars are all on one level of personality and animated existence." ... Ordinary kitchen salt is to us an inanimate substance, a mineral. To the Mesopotamian it was a fellow-being whose help might be sought if one had fallen victim to sorcery and witchcraft. The sufferer would then address it as follows:

> O Salt, created in a clean place,
> For food of gods did Enlil destine thee.
> Without thee no meal is set out in Ekur,
> Without thee god, king, lord, and prince do not smell incense.
> I am so-and-so, the son of so-and-so,
> Held captive by enchantment,
> Held in fever by bewitchment.
> O Salt, break my enchantment! Loose my spell!
> Take from me the bewitchment!—And as my Creator
> I shall extol thee.

As Salt, a fellow-creature with special powers, can be approached directly, so can Grain. When a man offered up flour to conciliate an angry deity, he might say to it:

> I will send thee to my angry god, my angry goddess,
> Whose heart is filled with furious rage against me.
> Do thou reconcile my angry god, my angry goddess.

Both Salt and Grain are thus not the inanimate substances for which we know them. They are alive, have personality and a will of their own. So had any phenomenon in the Mesopotamian world whenever it was approached in a spirit other than that of humdrum, practical, everyday pursuits: in magic, in religion, in speculative thought. In such a world it obviously gives better sense than it does in our world to speak of the relations between phenomena of nature as social relations, of the order in which they function as an order of wills, as a state.

By saying that the phenomena of the world were alive for the Mesopotamian, that they were personified, we have made things simpler than they actually are. We have glossed over a potential distinction which was felt by the Mesopotamian. It is not correct to say that each phenomenon was a person; we must say that there was a will and a personality in each phenomenon—in it and yet somehow behind it, for the single concrete phenomenon did not completely circumscribe and exhaust the will and personality associated with it. For instance, a particular lump of flint had a clearly recognizable personality and will. Dark, heavy, and hard, it would show a curious willingness to flake under the craftsman's tool though that tool was only of horn softer than the stone against which it was pressed. Now, this characteristic personality which confronts one here, in this particular lump of flint, may meet one also over there, in another lump of flint, which seems to say: "Here I am again—dark, heavy, hard, willing to flake, I, Flint!" Wherever one met it, its name was "Flint," and it would suffer itself to flake easily. That was because it had once fought the god Ninurta, and Ninurta had imposed flaking on it as a punishment.

We may consider another example—the reeds which grew in the Mesopotamian marshes. It is quite clear from our texts that, in themselves, they were never divine. Any individual reed counted merely as a plant, a thing, and so did all reeds. The concrete individual reed, however, had wonderful qualities which inspired awe. There was a mysterious power to grow luxuriantly in the marshes. A reed was capable of amazing things, such as the music which would come out of a shepherd's pipe, or the meaningful signs which would take form under the scribe's reed stylus and make a story or a poem. These powers, which were to be found in every reed and were always the same, combined for the Mesopotamian into a divine personality—that of the goddess Nidaba. It was Nidaba who made the reeds thrive in the marshes; if she were not near, the shepherd could not soothe the heart with music from his reed pipe. To her would the scribe give praise when a difficult piece of writing had come out from under his stylus and he saw it to be good. The goddess was thus the power in all reeds; she made them what they were, lent them her mysterious qualities. She was one with every reed in the sense that she permeated it as an animating and characterizing agent; but she did not lose her identity in that of the concrete phenomenon and was not limited by any or even all existing reeds. In a crude but quite effective manner the Mesopotamian artists suggested this relationship when they depicted the reed-goddess. She is shown in human form as a venerable matron. But the reeds also are there: they sprout from her shoulders—are bodily one with her and seem to derive directly from her.

In a great many individual phenomena, such as individual lumps of flint or individual reeds, the Mesopotamian thus felt that he was confronted by a single self. He sensed, as it were, a common power-center which was charged with a particular personality and was itself personal. This personal power-center pervaded the individual phenomena and gave them the character which they are seen to have: "Flint" all lumps of flint, Nidaba all reeds, etc.

Even more curious than this, however, is the fact that one such self might infuse itself into other different selves and, in a relation of partial identity, lend them of its character. We may illustrate by quoting a Mesopotamian incantation by which a man sought to become identical with Heaven and Earth:

> I am Heaven, you cannot touch me,
> I am Earth, you cannot bewitch me!

The man is trying to ward off sorcery from his body, and his attention is centered on a single quality of Heaven and Earth, their sacred inviolability. When he has made himself identical with them, this quality will flow into him and merge with his being, so that he will be secure from attacks by witchcraft.

Very similar is another incantation in which a man endeavors to drench every part of his body in immunity by such identification with gods and sacred emblems. It reads:

> Enlil is my head, my face is the day;
> Urash, the peerless god, is the protecting spirit leading my way.
> My neck is the necklace of the goddess Ninlil,
> My two arms are the sickle of the western moon,
> My fingers tamarisk, bone of the gods of heaven;
> They ward off the embrace of sorcery from my body;
> The gods Lugal-edinna and Latarak are my breast and knees;
> Muhra my ever-wandering feet.

Here again the identity sought is only partial. Qualities of these gods and sacred emblems are to infuse the man's members and make him inviolable.

As it was thought possible for a man to achieve partial identity with various gods, so could one god enjoy partial identity with other gods and thus share in their natures and abilities. We are told, for instance, that the face of the god Ninurta is Shamash, the sun-god; that one of Ninurta's ears is the god of wisdom, Ea—and so on through all of Ninurta's members. These curious statements may be taken to mean that Ninurta's face derived its dazzling radiance from, and thus shared in, that brilliance which is characteristically the sun-god's and concentrates itself in him. In similar manner, his ear—for the Mesopotamians believed the ear, not the brain, to be the seat of intelligence—shares in that supreme intelligence which is the outstanding characteristic of the god Ea.

Sometimes such statements of partial identity take a slightly different form. We are told, for instance, that the god Marduk is the god Enlil when there is question of ruling and taking counsel, but that he is Sîn, the moon-god, when he acts as illuminer of the night, etc. This apparently means that the god Marduk, when he rules and makes decisions, partakes of the personality, qualities, and abilities of the divine executive par excellence, the god Enlil. When, on the other hand, Marduk, as the planet Jupiter, shines in the nightly skies, he shares in those special powers which characterize the moon-god and have their center in him.

Any phenomenon which the Mesopotamian met in the world around him was thus alive, had its own personality and will, its distinct self. But the self which revealed itself, for example, in a particular lump of flint, was not limited by that particular lump; it was in it and yet behind it; it permeated it and gave it character as it did all lumps of flint. And as one such "self" could permeate many individual phenomena, so it might also permeate other selves and thereby give to them of its specific character to add to the qualities which they had in their own right.

To understand nature, the many and varied phenomena around man, was thus to understand the personalities in these phenomena, to know their characters, the direction of their wills, and also the range of their powers. It was a task not different from that of understanding other men, knowing their characters, their wills, the extent of their power and influence. And intuitively the Mesopotamian applied to nature the experience he had of his own human society, interpreting it in social terms. A particularly suggestive example will illustrate this. Under our eyes, as it were, objective reality assumes the form of a social type.

According to Mesopotamian beliefs, a man who had been bewitched could destroy the enemies who had bewitched him by burning images of them. The characteristic self of the enemy stared up at him from the image. He could get at it and harm it there, as well as in the person. And so he consigned the images to the fire while addressing it as follows:

> Scorching Fire, warlike son of Heaven,
> Thou, the fiercest of thy brethren,
> Who like Moon and Sun decidest lawsuits—
> Judge thou my case, hand down the verdict.
> Burn the man and woman who bewitched me;
> Burn, O Fire, the man and woman who bewitched me;
> Scorch, O Fire, the man and woman who bewitched me;
> Burn them, O Fire;
> Scorch them, O Fire;
> Take hold of them, O Fire;
> Consume them, O Fire;
> Destroy them, O Fire.

It is quite clear that the man approaches the fire for the destructive power he knows to be in it. But the fire has a will of its own; it will burn the images—and in them his enemies—only if it so chooses. And in deciding whether to burn the images or not, the fire becomes a judge between the man and his enemies: the situation becomes a lawsuit in which the man pleads his cause and asks the fire to vindicate him. The power which is in fire has taken definite form, has been interpreted in social terms; it is a judge.

As the fire here becomes a judge, other powers take form in similar pregnant situations. The thunderstorm was a warrior; he flung deadly lightning, and one could hear the roar emitted by the wheels of his war chariot. The earth was a woman, a mother; she gave birth each year to the new vegetation. In such cases the Mesopotamians did only what other people have done throughout the ages. "Men," as Aristotle says, "imagine not only the forms of the gods but their ways of life to be like their own."

If we were to try to single out a typically Mesopotamian feature, we should perhaps point to the degree to which this people found and emphasized organized relationships of the powers they recognized. While all people tend to humanize nonhuman powers and frequently visualize them as social types, Mesopotamian speculative thought seems to have brought out and systematized to an unusual degree the implications of social and political function latent in such typifying and to have elaborated them into clear-cut institutions. This particular emphasis would seem to be closely bound up with the nature of the society in which the Mesopotamian lived and from which he derived his terms and his evaluation.

When the universe was taking form for the Mesopotamian, he lived, we have argued, in a Primitive Democracy. All great undertakings, all important decisions, originated in a general assembly of all the citizens; they were not the affair of any single individual. It is accordingly natural that, in trying to understand how the great cosmic events were brought about, he should be especially intent upon the ways in which the individual forces of the cosmos co-operated to run the universe. Cosmic institutions would naturally come to loom important in his view of the universe, and the structure of the universe would stand out clearly as the structure of a state.

The Structure of the Cosmic State

The commonwealth of the Mesopotamian cosmos encompassed the whole existing world—in fact, anything that could be thought of as an entity: humans, animals, inanimate objects, natural phenomena, as well as notions such as justice, righteousness, the form of a circle, etc. How such entities could all be seen as members of a state we have just shown; they had in them will, character, and power. But though all things that could be imagined were members of the cosmic state, they were not all members on the same political level. The criterion of differentiation was power.

In the state on earth there were large groups of people who had no share in the government. Slaves, children, and perhaps women had no voice in the assembly. Only the adult freemen met there to decide on public affairs; they alone were citizens in the true sense. Quite similarly in the state which the universe constituted. Only those natural forces whose power inspired the Mesopotamian with awe, and whom he therefore ranked as gods, were considered full citizens of the universe, were thought to have political rights and to exercise political influence. The general assembly in the cosmic state was therefore an assembly of gods.

We hear about this assembly often in Mesopotamian literature, and we know in general how it functioned. It was the highest authority in the universe. Here the momentous decisions regarding the course of all things and the fates of all beings were made and were confirmed by the members of the assembly. Before that stage was reached, however, proposals were discussed, perhaps even heatedly, by gods who were for or against them. The leader of the assembly was the god of heaven, Anu. At his side stood his son Enlil, god of the storm. One of these usually broached the matters to be considered, and the gods would then discuss them. Through such discussions (the Mesopotamians called it "asking one another") the issues were clarified, and the consensus would begin to stand out. Of special weight in the discussion were the voices of a small group of the most prominent gods, "the seven gods who determine destinies." In this way, full agreement was finally reached, all the gods assented with a firm "Let it be," and the decision was announced by Anu and Enlil. It was now "the verdict, the word of the assembly of the gods, the command of Anu and Enlil." The executive duties (the task of carrying out the decisions) seem to have rested with Enlil.

Leaders of the Cosmic State

We have seen that the gods who constituted the divine assembly were powers which the Mesopotamians recognized in and behind the various phenomena of nature. Which of these powers, then, played the most prominent roles in the assembly, influenced most the course of the universe? In a sense we may answer: "The powers in those elements of the cosmos which were seen to be the greatest and most prominent."

Anu, the highest of the gods, was god of the sky, and his name was the everyday word for "sky." The dominant role which the sky plays—even in a merely spatial sense—in the composition of the visible universe, and the eminent position which it occupies, high above all other things, may well explain why Anu should rank as the most important force in the cosmos.

Enlil, the second highest of the gods, was god of the storm. His name means "Lord Storm," and he personifies the essence of the storm. No one who has experienced a storm in flat, open Mesopotamia can possibly doubt the might of this cosmic force. The storm, master of all free space under the sky, ranked naturally as the second great component of the cosmos.

As third basic component of the visible universe comes the earth. Earth, so near to man, so vitally important to him in so many of its aspects, was difficult to view and hold fast within the scope of a single concept. We meet it as "Mother Earth," the fertile giver of blessings to man, and as the "queen of the gods" and "lady of the mountains." But the earth is also the source of the life-giving waters in rivers, canals, and wells; waters which stream from a vast sea within. And as the source of these waters the earth was viewed as male, as *En-ki*, "lord of the earth," more originally perhaps "Lord Earth." The third and fourth in rank of the Mesopotamian gods were these two aspects of the earth, Ninhursaga and Enki. They round off the list of the most important cosmic elements that must rank highest and exercise the greatest influence on all that is.

A. THE POWER IN THE SKY: AUTHORITY

But considerations of size and position alone could hardly have suggested the specific character and the function which these powers were assumed to have in the universe. The Mesopotamian conceived both character and function in direct confrontation with the phenomena when they "revealed" themselves and deeply affected him.

The sky can, at moments when man is in a singularly receptive mood, reveal itself in an almost terrifying experience. The vast sky encircling one on all sides may be felt as a presence at once overwhelming and awesome, forcing one to his knees merely by its sheer being. And this feeling which the sky inspires is definite and can be named: it is that inspired by majesty. There is in it the experience of greatness or even of the tremendous. There comes a keen realization of one's own insignificance, of unbridgeable remoteness. The Mesopotamians express this well when they say, "Godhead awesome as the faraway heavens, as the broad sea." But, though a feeling of distance, this feeling is not one of absolute separation; it has a strong element of sympathy and of the most unqualified acceptance.

Beyond all, however, the experience of majesty is the experience of power, of power bordering on the tremendous, but power at rest, not consciously imposing its will. The power behind majesty is so great that it need not exert itself. Without any effort on its part it commands allegiance by its very presence; the onlooker obeys freely, through a categorical imperative rising from the depths of his own soul.

This majesty and absolute authority which can be experienced in the sky the Mesopotamians called Anu. Anu was the overpowering personality of the sky, the "Thou" which permeated it and could be felt through it. If the sky was considered apart from him, as it could be, it receded into the category of things and became a mere abode for the god.

The "Thou" which met the Mesopotamian when he confronted the sky was so powerfully experienced that it was felt to be the very center and source of all majesty. Wherever else he found majesty and authority he knew it to be that power in the sky, to be Anu. And he did find it elsewhere; indeed, authority, the power which produces automatic acceptance and obedience, is a basic constituent in all organized human society. Were it not for unquestioning obedience to customs, to laws, and to those "in authority," society would dissolve in anarchy and chaos. So in those persons in whom authority resided—the father in the family, the ruler in the state—the Mesopotamian recognized something of Anu and Anu's essence. As the father of the gods, Anu was the prototype of all fathers; as the "pristine king and ruler," he was the prototype of all rulers. To him belong the insignia in which the essence of royalty was embodied—the scepter, the crown, the headband, and the shepherd's staff—and from him did they derive. Before any king had yet been appointed among men these insignia already were, and they rested in heaven before Anu. From there they descended to earth. Anu also calls to kingship; and when the king commands and the command is unquestioningly and immediately obeyed, when it "comes true," it is again the essence of Anu which manifests itself. It is Anu's command that issues through the king's mouth; it is Anu's power that makes it immediately efficacious.

But human society was to the Mesopotamian merely a part of the larger society of the universe. The Mesopotamian universe—because it did not consist of dead matter, because every stone, every tree, every conceivable thing in it was a being with a will and character of its own—was likewise founded on authority; its members, too, willingly and automatically obeyed orders which made them act as they should act. These orders *we* call laws of nature. So the whole universe showed the influence of the essence peculiar to Anu.

When in the Babylonian creation story the god Marduk is given absolute authority, and all things and forces in the universe automatically conform themselves to his will so that whatever he orders immediately comes to pass, then his command has become identical in essence with Anu and the gods exclaim: "Thy word is Anu."

We see thus that Anu is the source of and active principle in all authority, both in human society and in the larger society which is the universe. He is the force which lifts it out of chaos and anarchy and makes it into a structure, an organized whole; he is the force which insures the necessary voluntary obedience to orders, laws, and customs in society and to the natural laws in the physical world, in short, to world order. As a building is supported by, and reveals in its structure the lines of, its foundation, so the Mesopotamian universe is upheld by, and reflects in *its* structure, a divine will. Anu's command is the foundation of heaven and earth.

What we have said here at some length about the function of Anu is said briefly and concisely by the Mesopotamians themselves. When the great gods address Anu in the "Myth of the Elevation of Inanna," they exclaim:

> What thou hast ordered (comes) true!
>   The utterance of prince and lord is (but)
>   what thou hast ordered, (that with which) thou art in agreement.
> O Anu! thy great command takes precedence,
>   who could say no (to it)?
> O father of the gods, thy command,
>   the very foundation of heaven and earth,
>   what god could spurn (it)?

As the absolute sovereign of the world, the highest power in the universe, Anu is described in such words as these:

> Wielder of the scepter, the ring, and the *palu*
>   who callest to kingship,
> Sovereign of the gods, whose word prevails
>   in the ordained assembly of the great gods,
> Lord of the glorious crown, astounding
>   through thine enchantment,
> Rider of great storms, who occupies the dais of sovereignty,
>   wondrously regal—
> To the pronouncements of thy holy mouth
>   are the Igigi attentive;
> In fear before thee move the Anunnaki,
> Like storm-swept reeds bow to thy orders
>   all the gods.

B. THE POWER IN THE STORM: FORCE

Turning from Anu, god of the sky, to Enlil, god of the storm, we meet a power of a somewhat different cast. As his name *En-lil*, "Lord Storm," suggests, he was in a sense the storm itself. As the storm, the undisputed master of all space between heaven and earth, Enlil was palpably the second greatest power of the visible universe, second only to the sky above him.

In the storm he "reveals" himself. The violence, the force, which fills it and is experienced in it was the god, was Enlil. It is thus through the storm, through its violence and force, that we must seek to understand the god and his function in the universe.

The city of Ur had long held sway over Babylonia. Then it fell before a merciless attack by Elamitic hordes which swept down upon it from the eastern mountains. The utter destruction of the city was wrought, in our terms, by the barbaric hordes which attacked it. Not so in terms of the Mesopotamian's own understanding of his universe: the wild destructive essence manifest in this attack was Enlil's. The enemy hordes were but a cloak, an outward form under which that essence realized itself. In a deeper, truer sense the barbaric hordes were a storm, Enlil's storm, wherewith the god himself was executing a verdict passed on Ur and its people by the assembly of the gods; and as that storm the enemy attack is seen and described:

> Enlil called the storm.
>   The people mourn.
> Exhilarating winds he took from the land.
>   The people mourn.
> Good winds he took away from Shumer.
>   The people mourn.
> He summoned evil winds.
>   The people mourn.
> Entrusted them to Kingaluda, tender of storms.
>
> He called the storm that will annihilate the land.
>   The people mourn.
> He called disastrous winds.
>   The people mourn.
> Enlil—choosing Gibil as his helper—
> Called the (great) hurricane of heaven.
>   The people mourn.
>
> The (blinding) hurricane howling across the skies,
>   —The people mourn—
> The shattering storm roaring across the land,
>   —The people mourn—
> The tempest which, relentless as a floodwave,
> Beats down upon, devours the city's ships,
> All these he gathered at the base of heaven.
>   The people mourn.
>
> (Great) fires he lit that heralded the storm.
>   The people mourn.
> And lit on either flank of furious winds
>   The searing heat of desert.
> Like flaming heat of noon this fire scorched.

This storm is the true cause of the city's downfall:

> The storm ordered by Enlil in hate, the storm
>   which wears away the country,
> covered Ur like a cloth, enveloped it like a linen sheet.

It is the cause of the destruction wrought:

> On that day did the storm leave the city;
> > that city was a ruin.
> O father Nanna, that town was left a ruin.
> > The people mourn.
> On that day did the storm leave the country.
> > The people mourn.
>
> (Dead) men, not potsherds,
> Covered the approaches.
> The walls were gaping,
> The high gates, the roads,
> Were piled with dead.
> In the wide streets, where feasting crowds would gather.
> Scattered they lay.
> In all the streets and roadways bodies lay.
> In open fields that used to fill with dancers,
> They lay in heaps.
>
> The country's blood now filled its holes,
> > like metal in a mold;
> Bodies dissolved — like fat left in the sun.

In the great catastrophes of history, in the crushing blows voted by the assembly of the gods, there is Enlil, essence of the storm. He is force, executor of the verdicts of the gods.

But not only as divine sheriff, as executor of all punitive decrees in the cosmic state, is Enlil active. He participates in all legitimate exercise of force, and thus it is he who leads the gods in war. The great Mesopotamian myth of creation, *Enuma elish*, has had a somewhat turbulent career; as its hero we find sometimes one, sometimes another, god. There can be little doubt, however, that the myth, in its original form, centered around Enlil. As such, it describes the dangers which once beset the gods when they were threatened with attack from the powers of chaos: how neither the command of Enki nor that of Anu, reinforced by the authority of the assembly of gods, could stay them; how the gods assembled and chose young Enlil to be their king and champion; and how Enlil vanquished the enemy, Ti'amat, by means of the storms, those forces which express the essence of his being.

Thus, in the society which the Mesopotamian universe constitutes, Anu represents authority, Enlil force. The subjective experience of the sky, of Anu, is, as we have seen, one of majesty, of absolute authority which commands allegiance by its very presence. The onlooker obeys it not through any outward pressure but through a categorical imperative which rises within his own soul. Not so with Enlil, the storm. Here, too, is power;

but it is the power of force, of compulsion. Opposing wills are crushed and beaten into submission. In the assembly of the gods, the ruling body of the universe, Anu presides and directs the proceedings. His will and authority, freely and voluntarily accepted, guide the assembly much as a constitution guides the actions of a lawmaking body. Indeed, his will is the unwritten, living constitution of the Mesopotamian world state. But whenever force enters the picture, when the cosmic state is enforcing its will against opposition, then Enlil takes the center of the stage. He executes the sentences imposed by the assembly; he leads the gods in war. Thus Anu and Enlil embody, on a cosmic level, the two powers which are the fundamental constituents of any state: authority and legitimate force; for, while authority alone may suffice to hold a community together, such a community becomes a state only when it develops organs to back up its authority with force, when its staff, to quote Max Weber, "successfully displays the monopoly of a legitimate physical compulsion." For this reason we can say that, while it is the powers of Anu that make the Mesopotamian universe an organized society, it is the complementary powers of Enlil that define this society as a state.

Because Enlil is force, his character is one of peculiar duality: he is at one and the same time the trust and the fear of man. He is force as legitimate force, upholder of the state, a rock of strength even to the gods. Man greets him in words like these:

> O Thou who dost encompass all heaven and earth, fleet god,
> Wise instructor of the people,
> Who dost survey the regions of the world;
> Prince, counselor, whose word is heeded,
> Whose spoken word .... gods cannot alter,
> The utterance of whose lips no god may spurn;
> Great Lord, ruler of gods in heaven,
> Counselor of gods on earth, judicious prince.

Yet, because Enlil is force, there lie hidden in the dark depths of his soul both violence and wildness. The normal Enlil upholds the cosmos, guarantees order against chaos; but suddenly and unpredictably the hidden wildness in him may break forth. This side of Enlil is truly and terribly the abnormal, a scattering of all life and of life's meaning. Therefore, man can never be fully at ease with Enlil but feels a lurking fear which finds expression frequently in the hymns which have come down to us:

> What has he planned ....?
> What is in my father's heart?
> What is in Enlil's holy mind?
> What has he planned against me in his holy mind?
> A net he spread: that is the net of an enemy.

> A snare he set: that is the snare of an enemy.
> He has stirred up the waters, and will catch the fishes.
> He cast his net, and will (bring) down the birds.

This same fear shows in other descriptions of Enlil, who may let his people perish in the merciless storm. The god's rage is almost pathological, an inner turmoil of the soul which renders him insensate, inaccessible to all appeals:

> O father Enlil, whose eyes are glaring (wildly),
> How long—till they will be at peace again?
> O thou who covered up thy head with a cloth—how long?
> O thou who laid thy head upon thy knees—how long?
> O thou who closed thy heart like an earthen box—how long?
> O mighty one who with thy fingers sealed thine ears—how long?
> O father Enlil, even now they perish!

C. THE POWER IN THE EARTH: FERTILITY

The third great component of the visible cosmos is the Earth, and the Mesopotamians acknowledged it as the third most important power in the universe. Their understanding of this power and its ways was gained, as with sky and storm, in direct experience of it as inner will and direction. Correspondingly, the ancient name of this deity, *Ki*, "Earth," had difficulty in maintaining itself and tended ever more to give way to other names based on significant characteristics. The earth revealed itself to the Mesopotamians before all as "Mother Earth," the great inexhaustible mysterious source of new life, of fertility in all its forms. Every year she gives birth anew to grass and plants. The arid desert becomes green overnight. The shepherds drive out their flocks. Ewes and goats give birth to lambs and kids. Everything thrives and increases. On the good fields of Shumer "grain, the green maiden, lifts her head in the furrow"; soon a rich harvest will fill granaries and storehouses to overflowing. Well-fed humanity, full of beer, bread, and milk, will feel abundant life surge through their bodies in a wave of profound well-being.

The force active in all this—the power manifesting itself in fertility, in birth, in new life—is the essence of the earth. The earth, as a divine power, is *Nin-tu*, "the lady who gives birth"; she is *Níg-zi-gál-dím-me*, "the fashioner of everything wherein is the breath of life." Reliefs show her as a woman suckling a child; other children are tucked away under her dress and peep out wherever they can; embryos surround her. As the incarnation of all reproductive forces in the universe, she is the "mother of the gods" and also the mother and creator of mankind; indeed, she is—as an inscription states—the "mother of all children." If she so wills, she may deny an evildoer offspring or even stop all birth in the land.

As the active principle in birth and fertility, in the continual renewal of vegetation, the growth of crops, the increase of flocks, the perpetuation of the human race, she holds with right her position as a dominant power, takes her seat with Anu and Enlil in the assembly of the gods, the ruling body of the universe. She is *Nin-mah*, "the exalted queen"; she is "queen of the gods," "queen of kings and lords," the "lady who determines fates," and the "lady who makes decisions concerning (all) heaven and earth."

D. THE POWER IN THE WATER: CREATIVITY

But the earth, so near to man, so varied and manifold in characteristics, is—as we have mentioned—not easily comprehended as an entity by the mind. It is too rich and diverse for any single concept to express fully. We have just described one of its basic aspects, the fertile soil, the active principle in birth and procreation, Mother Earth. But from the earth also come the life-giving sweet waters, the water in wells, in springs, in rivers; and in very early times these "waters which wander in the earth" seem to have been considered as part of its being, an aspect among many aspects under which it might be viewed. If so viewed, however, the power manifest in it was male, *En-ki*, "lord of the earth." In historical times only Enki's name and the role he plays in certain myths give any indication that he and the sweet water for which he stands were once merely an aspect of the earth as such. The waters and the power in them have emancipated themselves, have their own independent individuality and peculiar essence. The power which revealed itself to the Mesopotamian in his subjective experience of water was a creative power, a divine will to produce new life, new beings, new things. In this respect it was akin to the powers in the earth, in the fertile soil. And yet there was a difference—that between passive and active. The Earth, Ki, Ninhursaga, or whatever else we may choose to call her, was immobile; hers is the passive productivity, fertility. Water, on the other hand, comes and goes. It flows out over the field, irrigating it; then it trickles away and is gone. It is as though it were possessed of will and purpose. It typifies active productivity, conscious thought, creativity.

Moreover, the ways of water are devious. If avoids rather than surmounts obstacles, goes around and yet gets to its goal. The farmer, who works with it in irrigation, easing it along from canal to canal, knows how tricky it can be, how easily it slips away, takes unforeseen turns. And so, we may assume, the idea of cunning, of superior intelligence, came to be imparted to Enki. This aspect of his being would be further developed by contemplation of the dark, brooding, impenetrable waters of wells and lagoons, which suggested perhaps the more profound intellectual qualities, wisdom and knowledge. In the functioning of the universe the powers which are peculiarly Enki's manifest themselves often and in many places. They are directly active in the roles played by water everywhere: when it falls from heaven as rain, when it comes flowing down in the rivers, when it is led through canals out over fields and orchards where it produces the crops of the country and the prosperity of the people. But Enki's essence is also manifest in all knowledge. It is the creative element in thought, whether it produces new effective patterns of action, such as wise counsel (Enki is the one who gives to rulers their broad intelligence and "opens the door of understanding") or produces new things, as in the skill of the craftsman (Enki is the god of the craftsmen par excellence). Beyond all, however, his essence, his powers, show themselves in the powerful spells of the incantation priests. It is he who gives the powerful orders which constitute the priest's spells, orders which will assuage angry forces or drive away evil demons that have attacked man.

The range of the forces which are Enki's, the place which they occupy in the organized universe, is expressed with great precision in the office which Enki holds in the world state. He is a *nun*, that is, a great nobleman of the realm outstanding by experience and wisdom—a councilor, not unlike the Anglo-Saxon *witan*. But he is not a king, not a ruler in his own right. The position he holds in the world state he holds by appointment. His authority derives from Anu and Enlil; he is their minister. In modern terms one might perhaps call him Secretary of Agriculture in the universe. He is charged with overseeing rivers, canals, and irrigation and of organizing the productive forces of the country. He smooths out such difficulties as may arise by wise counsel, by arbitration, and by reconciliation. We may quote from a Sumerian hymn which describes him and his office clearly and well:

> O Lord, who with thy wizard's eyes, even when wrapped in thought,
>   immobile, yet dost penetrate all things,
> O Enki, with thy limitless awareness, exalted counsel
>   of the Anunnaki,
> Very knowing one, who dost exact obedience when turning his wit
>   to conciliation and decision,
> Settling of legal strife; counselor
>   from sunrise until sunset,
> O Enki, master over prudent words, to thee
>   I will give praise.
> Anu thy father, pristine king and ruler
>   over an inchoate world,
> Empowered thee, in heaven and on earth, to guide and form,
>   exalted thee to lordship over them.
> To clear the pure mouths of the Tigris and Euphrates,
>   to make verdure plentiful,
> Make dense the clouds, grant water in abundance
>   to all plowlands,
> To make corn lift its head in furrows and to make
>   pasture abundant in the desert,

> To make young saplings in plantations and in orchards
>   sprout, where planted like a forest—
> These acts did Anu, king of gods, entrust to thee;
>   while Enlil granted thee his potent awesome name....
> As ruler over all that has been born
>   thou art a younger Enlil,
> Younger brother of him, thou art, who is sole god
>   in heaven and on earth.
> To fix, like him, the fates of North and South
>   he truly has empowered thee.
> When thy righteous decision and pronouncement cause
>   deserted cities to be reinhabited,
> When, O Sabara, countless people have been settled
>   throughout the country far and wide,
> Thou dost concern thee with their sustenance,
>   a father, in truth, thou art to them.
> They praise the greatness of their Lord and God.

Summary: The Cosmic State And Its Structure

With Enki we may halt the detailed presentation of entities and powers in the Mesopotamian's universe. The list is long; some are powers within things and phenomena in nature, others—at least to our way of thinking—represent abstract concepts. Each of them influenced the course of the world in one particular way, within one well-defined sphere of action. All derived their authority from some power higher up in that hierarchy of powers which constituted the universe. In some cases, as in that of Enki, it was the highest authority, Anu, or Enlil, who had conferred the office in question. Frequently, however, it was somebody lower down in the scale; for just as a human state embodies many different subsidiary power-structures at various levels—families, great estates, etc.—each with its own organization but all integrated with the larger structure of the state, so did the cosmic state. It, too, had such minor power-groups: divine families, divine households, divine estates with stewards, overseers, servants, and other attendants.

But the basic lines of the view which the Mesopotamians took of their universe have, we hope, become clear. We may summarize as follows: The Mesopotamian universe did not, like ours, show a fundamental bipartition into animate and inanimate, living and dead, matter. Nor had it different levels of reality: anything that could be felt, experienced, or thought had thereby established its existence, was part of the cosmos. In the Mesopotamian universe, therefore, everything, whether living being, thing, or abstract concept—every stone, every tree, every notion—had a will and character of its own.

World order, the regularity and system observable in the universe, could accordingly—in a universe made up exclusively of individuals—be conceived of in only one fashion: as an order of wills. The universe as an organized whole was a society, a state.

The form of state under which the Mesopotamians viewed the universe, furthermore, was that of Primitive Democracy, which seems to have been the form of state prevalent in the age when Mesopotamian civilization itself came into being.

In the Primitive Democracy of early Mesopotamia—as in the fully developed democracies of the classical world—participation in government belonged to a large part of, but by no means to all, the members of the state. Slaves, children, and women, for instance, had no share in government in democratic Athens; neither had similar groups in the Mesopotamian city-states any voice in the popular assembly. Correspondingly, in the universal state there were many members who had no political influence, no share in its government. To these groups belonged, to mention one example, man. Man's position in the state of the universe precisely paralleled that of the slave in the human city-state.

Political influence was wielded in the universe only by those members who, by virtue of the power inherent in them, could be classed as gods. They alone were truly citizens in the political sense. We have mentioned a few of the most important: sky, storm, earth, water. Each god, furthermore, was seen as the expression or manifestation of a will and power to be thus and act thus. Enlil, for instance, is the will and power to rage in a storm and also the will and power to destroy a populous city in an attack by barbaric mountaineers; both storm and destruction were seen as manifestations of one and the same essence. But the realization of these many wills does not produce anarchy or chaos. Each power has limits within which it functions, a task and an office which it performs. Its will is integrated with those of other powers in the total pattern of conduct which makes the universe a structure, an organized whole.

The basic integration is traceable to Anu. The other powers voluntarily adapt themselves to his authority. He gives to each its task and office in the world state; and so his will is the "foundation" of the universe, reflected throughout its structure.

But, as any state *must* be, the Mesopotamian universe is dynamic, not static. Mere assignment of tasks and offices does not make a state. The state is, and functions through, the co-operation of the wills that hold the offices, in their readjustment to one another, in their alignment for concerted action in a given situation, in questions of general concern. For such alignment of wills the Mesopotamian universe has a general assembly of all citizens. In this assembly Anu presides and directs proceedings. Questions are discussed by the members pro and con until a consensus begins to stand out; the scales are weighted for it by assent from the seven most prominent gods, among them Anu and Enlil; and thus destinies, the great coming events, are shaped, are agreed to, are backed by the united wills of all the great powers of the universe, and are carried into effect by Enlil. Thus functions the universe.

Bibliography

F. M. CORNFORD, *From Religion to Philosophy* (1912).
HENRI FRANKFORT, *Birth of Civilization in the Near East* (1968).
HENRI FRANKFORT, et al., *Before Philosophy* (1949).
W. W. HALLO and W. K. SIMPSON, *The Ancient Near East: A History* (1971).
THORKILD JACOBSEN, *The Treasures of Darkness: A History of Mesopotamian Religion* (1976).
JOHN A. WILSON, *The Culture of Ancient Egypt* (1956).

Was Greek Civilization Based on Slave Labor?

M. I. FINLEY

When we think of Greek civilization, we think of the free, self-critical mind and high cultural achievement. We associate Greek philosophical and scientific writings with the most intellectually creative periods in Western history. However, there is another side of Greek civilization. Greek society was shot through with slaves, the great majority of whom had been taken captive in military conquests of foreign people.

As a percentage of the population, slaves in ancient Greece probably equalled the numbers in the American south in the nineteenth century. However, Greek slavery was far more diversified. So prominent a place did slaves hold in the Greek economy that the latter would not have functioned very effectively without them. Although most slaves were employed in agriculture, they could also be found in virtually every business, in banking and commerce as well as on the farm. Every Greek who could do so acquired one or more slaves to help at home and at work.

Unlike indigenous Greek helots (serfs) and American slaves, who could not escape their bondage, Greek slaves could rise to positions of near independence and even gain their freedom outright. That slaves could be flogged by their owners, that thousands were at all times fugitives, makes clear that Greek slavery was not a happy state. Nonetheless, both the Greek philosophers and the "man in the street" deemed slavery a morally tolerable institution.

The number of slaves in western Europe dwindled considerably between the ninth and twelfth centuries due to a greatly diminished supply of foreign captives and the growing influence of Christianity. Manumission came to be looked upon as an act of piety, and tenant-farming proved economically more viable than slave labor in agriculture. Although slavery persisted throughout the Middle Ages, after the ninth century it was a waning institution by comparison with ancient Greece and Rome.

From *Economy and Society in Ancient Greece* by M. I. Finley. Copyright © 1953, 1955, 1956, 1957, 1960, 1962, 1964, 1965, 1976, 1978, 1981 by M. I. Finley. Reprinted by permission of Viking Penguin Inc.

I

Two generalisations may be made at the outset. First: at all times and in all places the Greek world relied on some form (or forms) of dependent labour to meet its needs, both public and private. By this I mean that dependent labour was essential, in a significant measure, if the requirements of agriculture, trade, manufacture, public works, and war production were to be fulfilled. And by dependent labour I mean work performed under compulsions other than those of kinship or communal obligations. Second: with the rarest of exceptions, there were always substantial numbers of free men engaged in productive labour. By this I mean primarily not free hired labour but free men working on their own (or leased) land or in their shops or homes as craftsmen and shopkeepers. It is within the framework created by these two generalisations that the questions must be asked which seek to locate slavery in the society. And by slavery, finally, I mean the status in which a man is, in the eyes of the law and of public opinion and with respect to all parties, a possession, a chattel, of another man.

How completely the Greeks always took slavery for granted as one of the facts of human existence is abundantly evident to anyone who has read their literature. In the Homeric poems it is assumed (correctly) that captive women will be taken home as slaves, and that occasional male slaves—the victims of Phoenician merchant-pirates—will also be on hand. In the early seventh century BC, when Hesiod, the Boeotian 'peasant' poet, gets down to practical advice in his *Works and Days*, he tells his brother how to use slaves properly; that they will be available is simply assumed. The same is true of Xenophon's manual for the gentleman farmer, the *Oeconomicus*, written about 375 BC. A few years earlier, an Athenian cripple who was appealing a decision dropping him from the dole, said to the Council: 'I have a trade which brings me in a little, but I can hardly work at it myself and I cannot afford to buy someone to replace myself in it'. In the first book of the Pseudo-Aristotelian *Oeconomica*, a Peripatetic work probably of the late fourth or early third century BC, we find the following proposition about the organisation of the household, stated as baldly and flatly as it could possibly be done: 'Of property, the first and most necessary kind, the best and most manageable, is man. Therefore the first step is to procure good slaves. Of slaves there are two kinds, the overseer and the worker'. Polybius, discussing the strategic situation of Byzantium, speaks quite casually of 'the necessities of life—cattle and slaves' which come from the Black Sea region. And so on.

The Greek language had an astonishing range of vocabulary for slaves, unparalleled in my knowledge. In the earliest texts, Homer and Hesiod, there were two basic words for slave, *dmos* and *doulos*, used without any discoverable distinction between them, and both with uncertain etymologies. *Dmos* died out quickly, surviving only in poetry, whereas *doulos* remained the basic word, so to speak, all through Greek history, and the root on which there were built such words as *douleia*, 'slavery'. But Homer already has, in one possibly interpolated passage, the word (in the plural form) *andrapoda* ('man-footed' = human being) which became very common, having been constructed on the model of *tetrapoda* ('four-footed' = animal). These words were strictly servile, except in such metaphors as 'the Athenians enslaved the allies'. But there was still another group which could be used for both slaves and free men, depending on the context. Three of them are built on the household root, *oikos*—*oikeus*, *oiketes*, and *oikiatas*—and the pattern of usage is variegated and complicated. For example, these *oikos*-words sometimes meant merely 'servant' or 'slave' generally, and sometimes, though less often, they indicated narrower distinctions, such as houseborn slave (as against purchased) or privately owned (as against royal in the Hellenistic context).

If we think of ancient society as made up of a spectrum of statuses, with the free citizen at one end and the slave at the other, and with a considerable number of shades of dependence in between, we shall quickly discover different 'lines' on the spectrum: the Spartan helot (with such parallels as the *penestes* of Thessaly); the debt-bondsman, who was not a slave although under some conditions he could eventually be sold into slavery abroad; the conditionally manumitted slave; and, finally, the freedman. These categories rarely, if ever, appeared concurrently within the same community, nor were they equal in importance or equally significant in all periods of Greek history. By and large, the slave proper was the decisive figure (to the virtual exclusion of the others) in the economically and politically advanced communities; whereas helotage and debt-bondage were to be found in the more archaic communities, whether in Crete or Sparta or Thessaly at an even late date, or in Athens in its pre-Solonian period. There is also some correlation, though by no means a perfect one, between the various categories of dependent labour and their function. Slavery was the most flexible of the forms, adaptable to all kinds and levels of activity, whereas helotage and the rest were best suited to agriculture, pasturage, and household service, much less so to manufacture and trade.

II

With little exception, there was no activity, productive or unproductive, public or private, pleasant or unpleasant, which was not performed by slaves at some times and in some places in the Greek world. The major exception was, of course, political: no slave held public office or sat on the deliberative and judicial bodies (though slaves were commonly employed in the 'civil service', as secretaries and clerks, and as policemen and prison attendants). Slaves did not fight as a rule, either, unless freed (although helots apparently did), and they were very rare in the liberal professions, including medicine. On the other side, there was no activity which was not performed by free men at some times and in some places. That is sometimes denied, but the denial rests on a gross error, namely, the failure to differentiate between a free man working for himself and one working for another, for hire. In the Greek scale of values, the crucial test was not so much the nature of the work (within limits, of course) as the condition or status under which it was carried on. 'The condition of the free man', said Aristotle 'is that he does not live under the constraint of another.' On this point, Aristotle was expressing a nearly universal Greek notion. Although we find free Greeks doing every kind of work, the free wage-earner, the free man who regularly works for another and therefore 'lives under the constraint of another' is a rare figure in the sources, and he surely was a minor factor in the picture.

The basic economic activity was, of course, agriculture. Throughout Greek history, the overwhelming majority of the population had its main wealth in the land. And the majority were smallholders, depending on their own labour, the labour of other members of the family, and the occasional assistance (as in time of harvest) of neighbours and casual hired hands. Some proportion of these smallholders owned a slave, or even two, but we cannot possibly determine what the proportion was, and in this sector the whole issue is clearly not of the greatest importance. But the large landholders, a minority though they were, constituted the political (and often the intellectual) elite of the Greek world; our evidence reveals remarkably few names of any consequence whose economic base was outside the land. This landholding elite tended to become more and more of an absentee group in the course of Greek history; but early or late, whether they sat on their estates or in the cities, dependent labour worked their land as a basic rule (even when allowance is made for tenancy). In some areas it took the form of helotage, and in the archaic period, of debt-bondage, but generally the form was outright slavery.

I am aware, of course, that this view of slavery in Greek agriculture is contested. Nevertheless, I accept the evidence of the line of authors whom I have already cited, from Hesiod to the pseudo-Aristotelian *Oeconomica*. These are all matter-of-fact writings, not utopias or speculative statements of what ought to be. If slavery was not the customary labour form on the larger holdings, then I cannot imagine what Hesiod or Xenophone or the Peripatetic were doing, or why any Greek bothered to read their works. One similar piece of evidence is worth adding. There was a Greek harvest festival called the Kronia, which was celebrated in Athens and other places (especially among the Ionians). One feature, says the Athenian chronicler Philochorus, was that 'the heads of families ate the crops and fruits at the same table with their slaves, with whom they had shared the labours of cultivation. For the god is pleased with this honour from the slaves in contemplation of their labours.' Neither the practice nor Philochorus' explanation of it makes any sense whatever if slavery was as unimportant in agriculture as some modern writers pretend.

I had better be perfectly clear here: I am not saying that slaves outnumbered free men in agriculture, or that the bulk of farming was done by slaves, but that slavery dominated agriculture in so far as it was on a scale that transcended the labour of the householder and his sons. Nor am I suggesting that there was no hired free labour; rather that there was little of any significance. Among the slaves, furthermore, were the overseers, invariably so if the property was large enough or if the owner was an absentee. 'Of slaves,' said the author of the *Oeconomica*, 'there are two kinds, the overseer and the worker.'

In mining and quarrying the situation was decisively one-sided. There were free men, in Athens for example, who leased such small mining concessions that they were able to work them alone. The moment, however, additional labour was introduced (and that was by far the more common case), it seems always to have been slave. The largest individual holdings of slaves in Athens were workers in the mines, topped by the one thousand reported to have been leased out for this purpose by the fifth-century general Nicias. It has been suggested, indeed, that at one point there may have been as many as thirty thousand slaves at work in the Athenian silver mines and processing mills.

Manufacture was like agriculture in that the choice was (even more exclusively) between the independent craftsman working alone or with members of his family and the owner of slaves. The link with slavery was so close (and the absence of free hired labour so complete), that Demosthenes, for example, could say 'they caused the *ergasterion* (workshop) to disappear' and then he could follow, as an exact synonym and with no possible misunderstanding, by saying that 'they caused the slaves to disappear'. On the other hand, the proportion of operations employing slaves, as against the independent self-employed craftsmen, was probably greater than in agriculture, and in this respect more like mining. In commerce and banking, subordinates were invariably slaves, even in such posts as 'bank manager'. However the numbers were small.

In the domestic field, finally, we can take it as a rule that any free man who possibly could afford one, owned a slave attendant who accompanied him when he walked abroad in the town or when he travelled (including his military service), and also a slave woman for the household chores. There is no conceivable way of estimating how many such free men there were, or how many owned numbers of domestics, but the fact is taken for granted so completely and so often in the literature that I strongly believe that many owned slaves even when they could not afford them. (Modern parallels will come to mind readily.) I stress this for two reasons. First, the need for domestic slaves, often an unproductive element, should serve as a cautionary sign when one examines such questions as efficiency and cost of slave labour. Secondly, domestic slavery was by no means entirely unproductive. In the countryside in particular, but also in the towns, two important industries would often be in their hands in the larger households, on a straight production for household consumption basis. I refer to baking and textile making, and every medievalist, at least, will at once grasp the significance of the withdrawal of the latter from market production, even if the withdrawal was far from complete.

It would be very helpful if we had some idea how many slaves there were in any given Greek community to carry on all this work, and how they were divided among the branches of the economy. Unfortunately we have no reliable figures, and none at all for most of the *poleis* [city-states]. What I consider to be the best computations for Athens suggest that the total of slaves reached 60–80,000 in peak periods in the fifth and fourth centuries BC. Athens had the largest population in the classical Greek world and the largest number of slaves. Thucydides said that there were more slaves in his day on the island of Chios than in any other Greek community except Sparta, but I suggest that he was thinking of the density of the slave population measured against the free, not of absolute totals (and in Sparta he meant the helots, not chattel slaves). Other places, such as Aegina or Corinth, may at one time or another also have had a higher ratio of slaves than Athens. And there were surely communities in which the slaves were less dense.

More than that we can scarcely say about the numbers, but I think that is really enough. There is too much tendentious discussion of numbers in the literature already, as if a mere count of heads is the answer to all the complicated questions which flow from the existence of slavery. The Athenian figures I mentioned amount to an average of no less than three or four slaves to each free household (including all free men in the calculation, whether citizen or not). But even the smallest figure anyone has suggested, 20,000 slaves in Demosthenes' time—altogether too low in my opinion—would be roughly equivalent to one slave for each adult citizen, no negligible ratio. Within very broad limits, the numbers are irrelevant to the question of significance. When Starr, for example, objects to 'exaggerated guesses' and replies that 'the most careful estimates... reduce the proportion of slaves to far less than half the population, probably one third or one quarter at most', he is proving far less than he thinks. No one seriously believes that slaves did all the work in Athens (or anywhere else in Greece except for Sparta with its helots), and one merely confuses the issues when one pretends that somehow a reduction of the estimates to only a third or a quarter of the population is crucial. In 1860, according to official census figures, slightly less than one-third of the total population of the American slave states were slaves. Furthermore, 'nearly three-fourths of all free Southerners had no connection with slavery through either family ties or direct ownership. The "typical" Southerner was not only a small farmer but also a non-slaveholder.' Yet no one would think of denying that slavery was a decisive element in southern society. The analogy seems obvious for ancient Greece, where, it can be shown, ownership of slaves was even more widely spread among the free men and the use of slaves much more diversified, and where the estimates do not give a ratio significantly below the American one. Simply stated, there can be no denial that there were enough slaves about for them to be, of necessity, an integral factor in the society.

There were two main sources of supply. One was captives, the victims of war and sometimes piracy. One of the few generalisations about the ancient world to which there is no exception is this, that the victorious power had absolute right over the persons and the property of the vanquished. This right was not exercised to its full extent every time, but it was exercised often enough, and on a large enough scale, to throw a continuous and numerous supply of men, women, and children on to the slave market. Alongside the captives we must place the so-called barbarians who came into the Greek world in a steady stream—Thracians, Scythians, Cappadocians, etc.—through the activity of full-time traders, much like the process by which African slaves reached the new world in more modern times. Many were victims of wars among the barbarians themselves. Others came peacefully, so to speak: Herodotus says that the Thracians sold their children for export. The first steps all took place outside the Greek orbit, and our sources tell us virtually nothing about them, but there can be no doubt that large numbers and a steady supply were involved, for there is no other way to explain such facts as the high proportion of Paphlagonians and Thracians among the slaves in the Attic silver mines, many of them specialists, or the corps of Scythian archers (slaves owned by the state) who constituted the Athenian police force.

Merely to complete the picture, we must list penal servitude and the exposure of unwanted children. Beyond mere mention, however, they can be ignored because they were negligible in their importance. There then remains one more source, breeding, and that is a puzzle. One reads in the modern literature that there was very little breeding of slaves (as distinct from helots and the like) among the Greeks because, under their conditions, it was cheaper to buy slaves than to raise them. I am not altogether satisfied with the evidence for this view, and I am altogether dissatisfied with the economics which is supposed to justify it. There were conditions under which breeding was certainly rare, but for reasons which have nothing to do with economics. In the mines, for example, nearly all the slaves were men, and that is the explanation, simply enough. But what about domestics, among whom the proportion of women was surely high? I must leave the question unanswered, except to remove one fallacy. It is sometimes said that there is a demographic law that no slave population ever reproduces itself, that they must always be replenished from outside. Such a law is a myth: that can be said categorically on the evidence of the southern states, evidence which is statistical and reliable.

III

The impression one gets is clearly that the majority of the slaves were foreigners. That is to say, it was the rule (apart from debt-bondage) that Athenians were never kept as slaves in Athens, or Corinthians in Corinth. However, I am referring to the more basic sense, that the majority were not Greeks at all, but men and women from the races living outside the Greek world. It is idle to speculate about the proportions here, but there cannot be any reasonable doubt about the majority. In some places, such as the Laurium silver mines in Attica, this meant relatively large concentrations in a small area. The number of Thracian slaves in Laurium in Xenophon's time, for example, was greater than the total population of some of the smaller Greek city-states.

No wonder some Greeks came to identify slaves and barbarians (a synonym for all non-Greeks). The most serious effort, so far as we know, to justify this view as part of the natural arrangement of things, will be found in the first book of Aristotle's *Politics*. It was not a successful effort for several reasons, of which the most obvious is the fact, as Aristotle himself conceded, that too many were slaves 'by accident', by the chance of warfare or shipwreck or kidnapping. In the end, natural slavery was abandoned as a formal concept, defeated by the pragmatic view that slavery was a fact of life, a conventional institution universally practised. As the Roman jurist Florentinus phrased it, 'Slavery is an institution of the *ius gentium* (law of all nations) whereby someone is subject to the *dominium* of another, contrary to nature.' That view (and even sharper formulations) can be traced back to the sophistic literature of the fifth century BC, and, in a less formal way, to Greek tragedy. I chose Florentinus to quote instead because his definition appears in the *Digest*, in which slavery is so prominent that the Roman law of slavery has been called 'the most characteristic part of the most characteristic intellectual product of Rome'. Nothing illustrates more perfectly the inability of the ancient world to imagine that there could be a civilised society without slaves.

The Greek world was one of endless debate and challenge. Among the intellectuals, no belief or idea was self-evident: every conception and every institution sooner or later came under attack—religious beliefs, ethical values, political systems, aspects of the economy, even such bedrock institutions as the family and private property. Slavery, too, up to a point, but that point was invariably a good distance short of abolitionist proposals. Plato, who criticised society more radically than any other thinker, did not concern himself much with the question in the *Republic*, but even there he assumed the continuance of slavery. And in the *Laws*, 'the number of passages... that deal with slavery is surprisingly large' and the tenor of the legislation is generally more severe than the actual law of Athens at that time. 'Their effect, on the one hand, is to give greater authority to masters in the exercise of rule over slaves, and on the other hand to accentuate the distinction between slave and free man.' Paradoxically, neither were the believers in the brotherhood of man (whether Cynic, Stoic, or early Christian) opponents of slavery. In their eyes, all material concerns, including status, were a matter of essential indifference. Diogenes, it is said, was once seized by pirates and taken to Crete to be sold. At the auction, he pointed to a certain Corinthian among the buyers and said: 'Sell me to him; he needs a master.'

The question must then be faced, how much relevance has all this for the majority of Greeks, for those who were neither philosophers nor wealthy men of leisure? What did the little man think about slavery? It is no answer to argue that we must not take 'the political theorists of the philosophical schools too seriously as having established "the main line of Greek thought concerning slavery"'. No one pretends that Plato and Aristotle speak for all Greeks. But, equally, no one should pretend that lower-class Greeks necessarily rejected everything which we read in Greek literature and philosophy, simply because, with virtually no exceptions, the poets and philosophers were men of the leisure class. The history of ideology and belief is not so simple. It is a commonplace that the little man shares the ideals and aspirations of his betters—in his dreams if not in the hard reality of his daily life. By and large, the vast majority in all periods of history have always taken the basic institutions of society for granted. Men do not, as a rule, ask themselves whether monogamous marriage or a police force or machine production is necessary to their way of life. They accept them as facts, as self-evident. Only when there is a challenge from one source or another—from outside or from catastrophic famine or plague—do such facts become questions.

A large section of the Greek population was always on the edge of marginal subsistence. They worked hard for their livelihood and could not look forward to economic advancement as a reward for their labours; on the contrary, if they moved at all, it was likely to be downward. Famines, plagues, wars, political struggles, all were a threat, and social crisis was a common enough phenomenon in Greek history. Yet through the centuries no ideology of labour appeared, nothing that can in any sense be counterpoised to the negative judgments with which the writings of the leisure class are filled. There was neither a word in the Greek language with which to express the general notion of labour, nor the concept of labour 'as a general social function'. There was plenty of grumbling, of course, and there was pride of craftsmanship. Men could not survive psychologically without them. But neither developed into a belief: grumbling was not turned into a punishment for sin—'In the sweat of thy face shalt thou eat bread'—nor pride of craftsmanship into the virtue of labour, into the doctrine of the calling or anything comparable. The nearest to either will be found in Hesiod's *Works and Days*, and in this context the decisive fact about Hesiod is his unquestioning assumption that the farmer will have proper slave labour.

That was all there was to the poor man's counter-ideology: we live in the iron age when 'men never rest from toil and sorrow by day, and from perishing by night'; therefore it is better to toil than to idle and perish—but if we can we too will turn to the labour of slaves. Hesiod may not have been able, even in his imagination, to think beyond slavery as *supplementary* to his own labour, but that was the seventh century, still the early days of slavery. About 400 BC, however, Lysias' crippled client could make the serious argument in the Athenian Council that he required a dole because he could not afford a slave as a *replacement*. And half a century later Xenophon put forth a scheme whereby every citizen could be maintained by the state, chiefly from revenues to be derived from publicly owned slaves working in the mines.

When talk turned to action, even when crisis turned into civil war and revolution, slavery remained unchallenged. With absolute regularity, all through Greek history, the demand was 'Cancel debts and redistribute the land.' Never, to my knowledge, do we hear a protest from the free poor, not even in the deepest crises, against slave competition. There are no complaints—as there might well have been—that slaves deprive free man of a livelihood, or compel free men to work for lower wages and longer hours. There is nothing remotely resembling a workers' programme, no wage demands, no talk of working conditions or government employment measures or the like. In a city like Athens there was ample opportunity. The *demos* [the common people] had power, enough of them were poor, and they had leaders. But economic assistance took the form of pay for public office and for rowing in the fleet, free admission to the theatre (the so-called theoric fund), and various minor doles; while economic legislation was restricted to imports and exports, weights and measures, price controls. Not even the wildest of the accusations against the demagogues—and they were wholly unrestrained as every reader of Aristophanes or Plato knows—ever suggested anything which would hint at a working-class interest, or an anti-slavery bias.

Nor did the free poor take the other possible tack of joining with the slaves in a common struggle on a principled basis. The Solonic revolution in Athens at the beginning of the sixth century BC, for example, brought an end to debt-bondage and the return of Athenians who had been sold into slavery abroad, but not the emancipation of others, non-Athenians, who were in slavery in Athens. Centuries later, when the great wave of slave revolts came after 140 BC, starting in the Roman west and spreading to the Greek east, the free poor on the whole simply stood apart. It was no issue of theirs, they seem to have thought; correctly so, for the outcome of the revolts promised them nothing one way or the other. Numbers of free men may have taken advantage of the chaos to enrich themselves personally, by looting or otherwise. Essentially that is what they did, when the opportunity arose, in a military campaign, nothing more. The slaves were, in a basic sense, irrelevant to their behaviour at that moment.

In 464 BC a great helot revolt broke out, and in 462 Athens dispatched a hoplite [armed and armored foot-soldier] force under Cimon to help the Spartans suppress it. When the revolt ended, after nearly five years, a group of the rebels were permitted to escape, and it was Athens which provided them refuge, settling them in Naupactus. A comparable shift took place in the first phase of the Peloponnesian War. In 425 the Athenians seized Pylos, a harbour on the west coast of the Peloponnese. The garrison was a small one and Pylos was by no means an important port. Nevertheless, Sparta was so frightened that she soon sued for peace, because the Athenian foothold was a dangerous centre of infection, inviting desertion and eventual revolt among the Messenian helots. Athens finally agreed to peace in 421, and immediately afterwards concluded an alliance with Sparta, one of the terms of which was: 'Should the slave-class rise in rebellion, the Athenians will assist the Spartans with all their might, according to their power.'

Obviously the attitude of one city to the slaves of another lies largely outside our problem. Athens agreed to help suppress helots when she and Sparta were allies; she encouraged helot revolts when they were at war. That reflects elementary tactics, not a judgment about slavery. Much the same kind of distinction must be made in the instances, recurring in Spartan history, when helots were freed as pawns in an internal power struggle. So, too, of the instances which were apparently not uncommon in fourth-century Greece, but about which nothing concrete is known other than the clause in the agreement between Alexander and the Hellenic League, binding the members to guarantee that 'there shall be no killing or banishment contrary to the laws of each city, no confiscation of property, no redistribution of land, no cancellation of debts, no freeing of slaves for purposes of revolution'. These were mere tactics again. Slaves were resources, and they could be useful in a particular situation. But only a number of specific slaves, those who were available at the precise moment; not slaves in general, or all slaves, and surely not slaves in the future. Some slaves were freed, but slavery remained untouched. Exactly the same behaviour can be found in the reverse case, when a state (or ruling class) called upon its slaves to help protect it. Often enough in a military crisis, slaves were freed, conscripted into the army or navy, and called upon to fight. And again the result was that some slaves were freed while the institution continued exactly as before.

In sum under certain conditions of crisis and tension the society (or a sector of it) was faced with a conflict within its system of values and beliefs. It was sometimes necessary, in the interest of national safety or of a political programme, to surrender the normal use of, and approach to, slaves. When this happened, the institution itself survived without any noticeable weakening. The fact that it happened is not without significance;

it suggests that among the Greeks, even in Sparta, there was not that deep-rooted and often neurotic horror of the slaves known in other societies, which would have made the freeing and arming of slaves *en masse*, for whatever purpose, a virtual impossibility. It suggests, further, something about the slaves themselves. Some did fight for their masters, and that is not unimportant.

Nothing is more elusive than the psychology of the slave. Even when, as in the American South, there seems to be a lot of material—autobiographies of ex-slaves, impressions of travellers from non-slaveholding societies, and the like—no unambiguous picture emerges. For antiquity there is scarcely any evidence at all, and the bits are indirect and tangential, and far from easy to interpret. Thus, a favourite apology is to invoke the fact that, apart from very special instances as in Sparta, the record shows neither revolts of slaves nor a fear of uprisings. Even if the facts are granted, the rosy conclusion does not follow. Slaves have scarcely ever revolted, even in the southern states. A large-scale rebellion is impossible to organise and carry through except under very unusual circumstances. The right combination appeared but once in ancient history, during two generations of the late Roman Republic, when there were great concentrations of slaves in Italy and Sicily, many of them almost completely unattended and unguarded, many others professional fighters (gladiators), and when the whole society was in turmoil, with a very marked breakdown of social and moral values.

At this point it is necessary to recall that helots differed in certain key respects from chattel slaves. First, they had the necessary ties of solidarity that come from kinship and nationhood, intensified by the fact, not to be underestimated, that they were not foreigners but a subject people working their own lands in a state of servitude. This complex was lacking among the slaves of the Greek world. The Peripatetic author of the *Oeconomica* made the sensible recommendation that neither an individual nor a city should have many slaves of the same nationality. Secondly, the helots had property rights of a kind: the law, at least, permitted them to retain everything they produced beyond the fixed deliveries to their masters. Third, they outnumbered the free population on a scale without parallel in other Greek communities. These are the peculiar factors, in my opinion, which explain the revolts of the helots and the persistent Spartan concern with the question, more than Spartan cruelty. It is a fallacy to think that the threat of rebellion increases automatically with an increase in misery and oppression. Hunger and torture destroy the spirit; at most they stimulate efforts at flight or other forms of purely individual behaviour (including betrayal of fellow-victims), whereas revolt requires organisation and courage and persistence. Frederick Douglass, who in 1855 wrote the most penetrating analysis to come from an ex-slave, summed up the psychology in these words: 'Beat and cuff your slave, keep him hungry and spiritless, and he will follow the chain of his master like a dog; but feed and clothe him with physical comfort,—and dreams of freedom intrude. Give him a *bad* master, and he aspires to a *good* master; give him a good master, and he wishes to become his *own* master.'

There are many ways, other than revolt, in which slaves can protest. In particular they can flee, and though we have no figures whatsoever, it seems safe to say that the fugitive slave was a chronic and sufficiently numerous phenomenon in the Greek cities. Thucydides estimated that more than 20,000 Athenian slaves fled in the final decade of the Peloponnesian War. In this they were openly encouraged by the Spartan garrison established in Decelea, and Thucydides makes quite a point of the operation. Obviously he thought the harm to Athens was serious, intensified by the fact that many were skilled workers. My immediate concern is with the slaves themselves, not with Athens, and I should stress very heavily that so many skilled slaves (who must be presumed to have been, on the average, among the best treated) took the risk and tried to flee. The risk was no light one, at least for the barbarians among them: no Thracian or Carian wandering about the Greek countryside without credentials could be sure of what lay ahead in Boeotia or Thessaly. Indeed, there is a hint that these particular 20,000 and more may have been very badly treated after escaping under Spartan promise. A reliable fourth-century BC historian attributed the great Theban prosperity at the end of the fifth century to their having purchased very cheaply the slaves and other booty seized from the Athenians during the Spartan occupation of Decelea. Although there is no way to determine whether this is a reference to the 20,000, the suspicion is obvious. Ethics aside, there was no power, within or without the law, which could have prevented the re-enslavement of fugitive slaves even if they had been promised their freedom.

The *Oeconomica* sums up the life of the slave as consisting of three elements: work, punishment, and food. And there are more than enough floggings, and even tortures, in Greek literature, from one end to the other. Apart from psychological quirks (sadism and the like), flogging means simply that the slave, as slave, must be goaded into performing the function assigned to him. So, too, do the various incentive plans which were frequently adopted. The efficient, skilled, reliable slave could look forward to managerial status. In the cities, in particular, he could often achieve a curious sort of quasi-independence, living and working on his own, paying a kind of rental to his owner, and accumulating earnings with which, ultimately, to purchase his freedom. Manumission was, of course, the greatest incentive of all. Again we are baffled by the absence of numbers, but it is undisputed that manumission was a common phenomenon in most of the Greek world. This is an important difference between the Greek slave on the one hand, and the helot or American slave on the other. It is also important evidence about the degree of the slave's alleged "acceptance" of his status.

IV

It is now time to try to add all this up and form some judgment about the institution. This would be difficult enough to do under ordinary circumstances; it has become almost impossible because of two extraneous factors imposed by modern society. The first is the confusion of the historical study with moral judgments about slavery. We condemn slavery, and we are embarrassed for the Greeks, whom we admire so much; therefore we tend either to underestimate its role in their life, or we ignore it altogether, hoping that somehow it will quietly go away. The second factor is more political, and it goes back at least to 1848, when the *Communist Manifesto* declared that 'The history of all hitherto existing society is the history of class struggles. Free man and slave, patrician and plebeian, lord and serf, guild-master and journeyman, in a word, oppressor and oppressed, stood in constant opposition to one another....' Ever since, ancient slavery has been a battleground between Marxists and non-Marxists, a political issue rather than a historical phenomenon.

Now we observe that a sizable fraction of the population of the Greek world consisted of slaves, or other kinds of dependent labour, many of them barbarians; that by and large the elite in each city-state were men of leisure, completely free from any preoccupation with economic matters, thanks to a labour force which they bought and sold, over whom they had extensive property rights, and, equally important, what we may call physical rights; that the condition of servitude was one which no man, woman, or child, regardless of status or wealth, could be sure to escape in case of war or some other unpredictable and uncontrollable emergency. It seems to me that, seeing all this, if we could emancipate ourselves from the despotism of extraneous moral, intellectual, and political pressures, we would conclude, without hesitation, that slavery was a basic element in Greek civilisation.

Such a conclusion, however, should be the starting point of analysis, not the end of an argument, as it is so often at present. Perhaps it would be best to avoid the word 'basic' altogether, because it has been pre-empted as a technical term by the Marxist theory of history. Anyone else who used it in such a question as the one which is the title of this chapter, is compelled, by the intellectual (and political) situation in which we work, to qualify the term at once, to distinguish between *a* basic institution and *the* basic institution. In effect what has happened is that, in the guise of a discussion of ancient slavery, there has been a desultory discussion of Marxist theory, none of it, on either side, particularly illuminating about either Marxism or slavery. Neither our understanding of the historical process nor our knowledge of ancient society is significantly advanced by these repeated statements and counter-statements, affirmations and denials of the proposition, 'Ancient society was based on slave labour.' Nor have we gained much from the persistent debate about causes. Was slavery the cause of the decline of Greek science? or of loose sexual morality? or of the widespread contempt for gainful employment? These are essentially false questions, imposed by a naive kind of pseudo-scientific thinking.

The most fruitful approach, I suggest, is to think in terms of purpose, in Immanuel Kant's sense, or of function, as the social anthropologists use that concept. The question which is most promising for systematic investigation is not whether slavery was the basic element, or whether it caused this or that, but how it functioned. This eliminates the sterile attempts to decide which was historically prior, slavery or something else; it avoids imposing moral judgments on, and prior to, the historical analysis; and it should avoid the trap which I shall call the free-will error. There is a maxim of Emile Durkheim's that 'The voluntary character of a practice or an institution should never be assumed beforehand.' Given the existence of slavery—and it is given, for our sources do not permit us to go back to a stage in Greek history when it did not exist—the choice facing individual Greeks was socially and psychologically imposed. In the *Memorabilia* Xenophon says that 'those who can do so buy slaves so that they may have fellow workers'. That sentence is often quoted to prove that some Greeks owned no slaves, which needs no proof. It is much better cited to prove that *those who can*, buy slaves—Xenophon clearly places this whole phenomenon squarely in the realm of necessity.

The question of function permits no single answer. There are as many answers as there are contexts: function in relation to what? And when? And where? Buckland begins his work on the Roman law of slavery by noting that there 'is scarcely a problem which can present itself, in any branch of law, the solution of which may not be affected by the fact that one of the parties to the transaction is a slave.' That sums up the situation in its simplest, most naked form, and it is as correct a statement for Greek law as for Roman. Beyond that, I would argue, there is no problem or practice in any branch of Greek life which was not affected, in some fashion, by the fact that many people in that society, even if not in the specific situation under consideration, were (or had been or might be) slaves. The connection was not always simple or direct, nor was the impact necessarily 'bad' (or 'good'). The historian's problem is precisely to uncover what the connections were, in all their concreteness and complexity, their goodness or badness or moral neutrality.

I think we will find that, more often than not, the institution of slavery turned out to be ambiguous in its function. Certainly the Greek attitudes to it were shot through with ambiguity, and not rarely with tension. To the Greeks, Nietzsche said, both labour and slavery were 'a necessary disgrace, of which one feels *ashamed*, as a disgrace and as a necessity at the same time'. There was a lot of discussion: that is clear from the literature which has survived, and it was neither easy nor unequivocally one-sided, even though it did not end in abolitionism. In Roman law 'slavery is the only case in which, in the extant sources..., a conflict is declared to exist between the *Ius Gentium* [the law of the people] and the *Ius Naturale*' [the law of nature]. In a sense, that was an academic conflict, since slavery went right on; but no society can carry such a conflict within it, around so important a set of beliefs and institutions, without the stresses erupting in some fashion no matter how remote and extended the lines and connections may be from the original stimulus. Perhaps the most interesting sign among the Greeks can be found in the proposals, and to an extent the practice in the fourth century BC, to give up the enslavement of Greeks. They all came to nought in the Hellenistic world, and I suggest that this one fact reveals much about Greek civilisation after Alexander.

It is worth calling attention to two examples pregnant with ambiguity, neither of which has received the attention it deserves. The first comes from Locris, the Greek colony in southern Italy, where descent was said to be matrilineal, an anomaly which Aristotle explained historically. The reason, he said, was that the colony was originally founded by slaves and their children by free women. Timaeus wrote a violent protest against this insulting account, and Polybius, in turn, defended Aristotle in a long digression, of which unfortunately only fragments survive. One of his remarks is particularly worth quoting: 'To suppose, with Timaeus, that it was unlikely that men, who had been the slaves of the allies of the Spartans, would continue the kindly feelings and adopt the friendships of their late masters is foolish. For when they have had the good fortune to recover their freedom, and a certain time has elapsed, men, who had been slaves, not only endeavour to adopt the friendships of their late masters, but also their ties of hospitality and blood; in fact, their aim is to keep them up even more than the ties of nature, for the express purpose of thereby wiping out the remembrance of their former degradation and humble position, because they wish to pose as the descendants of their masters rather than as their freedmen.'

In the course of his polemic Timaeus had said that 'it was not customary for the Greeks of early times to be served by bought slaves.' This distinction, between slaves who were bought and slaves who were captured (or bred from captives), had severe moral overtones. Inevitably, as was their habit, the Greeks found a historical origin for the practice of buying slaves—in the island of Chios. The historian Theopompus, a native of the island, phrased it this way: 'The Chians were the first of the Greeks, after the Thessalians and Lacedaemonians, who used slaves. But they did not acquire them in the same manner as the latter; for the Lacedaemonians and Thessalians will be found to have derived their slaves from the Greeks who formerly inhabited the territory which they now possess,... calling them helots and *penestae*, respectively. But the Chians possessed barbarian slaves, for whom they paid a price.' This quotation is preserved by Athenaeus, who was writing about 200 AD and who went on to comment that the Chians ultimately received divine punishment for their innovation....

This is not very good history, but that does not make it any less important. By a remarkable coincidence Chios provides us with the earliest contemporary evidence of democratic institutions in the Greek world. In a Chian inscription dated, most probably, to the years 575–550 BC, there is unmistakable reference to a popular council and to the 'laws (or ordinances) of the *demos*'. I do not wish to assign any significance other than symbolic to this coincidence, but it is a symbol with enormous implications. I have already made the point that, the more advanced the Greek city-state, the more it will be found to have had true slavery rather than the 'hybrid' types like helotage. More bluntly put, the cities in which individual freedom reached its highest expression—most obviously Athens—were cities in which chattel slavery flourished. The Greeks, it is well known, discovered both the idea of individual freedom and the institutional framework in which it could be realised. The pre-Greek world—the world of the Sumerians, Babylonians, Egyptians, and Assyrians; and I cannot refrain from adding the Mycenaeans—was, in a very profound sense, a world without free men, in the sense in which the west has come to understand that concept. It was equally a world in which chattel slavery played no role of any consequence. That, too, was a Greek discovery. One aspect of Greek history, in short, is the advance, hand in hand, of freedom *and* slavery.

Bibliography

MARC BLOCH, "How and Why Ancient Slavery Came to an End," in *Slavery and Serfdom in the Middle Ages: Selected Essays by Marc Bloch*, trans. W. R. Beer (1975).
M. I. FINLEY, *Early Greece* (1970).
M. I. FINLEY, ed. *Slavery in Classical Antiquity* (1960).
H. D. F. KITTO, *The Greeks* (1979).
GREGORY VLASTOS, *The Philosophy of Socrates* (1971).
F. W. WALBANK, *The Hellenistic World* (1981).
A. E. ZIMMERN, *The Greek Commonwealth* (1961).

Who Were the First Christians?

WAYNE A. MEEKS

Was Christianity, as many have long maintained, originally a movement of the lowest classes of society, a revolt of the poor and homeless against the rich and propertied? According to Celsus, the early pagan critic of Christianity, the first Christians were "slaves, women, and children," society's weak and illiterate. When, however, one reads very carefully the letters of the apostle Paul, one finds evidence suggesting that the first Christians actually represented a fair cross section of urban society. Although the evidence is necessarily fragmentary and random, patient detective work permits the historian to discover with some precision who was who and who had what among Paul's followers. The resulting social profiles of identifiable individuals in Paul's letters, together with other internal evidence, indicate that the typical Christian came neither from the uppermost nor from the lowest levels of society, although there were both very rich and very poor Christians. The average Christian came rather from a middling group. Christians were largely upwardly mobile free artisans or small merchants, whose ultimate social position was indefinite at the time they became Christian.

"Proletarians" or "Middle Class"?

Celsus, the first pagan author we know of who took Christianity seriously enough to write a book against it, alleged that the church deliberately excluded educated people because the religion was attractive only to "the foolish, dishonourable and stupid, and only slaves, women, and little children." The Christian evangelists, he said, were "wool-workers, cobblers, laundry-workers, and the most illiterate and bucolic yokels," who enticed "children ... and stupid women" to come along "to the wooldresser's shop, or to the cobbler's or the washerwoman's shop, that they may learn perfection." Celsus lived in the second century, but he was sure that

Reprinted with the permission of Yale University Press from *The First Urban Christians: The Social World of the Apostle Paul* by Wayne A. Meeks. Copyright © 1983 by Yale University.

Christianity had always been a movement of the lowest classes, for Jesus himself had only been able to win disciples among "tax-collectors and sailors," people "who had not even a primary education." This was the sort of jeer to which the second-century apologists for Christianity had frequently to respond, and modern authors have more often than not assumed that the early critics were right. Did not Luke's Jesus pronounce a woe against the rich (Luke 6:24), James warn against kowtowing to "the rich who oppress you" (James 2:1–7), and Paul himself write that God had chosen "what is foolish in the world ... what is weak ... what is low and despised" 1 Cor. 1:27)? The notion of early Christianity as a proletarian movement was equally congenial, though for quite different reasons, to Marxist historians and to those bourgeois writers who tended to romanticize poverty.

Of particular importance in shaping this century's common view of Paul and his congregations was the opinion of Adolf Deissmann, professor of the New Testament at Heidelberg, then at Berlin. Deissmann saw that the hundreds of newly discovered documents written on papyrus or ostraca—letters, contracts, school lessons, bills of sale, magical spells—had revolutionary implications for understanding not only the vocabulary and grammar but also the social setting of the New Testament. He had a genius for popularizing the results of his own and others' research, and two extended trips through the Middle East enabled him to reconstruct "the world of St. Paul" in terms of a vivid, thoroughly romantic travelogue. In general his identification of the language of the New Testament with the vulgar $koin\bar{e}$[1] of the nonliterary papyri supported the view that the writers had belonged to the lower classes, but Deissmann had some difficulty in situating Paul himself. His occupation would have placed him among the lowest of the free poor, like the weaver whom Deissmann had watched in Tarsus in 1909, "making a coarse cloth on his poverty-stricken primitive loom," yet "the very fact that he was born a Roman citizen shows that his family cannot have lived in absolutely humble circumstances." Paul wrote unliterary Greek, yet "not vulgar to the degree that finds expression in many contemporary papyri. On the ground of his language Paul should rather be assigned to a higher class." Still, Deissmann was confident that Paul's closest ties were to the "middle and lower classes. ... As a missionary chiefly working amongst the unliterary masses of the great cities Paul did not patronizingly descend into a world strange to him: he remained in his own social world." Until recently most scholars who troubled to ask Deissmann's question at all ignored the ambiguities of the evidence that Deissmann had at least mentioned. The prevailing viewpoint has been that the constituency of early Christianity, the Pauline congregations included, came from the poor and dispossessed of the Roman provinces.

Within the past two decades, however, a number of scholars have looked at the evidence afresh and come to conclusions very different from Deissmann's about the social level of the first-century Christians. The

---

[1] A common Greek dialect used throughout the Hellenistic world.

convergence of these inquiries, which have been undertaken from diverse viewpoints, has led Abraham Malherbe to suggest that "a new consensus may be emerging" which would approve Floyd Filson's dictum of more than forty years ago, "The apostolic church was more nearly a cross section of society than we have sometimes thought." The role of the upper classes is particularly emphasized by E. A. Judge, who points to the pervasive but seldom-mentioned importance of *amicitia* [friendship] and *clientela* [clientage] in Roman society to support his conviction that "Christianity was a movement sponsored by local patrons to their social dependents." Robert M. Grant, looking primarily at evidence from the second through the fourth centuries, concurs: "The triumph of Christianity in a hierarchically organized society necessarily took place from the top down." He infers that, also in the earlier period, Christianity should be viewed "not as a proletarian mass movement but as a relatively small cluster of more or less intense groups, largely middle class in origin...."

If these studies and others like them are indeed moving toward a consensus, it it still not clear just what this consensus will tell us about the social characteristics of the Pauline groups. Some of the scholars just mentioned emphasize the status of the leading figures; others, the social distance between those figures and the majority of the members. To one observer the mixture of classes in the church simply shows that the Christian movement inevitably conforms to the social structure of the society as a whole; to another, it reveals a fundamental conflict between the values of the Christian group and those of the larger society....

A Profile of the First Christians

In the letters of Paul and his disciples written in the first century (that is, leaving aside the Pastorals) sixty-five individuals besides Paul are named or otherwise identified as persons active in local congregations, as traveling companions or agents of Paul, or as both. Some of these are also mentioned in Acts, which adds thirteen other names and an anonymous household. Thus it is possible to draw up a prosopography[2] of Pauline Christianity containing nearly eighty names. About most of them little information is to be found besides the name, and of some not even that. A close look at the whole list, however, does yield some clues about the social texture of the Pauline circle.

The long list of persons to whom Paul sends greetings in Romans 16 poses a problem. Paul may know some of these individuals or groups only by reputation; others he may have met only as individuals traveling in the East. Hence we should count only those whom the text specifically calls Paul's "fellow workers" or the equivalent, or who had earlier belonged to one of the Pauline congregations. That eliminates Apelles (vs. 10); the members

---

[2] A socio-economic profile of a particular group.

of the household of Aristobulus, probably including Herodion (vss. 10–11); the members of the household represented by Asyncritus, Phlegon, Hermes, Patrobas, and Hermas (vs. 14); Mary (vs. 6); the members of the household of Narcissus (vs. 11); Persis, Tryphaena, and Tryphosa (vs. 12); the members of the household represented by Philologus and Julia, Nereus and his sister, and Olympas (vs. 15); and Stachys (vs. 9).

Of the remaining persons mentioned in the letters, sixteen probably or certainly belong to the Pauline groups but lack any clear indicator of their social standing. These are Archippus of Colossae (Philem. 1; Col. 4:17); Aristarchus (Philem. 24; Col. 4:10f.; Acts 19:29; 20:4; 27:2); Demas (Philem. 24; Col. 4:14); Epaphras (Philem. 23; Col. 1:7; 4:12); Epaphroditus of Philippi (Phil. 2:25; 4:18); Jason (Rom. 16:21; not the Jason of Thessalonica in Acts 17:5, 9); Jesus Justus (Col. 4:11); Sosipater (Rom. 16:21; Acts 20:4?); Sosthenes (1 Cor. 1:1); Timothy (1 Thess. 1:1; 3:2, 6; 1 Cor. 4:17; 16:10; 2 Cor. 1:1, 19; Phil. 1:1; 2:19; 2 Thess. 1:1; Col. 1:1; Rom. 16:21; Philem. 1; Acts 16:1–17:14; 18:5; 19:22, 20:4); Titus (2 Cor. 2:13; 7:6–16; 8:6, 16–24; 12:18; Gal. 2:1–3); Tychicus (Col. 4:7f.; Eph. 6:21f.; Acts 20:4); Urbanus (Rom. 16:9); the anonymous "true yokefellow" (Phil. 4:3); and the two anonymous (in the extant text) "brothers" and "delegates of the churches" connected with the collection (2 Cor. 8:18f., 22f.).

We are left with thirty individuals about whose status we have at least a clue. For several the clue is nothing more than the name itself, which in the particular context may be significant. Thus Achaicus (1 Cor. 16:17), Fortunatus (ibid.), Quartus (Rom. 16:23), and Lucius (Rom. 16:21) in Corinth and Clement in Philippi (Phil. 4:3) have Latin names in the two Roman colonies where Latin was the dominant official language. This *may* indicate that their families belonged to the original stock of colonists, who tended to get ahead. One of these, Lucius, is a Jew besides.... On the other hand, the Greek names of Euodia and Syntyche (Phil. 4:2f.) may hint that they were among the merchant groups who were metics [resident aliens] in Philippi. It is to be noted besides that they were women who had sufficient independence to be recognized in their own right as activists in the Pauline mission. Tertius is another Latin name among the Corinthian Christians (Rom. 16:22); in his case we have the further hint of a profession, or at least training, as a scribe. Another professional with a Latin name is Luke (Philem. 24), a physician (Col. 4:14) with Paul, probably in Ephesus. Doctors were often slaves; we might speculate that Luke had been a *medicus* in some Roman *familia*, receiving the name of his master (Lucius, of which Lukas is a hypocorism) on his manumission.

The ability to travel bespeaks some financial means, but not necessarily the traveler's own. Many slaves and freedmen traveled as agents of their masters or mistresses, like the members of Chloe's household who told Paul in Ephesus about Corinthian troubles (1 Cor. 1:11). Ampliatus (Rom. 16:8), who is in Rome after Paul knew him in the East, may be a similar case, for his is a common Latin slave name. Andronicus and Junia(s) (Rom. 16:7) have also moved from the East, where they were imprisoned with Paul somewhere, sometime, to Rome.... Epaenetus (Rom. 16:5), honored as the first Christian convert in Asia, has also traveled to Rome. His name, like that of Ampliatus, suggests but does not prove servile origins. Silvanus (1 Thess. 1:1; 2 Cor. 1:19; 2 Thess. 1:1; cf. 1 Pet. 5:12 and often in Acts), who bears the name of a Latin deity, traveled widely with Paul but perhaps not at his own expense. Acts reports that he had been one of the leaders of the Jerusalem church (15:22) as well as a prophet (15:32), but neither necessarily implies anything about status in the larger society.

We can be slightly more definite about the status of the remaining individuals. Gaius (1 Cor. 1:14; Rom. 16:23) has a good Roman [first name], thus resembling several Corinthian Christians already mentioned, but in addition he has a house ample enough not only to put up Paul, but also to accommodate all the Christian groups in Corinth meeting together (Rom. 16:23). He is evidently a man of some wealth. The same is true of Crispus, whose office as *archisynagōgos* [leader of the synagogue] shows that he not only has high prestige in the Jewish community but is also probably well to do. It is noteworthy that these two are singled out by Paul as people whom he personally baptized at the beginning of Christianity in Corinth (1 Cor. 1:14). It is tempting to assume that the third person mentioned in the same context, Stephanas, the members of whose household were the very first converts... in Achaia (1 Cor. 16:15), was also a person of wealth. That would be too hasty an inference, however. His Greek name might indicate that his family was not part of the original colony, but either indigenous Greek or immigrant, in either case not of the highest social stratum. His having traveled with Achaicus and Fortunatus to see Paul in Ephesus suggests some independence, but they seem to be a more or less official delegation, so their expenses may have been paid by the Corinthian congregations. On the other hand, he heads a household important enough for Paul to mention twice. And the services he has rendered to the Corinthian Christians) (16:15b) seem from the context to be of the sort rendered by patrons rather than by charismatic gifts (*charismata*). It is precisely in contrast to the sometimes disruptive roles of the *pneumatikoi*[3] that Paul urges due recognition to "people like those" (*toioutoi*), namely Stephanas, Achaicus, and Fortunatus. We are probably safe, then, in placing Stephanas fairly high on the scale of wealth, though probably not so high as Gaius and Crispus....

It was also in Corinth, according to Acts 18:2f, that Paul met Prisca and Aquila. Two letters mention a Christian community in their house: 1 Corinthians, when Paul sends greetings from Ephesus (16:19); and Romans, when he sends greetings from Corinth (16:3–5). Moreover, we hear that they have "risked their necks" for Paul (Rom. 16:4). The author of

---

[3] People who are filled with the Spirit.

Acts has other information about them: that Aquila's family came from Pontus, that he was a Jew, that they lived in Rome until forced to leave by Claudius's expulsion of the Jews, and that they were tentmakers (18:2–3). Both have good Roman names, but in Rome that was quite common for Jews, Greek- as well as Latin-speaking, especially for women. We may summarize their known indicators of status as follows: wealth: relatively high. They have been able to move from place to place, and in three cities to establish a sizable household; they have acted as patrons for Paul and for Christian congregations. Occupation: low, but not at the bottom. They are artisans, but independent, and by ancient standards they operate on a fairly large scale. Extraction: middling to low. They are eastern provincials and Jews besides, but assimilated to Greco-Roman culture. One thing more: the fact that Prisca's name is mentioned before her husband's once by Paul and two out of three times in Acts suggests that she has higher status than her husband.

"Chloe's people" (1 Cor. 1:11) are slaves or freedmen or both who have brought news from Corinth to Ephesus. Whether the *familia* was situated in Corinth, with business in Ephesus, or vice versa, is not certain, but the fact that Paul expects the name to be recognized by the Corinthian Christians suggests that Chloe lived there. Whether she herself was a Christian is not stated and cannot be inferred with any confidence. The case of Onesimus and his owners is clearer. Onesimus of Colossae (Philem. 10 and passim; Col. 4:9) was not only a slave but a runaway. There is no indication what his particular task had been in Philemon's service, but Paul's eagerness to have him help in the mission suggests, despite the pun on his former uselessness (Philem. 11), that he may have had some education or special skills. Philemon himself ranks high at least on the dimension of wealth and on evaluation within the sect: he has a house large enough to accommodate a meeting of Christians (Philem. 2) and guests (22) and has been a patron of Christians in other ways as well (5–7). He owns at least one slave, probably a number of them, for Paul's strongly implied request to send the slave Onesimus back to work with him (8–14) evidently is not expected to be a great hardship for Philemon or the household. Apphia is usually taken to be Philemon's wife, but she is mentioned in her own right as "the sister," as Philemon is "beloved" and Timothy "the brother." Otherwise there is no separate indicator of her status.

Another "sister" is particularly interesting: Phoebe, who is recommended to the Roman Christians as *diakonos* of the church in Cenchreae and "*prostatis* of many [others] and myself as well" (Rom. 16:1–2). The two titles (if that is what they are) have evoked endless discussion. Whether *diakonos* represents an office, as perhaps in Phil. 1:1, or whether it means "missionary" or more generally "helper" is of considerable interest for questions of the internal governance of the early Christian groups and for questions about the role of women. It cannot, however, tell us anything directly about Phoebe's status in the macrosociety. Nor could *prostatis* if, as some commentators have recently urged, it is to be translated as "president" or the like. The term was used in that official sense in some Hellenistic cities, in the place of the more usual *prytaneis* ("executive officers"), and as a title, or in the general sense of "leader," of officers of clubs or guilds. If it were a title in Rom. 16:2, it would be in this latter sense, which is the way Paul uses the cognate participle in 1 Thess. 5:12: "those who labor among you and preside [*proistamenoi*] over you in the Lord and admonish you." That meaning, however, is rendered impossible by the context, for it is difficult to imagine what Paul could have meant by describing Phoebe as "also presiding over me." ... Paul says that Phoebe has been the protector or patroness of many Christians, including himself, and "for that reason" he asks that the Roman Christians provide her with whatever she needs during her stay in Rome. We may then infer that Phoebe is an independent woman (she is probably traveling to Rome on business of her own, not solely to carry Paul's letter), who has some wealth and is also one of the leaders of the Christian group in the harbor town of Cenchreae.

Another woman, then living in Rome, may have served as a patroness of Paul in the same loose sense. This is the mother of Rufus (Rom. 16:13). If what Paul means by calling her "my mother, too," is that she was his benefactress, then she, too, had traveled or resided for a time in the East and had some wealth. We obviously cannot put much weight on this possibility, however. We are in only a slightly more secure position to assess the status of Mark, sometime fellow worker of Paul and of Mark's cousin, Barnabas (Philem. 24; Col. 4:10). Mark's mother, according to Acts 12:12, had a house in Jerusalem that accommodated a meeting of the Christians. If that report is trustworthy, the family had some means, and the Latin surname, in a Jerusalem Jew, may imply some social ambition.

The last two persons to be considered from the letters can be reckoned as part of the Pauline circle only with some injustice to them, for they were missionaries in their own right before they met Paul. Barnabas was a leader of the Antioch groups before Paul's conversion; there is good reason to call Paul his fellow worker, in the early years, rather than the reverse. There is not much in the letters to indicate Barnabas's social standing, but 1 Cor. 9:6 says that he and Paul were alone among the apostles in their policy of working with their own hands rather than receiving regular support. Hock has argued that Paul's manner of talking about his own work resembles that found in rhetoricians and philosophers who come from higher social levels and thus think their decision to do menial work something worthy of comment. The parallel between Paul and Barnabas suggests that they might have determined this policy jointly in the earliest stage of their mission, in Antioch and its environs. The picture of Barnabas as a reasonably well-to-do man who deliberately chose the life of an itinerant artisan to support his mission is reinforced by the report in Acts that he was the owner of a farm that he sold, the proceeds going to the Jerusalem Christians (4:36f.). He is also described there as a Levite, of a family that had settled in Cyprus.

Apollos seems to have been more or less a free agent who was drawn into the Pauline orbit—according to Acts, through the good offices of Prisca. Despite a certain competitiveness among their partisans in Corinth (1 Cor. 1:12; 3:1–4:6), there seem to have been good relations between Paul and Apollos (16:12). Again we are dependent on the account in Acts for any clues about status. Acts describes him as an Alexandrian Jew, *logios* and "powerful in the scriptures" (18:24). *Logios* here implies at least rhetorical ability, perhaps also rhetorical training. There is some support for that claim in 1 Corinthians 1–4, where Paul contrasts the "wisdom of God" with, among other things, a human wisdom exhibited in rhetoric. Apollos's apparent ability to travel independently may further indicate some wealth.

The reports of the Pauline associates and converts in Acts must be treated with somewhat more caution, for the account is written a generation later than Paul's letters and depends on traditions that may have been distorted by time and the accidents of transmission. In addition, we must remember that the author of Luke-Acts evidently was interested in portraying the Christian sect as one that obtained favor from well-placed, substantial citizens. A number of women, including Joanna, the wife of Herod's *epitropos* [steward] Chuza, support Jesus and his companions from their own possessions (Luke 8:2f.). The proconsul of Cyprus, Sergius Paulus, summons Barnabas and Paul, is impressed by their miracle as well as by their teaching, and "believes" (Acts 13:7–12). "Not a few Greek women of high standing as well as men" become believers in Thessalonica (17:12, RSV); an Areopagite is converted in Athens (17:34); the procurator Felix converses with Paul often, if not for the highest of motives (24:26); King Agrippa is impressed by Paul's arguments (26:2–31); the "first man" of Malta entertains him, and he heals the official's father (28:7–10). Some or even all of these episodes may be true, but it is well to remember that the author of Luke-Acts is a sophisticated writer who is also capable of inventing typical occasions to make his points.

The list of early leaders of the Antioch congregation (Acts 13:1) is probably a reliable piece of tradition, but because Symeon Niger, Lucius of Cyrene, and Manaen ... were most likely active there before Paul's arrival, I include only Barnabas among the Pauline associates. The asiarchs of Ephesus who were "friends" of Paul (Acts 19:31) had best be left out of account as sounding a bit too much like a Lucan invention; besides, the story does not hint that they became Christians. It would be precarious, too, to draw inferences from the story of the Philippian jailer and his household, converted in response to a familiar sort of miracle (Acts 16:23–34).... A name we have, and a very prominent one, in Acts 13:17–12, which reports the impression made by yet another miracle on Sergius Paulus, proconsul of Cyprus. Still, we do not hear of his being baptized, nor anything else about him or Christianity in Cyprus—although Barnabas goes there later, 15:39—and again we should err on the side of caution by omitting him. The same is true of Dionysius of Athens, whose position as a member of the court of the Areopagus would otherwise have supplied good material for speculation, and with him Damaris, about whom we know nothing anyway (Acts 17:34).

Erastus, associated with Timothy as an assistant of Paul (19:22) ...; Sopater of Beroea (20:4); and Trophimus of Ephesus (20:4; 21:29; 2 Tim. 4:20) all certainly belonged to the Pauline circle, but we know too little about them to make judgments about their social level. Eutychus of Troas, famous forever as the first recorded Christian to fall asleep during a long-winded sermon (20:9–12), does not seriously warrant inclusion. Of Gaius of Macedonia (19:29) we have only the Latin name and the fact that he was free to travel with Paul. The same is true of Secundus of Thessalonica and Gaius of Derbe (20:4).

The three remaining persons named in Acts are all reported to have served as hosts or patrons of Paul and his associates. The most interesting is Lydia, the Thyatiran dealer in purple fabrics, who, as a gentile worshipper of the Jewish God, encounters Paul in Philippi and converts forthwith, with her *oikos* [household] (Acts 16:14f.). She persuades Paul, Silas, and their other companions to move into her house (vss. 15, 40). We have several indicators of her status. First, as a *porphyropōlis* [dealer in purple fabrics] she must have had some wealth, for purple was a luxury item; she also has a household in which several guests can be accommodated. Second, her name, occupation, and place of origin show that she belongs to the Greek-speaking merchants who have settled in Philippi alongside the Italian, agrarian colonists. Third, she is a pagan adherent of the Jewish synagogue. Finally, she is the female head of a household.

A certain Jason (not to be identified with the Jason of Rom. 16:21) is the host of the missionaries in Thessalonica, and consequently is held responsible for their conduct and forced to post bond for them (Acts 17:5–9). He is evidently a gentile, with a good Greek name. He has a house and some wealth. Titius Justus, like Lydia a "worshipper of God," has a house adjacent to the synagogue in Corinth which becomes the temporary domicile of Paul, Silas, and Timothy after their rebuff by the Jews. His name indicates that he may be a Roman citizen; he belongs to the dominant Latin group of the colony. Unfortunately, Acts does not say explicitly whether either Jason or Titius Justus became a Christian.

Our survey of the names mentioned in the Pauline letters and in Acts has yielded few data about the social level of typical Pauline Christians. A statistical analysis of the sort so important in modern, empirical sociology would be entirely unjustified. Yet some patterns have emerged that are not insignificant. Even though many inferences must remain tentative, we can form a cumulative impression of certain types of people who were prominent in the Pauline groups and mission. Before summarizing the results, however, it will be well to look at other, less direct evidence that can be gleaned from the letters. The prosopography may tend to give skewed evidence, for it is after all the leaders, the prominent, and the unusual who would be mentioned by name, and they may very well have stood out in part because their social rankings were different from those of the majority. The letters must be searched for evidence about the social level of anonymous groups within the congregations.

Indirect Evidence

Of the anonymous Christians mentioned in the Pauline letters, there is one group for which the text supplies a rather specific social location: the "saints" who belong to "the household of Caesar" and who join Paul in sending greetings from the place of his imprisonment to the Philippians (Phil. 4:22). Paul does not name any of them, nor does he say how many they are. We do not even know with certainty what city they were in, for some commentators have urged Ephesus or Caesarea as the place of writing, although Rome still seems the most likely. We also do not know whether the Christians in the *familia* were slaves, freedmen, or both, nor where they stood in the internal hierarchy of the *familia*, which ranged from menial domestics to heads of important state bureaus. Nevertheless, the imperial slaves and freedmen as a group had greater real opportunities for upward social mobility than did any other nonelite segment of Roman society, and it is a precious bit of information that some members of this group had found reason to be initiated into Christianity at so early a date.

Apart from the imperial household, we have already seen that there were both slaves and slaveowners among the Pauline Christians. Philemon and Apphia represent the latter category, as does probably Chloe; "Chloe's people" are slaves or former slaves, and Onesimus a slave who, though not a Christian in his master's house, became one as a runaway. How many or what proportion of each category may have been found in each congregation, we have no way of knowing. In 1 Cor. 7:20–24 Paul addresses a slave rhetorically. Although the slave, like the circumcised Jew of verse 18, is introduced [as an example], since the topic has to do with marriage, divorce, and celibacy, it would be a strange example if there were in fact no slaves among the addressees. On the other hand, it would be a mistake to infer from this passage that the majority of Corinthian Christians were slaves. There are no other admonitions in the authentic letters of Paul addressed explicitly to slaves, but in the later letters written in Paul's name (as in the similar one written in the name of Peter) the common Hellenistic moral topic on the duties of household members appears. In Colossians 3:22–25 the admonition to the slaves is much longer than the sentence addressed to masters (4:1), but this does not necessarily imply, as has sometimes been suggested, that the slaves were a majority of the congregation. The content of the admonitions would certainly be more readily approved by owners than by slaves. The parallel in the letter that later came to be known as Ephesians is more significant; the fact that that letter seems to have been designed as an encyclical addressed to several congregations of the Pauline mission area in western Asia Minor confirms the impression that the admonitions represent general expectations about Christian behavior rather than the situation in one particular congregation. In Ephesians 6:5–9 again the directives to the slaves are more extensive than those to the masters, but there is somewhat greater balance than in Colossians. Clearly the expectation is that a typical Pauline congregation would include both slave owners and slaves, and the ethos of the leaders is rather more that of the owners than of the slaves. It is also important to notice that these admonitions are within the context of advice for maintaining the proper—hierarchical—structure of a household.

Among the collections of moral advice, or *paraenesis*, in the letters there are a number of passages addressed to free handworkers or craftsmen. Since our prosopography includes several leaders of the Pauline mission—not least Paul himself—who belong to that category, these passages may repay a closer look. In what is usually taken to be the oldest of the extant letters, to the Christians in Thessalonica, Paul appeals to them "to strive to lead a quiet life, to mind your own business, and to work with your own hands, according to the instructions we gave you, that your behavior may be decent in the view of the outsiders and that you may not be in need" (4:11f.). This instruction probably implies, as Ernest Best says, "that the great majority of the Thessalonian Christians were manual workers, whether skilled or unskilled." It is also important to notice that this is a paraenetic reminder of instruction given the Thessalonian converts when the church was first organized there. It is not a unique admonition fitted to special needs of the Thessalonians, then, but represents the kind of instruction that Paul and his associates generally gave to new converts. That is confirmed by the appearance of a similar sentence in the paraenesis of the later deutero-Pauline encyclical, Eph. 4:28: "Let the thief no longer steal, but rather let him labor, working the good with his (own) hands, that he may have (the means) to share with anyone in need." On the other hand, 2 Thess. 3:6–13 (assuming that 2 Thessalonians is a real letter, whether or not Paul wrote it) presupposes the general teaching but applies it to a particular situation in which some Christians are behaving in a disorderly fashion by refusing to work. This behavior, the author says explicitly, violates the "tradition" which they received from Paul (vs. 6). Further, the example of Paul's own manual labor, which was implicitly a model to be imitated in 1 Thess. 2:9, here becomes that explicitly (vss. 7–9). The admonition is pointedly renewed: "That by working in quietness they should eat their own bread" (vs. 12). It is taken for granted that people work in order to eat, even though the prohibition of verse 10 may refer to the Eucharist or other communal meals.

There are a few passages in which the letters directly mention money. Several have to do with the collection for Jerusalem Christians. In 1 Cor. 16:1–4, Paul gives instructions which he says he also gave to the Galatians. Each person, on the first day of the week, is to "set aside and keep whatever he has succeeded in, so there need be no collections when I come" (vs. 2).... What we see clearly is that the collection is to be assembled little by little, week by week. This bespeaks the economy of small people, not destitute, but not commanding capital either. This, too, would fit the picture of fairly well-off artisans and tradespeople as the typical Christians.

The gift for the Jerusalem poor was intended to be quite substantial, as the term *hadrotēs* ("plenty, lavish gift"; 2 Cor. 8:20) suggests, and as the elaborate plans for collecting it confirm. The extant second letter to the Corinthians contains two appeals for participation in the collection, which may have stood originally in separate letters. In chapter 8, Paul uses the Macedonian Christians' generosity in the project to chide and encourage the Corinthians to do better. The size of the collection in Macedonia is the more remarkable, he says, because of their "abysmal poverty." He implicitly contrasts the economic situation of the addressees. The phrase, "from what one has," in verses 11–12, implies that the Corinthians have the means to "complete" that which was begun the year before. Verse 14 speaks of their abundance in contrast with the Jerusalem Christians' lack....

On the other hand, we should not take the "abysmal poverty" of the Macedonian Christians too literally, for 2 Cor. 9:2–4 suggests that Paul used the same sort of argument with the Macedonians, in reverse. He has bragged to them of the eagerness of the Corinthians. Moreover, we must remember that whereas Paul had been careful not to accept monetary support from the Corinthians, he had done so more than once from the Macedonians (2 Cor. 11:9; Phil. 4:14–19). Their "poverty" may be partly hyperbole occasioned by the structure of Paul's rhetoric in 2 Cor. 8, which depends upon the antithesis of "poverty" and "wealth," "abundance" and "lack," leading on to the goal, beloved also by Hellenistic moralists, of "equity"....

The fact that some members of the Corinthian groups conduct lawsuits against other members also implies some financial or mercantile transactions (1 Cor. 6:1–11). Paul's discussion gives no information about the kind of disputes involved, except that they involve *biōtika*, matters of everyday life. Nor can we infer the level of affluence of the parties, for, as the papyri show, it was a litigious age, when even small traders or village farmers could and did appear before magistrates to complain about the encroachments of their neighbors.

It may or may not be significant that the Pauline letters occasionally use commercial language both directly, to describe aspects of the relationship between the apostle and local congregations, and also metaphorically, to make theological statements. Paul makes a very direct promise to reimburse Philemon for any damages incurred by the defection of his slave Onesimus

(Philem. 18), but he also uses the formal language of partnership to reinforce the epistolary form of recommendation: "If you hold me as your partner, receive him as myself" (vs. 17). The language associated with commercial partnerships is especially evident in the letter to Philippi, both in the elaborate and carefully nuanced "receipt" that Paul gives for the gift the Philippian Christians have sent to help him in prison (4:15–19), and also, doubtless with that gift and the relationship it represented in view, in the general statements of the opening thanksgiving (1:5, 7). In the same letter Paul can speak of his conversion in terms of gain and loss (3:7f.), and his disciple writing to Colossae could speak of Christ's sacrifice as "canceling the note that was against us" (Col. 2:14). By themselves, these passages would prove nothing about the occupations or wealth of Christians, but they may add one small increment to the cumulative impression that many were artisans and merchants with a modest income. The same is true of the proverb Paul quotes in 2 Cor. 12:14b, "Children ought not save up for their parents, but the parents for their children." That does not sound like the ethos of people at the lowest end of the economic scale, who generally regarded their children, at least their sons, as economic assets, added hands in the workshop, and sometimes direct means for escape from financial straits by sale into slavery. It is wealthy misers whom Plutarch castigates for keeping and storing up their wealth for children and heirs.

It is also possible to infer something about social stratification from several of the conflicts that occurred in the Pauline communities. That is clearest in the case of the divisions which appeared when the Corinthian Christians gathered for the Lord's Supper, which Paul rebukes in 1 Cor. 11:17–34.... [J]ust what is the unacceptable behavior that Paul attacks with these heavy warnings and taboos? Instead of the Lord's Supper, "each proceeds with his private supper, and one goes hungry and another gets drunk" (vs. 21). These private suppers ought to be eaten "at home" (22a, 34). But what specific behavior is it that in Paul's view breaks up the communal Lord's meal? The nub of the problem seems to be stated in verse 22, a series of rhetorical questions. This form, of course, is used when the speaker wants to force his audience to draw conclusions for themselves, here, to acknowledge certain unacceptable inferences from their own behavior. Their actions imply that they "despise the congregation of God," because they "humiliate those who do not have.".... [T]his verse makes it clear that the basic division is between the (relatively) rich and the (relatively) poor.

We can go a bit further, thanks to a very illuminating study of this passage by Gerd Theissen. Theissen compares the divisions in the Corinthian Eucharist with two situations familiar in Roman society and therefore, he surmises, also in a Roman colony like Corinth. One was in collegia, where officers were sometimes assigned larger quantities of food than ordinary members. Theissen points out that most clubs and guilds were more socially homogeneous than the Corinthian congregation seems to have been, and therefore conflicting expectations might arise in the latter that would have no occasion in the former. The other situation was a banquet held by a patron, to which his freedmen clients as well as friends of his own social rank were invited. In the society of the principate it was apparently not uncommon for these to become occasions for conspicuous display of social distance and even for humiliation of the clients of the rich, by means of the quality and quantity of food provided to different tables. Theissen cites ... Pliny's letter of advice to a young friend, advocating a less offensive policy for the patronal class.

> ...I happened to be dining with a man—though no particular friend of his—whose elegant economy, as he called it, seemed to me a sort of stingy extravagance. The best dishes were set in front of himself and a select few, and cheap scraps of food before the rest of the company. He had even put the wine into tiny little flasks, divided into three categories, not with the idea of giving his guests the opportunity of choosing, but to make it impossible for them to refuse what they were given. One lot was intended for himself and for us, another for his lesser friends (all his friends are graded) and the third for his and our freedmen. My neighbor at table noticed this and asked me if I approved. I said I did not. "So what do you do?" he asked. "I serve the same to everyone, for when I invite guests it is for a meal, not to make class distinctions; I have brought them as equals to the same table, so I give them the same treatment in everything." "Even the freedmen?" "Of course, for then they are my fellow-diners, not freedmen." "That must cost you a lot." "On the contrary." "How is that?" "Because my freedmen do not drink the sort of wine I do, but I drink theirs."

If a person like Gaius, who opened his house for gatherings of the whole *ekklēsia* [church] of Corinthian Christians, regarded himself very much in the way that the wealthy patron of a private association or a pagan cultic society might do, that would not be surprising. If at the common meals of the Christian community, held in his dining room, he moreover made distinctions in the food he provided for those of his own social level and those who were of lower rank, that would not have been at all out of the ordinary, even though there were some voices even in pagan society who protested the practice. It was precisely the humiliation of the have-nots to which Pliny and the satirists objected. Paul objects on quite different grounds, but Theissen has given good reason for seeking the roots of the denounced behavior in the "status-specific expectations" of a sharply stratified society.

Theissen has argued that differing perspectives of people of different social levels were involved also in another of the conflicts that perturbed Christians at Corinth, the issue of "meat offered to idols," addressed in 1 Corinthians 8–10.... On one side are "the strong," who have "knowledge" (*gnōsis*) that "there is [really] no idol in the world" (8:1, 4) and who therefore insist upon their "right" and "freedom" to eat what they please. They are the ones to whom Paul directs his reply to the inquiry the Corinthians have sent, and with whom to some extent he identifies. On the other side are "the weak" (8:10f.), further specified as having "weak consciences," who lack this *gnōsis* and, because of their previous customs in paganism, regard the eating of sacrificed meat as a real and dangerous matter (8:7). Many attempts have been made to define these positions in terms of their theological beliefs or ideologies. Theissen does not dismiss all these efforts, but undertakes to show that there is also a social dimension of the conflict, to which the ideological factors would have to be related. In his reading, the "strong" are the socially powerful also referred to in 1 Cor. 1:26f. It is indeed plausible that those who, after conversion to Christianity, may still have had reason to accept invitations to dinner where meat would be served (10:27), perhaps in the shrine of a pagan deity (8:10), are likely to have been the more affluent members of the group, who would still have had some social or business obligations that were more important to their roles in the larger society than were comparable connections among people of lower status. The difference is not absolute, however, for Christian clients of non-Christian patrons would surely also sometimes have found themselves in this position. Theissen also argues, though, that the whole perception of what it meant to eat meat would have been different for people of different economic levels. The poor in fact rarely ate meat; the occasions when they did tended to be cultic, whether public or private. For wealthy people, who could have meat as a more or less regular item in their diet, it would have had far fewer numinous associations. For the poor, moreover, the Christian community provided a more than adequate substitute for the sort of friendly association, including common meals, that one might otherwise have sought in clubs, guilds, or cultic associations....

On the whole Theissen's case ... is convincing and makes the conflict between the "weak" and the "strong" further evidence for the presence within the Corinthian congregation of persons of significantly different strata. There is one problem with his construction, however, that may warrant a refinement in the concept of social stratification that he has employed. Theissen moves directly from his demonstration that the "strong" are relatively higher in economic status than the "weak" to the assumption that they are consequently better integrated socially into the larger society.... [But] is social status best understood as a single dimension or as the resultant of several different dimensions? Because Theissen has assumed a single dimension, or an average of several dimensions, he concludes that high status entails a high degee of integration, an assumption which other evidence seems to contradict. We would avoid these contradictions if we recognized that the "strong" of the Corinthian congregation are inconsistent in status. They may enjoy a high rank in some dimensions, such as wealth, identification with the Latin element in the colony, support by dependents and clients, and in one or two cases perhaps also civic office, but they may be ranked lower in others, such as origin, occupation, or sex. Such people would share many of the attitudes, values, and sentiments of unambiguously higher social levels yet still lack status crystallization. Other persons in the Corinthian congregation who were much lower on all these scales than the "strong" might suffer a much lower degree of inconsistency among their dimensions of status, and thus, within their own social circles, might be better integrated than those who were more mobile and more exposed.

Also in Corinth the status of women became a matter of controversy, as we see in 1 Cor. 11:2–16 and 14:33b–36. These are not the most lucid passages in the Pauline letters, and a small mountain of literature about them has by no means relieved their obscurity. Fortunately we do not have to solve all their problems in order to make the few observations that are germane to our present question. We have already seen that there were a number of women prominently involved in the Pauline circle who exhibited the sorts of status inconsistency that would inspire a Juvenal to eloquent indignation. There were women who headed households, who ran businesses and had independent wealth, who traveled with their own slaves and helpers. Some who are married have become converts to this exclusive religious cult without the consent of their husbands (1 Cor. 7:13), and they may, though Paul advises against it, initiate divorce (ibid.). Moreover, women have taken on some of the same roles as men within the sect itself. Some exercise charismatic functions like prayer and prophecy in the congregation (1 Cor. 11:2–16); others, as we have seen in our prosopography, are Paul's fellow workers as evangelists and teachers. Both in terms of their position in the larger society and in terms of their participation in the Christian communities, then, a number of women broke through the normal expectations of female roles.

It is not surprising that this produced tensions within the groups, and that the tortuous theological compromise stated by Paul in 1 Cor. 11:2–16 would not settle the issue. Later in the received form of the same letter, a discussion of ecstatic speech and prophecy in the assemblies is interrupted by an absolute prohibition of women from speaking in the meetings, requiring them to be "subordinate" and to "ask their own husbands at home if they want to learn something" (14:33b–36). The subordination of women within the household order was taught in the paraenesis of the Pauline congregations, and reinforced in the letters to Asian churches written by disciples of Paul (Col. 3:18; Eph. 5:22–24). In the second century the roles of women were still controversial among people who wrote fictional accounts claiming the authority of Paul. In the Acts of Paul and Thecla a virgin of Iconium on the eve of her marriage is won to celibate Christianity by Paul's preaching. After miraculously confounding the (male) authorities who try to silence her, but supported by the women of the city and saved on one occasion by a lioness, she baptizes herself. Then she cuts her hair short, dresses like a man, and goes off to follow Paul as an itinerant apostle. On the other hand, the author of the Pastoral Epistles rejects the sort of asceticism represented by Thecla and all teaching by women (1 Tim. 2:9–15; 4:3), except that older women should become "good teachers" by instructing younger women to be good wives and mothers, always subordinate to their husbands (Titus 2:3–5). These second-century documents furnish no direct evidence that can help to describe the social constituency of Pauline Christianity as I have defined it, but they do illustrate the variety and the strength of reactions to status inconsistency (and violation of conventions) of one kind....

Mixed Strata, Ambiguous Status

The evidence we have surveyed is fragmentary, random, and often unclear. We cannot draw up a statistical profile of the constituency of the Pauline communities nor fully describe the social level of a single Pauline Christian. We have found a number of converging clues, however, that permit an impressionistic sketch of these groups. It is a picture in which people of several social levels are brought together. The extreme top and bottom of the Greco-Roman social scale are missing from the picture. It is hardly surprising that we meet no landed aristocrats, no senators, *equites* [horse-soldiers, cavalry], nor (unless Erastus might qualify) decurions. But there is also no specific evidence of people who are destitute—such as the hired menials and dependent handworkers; the poorest of the poor, peasants, agricultural slaves, and hired agricultural day laborers, are absent because of the urban setting of the Pauline groups. There may well have been members of the Pauline communities who lived at the subsistence level, but we hear nothing of them.

The levels in between, however, are well represented. There are slaves, although we cannot tell how many. The "typical" Christian, however, the one who most often signals his presence in the letters by one or another small clue, is a free artisan or small trader. Some even in those occupational categories had houses, slaves, the ability to travel, and other signs of wealth. Some of the wealthy provided housing, meeting places, and other services for individual Christians and for whole groups. In effect, they filled the roles of patrons.

Not only was there a mixture of social levels in each congregation; but also, in each individual or category that we are able to identify there is evidence of divergent rankings in the different dimensions of status. Thus we find Christians in the *familia caesaris* [household of Caesar], whose members were so often among the few upwardly mobile people in the Roman Empire. We find, too, other probable freedmen or descendents of freedmen who have advanced in wealth and position, especially in the Roman colonies of Corinth and Philippi. We find wealthy artisans and traders: high in income, low in occupational prestige. We find wealthy, independent women. We find wealthy Jews. And, if we are to believe Acts, we find gentiles whose adherence to the synagogue testifies to some kind of dissonance in their relation to their society.

The "emerging consensus" that Malherbe reports seems to be valid: a Pauline congregation generally reflected a fair cross-section of urban society. Moreover, those persons prominent enough in the mission or in the local community for their names to be mentioned or to be identifiable in some other way usually—when we have evidence to make any judgment at all about them—exhibit signs of a high ranking in one or more dimensions of status. But that is typically accompanied by low rankings in other dimensions. Although the evidence is not abundant, we may venture the generalization that the most active and prominent members of Paul's circle (including Paul himself) are people of high status inconsistency (low status crystallization). They are upwardly mobile; their achieved status is higher than their attributed status. Is that more than accidental? Are there some specific characteristics of early Christianity that would be attractive to status-inconsistents? Or is it only that people with the sorts of drive, abilities, and opportunities that produced such mixed status would tend to stand out in any group they joined, and thus to be noticed for the record?

Bibliography

GUSTAV ADOLF DEISSMANN, *Paul: A Study in Social and Religious History* (1957).
ROBERT M. GRANT, *Early Christianity and Society: Seven Studies* (1977).
EDWIN A. JUDGE, *The Social Pattern of Christian Groups in the First Century* (1960).
EDWIN A. JUDGE, "The Social Identity of the First Christians: A Question of Method in Religious History," *Journal of Religious History* 11:201–217.
ABRAHAM J. MALHERBE, *Social Aspects of Early Christianity* (1975).
WAYNE A. MEEKS and ROBERT L. WILKEN, *Jews and Christians in Antioch in the First Four Centuries of the Common Era* (1978).
JOHN HOWARD SCHÜTZ, *Paul and the Anatomy of Apostolic Authority* (1975).
GERD THEISSEN, *The Social Setting of Pauline Christianity: Essays on Corinth* (1982).

The Vitality of Roman Paganism

RAMSAY MacMULLEN

A major event in Western civilization was the "triumph" of Christianity in the Roman Empire. One reason for its success was the readiness of people, the elite as well as the masses, to believe. But if such credulity assisted Christianity, it also permitted a complex system of pagan belief and practice to persist; Christianity's triumph was far from universal.

Unfortunately, evidence of internal belief and emotional life is thin in all pre-modern history. What there is of it for the three centuries after the birth of Christ, from literary, epigraphic, and papyrological sources, conveys the views of small elite groups far better than those of the masses. We learn from such sources that Roman philosophers and emperors liked to think that their religious beliefs were less crude than the "superstition" of the masses. But rationalism and skepticism were never the norm among the Roman elites and appear increasingly less so as one moves toward the third century AD. Belief in the gods, in solicitation of their favors, in enchantments and miracles, was shared by all. Christianity did not eradicate such belief. Pagan and Christian elements blended in the minds of many. Paganism continued to attract adherents after Constantine's conversion in 312 and pagans and Christians continued to live together peacefully in the cities of the Empire.

Beginning with the Epicureans, a sect skeptical of divine providence and a blissful afterlife and devoted above all to avoiding pain and anguish in the present life, MacMullen reveals the variety and vitality of pagan philosophy after the advent of Christianity.

The Epicureans represented the furthest extreme of disbelief. But aside from their name's being attached in obloquy to anyone who doubted a local oracle—"Atheist or Christian or Epicurean"—they hardly appear in the sources for our period. It is rather their company that calls for comment:

Reprinted with the permission of Yale University Press from *Paganism in the Roman Empire* by Ramsay MacMullen. Copyright © 1981 by Yale University.

they are close to Christians, and that, in mid-second century Pontus, was not good. They are close to atheists, and that was a great deal worse. In public, as many statements make clear, to deny the reality of the gods was absolutely unacceptable. You would be ostracized for that, even stoned in the streets. There is no need to recall the scenes of persecution in Smyrna, Rome, and Lyon in which the mob rails at Christians as godless. An Apologist acknowledges his opponent's feelings: you "believe that to worship no god at all is impious and unholy." A contemporary, but a pagan, Aelian, condemns the atheist who, with alien "wisdom," disputes whether the gods exist or not, and Lucian, a half-century later, declares that "the great majority of Greeks and all the non-Greeks" (which includes Romans) are believers.

To have the same author, in contradiction of himself, tell us there were no worshipers left to Zeus any more is certainly puzzling; puzzling, that our learned friend the Epicurean of Oenoanda, Diogenes, should have dared instruct his fellow citizens in the freethinking of his sect, spelled out across the most public walls in town; and puzzling, that the same ardent Romans who burnt the "atheist" Justin should, in Juvenal's day, have laughed at anyone professing faith in an altar or temple. So the poet tells us, anyway. Pompeian walls display dozens of blasphemous graffiti, insults to Venus (patron deity of the town), or, in a tavern, an obscene painting at Isis's expense. We may take their like for granted elsewhere, if there were other sites so well preserved. In Africa, down the coast from Carthage, a rich man commissioned a semipermanent, semipublic bit of humor: a mosaic wall with figures and captions making fun of the gods at their feasting.

This is the kind of mixed bag of facts that renders general statements about religious life so hard to frame or so easily criticized if they are framed too narrowly. What, for instance, can one make of the assertion that oracles, "it is true, enjoyed a recovery in popularity in the second century"—for which a single inscription is cited, recording help sought by a city in Sardinia from Apollo in Claros? Such characterizing of the feelings and thoughts of fifty million people on any day out of thirty-six thousand has something ludicrous about it, as if one were to measure the pulse of the western world on the basis of a single headline in the *St. Albans Sentinel*. Worse than that, perhaps: since religious feelings are not something to talk about in public, in some of their aspects, they must prove all the harder to assess from the outside. The more need for care.

Let us consider a few further contradictions suggested by the important role of inner emotions in religion. Lactantius tells pagans to their face (and there is a sort of reliability in such testimony, out in the open and instantly subject to challenge by contemporary readers) that theirs is "a superstition about those gods of theirs... in which, for all I can see, there is no more than worship by the finger-tips..., nothing required but the blood of one's flocks, and smoke, and foolish libations." In contrast, Porphyry declares "the one who loves god cannot love pleasure or body; but the latter sort of man will love money and so be unjust, and the unjust man is unholy, both toward god and his ancestors, and a criminal in his conduct toward others. So he may sacrifice hecatombs and adorn the temples with myriad offerings, but he remains impious and godless and, in true calling, a sacrilegious person."

Or we may turn back from the later Empire to the earlier, there to read, "Vesta, be gracious! To you we now open our lips for worship—if indeed we may join your ceremonies. I was completely absorbed in prayer, I was aware of the divine powers; and the earth, joyful, shone back with a dark red glow." And another's assertion that "all men feel a powerful longing to honor deity and pay cult from close up, drawing near and seizing hold with persuasion, offering sacrifices and crowning with wreaths. Just as tiny children, torn away from father or mother, feel a terrible longing and desire, and often reach out their hands in their very dreams to the absent ones, so to the gods, men who rightly love them for their beneficence and kinship are eager to be and to talk with them by any means."

Moving passages, reminders to their audience, western or eastern, of emotions shared in the innermost heart! But consider for comparison the scene of devotion that Seneca painted, in which simplicity of feeling and intensity itself are derided as madness. And in other pages too long to quote, leading up to that scene, he dismisses the dancing or howling or bloodied priests of Cybele or Isis or Bellona, all of them as revolting as they are demented—the very manifestations of "true" piety that modern students most often point to! Even Porphyry's plea for god and ancestors, almost equating the terms of the two,... Seneca denies head on: "What of the fact that we even join the gods in marriage, and dishonorable marriage at that, the marriage of brother and sister? We give Bellona in marriage to Mars, Venus to Vulcan, and Salacia to Neptune. But some we leave unwed, as if no match could be arranged, especially since some are widows, such as Populonia, Fulgora and the goddess Rumina. I am not at all surprised that there has been no suitor for these. As for all this obscure throng of gods, assembled through long years of ancient superstition, we shall invoke them, but with the reservation in mind that their worship belongs rather to custom than truth." The repudiation of mythology here is echoed by other writers as well.

Enough of such contradictions—which, useful though they may be to indicate the bounds of the possible, chiefly demand resolution. It cannot be found, however often sought, in the change from one century to another—from "the religious crisis in the Roman world at the end of the Republic and beginning of the Empire" to "the second century with its powerful upsurge in religious life," then the mid-second century to the early fourth, all one "age of anxiety," in its later phases coinciding with "the decline of paganism in the second half of the third century." Conventional and representative of a sort of scholarly consensus regarding successive developments within our subject, that succession of periods must nevertheless be looked at critically. All of its parts are made of, or meant to describe, religiosity, not only the whole nexus of thoughts and feelings about the divine, but their intensity or vitality as well. For the final period of decline, substantiation is sought in the much-diminished epigraphic record, not in what it says but in its very silence. The silence itself is a fact plain and uncontested, though its interpretation is something else again.... But for the other periods, the sources used are almost wholly literary, since "inscriptions seldom tell us much about the underlying personal experience." Here too is a fact uncontested, witness the passages called on in the last few pages to convey a sense of what emotions characterized moments of active worship. They are drawn from a metaphysician, Porphyry; a poet, Ovid; a rhetor, Dio Chrysostom; and still others that display or suggest deep attachments or experiences might be found in a novelist and rhetor, Apuleius, in a natural philosopher, Aelian, or in other poets. Inscriptions provide no match.

There are, however, two objections to be raised against reliance on such authorities. First, they represent only a small group.... Second, even that small group they do not represent accurately.

To examine the latter objection: as is clear in the opposing pairs of quotations that were presented above, the religious feelings most common in the Empire, and those considered suitable or "true," covered a very wide spectrum indeed. Explanation lies in plain human variety, not in place or period. Moreover, the range indicated in the comparisons could be easily extended by the inclusion of prinking and frivolity in sacred processions, erotic or abnormal titillation in cult groups (or in novelistic fantasies about them), exaltation roused by concentrated and emotive word pictures describing the great powers and loving kindness of a god—and so forth. Examples of all such passages in the literature of our two centuries of study have been offered above. Except from a sectarian point of view, then, it would be wrong to pick out one or a few particular dispositions as characteristic of paganism.

Indeed, it is my guess that the variety of feelings satisfied in the practice of religion differs inconsequentially from age to age, however much accepted patterns of behavior to receive those feelings change in shape; for, as Nock wrote, "there are fashions in religion as in everything else." If my guess should be right, religiosity in any society as a whole would likewise differ inconsequentially across time, and the several phases or periods which it is conventional to distinguish in the religious history of the Roman Empire would lose all meaning. Whether one age is "more religious" than another, that is, whether it actually stimulates its inhabitants to significantly different levels of emotion in the service of their god or gods, is a question almost too important to leave alone; but surely even those who choose to offer an answer to it for their own generation, if they were really pressed, would admit they had no evidence anywhere near adequate in scope or weight to support any opinion. Hope of discovering the truth about a remote and ill-documented period it would be foolish to entertain.

Let us rejoin the circle of writers from whom we turned aside a moment ago. None in the present connection is better known or more certain to be referred to than Marcus Aurelius, the Stoic emperor. His Stoicism, however, stands out in isolation. There are no signs of a similar devotion in the preceding half-century. Suppose that we knew nothing of his meditations, or that another spiritual diary of the same bent but from a half-century later were discovered, would historians have any difficulty in accommodating either possibility? Surely not. There is a quite inadequate, and therefore indiscriminately welcoming, texture of evidence across the whole period of this study. Accordingly, the emperor's religion has human interest but not historical. Even—or perhaps one should say, especially—a careful examination of the man and his time must conclude by admitting that we do not know to what extent he typified his own aristocratic circle. The same admission should guide the student of Plutarch's circle, earlier, or Porphyry's, later.

Marcus Aurelius and the other names most likely to occur in a book about the cults of the Empire are in any case self-selected for the interest they felt in their own spiritual life and things divine. They wrote on those subjects. Not everybody did. Some people are simply more given to belief than others, like Teucrus of Cyzicus, who journeyed to Pergamon in search of relief from epilepsy. There Asclepius "appeared to him, and they struck up a conversation, and he developed a quartan fever, and through it recovered from epilepsy." They "struck up a conversation"—extraordinary! Or D. A. Lazurkina at a congress of the Communist party not many years ago, who reported, "Yesterday I consulted Lenin again... and he said to me...."

There is epigraphic confirmation for the point, perhaps. Among vows paid to the more prominent deities, where some very rough statistical tests are possible, and particularly among those vows that depart at all from the bare formulas of dedication, dedicants who identify themselves as servants of the god—priests or the like—are present disproportionately, in comparison to ordinary dedicants. Some of them are quite lowly. The cult of Asclepius at Epidaurus presents a striking case: the sanctuary is filled with scores of altars set up by the priests themselves. Another illustration lies in the cult of Jupiter Dolichenus, whose priests made themselves exceptionally prominent. It was naturally to their advantage to celebrate the deity who fed and sheltered them; no less natural, we should grant them, to feel a genuine faith. That faith prevailed over advantage is suggested by those priests of one deity who offered tribute to another. Taken as a class, they were surely representatives of human nature at its most devout.

It would not be too cynical, but simply wrong, to attribute to the professional servant of the gods real doubt about their existence or efficacy; for most of the most highly admired and educated people in the world about him were quite at one with his convictions—at the top, the emperor Marcus Aurelius, who doubted wonder-workers but credited healing dreams, above all, those sent by Asclepius. Everyone agreed: Marcus's teacher Fronto, for one. But there is no need to call up from earlier pages the proofs of unfeigned belief to be found in virtually every writer of the second and third centuries whose works survive. They all believed; which cannot be expected to mean that they all believed everything. The variety of religious convictions or systems... matches the variety of emotions regarding the divine; but the former can be examined with some hope of understanding them. The latter, as has been said, lie beyond reach of profitable discussion.

What literate circles thought about religion must be learned, almost by definition, out of their writings. Some of their writings, however, in the Greek-speaking world and occasionally beyond, as known only on stone. There, the same substance and style appear unchanged. The sources epigraphic and literary join without a seam. It is no cause for surprise, then, that the acceptance of the gods should be as widespread in inscriptions as is implied, for instance, by Lucian, when he counts listeners to atheism as so few. Here is one respect in which reliance only on a small selection of writers would be misleading. And (for a second illustration) it should not be surprising that the deities addressed in inscriptions are described only in very broad strokes and simple affirmations, in a shouted phrase, for example—"The One," "Greatest," "Savior"—or in a string of epithets without integration: "swift-running," "dwelling on high." The resulting picture of the gods is oddly pointillist, as if in acceptance of each one's birth and growth out of the visions of all his votaries, individually, by quite uncontrolled accretion—pointillist and motionless: it is rare that the gods are seen in action in any episode of their story, though a life or biography many of them are indeed known to have possessed. The literary treatment of religion—not merely the treatment offered by certain authors in certain works—in this respect also matches the epigraphic. After Ovid, back at the turn of the era, and all the way up to Claudian and Nonnus at the edge of another great break in history, writers show little interest in anecdotes from "mythology," as we would call it.

Literary evidence, at least in Greek, joins closely with one other type, papyrological. There is no sharp break detectable in moving from the style and interests that broadly prevail in one, to the other. Good reason, therefore, to trust to Egypt for some impression of the place of religion in literature—though that province was famed for being particularly addicted to sacred lore and studies. Out of some thousands of papyri, whole or fragments, that are of literary character, only a small number focus directly on religion. Numenius, Ammonius, Plotinus, and Porphyry make no appearance; other philosophers very rarely and for treatises on government or ethics or logic. There is a Hellenistic scrap of Orphism,[4] there are two or three scraps of aretology,[5] quite a few hymns and paeans (so far, the same mix found in inscriptions, minus the votive), plus bits and pieces of fiction

---

[4] An eclectic mystery or secret religion.
[5] In philosophy, the study of virtue.

describing scenes of worship. Throughout this little corpus of texts there is a distinctly regional quality, to which Isis and Osiris especially contribute. Had anyone demanded a larger share of the written word for piety, there was an answer ready to meet him: all the big temples had their own libraries, containing no doubt the same sort of prose and verse in praise of native deities that still survives, but in much, much greater abundance; beyond that, representing Hellenic culture in a broad sense, there was Homer. A majority of all identifiable literary papyri are the two epics, or commentary; and Hesiod is high in popularity, too. Those, it might have been said, were the old and the new testaments of truest Hellenism.

In trying to understand the faith prevailing in the lettered classes, use is commonly made of Gnostic, Hermetic, Chaldaean, Neoplatonic, Orphic, or Neopythagorean texts. With favorite selections drawn from other genres, they constitute the material from which the modern account of religious feeling in our period of study is typically composed. They are, however, given an importance quite out of scale with what contemporaries conceived their faith to be. "The underlying personal experience" is indeed far better found, at its very deepest, in Gnostic texts and the like. To call this deepest level "religion" without further qualification misrepresents the subject.

So much for the first objection that must be raised against choosing one's sources to fit one's modern preconceptions—against reliance, that is, on a small group of writers. The choice must rather widen to include experiences by no means intense, but no less a fact; concerns by no means profound, but no less sincerely expressed; and indifference or positive rejection almost as strongly represented as high-wrought religiosity. This said, nothing is subtracted from the subject. It is only taken away from a little, rather peculiar collection of books, and restored to a very much larger circle of real people, some of whom (like any sampling from the *Canterbury Tales, Simplicissimus*, or *War and Peace*) felt religion at the heart always; most, at the fingertips, as Lactantius puts it; and a few, never at all.

The second objection lies against the presenting of religion in our period only through the testimony of writers and readers. How few they were in the entire population has already been emphasized. That they were different remains to be asserted.

Plutarch may stand for a type thoroughly accepted among the well educated and well-to-do. He had a broad range of friends and interests Roman and Greek, even (but not untypically) reaching beyond, to write our only extant essay on Isiacism. He counted as more devout than most. In his collection of antiquarian oddments called *Quaestiones Romanae* [*Questions for Romans*], he takes up about a hundred customs having to do with Roman religion. For example: (1) Why do the Romans consider Kronos the father of truth? (Because they suppose Kronos is Chronos, Time, and time discovers truth?) (2) Why do they pay honor to the dead in December? (Because in that month all growing things have done with their lives?) (3) Why may the priest of Jupiter never anoint himself in the open? (Because it is not decent for a son to strip before a father, and Jupiter is the father of all?) (4) Why are slave women barred from the shrine of Matuta? (Because her Greek equivalent, Ino, was jealous of a slave woman on her husband's account?) (5) Why may the King of Sacrifices never address the people? (Because the Romans expelled their kings, and wish to limit his semblance to cult acts?) And (6) Why is Rome's guardian deity never named? (Because that protects him from being conjured away?)

The answers he offers to his questions he arrives at through six characteristic modes of thought. They lie in punning, in symbolic or esthetic appropriateness, in analogy with mortal customs, in echo of myth or a deity's life story, in historical accident, and in suitability for achieving some result, through binding or pleasing a deity. Only that last could be called functional, that is, only in that category of explanation does Plutarch consider the gods and their will as really existing. All the others (the next to last being the most often invoked) assume that cult is wholly man-made. His approach, not only in the first category, is bookish in the extreme, and in a sense also extremely rational.

By contrast, an inscription from third-century Dacia in semiliterate Latin describes how Aurelius Martinus Basus and Aurelius Castor Polydeuces, "standing about, saw the spirit of an eagle come down from a hill upon three snakes. One big viper tangled up the eagle. The aforementioned freed the eagle from danger. They set this up as their vow deserved, willingly," to the sky god Jupiter of Doliche. Somehow they felt the divine had entered their lives, and in a fashion far from bookish and rational, they did what needed to be done.

The differences in religion separating the upper class from the lower (and no middle really existed) can be more easily sensed than brought out explicitly through the evidence. That they existed, at least one of the two well knew, and reminded the other in clear and often scornful terms. They may all be gathered under one alone: "superstition." In turn, however, what we and the ancients, too, indicate by that term is a crudeness of conviction in regard to both the gods' sphere of action and their nature. The two elements in "superstition" now to be examined should be kept distinct so as to grasp the meaning of the word clearly and to understand the chief class differences in religious views.

The wonderful happening in which the two Aurelii participated brought the god of Doliche down from the sky to the very roadside. It was a sign that they could touch—as Timoleon's soldiers could touch the load of parsley on the mule's back, when they passed it on their way. They took it for a portent. Plutarch tells the story (the explanation does not concern us), calling it an instance of superstition. He uses the word to express his disagreement with those who would take a perfectly ordinary event, as he saw it, and ascribe divine dimensions to it. The more a person saw the gods at work in the material world—moving things around, for instance—and the less a person explained in terms of natural causes, the clearer was the presence of superstition.

THE VITALITY OF ROMAN PAGANISM

Over the course of the centuries chosen for examination here, superstition within this meaning certainly increased. The fact is best sensed (to say "measured" would imply a degree of accuracy beyond our reach) in the greater prominence of magic; for magic, after all, is most shortly defined as the art that brings about the intervention of superhuman powers in the material world—"moving things around, for instance." Proof of the practice of the art grows more abundant, most obviously in recipes and handbooks written on papyrus. It is to be found in every province, for example, in leaden curse tablets. And people who should have known better come to credit invocations with an efficacy that, in some previous century, would never have been believed. It means nothing that a late orator attributed an ineffectual speech to hexing by jealous detractors; an early orator, consul in Cicero's day, offered the same excuse; but when the very emperor resorted to wizards to aid him in his wars, times had changed. Perhaps no new ideas are to be discovered, but old ones are found in circles previously immune to them, now ready to acknowledge the direct, visible intervention of superhuman powers in the world at human bidding.

With the change, no doubt partly cause and partly effect, philosophy in the old sense fell out of favor. This too is a phenomenon well known. It is often remarked among the upper classes. It shows itself in times of peace and prosperity in the later second century, or at least the symptoms that characterize the developed disease are by that period already discoverable. Its origins therefore cannot lie in the decline of wealth, schools, libraries, endowed chairs of learning, and the like, although all these latter indeed suffered in the third century. Alternatively, to explain the waning of philosophy as a mere fashion, in Nock's term (above), provides no serious answer unless the fashion itself can be derived. But contemporaries had their own explanation: "philosophers agree about nothing—one of them even says that silver is black. You can hear more uproar from a household of philosophers than from a household of madmen." And variations on the theme: "I frequented the schools of the philosophers [at Rome] and found nothing but preparation for the overthrow of doctrines; competing and arguing; and tricks of syllogizing and the imagining of premises"—from all of which the wise man would turn away to more profitable studies. At the end of our period, the emperor himself before a learned gathering could describe "Socrates, elated by his debating powers, making the weaker reasoning appear the stronger, and playing about with mutually contradictory arguments..., and Pythagoras as well, while pretending to practise self-control in a special degree, and silence, too, was caught in imposture..., and finally Plato, up to a point, was wise, but in other matters he is found to have erred from the truth." They had all been wrong, every one.

Disciplined abstract thought, tested by challenges made sharp in the course of fierce fights over many, many centuries, the challenges themselves not to be handled or even understood by the casual observer, had passed from favor. As in the history of warfare periods emerge in which attack prevails over defense, so in the history of thought a time had come in which the nays had it. Every proposition could be overthrown by ten different arguments. All the arguments were in every student's hands or handbooks. And the casual observer whose interest counted for most had spent his youth, not in a university, but in some catechetical school or, more likely, in a barracks. Thus the balance of techniques of debate, and then political and economic troubles, and the hastening advancement of people new to wealth and cultural leadership, combined to bring on the moment when Constantine could simply wave philosophy aside without being laughed at.

That was the test: ridicule. Fully to sense the meaning of Constantine's preposterous pontification, he must be imagined speaking at Plutarch's table. There, his views would have produced delighted grins; likewise, no doubt, in the company of Lucian or Apuleius. Lucian knew of opinionated ignoramuses in very high places indeed, followers of the pious fraud Alexander. They were the equal in gullibility of the population of Abonuteichus where Alexander set up shop. Lucian expects his readers to laugh at them, as Apuleius could hope (a little anxiously, in a small town like Oea) to raise a laugh at yokel accusations of magic. He practiced no magic, he insisted in his defense, but scientific experiment in the tradition of Aristotle. Who but a clod could misinterpret that? With his trial, we have passed the mid-second century. We still feel a difference—the difference between "religion" and "superstition"—separating the literate few of Athens, Rome, or Carthage from the people of remote centers like Oea in Tripolitania or Abonuteichus in Pontus. Another hundred years pass, and gullibility is no longer a target for ridicule. In the most educated circles that the Empire has to show, enchantments, trances, and wonder-working raise no laugh; rather, fear and awe. It is rationalism, as we would call it, that now must defend itself; and it is easily put to rout by Constantine. Most of his listeners—not all, for such large changes come about very gradually—no doubt shared his views.

To return, then, to our point of departure, in the contrast between the lettered elite and the broad masses of the population, and between the religion of the one and the superstition of the other: it is clear that the differences were sharper at the beginning of our period than at the end. It follows that a sharper objection must be raised against the use of some member of Plutarch's circle than of Constantine's, to represent the whole world of the Apologists. Elite and masses, in their views about the supernatural at work, had at the end drawn much closer to each other. What divided them still was only a matter of complexity or depth of explanation.

A final sign of their approximation: by piety, that is, by a life lived in accord with divine will and laws, one could draw down upon one's whole community all sorts of blessings—wonderful happenings, or good crops and bread at low prices. "The priestess Alexandra of Demeter Thesmophoros asks"—so begins an inscription of the second century from the oracle of Apollo at Didyma. And her question follows: "Because, since first I assumed the priesthood, the gods as never before have been visible through their attentions—and this, sometimes through the virgins and matrons, sometimes through men and boys—what means such a thing, and toward what destiny?" The answer, though largely lost, can perhaps be reconstructed: the cause of the phenomena she asks about was the devotion of the priestess herself, here, as reported also of others in other inscriptions, at Stratonicea (for a specific miracle vouchsafed) and elsewhere. We can recall, too, a traveler of the period talking with a Greek shepherdess who claimed "the power of prophecy given her by the Mother of the Gods; and all the shepherds in the region and the farmers used her for the fertility and security of their crops and flocks." Or we can compare another tourist at Atargatis's shrine, seeing the pillar saints atop their pillars, "whom *hoi polloi* [the masses] believe to be up there in the company of the gods, requesting benefits for the whole of Syria."

Intercessors for divine favor thus appear widespread in the eastern provinces—but more easily to be found in the hinterlands and periphery (Olbia, Cyrene, Caria, and the islands) than at the center of things; move venerated, too, by the ignorant and simple. It is not till the third century that the very emperors are acclaimed in open ceremonies as winning bountiful harvests for their farmers and calm seas for their sailors by their piety. The change is not abrupt, a matter of emphasis rather than of innovation; but it assumes in the gods accessibility to direct and specific appeal, it assumes their willingness to make their favor felt by visible tinkering in the natural world. Earlier, by contrast, when a panegyrist credited Trajan with averting famine, it was not the emperor's prayers that had brought supernatural aid, but his shrewd administration that had mobilized quite human forces.

Bibliography

PETER BROWN, *The World of Late Antiquity A.D. 150–750* (1971).
PETER BROWN, *Religion and Society in the Age of St. Augustine* (1972).
A. B. COOK, *Zeus: A Study in Ancient Religion*, 3 vols. (1914–1940)
E. R. DODDS, *Pagan and Christian in an Age of Anxiety: Some Aspects of Religious Experience from Marcus Aurelius to Constantine* (1965).
J. FERGUSON, *The Religions of the Roman Empire* (1970).
M. GRANT, *The Climax of Rome: The Final Achievements of the Ancient World A.D. 161–337* (1968).
A. H. M. JONES, *Constantine and the Conversion of Europe* (1962).
RAMSAY MACMULLEN, *Roman Social Relations 50 B.C. to A.D. 284* (1974).
M. J. VERMASEREN, "Paganism's Death Struggle: Religions in Competition with Christianity," in *The Crucible of Christianity*, ed. A. Toynbee (1969); pp. 235–260.

Ninth-century mosaic depicting St. Peter giving spiritual authority to Pope Leo III and temporal power to the emperor Charlemagne. *Vatican Library*

PART TWO

The Middle Ages

During the Middle Ages political, social, and religious institutions as we know them today took shape. By the eleventh and twelfth centuries monarchies existed with enough military strength and administrative personnel to begin the long process of subjecting their territories to one rule and law. Representative bodies also formed in opposition to protect the interests of noblemen and towns, particularly in England and France. The many bloody conflicts over the boundaries of political power were accompanied by much theorizing about its nature, particularly as regarded the origins and limits of a ruler's power. Francis Oakley takes us on a grand tour of the world of medieval political thought.

During the Middle Ages the Christian church ceased to be the politically timorous spiritual institution it had been under the Franks and became an independent worldly power capable of contesting the new secular monarchies on their own terms as well as spiritually. The church inspired military crusades to the Holy Land, deposed kings and emperors, and subjected laypeople to a uniform system of penance for their moral sins and crimes. Even in its innermost spiritual nature and functions, however, the church revealed itself to be very much a part of the world it sought to discipline and redeem. The Benedictine order of the eleventh and twelfth centuries and the Franciscan and Dominican friars of the thirteenth and fourteenth appear also to have been deeply influenced by the secular values they so strongly condemned. The inescapable intertwining of social reality and spiritual ideals is the theme of Barbara Rosenwein and Lester Little's investigation.

Basic social institutions evolved during the Middle Ages under growing Christian influence. When the Carolingians adopted the Christian concept of marriage as an indissoluble monogamous union, the Christian ideal of a tightly knit nuclear family became also the Western ideal. The result was an enhancement of the home and family life. This had both positive and negative consequences for women, who found themselves exalted but also somewhat trapped in the roles of mother and housewife. This conflict is the subject of Suzanne Wemple's essay. By the eleventh and twelfth centuries, however, women's work reached well beyond the home. It found expression in an enormous variety of jobs which the many women leading independent professional lives in trades and crafts seem to have found satisfying. On the other hand, the most socially prestigious professions remained the preserve of men, who also received more pay than women for the same work. Shulamith Shahar describes both the growing opportunities for women and the continuing restrictions on their lives during the high and later Middle Ages.

Finally, the care and rearing of children improved significantly during the Middle Ages under both secular and Christian influence. Whereas neglect of children and even cruelty toward them can be documented in late antiquity and the early Middle Ages, by the eleventh and twelfth centuries the special needs of children were widely recognized. It was then, as David Herlihy demonstrates, that institutions devoted to the nurture and protection of children began to multiply.

A Vision of Medieval Politics

FRANCIS OAKLEY

In every field of scholarship authorities hold sway. On the subject of medieval politics Walter Ullmann is such an authority. He is widely known for his controversial interpretation of medieval political history as a clash between allegedly diametrically opposed concepts of government and law. On the one hand, he finds an "ascending" concept of political power throughout the thought and practice of the Middle Ages. This point of view, which Ullmann closely identifies with Aristotle and his followers, derives all political power from "the people," who extend it to a sovereign. In competition with this viewpoint Ullmann finds a "descending" concept of political power. Here power originates in a sovereign and flows from him to subordinates, the least authoritative of whom are the masses of ordinary people; Ullmann closely identifies this descending view with Christianity. Ullmann divides the major religious and political thinkers and traditions of the Middle Ages into these two camps.

Francis Oakley challenges the accuracy of this grand thesis as an interpretation of medieval political history. On the one hand, he recognizes its richness, while on the other he asks whether it is guilty of oversimplification. By contrast, he stresses the integrated character of medieval political thought.

Over the course of the last dozen years, with a contempt for his critics at once both admirable and deplorable, Walter Ullmann has set out to reshape our understanding of medieval political and constitutional thinking .... Of course, like many another intellectual pace-setter, Ullmann is now in danger of being both quoted and criticized more often than he is read. But I have read him; I have read him at length, with attention, and with deepening bewilderment. For if the density of his scholarship nearly always succeeds in intimidating, with surprising frequency it also fails to convince.

From "Celestial Hierarchies Revisited: Walter Ullman's Vision of Medieval Politics" by Francis Oakley. World copyright: The Past and Present Society, Corpus Christi College, Oxford, England. This article is reprinted with the permission of the Society and the author from *Past and Present: A Journal of Historical Studies*, no. 60 (August 1973).

The omissions and mistakes of fact are simply too striking; some of the most confident assertions simply too bizarre. The interpretations given to familiar texts are all too frequently idiosyncratic, and, "semantic method" notwithstanding, the meanings accorded to such crucial terms as "nature" and "grace" are altogether too pliable....

... It would be improper, [however,] to pass too swift a judgment upon Ullmann's reading of any particular text without having attempted to evaluate the general interpretative structure in terms of which it has been understood.... It is, then, to the adequacy of this conceptual framework, the component central to Ullmann's whole contribution, that I propose in this essay to address myself.

Fortunately enough, its main outlines stand out in bold relief.... [M]edieval political thinking was in his view dominated by two competing "conceptions of government and law", conceptions which, being "diametrically opposed" to one another, were mutually exclusive. These he refers to as the "ascending" and "descending" themes or theses. According to the former of these, which he designates also as the "populist" conception, "governmental authority and law-creating competence" are attributed to the people or community and ascend to the top of the political structure "from the broad base in the shape of a pyramid". With this theme are associated consent, representation, and the notion of the individual as citizen, as participant in public government, occupying within society a status characterized by autonomy and independence, endowed, therefore, with a battery of "inalienable rights" proof even against the encroachments of the powers that be. According to the latter thesis, on the other hand, all power is located ultimately in God, who, by means of an earthly vicegerent himself endowed to this end with a plenitude of power, distributes it downwards *via* a hierarchy of officials "again in the shape of a pyramid". In the context of this theme, faith is substituted for consent, the notion of office delivered from above replaces that of representation, and instead of the autonomous, right-bearing individual, we encounter the faithful Christian, recipient of the favours of an absolutist government, subject rather than citizen.

Of the two, the ascending theme is taken by Ullmann to be the more fundamental—prevalent, it would seem, both over longer stretches of time and over broader expanses of space, rooted more deeply in the soil of mundane human existence, attached more firmly to the very bedrock of the human psyche. Thus, in "unadulterated" form, it has prevailed in the modern era, in Republican Rome, and also (or so one must presume) in the world of the Greek *polis* as well. It prevailed likewise among the Germanic peoples of the pre-Christian era among whom kingship was "based on the popular will"—so much so, indeed, that long after the descending thesis had triumphed over "the whole of Southern and Western Europe", not only did the "populist kingship" survive in the Scandinavian North, but even in the West, at the village level and in the "lower regions of society", remnants of populism eked out "a somewhat subterranean existence throughout the medieval period". And, in the thirteenth and early-fourteenth centuries, it was those populist remnants, fortified long since by the growth of feudalism, which made possible the full-scale appropriation of "Aristotelian naturalism"—itself the single most important factor making for the recovery of the ascending theme, and, as a result, for the "advance of political reasoning toward what might well be called a Lockean position".

The expressions which Ullmann uses in connection with the ascending or populist theme, and the adjectives with which he qualifies it, suggest very strongly that there was nothing accidental about either its popularity or its staying power. On the contrary, he seems to view it as nothing other than the "natural" way of thinking about matters political. Thus, he speaks of its "earthiness", its "practicality", its immediate appeal to the "unsophisticated", to "ordinary humanity". He associates it with "subjectivity", with "individualism", with "humanism", with the vernacular languages, with the working of "natural forces", with the lay rather than the clerical mind. Grounded in nature itself rather than in any notion of the divine, it is, accordingly, "realistic", flexible, "unspeculative", "earth-bound", reflecting the "ordinary laws of nature" and the natural diversities and "variations of human development", pressing itself imperatively upon those who are open to the promptings of "empirical" or "inductive" reason—or responsive, as he puts it elsewhere, to "the laws of human natural reasoning".

In contrast with the homely features of this naturalistic norm, the rival "descending" thesis is of grander mien, conveying a sense of majesty, evoking a feeling of awe. For it stands out as extremely "doctrinaire", a characteristic product of the clerical mind, associated with "the Latin of the academics", with the "a-natural", the "objective", the "extra-human", the world of spirit, the divine. It is "sophisticated", "monolithic", "a rarified doctrine", a "speculative theorem" deduced from "abstract principles", the outcome, in fact, of rigid adherence to "the laws of logical reasoning". This being so, the fact that it succeeded in dominating Byzantine political thinking and in displacing the ascending theme in Southern and Western Europe so effectively and for so long clearly calls for some extraordinary explanation. And that explanation Ullmann finds in the influence exerted upon political thinking by Christianity in general and by certain New Testament motifs in particular. Thus, given the papal claim to a "direct link" with divinity, "a provable title-deed" provided by the very words of Christ as reported in the Bible, it is no accident that in medieval papal government we meet with "the descending theme in its purest form". Again, although "the unadulterated ascending thesis" prevailing in Republican Rome was modified under the Principate, it was only "through the adoption of Christianity" that it finally gave way to "the fully-fledged descending (theocratic)" doctrine which "gained momentum from the late fourth century onwards" and triumphed at Byzantium. Finally, in the early Middle Ages it was again "as a result of the overpowering influence of Christianity" that the Germanic peoples adopted the descending or theocratic theory "inherent in Christian doctrine" and that the ascending theme was "driven underground, not to emerge as a theoretical proposition until the late thirteenth century". It is true that the Western theocratic monarchs who thus emerged lacked, like their Byzantine counterparts, that direct link with divinity which the papacy possessed in its Biblical title deeds. Nevertheless, the West Frankish bishops of the ninth century, by introducing the practice of anointing and crowning these monarchs, did much to remedy that deficiency, effecting nothing less, indeed, than "the visible and concrete sacralization of the kingly office". By so doing, they finally succeeded then in substituting "the ecclesiastical unction and coronation as king-creating agencies in place of conquest and election". So that, from the mid-ninth century onwards, these Western monarchs, like their Byzantine counterparts, enjoyed in the sacrament of unction an outward and public sign of the divine grace transmitted to them as "kings by the grace of God" *via* the mediation of the clerical hierarchy.

Such, then, is the general conceptual framework upon which Ullmann constructs his interpretation of medieval political thinking. It is easy enough to perceive its value as an explanatory tool when confronting the differences between the medieval political vision and those of the modern world or of classical antiquity; or, again, when confronting the more specific differences between Scandinavia and Southern and Western Europe, or between the earlier and later Middle Ages....

... [T]he value of Ullmann's interpretative schema is undercut by his failure to perceive that "consent" is a word with more than one meaning and by his related insistence on denying it any rôle within those forms of monarchy—papal, imperial, "national"—which he wishes to call "theocratic" and to view as manifestations exclusively of the descending theme. Hence, having asserted that it is in the papal government that we encounter the theocratic-descending theme "in its purest form", he is understandably reluctant to admit that late-medieval Conciliarism marked any unambiguous assertion of his ascending theme. But ... I propose here to exclude from consideration what he has to say about ecclesiastical government and to concentrate instead on his picture of the rise of imperial and royal theocracy, and of the challenge posed to it by that later re-emergence of the ascending or populist theme. More precisely, I propose to focus first on what he has to say about the emergence and re-emergence of the fully-fledged theocratic-descending theme in the latter years of the Roman empire and in the monarchies of the early-medieval Latin West; and secondly, on what he has to say about the decisive reassertion of the populist-ascending theme by the Aristotelian thinkers of the later Middle Ages.

(a) The Triumph of Theocracy

Although Ullmann nowhere really addresses himself to them, he is apparently willing to concede some rôle to the Principate and to "the sacral nature of pagan Germanic kingship", respectively, in promoting the ultimate victory of the theocratic-descending theme in the Roman empire and later on in the early-medieval Latin West. But, as we have seen, the truly vital factor he believes to have been the influence of Christianity. It was, he says, "the overpowering force of the Christian idea" which "itself was responsible for the very institution of theocratic kingship". By the Christian "idea" or "theme" he means, in effect, the Pauline teaching that "there is no power but of God", a teaching which, in his discussion of medieval kingship by the grace of God, he links up with the other Pauline statement: "What I am, I am by the grace of God". And at once we encounter a puzzle of major proportions concerning the way in which he goes about constructing his conceptual framework.

When speaking of "the principles with which and on which the medieval papacy" functioned, he is careful to insist that "the prerequisite... for a proper historical presentation... is to see the institution from within itself". Thus 'the question whether a particular papal tenet can be squared with biblical data" is one that belongs, not to the historian, but to the theologian. The question which "comes within the precinct of the historian's quest" is a rather different one—namely, whether or not "the papacy based the tenet on the Bible". Now Ullmann does not repeat this *caveat* when he comes to discuss medieval theocratic monarchy, but even had he done so, we should still be entitled to accuse him of using this attractively economical division of scholarly labour to avoid facing up to a quite properly historical question, and an important one at that.

In some of his most interesting passages he illustrates the ingenious ways in which medieval propagandists aligned on the side of the "theocratic" idea the Pauline texts to which he refers. But nowhere does he really explain what it was that disposed them to manipulate these texts in such a fashion. And yet this cries out for an explanation. For, despite the use to which they could often be (and frequently were) put during the medieval and early modern centuries, these texts say nothing at all about monarchy, still less about absolute monarchy. Nor... does Romans xiii necessarily say anything more about the historical origin or derivation of power than it does about its form. Instead, it simply asserts that there is something sacred about the authority which rulers possess. Moreover, it reflects only the most positive of the several attitudes towards political authority which find expression in the New Testament. Side by side with it should be placed those other New Testament texts which cover a whole doctrinal spectrum, ranging from the more guarded affirmations of Peter's First Epistle to the blank hostility of the Apocalypse of John, which, in the name of the

Kingship of God, denounces as Satanic the blasphemously deified emperors of Rome. If these texts are to be regarded as any less "Christian" than those of Paul, then the reason for so discriminating should clearly be stated. As it is, their existence should serve to remind us that New Testament political views (including the Pauline) were predicated upon the assumption that the empire was a heathen power. It should serve to remind us, too, that when compared with the classical political vision, those views are markedly negative in tone—certainly ill-designed to engineer the triumph of the type of theocratic-descending conception which Ullmann describes. A far better index of the nature of their influence, it may be urged, is the fundamentally negative political vision that found expression, long after the accession of the Christian emperors, in Augustine's *De civitate dei* [*The City of God*], and one cannot help wondering if Ullmann's silence on that work is indicative of his inability to align it with his general conceptual framework.

If, then, we wish at all to speak in terms of the dominance of the theocratic-descending theme in "the later Roman and Christianized empire", we must look elsewhere for its origins than in the pages of the New Testament. Instead, we must ask ourselves what it was that led such Christian thinkers as Eusebius of Caesarea (whom Ullmann cites) to ignore the more negative aspects of New Testament political teaching and to marshal in support of absolute sacral monarchy those Biblical texts susceptible of a sympathetic interpretation. And the critical factor at work, as Eusebius's writings make abundantly clear, was the pervasive influence of those Hellenistic ideas of kingship which, awakening native resonances, had by the fourth century A.D. triumphed in the Roman world, and which, themselves in tension with Judaic and Christian beliefs, had their roots deep both in Pythagorean-Platonic speculation and in ancient Near Eastern notions of divine or sacral monarchy.

Ullmann, it is true, is uneasily aware of the importance of such Romano-Hellenistic conceptions. But he appears unconscious of the degree to which they pre-empted motifs which he regards as manifestations of "the specifically Christian idea". Thus when he attributes to Eusebius in the fourth century the chief responsibility for "linking monotheism with the concept of the Roman emperorship", he makes no mention of Eusebius's well-attested indebtedness to the political thinking of Philo Judaeus, who, four centuries earlier and without benefit, it need hardly be added, of the Pauline Epistles, had not only correlated monarchy with monotheism and described rulership as a special gift of God but also, in remarks actually quoted by Eusebius, introduced what it is tempting to think of as the characteristically "Pauline" notion that God permits even the rule of tyrants as punishment for a people's wickedness. Similarly, while Ullmann makes much of the importance of Paul's description of the ruler as a "servant of God", he makes no mention, for example, of Pliny the Younger's description of the emperor Nerva's acting as a "servant of the gods" or of the fact that the notions expressed by this and by such related titles as "vicar of

God" and "image of God" were of Hellenistic provenance, or, indeed, more ancient still. And to say this is to say also that even if "king by the grace of God" did not become a standard royal title until the eighth century, the idea which it conveyed was a much more ancient one and by no means the creation of Christian thinkers. Ullmann can say that "the first pictorial representation" of the appointment of the emperor by God "occurred in fact soon after Constantine the Great, when on a medallion a hand was seen to reach down from the clouds and put a crown on the head of the emperor". But in this he is simply mistaken. For the same notion finds visual expression on numerous Roman coins ranging from the time of the emperor Trajan (d. 117) to that of Galerius Maximianus, many of them bearing the legend "by the providence of the gods" and depicting Jupiter conferring upon the emperor the imperial insignia. Alföldi has suggested a coin dating back to the last century of the Republic as a Roman prototype for this motif and has noted its deeper roots in a more ancient iconographic tradition of Assyro-Babylonian origin.

That Ullmann misconceives not only the importance but also the nature of the ancient pattern of divine or sacral monarchy to which these iconographical materials witness, is evidenced by his summary formulation that, with their adoption of Christianity, the Roman emperors "changed from considering themselves divine emperors to considering themselves emperors by the grace of God", the significance of that change lying in the fact that they "abandoned their claim to be true divinity on earth and recognized instead in God the origin of their power". For to put the matter in such a way is erroneously to assume that the attribution of a divine status to a ruler, on the one hand, and the derivation of his authority from a god on the other are incompatible ideas. And to assume that is, in turn, to be committed to the prior assumption that pagan notions of what it is to be divine are commensurate with that narrower, more exclusive, and historically much more peculiar conception of divinity which emerges in the pages of the Bible—the conception, that is, of a unique God, a single and impenetrable entity, who, suffering no alienation and admitting of no degree, transcends the natural world which of his omnipotence he has created out of nothing and at every moment sustains in being. In making this assumption Ullmann is by no means alone. But the assumption itself is no less misleading for being commonly or even unconsciously held, and it vitiates much of what he has to say about the triumph of his "theocratic-descending theme" not only in the later Roman world but also in the early-medieval Latin West. For there, too, analogous considerations apply.

Evidence concerning the nature of kingship in ancient and early-medieval Scandinavia, though late in date, is comparatively abundant. As a result, there is enough of a scholarly consensus for one scholar recently to assert: "That kingship in Old Scandinavia was entirely sacral is nowadays considered as a mere matter of fact". Certainly, it is clear that the Scandinavian monarchs of the early medieval period played a prominent rôle in the religious cult, were sometimes revered as gods after their death, were regarded as being of divine descent, and, in accordance with a pattern familiar also to the ancient Near East (and, indeed, at one time or another to most parts of the world) were held responsible for the rotation of the seasons, the fertility of the crops, and the general prosperity and well-being of their subjects. Consensus evaporates, however, when one turns to the Germanic kingship in Southern and Western Europe during the early imperial age and during the later era of barbarian migrations. The picture is more complex, the evidence much scantier. Moreover, how it is interpreted depends very much on the position taken concerning the admissibility of evidence based on later Scandinavian parallels. It depends, too, upon the preconceptions concerning the nature of the divine with which it is approached. Now Ullmann clearly sides with those who argue that pagan Germanic kingship did indeed possess some sort of sacral dimension. In this he is, I believe, quite correct. And in his most recent and impressive analysis of "the clericalization of the royal office" in the Carolingian era he asserts that it was precisely because Pepin the Short lacked the "blood charisma" possessed by his Merovingian predecessors and needed, if his title was to be legitimized in the eyes of the people, some substitute religious character, that unction was administered to him in 751. Here again, I believe, he is not mistaken. Unfortunately, however, he nowhere addresses himself explicitly to the nature of Germanic sacral monarchy. And what little he does say about it—even more, what he implies—may be criticized on three grounds at least.

In the first place, while he assigns some vague rôle to the sacral nature of Germanic kingship in accounting for the triumph of the theocratic-descending theme in Southern and Western Europe, he can still assert that "there was no trace of a theocratic-descending form of government" in Scandinavia until "very much later" and that "in the Scandinavian countries the populist kingship never died out". It is surely not unreasonable to infer from this that he ascribes no sacral character to Scandinavian kingship. And given the strength of the evidence to the contrary, it seems legitimate, therefore, to wonder why.

In the second place, he characterizes the contrast which he draws between the Carolingian monarchy and the Merovingian and older Germanic kingship as being cognate at least to the distinctions between the spiritual and material, the supernatural and natural. Thus he persistently correlates the so-called pagan blood-right, right of descent, or "blood-charisma" not with the Germanic notion of royal descent from divinity, not, indeed, with any notion of divinity at all, but rather with the human, the physical, the biological, the natural. So that, over and against the "theocratic" kings of the Carolingian era and later—divine appointees, ruling by "gift of God", by virtue of "divine intervention" and the "transmission of divine grace"—he sets those earlier Germanic rulers whom he characterizes as the products of merely "natural-biological forces", their kingship resting only on foundations "of a physical and purely human kind". In so doing, in attempting to assimilate to "the natural" the god-sprung, priestly kings of the Germanic world—*mana*-filled mediators between their gods and their peoples—he is once more guilty of anachronistically imposing on a less differentiated world of thought to which it was alien that firm distinction between the realms of nature and supernature which is grounded in the Hebraic and Christian doctrine of creation and the peculiarly exclusive conception of God which that doctrine, philosophically speaking, both presupposes and entails.

The fact that he should be betrayed into so doing should be correlated, moreover, with the implicit assumption which constitutes the third ground for criticizing his handling of these issues—the assumption, namely, that the conceptual relationship between forms of kingship rooted in the divine and those rooted in popular election and limited in some sense by popular will must necessarily be one of opposition or contradiction. So that, because medieval Scandinavian kings and their ancient Germanic forebears were often "elected", or because there were limitations of some sort upon their power, the implication is that they cannot be regarded as truly sacral kings. And yet, despite the example of ancient Near Eastern monarchies or of early-modern divine right theory, there is nothing *a priori* necessary about the opposition presupposed in this assumption. After all, in what has been called "the first Indo-European contribution" to the development of ideas of kingship, the Hittite *pankus*, or assembly of nobles, which we know to have existed at least in the Old Kingdom, may have had a voice in the making of the Hittite kings (on this there is some scholarly disagreement), and certainly "had jurisdiction over the king if the latter committed a crime". And this despite the fact that the Hittite king was unquestionably a fundamentally sacral figure "regarded during his lifetime as the incarnation of his deified ancestor" and himself worshipped after death as a god. Nor should we slip into the anachronistic assumption that the *thing*, or popular assembly, which is described as "electing" Germanic or Scandinavian kings was necessarily itself some sort of "secular" and "democratic" body, lacking a sacral status and bereft of sacral functions, or that the act of "election" —even apart from the limitation of choice to members of royal families claiming divine descent—was itself devoid of a sacred dimension. And as for allegedly populist limitations on the power of pre-Christian Germanic kings in Western and Southern Europe, the most definite evidence that has come down to us again suggests very strongly that such limitations... sprang precisely from their sacral status. The king of the Burgundians, as the fourth-century Roman historian, Ammianus Marcellinus, tells us,

> according to an ancient custom, lays down his power and is deposed, if under him the fortune of war has wavered, or the earth has denied sufficient crops; just as the Egyptians commonly blame their rulers for such occurrences.

Just as consent could in the Middle Ages signify many things, so too, it should be remembered, could accountability.

But if the pagan Germanic and Scandinavian kingship was by no means as unqualifiedly "populist" (in Ullmann's sense of that word) as he claims, are we not entitled, then, to feel some misgivings about the allegedly "theocratic" purity of the medieval Christian monarchy, which he contrasts with it as a manifestation of the descending rather than the ascending theme? Ullmann is not alone in stressing the fact that the Christian emphasis on the derivation of the king's powers from God, symbolized so effectively in the reception of unction and the adoption of the title "king by the grace of God", involved also an emphasis on the independence of the king in his relations with his people. Fritz Kern said as much long ago, and in a statement of classic balance. But, then, Kern was also at pains to stress the interdependence during the greater part of the Middle Ages of the divine and popular sanctions which the monarchy enjoyed, insisting that the monarch's dependence upon God "was broadly enough conceived to allow the monarch to be dependent also upon the will of the community in so far as monarchy itself was based upon a popular as well as a divine mandate"....

(b) Aristotelian Naturalism and the Recovery of the Ascending Theme

The rigidities, however, of Ullmann's over-arching conceptual framework are not only exclusivist; they are also interlocking. It follows, therefore, that the price which he must pay for them, evident as it is in his depiction of the triumph of the theocratic-descending thesis in the late Roman and early medieval eras, must accordingly be manifest also in what he has to say in general about the recovery of the populist-ascending theme in the later-medieval period, and in particular about the rôle of what he calls "Aristotelian naturalism" in sponsoring that recovery. Having set up his purely theocratic kingship in stark contrast to the supposedly pure populism of the archaic Germanic past, he must now turn to the dramatic intervention of a novel factor to render intelligible that "return" to the populist-ascending theme which, he argues, characterized late-medieval political thinking. The novel factor he has in mind is, of course, the recovery of the works of Aristotle, and he argues that the attitude they conveyed was able to make so profound an impact upon later-medieval political thinking because of the prior undermining of the theocratic-descending theme by factors indigenous to Western Europe, most notably by feudalism.

... It remains ... to demonstrate that the rôle he ascribes to the recovery of Aristotelian views sponsors severe distortions—in his assessment of the nature and importance of their impact, in his treatment of the medieval Aristotelian thinkers on whom he repeatedly focuses, and even in his understanding of the political thinking of Aristotle himself. For, given his insistent correlation of the descending thesis with the supernatural and the ascending with the natural, Ullmann's Aristotle and his medieval disciples must bear the burden of accounting at the same time for the recovery of a "naturalistic" view of political life and for the emphasis on popular consent as the source of political power that is assumed to go with it. This despite the fact that canonist and civilian authors, long before the translation of Aristotle's *Politics*, had undoubtedly begun to appropriate the notion that man is by nature a political animal. This despite the fact, too, that, "Aristotelian naturalism" notwithstanding, it was possible to employ Aristotelian ideas to buttress the theocratic-descending theme. Thus the papalist theologian, James of Viterbo, while adopting the Aristotelian teleological approach and agreeing with Aristotle and Aquinas that the state was natural and possessed a positive ethical value of its own, argued from the superior end pursued in the Christian society by the spiritual power to its ultimate supreme control over the temporal, believing that only in this way could nature be perfected.

But we hear little from Ullmann about political "naturalism" in medieval Europe before the advent of Aristotle's *Politics* and nothing at all about James of Viterbo. His chosen Aristotelians, instead, are Aquinas, John of Paris, Dante and Marsilius of Padua, and he uses them to illustrate the process by which Aristotelian ideas, after an initial phase of hostility, were first received and absorbed "into Christian cosmology", and then, in the fourteenth century, released "from the Christian grab". So that, whether or not John of Paris is taken to be more "progressive" or advanced than Dante, we are given to understand that what occurred on the road from Aquinas to Marsilius was a progressive de-Christianizing of Aristotle. "The Christian elements faded into the background more and more, and what remained was Aristotle"....

Unfortunately, even though they are of his own choosing, the first three of his Aristotelians prove to be ungratefully recalcitrant and he elicits the desired answers from them only by dint of applying considerable pressure to their texts. Thus, though he is quite correct in his emphasis on the Thomistic commitment to the viewpoint that man is by nature a social and political animal, may one not cavil, even while admitting the complexity of Dante's thought, at a reading... which, because of an obsessive preoccupation with Dante's "naturalism", refuses any recognition to the quasi-religious character of his world-empire ...? [O]ne cannot help wondering at the repeated emphasis on John of Paris's remark to the effect that the disposition of temporal power must reflect or accommodate itself to such natural diversities, a remark on the basis of which Ullmann can conclude that "the rigidity of political thought" was giving way to a more naturalistic "flexibility" and that "into the place of the hitherto prevalent monolithic thesis of absoluteness" was now stepping "the dominant note of relativity".

But, then, it should be noted that the context in which he addresses himself to this issue has been set by his prior insistence that John of Paris, even more sharply it would seem than Aquinas before him, distinguished between "the natural body politic and the supranatural mystical body of Christ", so that to him, as Ullmann puts it:

> The Church... was a mystical body pure and simple—a concept that had come more and more in evidence in the thirteenth century—and as such contrasted sharply with the natural body politic. Since the Church was purely mystical, its ministers had similarly purely sacramental functions. Negatively expressed, the Church was, for John of Paris, no organic juristic body in the traditional sense.

Unfortunately, the chapter... to which he refers in support of this claim is not itself concerned at all to distinguish between the Church and the "natural body politic" nor does it make any reference to the Church as a mystical body. Indeed, in John's entire treatise only three such references occur, and they tell a story directly opposed to Ullmann's.... [T]he Church for John of Paris was very much a "juristic body", a corporate entity, and, *as such*, a mystical body....

Ironically enough, it is in connection with the power of jurisdiction which popes and prelates exercise in the ecclesiastical mystical body which is the Church that Ullmann can find his most striking evidence of John of Paris's advocacy of the populist-ascending thesis. For, by consistently applying canonistic corporational theory to the structure of the whole Church, John developed what has been called "by far the most consistent and complete formulation of conciliar doctrine before the outbreak of the Great Schism". In comparison, what he has to say about the popular source of royal power is not very extensive. But is it clear and, indeed, traditional enough. Royal power is from God and from the people. What he wishes to exclude by this formula is not, as Ullmann seems to imply, the derivation of royal power from God, but the high papalist claim that that power was mediated to the king *via* the pope, and he drives his point home appropriately by reminding us that Paul in his famous statement to the Romans had not said that the ruler was a "servant of the pope" but a "servant of God".

That Ullmann, however, should make so much of these statements is understandable enough. Fragmentary though they are, they constitute by far the most explicit affirmations of the derivation of political power from the people to be found in the first three of his Aristotelians. For it is only by sailing rather too close to the dialectical wind that he can elicit from Aquinas and Dante truly convincing intimations of his populist-ascending thesis. Thus, for example, he classifies as an enviably clear elaboration of the populist-ascending theme Aquinas's commentary on Aristotle's genetic account of the emergence of the *polis* as the completion of such other natural associations as the family, village and so on—an analysis which is, in fact, concerned rather with the goal than with the derivation of power. Or, again, he stresses Aquinas's definition of democracy in the *Summa Theologica* without noting that elsewhere Aquinas, following Aristotle, classifies democracy as one of the unjust or perverted forms of government. At the same time, he implies that the words "and this was established by the divine law" apply to democracy when in fact they apply to the "mixed" form of constitution, and then, not because Aquinas was himself willing to describe it (here and in one other text) as the "best polity", but simply because it was the constitutional form which he believed to have been instituted among the Jews under Moses and his successors. Moreover, Ullmann's further suggestion that "the principle of representation" necessarily follows from Aquinas's alleged flirtation with democracy involves the imposition of a further strain on two unrelated texts which, while they certainly reflect the older medieval view of representation as personification, in no way indicate any adhesion to the newer notion of representation as delegation—a notion which one would have thought to be more germane to his concern with popular consent. Similarly, in an effort to imply (he never quite says as much) that Dante, too, can be numbered among the supporters of the populist-ascending thesis, he sharply contrasts Dante's description of the ruler as the "servant of all" with the Pauline statement that he was the "servant of God".... He does so ... without noting that ... Dante himself clearly regards the emperor as the servant or minister of God and elsewhere explicitly describes Henry VII as such....

It may be, of course, that Ullmann would account for his difficulties with these three Aristotelians on the grounds that their views were transitional ones which, "precisely because they set out from the theocentric origin, could not exhibit a genuine populism, could not arrive at a genuine popular sovereignty". This could not emerge "as long as there was, conceptually at least, the idea of nature being created by God, as long as the natural inclination of man to form the State was eventually of divine provenance". Aristotelian ideas had still, therefore, to be released from "their Christian garb". What was needed was "a radical operation". And what better a candidate for that task than Marsilius of Padua who "set out from the axiom that the link between nature and God was a matter of faith, and not a matter capable of rational proof", and, as a result, not "an operational principle in political science"?

Certainly, with Marsilius, Ullmann has no difficulty in documenting the political "naturalism" and the preoccupation with popular consent which he regards as integral to the populist-ascending theme. Instead, the trouble here is that we are given the impression, and overwhelmingly so, that with Marsilius we encounter once more the political teaching of Aristotle himself, an impression bolstered by a highly tendentious reading of Aristotle's *Politics* which succeeds in transforming even the Stagirite himself into an advocate of "Aristotelian naturalism". For, to take only three crucial points which Ullmann emphasizes, it must be insisted that neither in his separation of law and politics from morals, nor in his attribution of legislative sovereignty to the people, nor in his own particular version of political naturalism is Marsilius at one with Aristotle.

Thus, in the first place, if, by distinguishing between "transient" and "immanent" acts and limiting government almost entirely to the moderation of "the excesses" of men's "transient" acts, or, again, if by identifying enforceable, coercive command as the very essence of law, one can argue that Marsilius did indeed engineer a separation between politics and morals, Aristotle most certainly did not.... A state which limited itself to "preventing mutual injustice and easing exchange" would be for him no state at all. For "the end of the state is not mere life; it is, rather, a good quality of life". That is to say, the state exists to make possible not merely man's physical survival but also his moral and spiritual perfection....

In the second place, if Marsilius defines law as in its very essence enforceable, coercive command and regards the people as alone endowed with the power so to command, Aristotle really does neither. For him law is the voice of Reason and of God. It can be defined as "Reason free from all passion", and the qualities essential to the art of legislation are, therefore, intelligence and "right judgment". The texts which Ullmann cites to support his own contention that for Aristotle it is the "will" of the people which "determines what should be law" say nothing of the sort—even if Marsilius, before him, had thought that they did. What they convey, instead, is a rather tentative statement coming from an Aristotle who has just classified democracy as a perverted constitution, to the effect that there may be something to be said after all for the idea that the people at large should wield the dominant authority in the state. At least, even if they should not be permitted "themselves in their individual capacity" to hold office, it would be appropriate to let them "share in the deliberative and judicial functions"—in particular, to elect the magistrates to office and to call them "to account at the end of their tenure of office".... In contrast with this, and despite his frequently attested dependence on Aristotle, Marsilius persistently reorients his own political thinking from final to efficient causes; it is "an efficient cause called the 'legislator'" which occupies "the dominant position" in his doctrine. And this in turn, it should be noted, reflects (or accounts for) the difference, in the third place, between the types of political "naturalism" espoused by the two thinkers.

In embarking upon his discussion of Aristotle, Ullmann rightly stresses the relevance of his natural philosophy to his political thinking. He does so in order to stress Aristotle's fundamental "empiricism", but fails to note that, unlike modern behaviourist empiricism, Aristotle's is not of the "mechanistic" or "instrumental" variety. For him the concern with efficient causality, though necessary, can never by itself suffice to convey an adequate understanding of any process.... For it is in the end or outcome of a process that the nature of a thing resides; it is on ends or outcomes, therefore, that Aristotle's emphasis characteristically lies....

On this matter, Marsilius provides a striking contrast. For along with his orientation of politics to efficient causes goes a cognate inclination to interpret the "natural" less as the completed or perfect than as the primitive....

The point at issue here concerns fundamental metaphysical assumptions. Ullmann, it would seem, in his concern with the destructive impact of Aristotelian ideas on traditional Christian modes of thought, has underestimated the degree to which those ideas were themselves transformed into something rich and strange under the impress of the profoundly alien metaphysic into which the scholastic thinkers strove to insert them. It should not be forgotten that Aristotle's world of nature, before it was "absorbed into the Christian cosmology", was a world which in its ceaseless striving to emulate the perfection of God itself pulsated to the rhythm of the divine. It was a restless but intelligible world, one in which final causes were ceaselessly at work, one dependent for its very motion upon that ultimate final cause, the unmoved mover, the final good which he himself calls God. For "upon such a principle", he tells us, "depend the heavens and the world of nature". It was not, therefore, the natural world which the Hebraic and Christian tradition bequeathed to the modern era, a world which, precisely because it was regarded as having been created out of nothing by an omnipotent and transcendent God, was a "disenchanted" one—one from which the divine had finally been banished. Instead, it was a world which at once both yearned towards the divine, the transcendent good which was its final end, and, at the same time, by virtue of its immanent order, was in some sense suffused with it. As a result, if we choose to talk at all about "Aristotelian naturalism", we must be careful to do so in the knowledge that Aristotle's idea of "the natural" was one which can itself be said in some degree to have comprehended that which under the influence of the Christian tradition we ourselves have become accustomed to classify as "the supernatural".

... [Ullmann's] identification of the ascending thesis with the natural and the descending with the supernatural, the adjectives he characteristically applies to both, and the periods during which he asserts them to have been prevalent, suggest very strongly that for him there is, despite all surface differences, a fundamental continuity between the modes of political thinking characteristic of the modern world and those characteristic of the classical world, at least from Aristotle onwards—both periods being committed, presumably, to the "natural" and "secular" modes of explanation appropriate to any properly *political* thinking. In addition, they suggest, too, that for him the medieval period stands out in the history of Western political thinking as an exceptional one, something of an interruption, a deviation from the norm, a period during which the "natural" categories of political philosophy as we know it were pushed to one side by motifs of a supernatural bent. In assuming this picture of the larger historical process, Ullmann is by no means alone. Its tidiness continues, it would seem, to beguile. And yet it is now a hundred years and more since Fustel de Coulanges, in a classic evocation of the centrality of religion to the political life of the ancient world, warned his own contemporaries of the dangers of anachronism, of historical narcissism, of finding their own attitudes reflected all too readily in those of ancient peoples whose modes of thought were in reality fundamentally alien to theirs. Since he wrote, moreover, the findings of the cultural anthropologists, the sociologists, the students of primitive and comparative religion have converged to confirm the precocious acuteness of his vision, and to make clear that the transition from the archaic and classical outlook to the Christian was not so much a shift from a "secular" to a "religious" viewpoint as from one ancient and widespread mode of religious consciousness to another and radically different one. The same is true of the transition from the world of Germanic paganism to that of early-medieval Christianity. Once this is understood, of course, it is no longer, *pace* Ullmann, the "religious" nature of medieval political thinking that cries out for explanation, but rather the emergence in the modern era of that uniquely secularized political vision which has so succeeded in shaping the common political sense of the Western world that we are persistently tempted, even at the cost of rampant anachronism, to see it as something grounded in the very nature of man. But, then, it is properly the task of historical reflection rather to deliver us from such delusions than to strengthen our bondage to them. That in this respect it should fail us may well, therefore, be the gravest defect in Ullmann's whole over-arching conceptual apparatus.

Harsh judgements, perhaps, and ones made, it must certainly be admitted, with intimations of fallibility more than usually insistent. Nonetheless, they are judgements I am prepared to stand by — not unmindful, however, of the need to insist that they are judgements the specific concern of which is the adequacy of Ullmann's conceptual apparatus as a guide to the intricacies of medieval political thought. Even at their most negative, therefore, they should not be taken to impugn either the desirability or the significance of the whole interpretative enterprise upon which he has been bold enough to embark. Nor, for that matter, should the persistent identification of weaknesses which precedes them be taken to preclude the admiring recognition of strengths. For, in this respect, I am struck with the pertinence of a remark once made by John Stuart Mill. "For our own part", he said,

> we have a large tolerance for one-eyed men, provided their one eye is a penetrating one: if they saw more, they probably would not see so keenly, nor so eagerly pursue one course of inquiry. Almost all rich veins of original and striking speculation have been opened up by systematic half-thinkers.

Taking this statement, then, and applying it to Ullmann's vision of medieval politics, my own verdict overall would run very much as follows: Rich? Undoubtedly. Striking? Without question. Original? In no small degree. Speculative? More, perhaps, than he would care to admit. But fundamentally valid as a key to the understanding of medieval political thought? I would argue not.

Bibliography

ARTHUR S. McGRADE, *The Political Thought of William of Ockham* (1974).
JOHN MORRALL, *Political Thought in Medieval Times* (1962).
ALEXANDER MURRAY, *Reason and Society in the Middle Ages* (1978).
FRANCIS OAKLEY, *The Western Church in the Later Middle Ages* (1979).
BRIAN TIERNEY, *Foundation of the Conciliar Theory* (1955).
WALTER ULLMANN, *A History of Political Thought: The Middle Ages* (1965).
WALTER ULLMANN, *The Growth of Papal Government in the Middle Ages* (1970).
MICHAEL WILKS, *The Problem of Sovereignty in the Later Middle Ages* (1963).

The Social Meaning of Monks and Friars

BARBARA H. ROSENWEIN AND LESTER K. LITTLE

Monks and friars were integral parts of their respective societies even when they rejected them, but how were their religious practices related to their societies? Rosenwein and Little explain the relationship in the following way.

For the Benedictine monks of Cluny in the tenth and eleventh centuries, the essence of spirituality was prayer and patience. They espoused humility in place of pride and endured oppression rather than afflict it on others. On the surface a monastic life devoted to these values was the ultimate rejection of the violence that pervaded medieval society, a condemnation of the knightly life the monks knew all too well through parents and siblings. Beneath the surface, however, these same monks also adopted and modified violence so that it became acceptable under certain conditions. They, too, were violent men, but on a spiritual plane. The liturgy of Cluny enacted a ritualized battle with the Devil for the souls of people, a bloodless conflict on behalf of those too weak to save themselves. The monks of Cluny thus modelled themselves on the knighthood they rejected. They also remodelled acceptable knighthood on the new values they espoused: the knight, they taught, should be a peaceful man with high ideals, who raised his sword only in defense of the weak.

For the mendicant spirituality of the thirteenth and fourteenth centuries the standard was apostolic poverty and preaching. Those who chose such poverty deliberately rejected the materialistic values of the commercial society of the towns. At the same time, however, these same friars also adopted for themselves and modified the model of the merchant as negotiator and tradesman, integrating it into their own spirituality. Their preaching and particularly their penitential system also became commercial transactions, business deals between man and God, often sealed with the gift of money. The friars employed the mercantile techniques of bargaining, persuading, and contracting to religious ends.

From "Social Meaning in Monastic and Mendicant Spiritualites" by B. H. Rosenwein and L. K. Little. World copyright: The Past and Present Society, Corpus Christi College, Oxford, England. This article is reprinted with the permission of the Society and the author from *Past and Present: A Journal of Historical Studies*, no. 63 (May 1974).

The religious beliefs of Benedictines, on the one hand, and those of Franciscans and Dominicans, on the other, were basically the same. Because they lived in different societies under altered social conditions their respective spiritualities developed in profoundly different ways. Society is as influential in molding religious beliefs and organizations as the latter are in shaping society.

Spiritualities—the ideals, beliefs, and practices of persons who devote themselves fully to religion—are integral components of the societies in which they appear. The task of the social historian is to determine the precise nature of this integration in particular instances. Two cases from early European history provide an opportunity for study and comparison: the Benedictine monks and the Franciscan and Dominican friars. Between the Viking invasions and the First Crusade, the leading form of spirituality was the one defined and engaged in by the Benedictines; later, during the thirteenth and early fourteenth centuries, the spirituality of the Franciscans and Dominicans was similarly dominant. Both monks and friars gave expression to the deepest religious feelings of their times, but the social contexts in which they thrived were markedly different.

Specialists in various fields of history have already shown how thoroughly a part of feudal, agrarian society were the Benedictine monasteries, chief among them Cluny with its vast network of dependent priories. An analogous set of observations has been made about the mendicant orders and their ties with the more recent urban, commercial society. But establishing that a spirituality fits, in a general way, into its social context still leaves unanswered the question of how a specific form of spiritual life is causally related to particular social phenomena. The answer to this question will be sought by isolating and analysing the unique features of Benedictine spirituality, namely patience and prayer, and of mendicant spirituality, namely poverty and preaching. These will then be correlated with the unique features of the societies that incorporated them. We intend to show that, within certain well-defined temporal and ideological limits, monastic prayer was part of a complex of responses to feudal warfare, while the preaching of the mendicants, delimited in a similar way, was one of a number of related responses to urban money-making.

I. Monastic Patience and Prayer

In the tenth and eleventh centuries, Cluny was the major model and propagator of the religious life in France, England, Spain and Italy. In accordance with the Benedictine Rule, which was the ultimate foundation for Benedictine spiritual forms, the Cluniacs practised "humility" and performed the "work of God (*opus Dei*)", that is prayer, but in both instances they did so with notable modifications.

In the Benedictine Rule humility had twelve clearly defined degrees, one of which was patience (*patientia*), the aspect of humility necessary for achieving perfect obedience. It was defined as the willingness to endure afflictions or injustices silently. In early Cluniac writings patience came to subsume the notion of humility. Whereas the traditional scheme of Gregory the Great had seen humility as "the source of virtue" (just as pride was the root of all vice), John of Salerno, the biographer of St. Odo (Cluny's second abbot), wrote instead that "patience is the source of all virtues". Odo himself explained why this was so by elaborating on the theme of patience in his *Collationes*, written, indeed, with the specific purpose of consoling victims of wanton violence by explaining to them why they should endure their troubles patiently. The Augustinian division of men into the generations of Cain and Abel was used by Odo to delineate (among other things) two different attitudes toward afflictions: the generation of Cain inflicted injuries but did not receive them; the generation of Abel welcomed afflictions but never injured others. The one included the "powerful oppressors of the poor", the "rich men" who were "swollen with proud thoughts". The other consisted of those whose lot it was to be scourged by the generation of Cain: "You see the humble and weak and poorer men oppressed, afflicted, and unjustly hurt by the proud and powerful and rich". The patient man, willingly powerless, passive and poor, was punished for his sins temporally but was thereby spared eternal punishment.

The other main aspect of Cluniac spirituality, the *opus Dei*, was the principal monastic occupation. The Rule had prescribed about three and one half hours of liturgy, but the Cluniacs, while performing the offices in the Rule, added before and after them so many extra liturgical acts that virtually the entire monastic day was spent in the choir. The development from the mixture of work and prayer in the Benedictine Rule to the Cluniac preoccupation with prayer had taken place gradually. The process began with the reforms of St. Benedict of Aniane in the early ninth century. Benedict had his monks at Inden recite the Gradual Psalms (psalms 119–33) before nocturns as well as add a number of prayers and perform a daily office of the dead. His ideas, promulgated in the monastic reforms of Louis the Pious, were forgotten during the course of the ninth-century invasions and Carolingian dynastic wars, but were revived at isolated monasteries such as Baume at the end of the ninth century. The monks at Baume sang 138 psalms daily, a considerable increase over the 40 psalms per day prescribed in the Rule. It was only a short step from this to the some 170 psalms sung by the Cluniacs each day.

The expansion of the liturgical ritual at Cluny was accompanied by the ritualization of activities outside the choir as well. The normal activities of everyday life—waking, dressing, sitting and eating—became ceremonialized. Occupations that had once been necessary but had subsequently become superfluous were retained in ceremonial form. Ritual, dependent as it was on symbol and gesture, was also behind the Cluniac propensity toward extravagant garb and splendid ceremonial objects. Doubtless too it was partially responsible for the Cluniac sign language, a language of acts rather than words. Not all these practices were original or peculiar to Cluny. At Baume, John reports, the monks "made various signs to each other that grammarians I suppose would call the language of the fingers and eyes".

The unique character of Cluniac prayer consisted not only in its length but also in the new use to which the additional liturgy—for the most part traditional collects and psalms—was put, namely intercession. The new prayers were chanted for the salvation of the souls of the dead and the living. The fifteen Gradual Psalms added before nocturns are an instructive example. The first five psalms were sung for departed brothers and other faithful, the next five for the monks themselves, and the last five for "the kings and all our benefactors still living". Most of the other psalms and collects in the day were similarly performed on someone's behalf. Further, an entire office "of the dead" consisting of both matins and vespers, and a morning mass for the same intention, were added to the daily schedule. Beginning in the early eleventh century an entire day was set aside for All Souls, to be spent in prayer and almsgiving "for the redemption of the souls of all the faithful".

The notion that the monks could help save souls through intercessionary prayer was part of a theology of redemption that pitted God against the Devil in a battle for the souls of men. In the thick of the fray were the monks with their prayers: the demons, wrote the Cluniac monk Jotsaldus, "lamented and made many complaints that due to prayers of religious men ... often the souls of the damned were freed from their punishment through God's mercy". And because of the monks' prayers on All Souls' Day, Jotsaldus wrote, "the adversary [the Devil] laments that more and more he appears a failure to himself".

The paradox that peaceful monks should daily engage in battle was not lost on one contemporary. Adalbero of Laon satirized the "bellicose order of monks" at Cluny: off they went to battle, javelins behind their backs, shields hanging from their necks, swords in their teeth. But Adalbero's jaundiced view was one-sided. If the Cluniac monks were powerful warriors in their liturgy, they were also powerless victims in their humility. That these two contradictory characteristics should co-exist within the spirituality of tenth- and eleventh-century monasticism was the result of historical circumstances.

The Viking invasions and the Carolingian dynastic wars of the ninth and tenth centuries intensified the already violent character of Frankish society. The invasions brought burning, murder and pillage to nearly all areas of France. Rouen was burned in 841; Bordeaux, Aquitaine and Poitou in 848.

The areas contiguous to the Scheldt, Somme, Seine, Loire and Garonne were continually attacked. Paris, burned in 857 and 861, was subjected to a prolonged siege in 885–7 that was raised only when the Vikings were allowed to withdraw to Burgundy and pillage there.

The dynastic wars of the Carolingians had a similar, if less devastating, effect. When, for example, the smouldering feud between Charles the Bald and his brother Louis the German over Aquitaine flamed into war in 854, Charles's men "devoted all their energy", as a contemporary observer put it, "to pillaging, burning and taking captives. And they did not restrain their cupidity and audacity from the very churches and altars of God". Such behaviour was normal in a society where violence was deep-rooted and unchecked.

Both the invasions and the dynastic wars were symptoms of the impotence of late Carolingian government, and both led to the same result: the enrichment of an élite group of laymen. These men, some of them "new", others from them members of the old Carolingian aristocracy, benefited from the anarchy by usurping, extending or consolidating territories and powers. They were further enriched by fiefs from the Carolingian kings, who were desperate to ensure the support, or at least the neutrality, of the great men of the realm. But the kings' intentions were thwarted; the magnates did not scruple to switch allegiance from one king to another. In 858, for example, Charles's men abandoned him for the rich domains promised them by Louis.

The result of these developments was the devolution of power into the hands of local strong men, and the use of that power for private purposes. The late Carolingian kings might continue to promulgate statutes to keep the peace, but, as one of their capitularies complained, the laws were "virtually void", for "everyone plunders his neighbour". The duchy of Burgundy in the early days of Cluny was no exception. It was described by a contemporary in ominous terms:

> After [Duke] Richard the Great died [in 921] ... unseen tyrants began to come out from everywhere and in turn to contend with each other in mutual slaughter. The church of God is confounded, rights are annulled, statutes are violated, the possessions of the church are everywhere invaded and plundered by these impious men.

Violence was a characteristic of all classes, but in the wake of the Viking invasions and the feudalization of society, it had come to be the profession of only one. In the theme of the tripartite division of society popular in the tenth and eleventh centuries, the Christian community was said to be composed of those who prayed, those who fought, and those who worked. Those who worked—the peasants—did at times pick up arms and fight as foot-soldiers in the host. But for the most part their lives were spent tilling the fields. Similarly those who prayed—the monks—took part in the violence of their time by praying for the harm of their enemies and even, on occasion, by killing their oppressors with force of arms. But again, their lives were spent primarily in the choir. Only for those who fought—the knights (*milites*)—was armed violence a way of life. It would perhaps not be fair to say that knights lived on "plunder or oppression", but documents from the Peace of God leave no doubt that the knights were, as Georges Duby has concluded, "those whose aggressive tendencies it was necessary to repress".

The knight rode a horse and bore arms. Thus when Bishop Jordon of Limoges excommunicated some nobles for breaking the peace, he anathematized their arms and horses as well. Odo of Cluny, doubtless aware of the conditions in Burgundy after the death of Richard the Great, told of a miracle in which horsemen (*equites*) who attempted to rob some merchants (*negotiatores*) of their pigs came to a just end: in their robbery attempt two of the knights were badly injured (one by falling off his horse) while the merchants eventually marched off with their pigs. "These things have been said", Odo wrote, "concerning the persecutors of the poor". Thus for Odo the "poor man" (*pauper*) was not materially poor so much as powerless. Unarmed and weak, he was the victim of violence. It was for this reason that Odo was able to identify the poor as the humble and patient members of the generation of Abel. The church, too, belonged in this category. The miraculous story about the knights and merchants was only part of a general diatribe against powerful men who "lay waste the belongings of the church or of the poor".

Complaint against the armed violence of powerful men did not betray an opposition to warfare in general; Latin Christianity had early repudiated pacifism. But wars were to be waged only by duly constituted authorities. Between the eighth and the tenth centuries this authority had come to be vested in the Germanic kings, whose anointment gave them a quasi-sacred character that set them off from all laymen, no matter how powerful. The anointed king could properly and legitimately exercise armed violence. The coronation ceremony itself expressly entreated the king to "take up the sword". But the violence of the lay soldier, though carried out under the banner of the anointed king, was not similarly sanctioned. Penitentials from the seventh to the tenth century reveal the prevailing attitude. The First Vallicellian Penitential, written in Italy in the eighth or ninth century, declared that "if anyone in company with his king kills a man in battle, he should do penance for forty days". The identical words were used in the *Capitula Iudiciorum* (*The Penitential of Thirty-Five Chapters*), a Frankish composite penitential written in the same period. The seventh-century English penitential of Theodore of Tarsus said, "he who kills a man in public war should do penance for forty days". There are further examples. The implications of such an attitude were clear: the soldier could hardly be expected realistically to refrain from shedding blood in battle; the penitentials thus called the military career itself into question. The soldier was a sinner by profession.

In the beginning of the ninth century, when the spiritual and temporal orders were closely allied under the Carolingians, and when the social status of the king's warriors was rapidly rising, Rhabanus Maurus deliberately challenged the prevailing view. It should not be sinful, he argued, for a man to shed blood in a war called by a legitimate prince. But the Viking invasions and the consequent weakening of royal authority in the western half of the Carolingian Empire made Rhabanus's view unrealistic. When the tenth-century lay knight took up arms, his battles could no longer come under the rubric of "public war"; indeed technically speaking, killing in a private war was nothing other than homicide. Thus by the eleventh century Burchard of Worms, noting the new situation, was to prescribe two separate penances for two different kinds of war: three forty-day periods of penance were due from soldiers who shed blood in a war declared by a legitimate prince; atonement as if for a murder—periodic fasting for seven years—was required from the soldier who killed without the order of a legitimate ruler.

Cluniac spirituality may be seen as an outgrowth of this attitude against the violence of the lay knight. Odo's fulminations against the plundering knight found their most radical expression in a repudiation of the battlefield in favour of the reformed and peaceful monastery. Odo's own conversion to the religious life was the result of a profound revulsion against his military training. A century and a half later St. Hugh, Cluny's sixth abbot, was to be equally repelled by the violence of the knightly profession in which he was brought up by his father. Unfortunately, evidence for other Cluniac monks is scanty. The abbots between Odo and Hugh seem to have been from knightly familes, but we do not know if their monastic conversion involved a deliberate repudiation of the knightly life. We know even less about the concrete motives of most of the men who became simple monks or sent their children to monasteries as oblates. However, what evidence there is tends to show that tenth- and eleventh-century monks were often from knightly families. The patrons and supporters of these monasteries also generally came from the order of fighters.

In the process of becoming peaceful monks, the knights (or sons of knights) gave up the most characteristic element of their class, namely power. The Cluniac notion of patience was an expression of the transformation of the monk from oppressor to willingly oppressed; patience was the precise opposite of knightly pride. Yet the monasteries, which were sought out and sustained by penitent warriors, were the ones to elaborate a bellicose liturgy. What seems to be a contradiction is from another point of view a solution to the knightly dilemma; the liturgy was a carefully circumscribed and modified form of the exercise of violence. The Cluniacs battled, but the battles were bloodless and contributed to the salvation of men. In the sphere of the supernatural, the monks were Christian knights. By ritualizing violence, the liturgy confined and bound the battle, rendering it predictable, controlled, and, in practical terms, harmless. Nevertheless, it was considered enormously efficacious.

Cluniac spirituality did not stop at the walls of the monastery. In the first place, Cluniac liturgy offered the possibility of vicarious expiation for the sins of non-monastic members of the knightly class. It was an important link between the sinner and God in the tenth- and eleventh-century penitential system. Men who joined a confraternity with Cluny, or simply made a donation there, were assured of prayers on behalf of their souls.

Moreover, the Cluniacs attempted to apply the principle behind Cluniac liturgy to the battles waged by knights in the world. On this point St. Odo's writings were seminal. In both his *Collationes* and his *Vita Geraldi* he suggested a way to legitimize the violence of the knight. Wanton violence, said Odo, violated the commandments of God and had to be stopped. Odo looked first to the clergy and to church sanctions to solve the problem; he threatened violent men with excommunication and eternal damnation in hell:

> Let [the violent man] go now and trustingly commit any sort of violence. Let him fulfill the wickedness of his will, plunder others, be sated with the oppression of innocents; and because he is not punished [in this world] let him think that his ways either are not seen by the Lord or, worse, are approved. It will surely come; the eternal and sudden scourge will come, and he will see that everything has been seen by God when, at his unexpected end, he sees that he is damned, in retribution for everything.

But, Odo recognized, the threat was ineffective: instead of listening, the plunderers despised the clergy and ridiculed them. The church had to find more forceful means; it would itself have to exercise violence against the breakers of the peace or else harness the violence of others to do the job. Odo opted for the latter. Violent men were to learn to use their violence properly. There was an important place in society for violent laymen: they were not to lay down their arms but rather were to limit their violent behaviour to appropriate victims and purposes. Lay violence became justifiable if it was used against those knights over whom the church was too weak to enforce its own rules. Odo's model knight, St. Gerald, fought on behalf of the non-violent church:

> [Gerald knew] that the rhinoceros, that is, any powerful man, is to be bound with a thong that he may break the clods of the valley, that is, the oppressors of the humble.... It was lawful, therefore, for a layman belonging to the order of fighters to carry the sword so that he might protect defenceless people, and so that he might restrain either by the outcome of war or by the force of the judiciary those whom ecclesiastical censure was not able to subdue.

Thus Odo's solution to the problem of lay violence consisted in carefully delimiting its proper use. It had to be used by knights against other armed members of society (*oppressores*), and only to enforce the peace-keeping functions of the church, which had now taken over the role of the king in this regard. The soldier was to become part of a church-sponsored and church-directed police force just as he once had been part of the king's army. As a fighter for the church, his warfare would no longer come under the rubrics of either "public" or "private" but would be, according to Odo, "a new kind of fighting mingled with piety". Thus Odo opened the way for the moral approval of certain forms of knightly violence. But Odo's notion of permissible violence was so narrow that his "real" knight, St. Gerald, who "never stained his sword with human blood", could hardly have survived in the world. Like the liturgy at Cluny, Gerald's battles were rituals, the outcome of which depended on a symbolic display of power —Gerald bared his weapons—but excluded actual bloodshed. It remained for the peace movement to relax these limitations somewhat to make a reality of Odo's model. Sworn associations to keep the peace by protecting unarmed members of society were set up by local churches, often with some form of ecclesiastical blessing. Clerics themselves might join in the fighting, as when Burchard, archbishop of Vienne, personally led a body of knights against breakers of the peace.

There is no evidence of a direct link between Odo's writings and the later peace organizations, but under abbot Odilo, in the eleventh century, the Cluniacs became actively involved in both the Peace and Truce of God. The Truce of God added a new dimension to the sanction of limited violence. While the Peace of God prohibited the use of arms against unarmed members of society, the Truce of God limited knightly warfare to certain days of the week. But this meant that private warfare was legitimate on the other days. Such a development marked a shift from Odo's highly constricted notion of permissible violence to an acceptance of bloodshed in a still very carefully delimited form. The regulated fighting of the peace movement—conforming to the rhythms of the church calendar—and the ceremonies of chivalry turned the knightly life into a secular liturgy. The modification of knightly violence through restrictions and rituals allowed the formation of a Christian knighthood to begin.

The peace movement had set up church-sponsored police forces within Christendom. But in the second half of the eleventh century, the reformed, centralized papacy began to sponsor wars that it thought to be in the interest of the church against non-Christians. The most important of these was the Spanish *reconquista*. Cluny put its unrivalled prestige behind the *reconquista*, becoming purveyors of knights for the Christian armies and propagandists of a religious justification for them. The knights slain in battle against the Saracens, the Cluniacs said, "were transported to the condition of the blessed".

These movements, directed by the papacy, ultimately culminated in the First Crusade, which in turn would lead to the completion of the moral justification of the Christian warrior. If the Cluniac monks could not bring themselves to support completely the notion of a holy war, contenting themselves instead with praying for the success of the holy warriors, nevertheless it was a former Cluniac prior, Urban II, who launched the First Crusade. Thus the Cluniacs first rejected, then modified, and ultimately helped to justify a limited form of knightly violence.

II. Foundations of a New Spirituality

At the very time monasticism reached its greatest heights, three major social phenomena—ones that would bridge the years between the full maturity of the monks and the birth of the friars—began to develop. The first of these was the market economy; the second, the apostolic religious movements; and the third, the urban schools.

The end of Europe's external invasions and the subsequent rise of strong governments together provided for a new political and social order, or for a sense, at least, of such order. This is not to say that violence subsided; indeed as it was increasingly legitimized and institutionalized, it became, in the hands of secular and ecclesiastical governments alike, one of the principal instruments of the new stability. The relative safety of roads encouraged travel and provided the necessary circumstances for rapid commercial growth, and this growth, with local variations and temporary set-backs, was steady from the eleventh to the late thirteenth century. The urban culture that then appeared probably never embraced more than 5 per cent of the total population, but it had a far greater impact on society at large than that small percentage would imply.

Except for the universal misery brought on by natural disaster, the problems of city life were profoundly different from those of country life. Crucial to this difference were the sources of urban, as opposed to rural, poverty. While the wage-earner in the city was vulnerable to the fluctuations of a market economy, the peasant on the manor had been rather more threatened by the wanton attacks of mounted, heavily armed fighters. Whereas such fighting men had constituted the dominant class in feudal society, the dominant class in this small but increasingly influential commercial society consisted mainly of merchants, bankers, notaries and lawyers, as well as those landlords who organized production on their lands for the market. The successful participants in the new economy, which was effectively free from externally imposed restraints, assembled vast fortunes, sometimes with conspicuous speed; and some of these fortunes, following the simple law of supply and demand, were derived from the weakness or misfortune of others. In addition, the immediate proximity of wealth and poverty in the city made such conditions more obvious there than in the countryside. Money-making rather than violence, therefore, seemed to be the source of poverty in urban society, and the urban poor could easily see themselves as victims of the avarice of those who prospered in the new economy.

Contemporaneous with this new market economy and its concomitant problems was a richly varied flowering of new forms of religious life. These began early in the eleventh century with the hermits of northern Italy, most notably Romuald of Ravenna and Peter Damian. What may seem at first glance to have been mere withdrawal from society was for them a temporary withdrawal from corrupt institutions that they hoped to reform. For models they looked to the past, going beyond the accumulated traditions of recent centuries and settling first on the early forms of Christian monasticism and eremitism, and ultimately on the exemplary lives of Jesus and the Apostles. Others who made a similar quest but with a variety of results included the monastic and canonical reformers, the wandering evangelical preachers, and companies of lay Christians like the Humiliati and the Waldenses. The history of these various movements, seen as a whole, reveals the emergence of an apostolate of poverty and preaching. It was Peter Damian who perceived the critical connection between these two pursuits when he argued that only those who own nothing whatever of their own, like the members of the first Christian community at Jerusalem (Acts iv. 32), are fit for the office of preaching. Such a programme lay at the core of the canonical reform; it was also undertaken on an individual level by the wandering preachers, most of whom ran into difficulty on the issue of their authority to preach, although a few gained temporary approbation, as Robert of Arbrissel did from Urban II in 1096 or as Norbert of Xanten did from Gelasius II in 1119. A century later, the major themes of the various apostolic religious movements found fulfillment in the Dominican and Franciscan orders. For all their great originality, these two orders were discernably derivative. The Dominicans were regular canons, living by the so-called Rule of St. Augustine, having absorbed important elements from the religious life of the canonical reformers, the itinerant preachers, and the Cathar heretics. The Franciscans drew heavily on the traditions of the hermits, the itinerant preachers, the Humiliati, and the Waldenses. In the early 1220s, James of Vitry, a knowledgeable reporter on the religious life, would describe the Franciscans as an order of preachers. Another early thirteenth-century observer, Burchard of Ursperg, stated—inaccurately but not without historical interest—that Pope Innocent III approved the Dominicans as a replacement for the Humiliati, and the Franciscans as a replacement for the Waldenses. The friars thus came at the end of a lengthy development, one whose continuity was apparent to some of their contemporaries.

That development did not pass along one route only, however. The main route, to be sure, was that of a new apostolic religious programme. But another of the crucial elements of Dominican and Franciscan life, namely education, had travelled by the separate route of the urban schools. The Benedictines had earlier worked out a programme of education that was wholly appropriate to the demands of their spiritual life. The novice had to be prepared for a life of contemplation and liturgical intercession. He studied the sacred texts of the Bible and the virtually sacred texts of the Fathers by intensive reading and repetition, in effect by memorization. He sought thereby to incorporate as much of this tradition as he could, to absorb into his mind and being a spiritual vocabulary and literature that in turn would supply the idiom for his specialized vocation in the cloister. Analysis, criticism, debate and persuasion were all foreign to this type of schooling and the spirituality it served.

Those many new religious groups to appear in the eleventh and twelfth centuries, including the Cistercians, did not work out corresponding programmes of education to meet their respective needs. Educational change, instead, went by way of the towns, specifically of the cathedral schools. There it underwent a period of dazzling accomplishment. Yet, while many of the leading religious innovators of the eleventh and twelfth centuries were educated in urban schools, the groups they organized tended either to be divorced from the new intellectual trends or absorbed in denouncing them.

The city schools gave training in rhetoric and dialectic, that is discourse and disputation, techniques that would later serve an expanded and improved order of preachers. Indeed it was Peter Damian who observed that the order of preachers, which since patristic times had coincided with the order of bishops, needed to be greatly enlarged in size and improved in intellectual and moral quality. The study of history in the city schools led to a new appreciation of the apostolic era, in particular the example of the Apostles' poverty and the historic connection between poverty and preaching. Perhaps the most radical intellectual change fostered by the new schools was a phenomenon that Père Chenu has called "the awakening of the conscience", a new self-awareness that called for the simultaneous cultivation of the individual conscience and an internalization of Christian morality. The very conception of sin itself changed by shifting attention from the external act to the inner intention. The drama of Christian morality was starting to move from the open field of bad actions and penitential counteractions to the private chamber of intention and contrition. In the closing years of the twelfth century, a coterie of theologians who were gathered about Master Peter the Chanter at Paris devoted their attention to complex and immediately pressing moral problems, both individual and social. Moral theology—the very term dates from the 1160s—was just then coming into its own. The schools thus had the capacity to give the religious life new techniques of analysis and expression, new historical perspectives, and new psychological insights into morality. The schools, together with the commercial economy and the apostolic religious movements, provided the basis for a carefully reasoned spirituality of preaching and penance, based on poverty.

III. Mendicant Poverty and Preaching

Poverty was the essential element in both the Dominican and Franciscan orders, though it came to be so for a separate reason in each case. At Montpellier in 1206, Bishop Diego of Osma made an analysis of the failure of a Cistercian mission sent by the pope to reconvert dualist heretics. He attributed this failure neither to a lack of sincerity nor to a lack of ability on the part of the missionaries, but rather to the material splendour in which they appeared before the Cathars and which, he thought, compromised their evangelical message. He proposed that they divest themselves of all their possessions and then go about preaching, dressed simply and on foot, in the manner of the Apostles. The Cistercians agreed with this idea in principle but none of them ventured to lead the way. Thereupon Diego dismissed his entourage—he had been on a royal diplomatic mission—and gave a personal demonstration of his plan. Even then the Cistercians held back, but the lesson was not lost on Diego's protégé Dominic of Guzman. What began as a tactic on the part of a capable, experienced administrator became the ideal on which Dominic based his small band of preachers, which in turn a decade later would become the Order of Preachers. More familiar is the story of how Francis of Assisi in the years 1206 to 1209 underwent an intense personal crisis, which he resolved by dramatically repudiating his patrimony and adopting a code of absolute personal poverty. Francis had an incomparably more magnetic personality than did Dominic, one of the least charismatic of saints, and indeed the Order of Lesser Brothers that he established attracted many more recruits than did the Order of Preachers. The Franciscans would have the great advantage of always having before them the immediate, personal example of their Christ-like founder, regardless of the widely varying views they took of that example in their internal disputes, which turned principally on the interpretation of poverty. For the Dominicans, who in the second generation had practically to re-invent the legend of their founder before all memory of him had faded, poverty would always retain something of its original character as a tactic. These and other distinctions between Franciscan and Dominican conceptions of poverty are not negligible, but in the present context they are relatively unimportant, for these conceptions stand close together in contrast to those held in the older, monastic order. There, as we have seen, poverty meant the abandonment of worldly power and the pursuit of humility more than it did the abandonment of material riches. The friars in both orders thought of themselves as mendicants, determined to lead full lives each day without stocking supplies for the following day. In times when practice veered far from this ideal, the view of the friars as mendicants was maintained both by the friars themselves and by their detractors, some of whom opposed begging as a proper component of the religious life while others argued against the friars being allowed to monopolize mendicancy.

The principal spiritual task of the Order of Preachers was, obviously, to preach; but preaching was really not less important to the Franciscans though they placed it within a larger programme of apostolic activities. The Dominicans began as specialists in learned theological debate with the Cathars, but in 1215 became evangelical preachers for the diocese of Toulouse, and in 1217 branched out to become evangelical preachers throughout Latin Christendom and eventually beyond. The Franciscans were always popular preachers: first in Umbria in 1210, then throughout the Italian peninsula during the next few years, and beyond the confines of Italy starting in 1217.

Quite inseparable from preaching for both orders was the administration of penance. The preaching of the Apostles in the Primitive Church had been directed toward converting listeners to the Christian religion. But preaching directed to Christians within thirteenth-century Europe had as its goal an inner conversion of the individual listener to a deeper involvement in the faith that he already professed; a necessary first stage of such a conversion would be an awareness of his own shortcomings in keeping that faith. Thus the immediate rhetorical goal of the preacher was to move members of his audience to make confession and to do penance. The Dominican Master-General Humbert of Romans made the connection succinctly when he wrote: "The seed is sown in preaching, the fruit is harvested in penance".

The movements started by Francis and Dominic seem to have grown organically out of the religious movements that had gone before, particularly with respect to their emphasis on poverty and preaching. The point at which they differed significantly from their fore-runners came in 1217, when men from both groups headed for the major intellectual centres, Paris and Bologna, which had the most important schools in Europe. In the schools they found recruits and they also made contact with the latest developments in canon law and in theology, especially moral theology, which would form the basis for their sophisticated handling of penance. Out of this rapprochement between intellectual and spiritual movements grew a collaboration that gave the orders an intellectual orientation and character, and the schools a new spiritual purpose. The astounding success of the new mendicant orders came in part from their integration of the most advanced religious sensibility with the most advanced intellectual activity of their time.

While the friars joined actively in the intellectual life of the towns, the commercial aspect of town life repelled them. The conversion of St. Francis had been a repudiation of the life of a merchant, and the friars subsequently, whether as individuals or as a group, would always constitute something of a living or continuing rejection of such pursuits. Yet the spirituality developed by the friars belonged unmistakably to the very society that they rejected. This is first of all apparent in their language, heavily impregnated with a market-place vocabulary, for example in the title of an early Franciscan allegorical work on poverty, *The Holy Commerce* (*Sacrum Commercium*), or as a fourteenth-century writer once called it, *The Business of Poverty* (*Commercium Paupertatis*). Starting around 1240, the stories about St. Dominic included mention of a will he was purported to have made out to his followers; "Have charity", he is supposed to have told them, "keep humility, and possess voluntary poverty".

The practice of making such allusions had gained authority and impetus in its frequent use by that one-time cloth merchant, Francis of Assisi. In addition to certain terms and images, the very forms of the friars' ministry were borrowed from the activities of towns-people. Above all, the friars talked and argued and negotiated. Success in preaching, just as in commercial bargaining or legal pleading, depended on one's skill in the art of persuasion. People already knew what the Christian Gospel was, just as they knew how to recognize a piece of cloth or knew that a person is supposed to obey the law. But if there were differing views of what the Gospel meant and of how it was to be followed in a concrete situation, persuasive discourse had to intervene to influence the choices people made, just as it did in a market-place filled with competing sellers of cloth or in a court where two opposing parties both claimed to be on the right side of the law. Penance, similarly, which had once been a simple matter of right and wrong, of a fixed list of sins and appropriate penalties, became increasingly in the thirteenth century a sort of negotiation. The confessor, like a judge, asked a series of questions about the circumstances, such as the frame of mind of the confessee, surrounding the act under discussion, so as to arrive at some understanding of the relative gravity of the fault. Even more clearly reflecting his commercial surroundings, one Dominican would explain the system of indulgences, coming into more frequent use around 1230, as transactions with the church's Treasury of Merits. For a cash payment the penitent person could get credit against his penitential debt from the store of supplemental merit and good works on deposit there from the lives of Christ, Mary, and the saints.

The friars would not have seen or described their spirituality as buying and selling and pleading and negotiating, but the point did not altogether elude their critics. In the previous generations, conservatives opposed to the newer kinds of preaching and teaching had objected that the Gospel was being retailed and that the Holy Trinity was being torn to pieces in public view. Similarly in the thirteenth century there were critics of the friars who denounced these newcomers as rabble-rousers, trouble-makers, hypocrites, entertainers and enterprising merchants. Matthew Paris, for example, said they were selling crusade indulgences as one would sell sheep on the wool market. A priest at Dieppe drew a sharp rebuke from the pope in 1289 for preaching angrily against St. Francis, gesturing irreverently at a representation of the saint in a window and referring to him as an avaricious merchant. Certain critics thus associated the friars with precisely the sort of urban activities that the friars themselves were criticizing. This paradox of enterprising mendicants, like that of bellicose monks, calls for historical explanation.

The friars were born of a spiritual crisis brought on by the spread of the cash nexus. While some individuals rushed in to benefit from the new developments, many others held back approval, either because they were opposed to these developments or because they felt ambivalent about them.

Opposition to money-making came not only from those with specific, economic grievances, but from those who, even if they did not suffer materially, were sensitive to the moral problems involved. The iconographic and written sources produced by such people give ample testimony to the prevailing feeling that the merchants' desire for money was insatiable. Satirical poems pressed the attack against corrupt clerics and greedy lawyers, just as sculptured allegorical figures of avarice, for example on church facades, pointedly showed these various types of people who profited from the money economy grasping desperately on to money-bags and chests while devils and snakes lurked about them menacingly.

The root of the problem seems to have been two-fold: first, there was a disgust with money itself; and second, the new urban professions lacked moral justification. Money was the life-blood of the new economy, a medium whose compactness, durability, and consistent, recognizable appearance allowed wealth to circulate freely and conveniently. For the same reasons it made large concentrations of population, that is cities, possible. But this same tool of convenience, while not unknown in the pre-commercial age, was then very little used. When it did come into circulation in massive quantities starting in the eleventh century, it came as something both new and strange. The quantitative change was so great as to become qualitative. The use of money extended well beyond the cities, as we have observed, for agriculture now became organized for the market economy instead of merely for subsistence. All this may explain why there was new concern over the use of money, but concern often took the form of revulsion. Poems, drawings and ecclesiastical polemics alike made the point that money was filthy and disgusting waste, that while it might glitter deceptively, it was an agent of rot and decay. The allegorical figure of avarice had the characteristics of an anal compulsive accumulator, so we should not be surprised to see him tormented by devils, those eminently disgusting and foul-smelling creatures. Such an association between money and excrement was not peculiar to western Europe; anthropologists have noted the same phenomenon in several other societies. Thus the essential tool of the new kind of economy repulsed people even as it attracted them.

The leading urban professions were similarly pursued and scorned. The moral legacy from earlier centuries held that a merchant's job almost necessarily entailed lying and cheating. With the growing number of merchants came a growing concern over whether their business activity could legitimately be considered work. And though the practice of law had not been regarded as dishonourable, once lawyers started to collect fees some people wondered if lawyers had the right to sell knowledge, which was considered a gift freely given them by God; an analogous dilemma faced the masters who taught in city schools. Throughout the twelfth and thirteenth centuries, commercial activity, the study and practice of law, and the urban schools all expanded aggressively. No evidence allows one to think that the growth of these activities and institutions was stunted by centuries-old moral maxims. Yet the questions raised were serious, and the cost seems to have been borne not in restricted activities but in the troubled consciences of the individuals centrally involved. Just as knights once had the problem of living in a society whose morality condemned lay warfare, urban professionals were now confronted with a morality that condemned commercial transactions. While some of these city people entertained old-fashioned fears of going to hell, still others, as they cultivated an awareness of their conscience and sharpened their aptitude for calculation, came to worry about their own intentions as well as their time-payments in purgatory. The price of better education and more sophistication was a more complex and potentially more tormenting form of guilt.

The directing groups of urban society were confronted with a severe conflict between their characteristic activities and their perception of the religious faith they professed. The most immediate and absolutely satisfying way to resolve this conflict was to abandon the compromising activity altogether, to abandon all wealth (also compromising), and to become a poor man in imitation of Christ and the Apostles. This is what Francis the merchant did; this is what Raymond of Peñafort, a master of law from Bologna, did in becoming a Dominican; this is what several university masters did, for example the theologian Alexander of Hales, in becoming Franciscans; and this is what John of Paris, the son of a great burgher family, did in joining the Dominicans. Those of their contemporaries who sought a radical religious conversion were generally not content to join the secular clergy, for prelates and simple priests alike were currently the targets of merciless attacks precisely for being too deeply involved in the money economy. As for joining the regular clergy, not only had the old Benedictines long been seen and criticized as too comfortable, but even the new monks, the Cistercians, had become hopelessly wealthy and thus also compromised. Meanwhile the hermit life itself had become so organized as to be barely distinguishable from the monastic life. By 1200, not only the intellectual future lay in the towns but also the future of the religious life, whose uncompromised goal remained a literal imitation of the life led by the Apostles. As only towns had a sufficient margin of wealth to support those who chose to be poor and only towns could regularly supply audiences to preachers, the setting for this revived *vita apostolica* was going to be urban.

But beyond certain inadequacies in other available forms of the religious life and the sociological pull of urban areas, the friars were drawn to towns because they did not completely repudiate the money economy, indeed precisely because they did accept and did participate in some of its crucial aspects. The spirituality of the friars, as described previously, was not strictly a rejection of commerce, nor strictly a form of commercial activity (as some of their critics liked to say), but rather an amalgamation of the two. With the apostolic life the friars combined a modified form of the unacceptable behaviour of merchants. Extracting the use of money and legal contention from urban professional behaviour, they kept argument, persuasion, discussion and negotiation. If the ideal of poverty determined that the friars would not be able to handle money, itinerancy in combination with poverty was efficacious precisely because it removed all possibility of a life based on calculation. Even in begging, one could calculate the best times and places at which to beg, or one could return regularly to a sure source of patronage. And so the friars espoused, as an ideal, the principle that begging should be irregular, unplanned, and indiscriminate. In rooting out the calculating aspect of commercial activity, the friars further demonstrated the subtlety of the solution they were elaborating. Within the framework of the present analysis, the Spiritual Franciscans can be seen as those who kept to a literal imitation of the Apostles but who refused to merge with it any form whatever of urban activity. The achievement of the main line of the mendicant orders was to bring into balance and to keep in balance their strict refusals to touch money or participate in legal proceedings with their exploitation of the techniques of selling, bargaining and persuading.

Each of the major mendicant orders had a second order, which was for women, and a third order, for the laity. The third orders provided alternatives to embracing fully the religious life; their members would continue in worldly pursuits but at the same time engage in some of the friars' religious observances and enjoy some of their spiritual benefits, in a way analogous to that in which knights had associated themselves with the monks by joining Cluniac confraternities. In the third orders perhaps more clearly than among the friars themselves we can see the true descendents of the Humiliati, the Beguines and Beghards, and the orders of penitents. But joining either of the mendicant orders at any level was exceptional; a more usual pattern to follow was that of patronizing the friars so as to gain vicarious satisfaction from expressing approval and giving support for those who had made a more radical break. No one social order had an exclusive hold on membership in or support of the friars. The leaders of the German friars came from the lesser nobility and the urban patriciate, while the rank and file emerged from ordinary burgher families. Detailed lists of third-order membership in Italy show a heavy predominance of tradesmen and lesser professionals. There is little evidence anywhere, however, of poor people being involved either as members or donors. The real strength of the movement came from the better-off inhabitants of cities, whether bourgeois or noble. Indeed the archbishop of Pisa went so far as to proclaim, in 1261, that St. Francis was the patron and protector of merchants.

Beyond the alternatives of membership in a mendicant order and vicarious expiation through material support of these confident poor by the troubled rich, the friars offered their greatest service to the dominant members of urban society by providing a fully developed justification for most forms of urban activity. Here above all is where they followed on the inquiries already being conducted during the previous generation by such intellectuals as Peter the Chanter. The professors of theology and law now found legitimate reasons for lawyers and teachers to accept fees. They reasoned that such professionals did not indeed sell knowledge, but instead charged legitimately for the advice, effort, and time they put at the disposal of their clients. One of the critical elements here was a new appreciation of the value of time, an appreciation that emerged from the need to calculate so characteristic of the new forms of commercial and industrial activity. With regard to that commercial activity, the task of finding justification was more complicated, for it involved such issues as lending money, investing money, and determining a just price in buying and selling. But while official condemnations of usury grew stronger, Dominican and Franciscan schoolmen were in fact identifying a whole series of practices, hitherto regarded indiscriminately as usurious, as not being usurious and therefore as being legitimate. They did so by combining a new methodology with new (or newly revived) ideas. Raymond of Peñafort redirected much of prevailing thought on penance in the *summa* he composed in 1220–1; it contained a programme for the methodical examination of conscience and a systematic use of specific cases. A similar casuistry found its way into theology about two decades later in the influential work of the Franciscan doctor Alexander of Hales. The new translations of Aristotle, mainly the work of the Dominican scholar William of Moerbeke, supplied the schoolmen with a whole theory of social utility.

By building on this theory and exploiting the new casuistry, Albert the Great and Thomas Aquinas emancipated private property and the Christian merchant. They came to view private property as a necessary instrument of the good life and of an orderly society. They defined the merchant's activities of transferring goods and making them available on the market not only as useful and necessary but also as worthy to be designated as work. The key to these judgements of the schoolmen was intention; if the merchant sought his modest and honest profit in order to perform these needed services as well as to support his family and charitable enterprises, then he was entitled to that profit as a payment for his labour. No justification was granted the profit motive as such. Similarly, while the schoolmen did not arrive at a theory of credit operations, they approved certain forms of compensation—as distinguished from interest for profit—for lenders of money. At first they developed these matters in the course of comprehensive surveys of theological problems, but in 1278 a Dominican named Giles of Lessines devoted an entire tract, *De usuris*, to questions related to the money economy. A Franciscan counterpart to this work was composed by Alexander Lombard in 1307. One notably influential work of the late thirteenth century, by the Dominican scholar John of Freiburg, wove together into a clear, relatively simple pattern the various legal and theological strands relating to commercial matters, using an especially rich array of illustrative cases; in order to make his book more readily usable, the author himself added an alphabetically arranged subject index.

John of Freiburg's concern about propagating the new scholarship was not unique; on this point we see exposed perhaps the greatest single difference separating the scholastic doctors of the thirteenth-century universities from the twelfth-century school masters. The discontinuity comes with neither subject matter nor methods used, but with clientele and purpose. The twelfth-century masters trained priests, ecclesiastical administrators, lawyers, notaries, teachers and some merchants. A few of the students went on to distinguished preaching careers. The same groups were still represented in lecture audiences in the thirteenth century, but along with the important addition of a large, organized corps of dedicated evangelical preachers. The sometimes very abstruse and sophisticated solutions worked out by friar-intellectuals in the universities found the way to their ultimate audience, the laity, via these student friars, subsequently placed in the nearly two thousand convents established by their orders in the cities of Latin Christendom. In addition to direct teaching in the universities, the friars developed another means of communication in their handbooks for preachers and confessors. In these works, some in Latin but others —increasingly as time went by—in vernacular languages, the individual friar or parish priest could find model sermons, *exempla* for use in illustrating sermons, discussions of the principles of hearing confession, and illustrative cases of what he might encounter in the confessional. One such handbook, composed by a Dominican early in the fourteenth century and dealing especially with price-setting and money-lending, bore the significant title *Regula mercatorum* (*Rule for Merchants*); by co-opting the technical monastic term "rule", this title gave eloquent testimony to the devolution of the religious life from the monks to merchants. The social achievement of the friars thus consisted in their confronting and eventually de-mystifying the taboo of monetary commercial transactions, starting by outright rejection, then by incorporating elements of commercial practice into their spirituality, and finally by helping to justify worldly commerce in a modified and carefully circumscribed form.

The religious life of the friars, like that of the monks before them, involved the Christianizing of an activity that had been seen as wholly exploitative and therefore morally unacceptable. In both instances this activity was the occupation of the dominant class of a sector of society. In urban society, dominated by merchants and professionals, money-making had been condemned, while in feudal society, dominated by knights, lay violence had been unacceptable. The spiritualities that responded to these conditions did so, on one level, by repudiating the unacceptable activities: the friars rejected money; the monks abandoned the battlefield. But on a second level, the response was less sharply disapproving. Both monks and friars nourished a deep sensitivity to the positive possibilities inherent in these hitherto indiscriminately condemned activities. They developed spiritualities that in themselves suggested a way to separate out the useful aspects from the exploitative ones. The monks fought spiritual battles without shedding blood, thus exercising violence as truly Christian knights. The friars negotiated the Gospel without using money, thus exercising commerce as truly Christian merchants.

But neither the monks nor the friars stopped with a solution valid only for themselves. Other sections of society had not been unaware of the moral problems of their age, and the monks and friars joined with them in working out for the ruling classes an acceptable version of the previously objectionable activities. Money-making and warfare were carefully examined to determine precisely which of their aspects should continue to be condemned and which, on the other hand, merited religious and moral justification. In each case, once this task had been accomplished—once the Christian knight (who did not fight all the time, but only on behalf of the church) and the Christian merchant (who did not get rich in any way he could, but only by charging a just price) had been defined and justified—the vitality of the religious order began to wane. Hence the assertion that different forms of the religious life develop in response to particular social problems is corroborated by the pattern of decline that sets in once the problems have been met.

The Franciscans and Dominicans assuredly professed the same basic beliefs of the same religion as those professed by the Benedictines in the eleventh century. But just as assuredly, the spiritual lives led by monks and friars were fundamentally different. The key to understanding their peculiar characteristics lies not in their shared religious beliefs but in the ways they reflected and modified two distinctly different societies.

Bibliography

MARC BLOCH, *Feudal Society* (1964).
GEORGE DUBY, *The Early Growth of the European Economy: Warriors and Peasants from the Seventh to the Twelfth Century* (1974).
JOHN B. FREED, *The Friars and German Society* (1977).
RICHARD KIECKHEFER, *Unquiet Souls, Fourteenth Century Saints and Their Religious Milieu* (1984).
DAVID KNOWLES, *From Pachomius to Ignatius: A Study in the Constitutional History of the Religious Orders* (1966).
M. D. LAMBERT, *Franciscan Poverty* (1961).
JEAN LECLERCQ, *The Love of Learning and the Desire for God: A Study in Monastic Culture* (1961).
LESTER K. LITTLE, *Religious Poverty and the Profit Economy in Medieval Europe* (1978).
JOHN MOORMAN, *A History of the Franciscan Order* (1968).
BARBARA H. ROSENWEIN, *Rhinoceros Bound: Cluny in the Tenth Century* (1982).

Monogamous Marriage Among the Franks

SUZANNE WEMPLE

Marriage in Merovingian times remained free of Christian influence. Polygyny and concubinage were tolerated and divorce was sanctioned. The Carolingians changed all that by embracing the Church's doctrine of indissoluble, monogamous marriage and opposing divorce. To do so was politically attractive; monogamy reduced the ability of nobles to form political alliances against Carolingian kings.

As a consequence, aristocrats were forced to develop new marriage strategies. Wives now had to be chosen more carefully and with an eye to their upward social mobility or at least parity. Monogamous marriage gave women greater legal security, increased their domestic responsibilities, and elevated women's role as household manager to a new dignity. In support of these changes the church downplayed virginity and Mary became a focus of devotion as a model mother. A new type of female saint came into being: the good homemaker.

On the negative side, being the only wife also meant having sole responsibility for propagating heirs, and the increased child-bearing seems to have undermined female health. Carolingian aristocratic women lived shorter lives than their predecessors and women in other contemporary societies. A woman now also became the sole object of a cruel husband's attention, and churches and cloisters began to provide sanctuary for abused wives. Some men, resenting monogamy and having no escape from it through divorce, falsely accused their wives of adultery and had them killed.

As monogamy exalted the conjugal family, it brought about a decline in the extended family, and this reduced the security of widows. They too sought sanctuary in churches and cloisters. Women also became less active in the land market because the occurrence of fewer marriages and the absence of divorce meant fewer opportunities for women to gain control of property. Over time, however, as they

---

Reprinted with the permission of the University of Pennsylvania Press from *Women in the Frankish Empire: Marriage and the Cloister, 500–900* by Suzanne Wemple. Copyrigth © 1981 by Suzanne Foray Wemple.

accumulated and consolidated landed wealth, aristocratic wives and widows came to exercise new and greater political and economic powers.

The rise of the Carolingian dynasty during the second half of the eighth century opened a new chapter in the history of marriage in the Latin West. Marriages in the Merovingian period had remained remarkably free from the influence of Christianity. They were arrangements made for the maintenance and enlargement of kin or the working force through the procreation of children. By tolerating polygyny and concubinage, as well as sanctioning divorce, practices which assured that the male genetic power of the great aristocratic families was widely disseminated, secular laws came into conflict with the Christian ideal of lifelong monogamy. The laws in effect in the Merovingian kingdom coincided with Christian principles only in their condemnation of abortion, abduction, and female unchastity. The aim of these laws was not to translate Christian teachings into practice, but to ensure the growth of population and to eliminate vendettas resulting from rivalry over women and disputes over paternity....

Carolingian legislation on the indissolubility of marriage and the exclusion of illegitimate children from inheritance brought about a new concept of the family in the ninth century. Although the kin as a social and political force remained as influential as in Merovingian times, the conjugal unit came to be recognized as the fundamental unit of soceity. Acknowledged as an essential member of this unit, a wife had many responsibilities, which were carefully delineated, at least on the highest level of society. Her legal position was secure. Unlike her female ancestors, she could not be repudiated, although she could still be neglected or mistreated.

The purpose of this chapter is to examine whether or not this new concept of the family was paralleled by increased female influence within and outside the family. Of equal interest is the fate of women in the new monogamous structure if they did not marry, or if their husbands abandoned them or died. Because the economic activities of women provide a fairly reliable index of female influence and status, I have sought answers to these questions not only in legal and narrative sources but also in donations preserved in ecclesiastical cartularies.

The introduction of the Christian model of marriage did not alter the role of the wife, even though it increased her responsibilities. Bearing children, which might have been done by a succession of wives or simultaneous wives in an earlier period, and supervising domestic activities, which had been previously shared by all female members of the family, were now the exclusive duty of one wife. Further, a married woman in the ninth century had greater responsibility for land management than her Merovingian ancestors. She was thus expected not only to produce children but also to administer a complex family economy.

On the highest level of society, the position of the queen as her husband's partner, *augusta* or *consors regis* [wife or partner of the king], was formalized in the middle of the ninth century by instituting the ceremony of anointment and coronation and incorporating the queen's name in the *laudes*, litanies sung in praise of kings. Charlemagne set the precedent for the official recognition of the queen's position. Although his own family remained extended and multigenerational, including bastards, concubines, his daughters' lovers, grandchildren, and his own mother, Charlemagne made possible the concentration of power in the conjugal unit by delegating to his last queen, Liutgard, a line of command second only to his own. In the *Capitulare de villis* [Ordinance for the Villages], Charlemagne declared that "anything ordered by us or by the queen to one of our judges, or anything ordered to the ministers, seneschals, and cupbearers, must be carried out to the last word."

Charlemagne's purpose was to ensure that his queen's commands concerning the administration of the palace and royal estates would be carried out promptly by royal officials. In an age when no distinction was made between a ruler's private property and public domains, these were great powers indeed. Two generations later, when Hincmar of Reims described the administration of the palace, he explained that the queen, with the assistance of the chamberlain, was in charge of the royal treasury. She was entrusted with these powers because the king was occupied with the ordering of the whole kingdom and could not be concerned with domestic trifles.

Merovingian queens also had access to the treasury but they were not entrusted with formal administrative functions. Whereas Merovingian queens acquired visibility in the economic sphere primarily through force of character, Carolingian empresses and queens were expected to serve as economic assistants to their husbands as a matter of course. Instead of being cloistered in the protective setting of their own residences, they were constantly on the move, accompanying their husbands on visits to different parts of the realm. For a queen or empress to remain at home was unusual enough for the chroniclers to take notice of it. Traveling with her husband, the queen participated in assemblies and issued donations jointly with the king. She also managed crown lands. Only illness exempted her from her duties. Ermengard, Louis the Pious's first wife, died en route to Tours with the imperial court. Taken ill at Angers, she stayed behind in a monastery, the emperor returning to her side only shortly before her death six weeks later.

In the ranks of the aristocracy, royal service and warfare absorbed the energies of the men, often leaving the supervision of the family estates in the hands of women. For example, the domains of Bernard of Septimania, imperial chamberlain and the most influential member of Louis the Pious's court, were run by his wife. Loyal and competent, Dhuoda accepted her husband's command to remain at home at Uzès. With perspicacity and skill, she kept his patrimony intact, despite his persistent demands for cash. Although she was conscience-stricken for having to borrow constantly from Jews and other moneylenders, she succeeded in covering Bernard's staggering expenses and continued to finance his royal way of life. As she explained with pathetic candor in her *Manual*, an educational guide addressed to her oldest son, William, she did all this to prevent the lord Bernard, her seignior, from abandoning her and William....

... [O]ther aristocratic women had to carry equally heavy administrative burdens. A capitulary of Charlemagne made it clear that, when a count was summoned to participate in a campaign, he was to leave behind only four of his men, two to protect his wife, and two to carry on the local administration. Handling the myriad details of land management alone, countesses acquired enough expertise to continue as the head steward even after their husbands returned. Gisla, daughter of the Saxon Count Hessi and widow of Unwan, traveled constantly to oversee the cultivation of her own and her son's estates. She chose as her assistant, not her son, but a young woman of lesser stature, Liutberga, whom she removed from a convent and trained specifically for this task. Even if the husband chose to exercise his prerogatives as a landowner, the wife remained in charge of the inner economy of the household.

The expression "he married her to rule his home," used by the biographer of Saint Glodesinda in 882, was not mere hyperbole. It accurately described the function of a wife in the great families. Once married, even though she was normally only a teenager who had barely reached the age of menarche, a young wife became responsible not only for the material comfort of her husband but also for the organization of his extensive household. She had to ensure that the storehouse was well stocked, the staff at the workshop was kept busy, and the kitchen was well run. Training for her executive tasks involved practical work experience from which even princesses were not exempt. Einhard made it clear that Charlemagne "made his daughters learn to spin and weave wool, use the distaff and spindle, and acquire every womanly accomplishment, rather than fritter away their time in idleness."

Skill in household management and handicrafts were so much appreciated that a new type of female saint made her appearance in the ninth century, the professional housekeeper and teacher of domestic "science." Saint Liutberga, Countess Gisla's assistant, earned her sainthood by supervising her patron's household and estates during the day and devoting her nights to prayer. When, in her old age, Liutberga was finally allowed to retire to the convent of Wendhausen, she was visited there by the great men and women of the area, who sought her counsel and brought their daughters to learn from her the secrets of wool dyeing and similar arts....

The supervision of a child's upbringing was also the responsibility of wives. Children had to be placed in the care of governors and governesses and given a proper education. To keep peace between the children and servants was, according to Sedulius Scottus, also one of the duties of royal wives. Moreover, solicitude for the religious training of children fell within the province of women. The ninth-century biographer of Saint Salaberga, after transforming the saint into a married woman with five children, praised her for converting her husband and children to monasticism. The biographer of Saint Waldtrud mentioned as a matter of course that the saint postponed her vocation until her children had grown up, although the father of the children had felt free to join a monastery much earlier. Nunneries and monasteries usually would not take children below the age of six or seven, although exceptions were made for children whose mothers had joined the institution. . . .

Carolingian women also lived shorter lives. On the basis of the life spans of four generations of Charlemagne's descendants, the only family group in the ninth century for which rudimentary biographical information is available, we can conclude that the average age of women at death was about thirty-six. In five generations of the Carolingian dynasty beginning with Charlemagne, K. F. Werner lists 176 people, including wives, husbands, concubines, and lovers. Of these, sufficient information exists for calculating the approximate age at death of 53 males and 47 females.

The early childhood mortality rate was higher for males than for females; six boys and two girls died before age five. The ratio was reversed in the early teens, with one boy and four girls dying between the ages of ten and fourteen. A higher mortality rate also prevailed for women between the ages of fifteen and thirty-nine, with 31 percent of the men as opposed to 48 percent of the women dying. Only 39 percent of the women lived to age forty and beyond, compared to 57 percent of the men. The highest proportion of male mortality occurred between the ages of forty and fifty-four, and of female mortality between the ages of twenty-five and thirty-nine. Clearly the disparity between the two mortality rates had some connection with women's biological function.

The shorter life span of a woman was by no means a general rule in the early medieval royalty and aristocracy. K. J. Leyser's study of the survival rate for the Saxon nobility and royalty has shown that men died earlier than women in the tenth and eleventh centuries. With their husbands and brothers perishing in wars and feuds, there was an abundance of elderly widows and spinster heiresses exercising influence, prestige, and even authority in Ottonian Saxony. Although Carolingian princes also plunged into wars and feuds, they were more fortunate in escaping violent death than the Saxon nobility.

A lower average age of mortality for women was also the pattern in families of lesser stature. David Herlihy's study of the life expectancy of peasant women in the ninth century reveals that men lived longer than women also on the lowest level of Carolingian society. It is not altogether possible to draw a direct correlation between the mortality rate of women and their childbearing function. No royal descendant, wife, or concubine is known to have died during childbirth. It would be equally wrong to assume that a woman who bore many children would die sooner than one who had none. In contrast to Hildegard's death at twenty-five, her granddaughter, the equally fertile Gisla, lived to a ripe age of fifty-two to fifty-five. Fastrada, the mother of two, died at twenty-five or twenty-seven, while the childless Liutgard died at twenty or twenty-two. Since women, at least in the royal family, were not more prone than men to be victims of violence, their relatively low survival rate must be attributed to the combined effect of inadequate health care and an iron deficiency in the Carolingian diet, aggravated by menstruation, gynecological problems, and childbearing.

As the responsibilities of a married woman increased, her contributions to the well-being of the conjugal unit gained recognition. Virginity as a more perfect state than marriage, a theme of patristic and Merovingian writings, received less emphasis in the ninth century. Indeed, Haimo of Auxerre declared that a married woman pleased God as much as one who espoused chastity. By bearing children and giving them a religious education, a married woman carried out the work of God, according to Haimo. The first poem celebrating women in every role was composed at this time. Virgins, married women bearing sons to please God, widows loyal to the memory of their husbands who encouraged their sons to serve God, and even reformed courtesans were, according to the court poet Notker, capable of defeating Satan and ascending to heaven on the ladder that the love of Christ made especially accessible to women.

Another aspect of the celebration of women as wives and mothers was the veneration of Mary, which gained prominence in the ninth century. Ilene Forsyth has assembled evidence showing that manuscripts, ivories, and reliefs representing Mary in majesty with the child Jesus on her lap were produced in Carolingian ateliers. Hincmar had at Reims a gold altar portraying Mary as the mother of Jesus, a gold relief of Mary served as an altar frontal in the cathedral of Metz, and the monks of Luxeuil prized a silver retable of Mary. Even earlier, on a reliquary given by Charlemagne to Witikind in 785, the matronly figure of the Virgin holding the Child appeared between the apostles Peter and Paul. A homily on the assumption of Mary, composed by Paschasius Radbertus, enjoyed such popularity that Hincmar had it transcribed, and extracts from it were sung as antiphons at matins on the Feast of the Assumption. Mary's nativity and purification were also commemorated from the time of Charlemagne. Her merits were sung, moreover, not only by Paschasius Radbertus but also by Alcuin, Hrabanus Maurus, Walafrid of Strabo, Sedulius of Liège, and Hincmar of Reims.

Ninth-century writers venerated Mary and praised women's accomplishments as mothers and wives but did not think of husbands and wives as equals. The subjection of wives to their husbands continued to be justified on the basis of the Pauline passages and the third chapter of Genesis. Even the champion of women, Hincmar of Reims, while stressing equality of men and women before the law, referred to women as the weaker vessel and upheld the notion that a husband was the ruler of his wife.

Complaints registered by wives against their husbands were handled with great caution by the Carolingian courts. A well-known case is that of Northilda, who brought charges against her husband to an assembly of lay nobles and bishops in 822. She accused him of forcing her to have sex with him in a shameful manner. Although unnatural intercourse was considered a grave sin, the lady's scruples did not move the judges. They refused to suspend marital relations between the couple, referring Northilda to a secular court, which, in their opinion, was more qualified to handle the case.

Only when a woman was threatened with divorce or physical danger were the courts quick to intervene. Hincmar's bloodcurdling account of the atrocities committed by husbands suggests that the bonds of permanent marriage proved to be too much for some men to bear. When a wife was a burden or a nuisance, there were ways other than divorce to get rid of her. Hincmar pointed out that men, accusing their wives of adultery,

> lead them to the slaughterhouse to be butchered and they bid the cooks to kill them with swords as it is the practice with sheep and pigs, or they personally murder them with the edge of their own swords, cutting them to pieces.

To defend women in fear of their lives, the Council of Tribur in 895 authorized bishops to make churches available as sanctuaries.

A woman could also seek shelter in a monastery if she were mistreated by her husband. Theutberga finally withdrew to Avenay. Another barren royal wife, the Empress Richardis, entered Andelau after she had successfully defended herself against the accusation of her husband, Charles III, the Fat, that she had committed adultery with Bishop Liudward of Vercelli. As earlier, wives were shielded also by their own kin. In a case of extreme brutality brought before the courts, a priest who had sought to reunite a woman with her husband suffered the greatest injury. The woman in question sought refuge with her brother, who became so enraged by the priest's entreaties that he had him castrated.

If a woman were lucky enough to survive her husband, she did not fare much better than her predecessors in the Merovingian era. Even though the Carolingians placed them under special royal protection, widows still might be robbed of their property. To guard the interests of women bereft of husbands, the capitularies entitled them to seek the services of royal officials as their "defenders." The sad story of the noble widow, recorded by

Paschasius Radbertus, indicates, however, that the officials often extorted enormous fees from the women they were supposed to protect. The lady in question had been dispossessed of all her lands by a justiciar she had chosen as her "defender." When she complained to the emperor, he entrusted the case to his judges, who did not sympathize with the widow's plight. Her testimony that she had adequately compensated her "defender" by turning over to him half her possessions was discounted, and the case was adjudicated in favor of the justiciar.

To be protected by the church, a widow had to join a convent. Earlier, she could take a vow of chastity and remain in the world as a *Deo devota*. Reforming synods, beginning in the late eighth century, required women to enter nunneries if they wished to devote themselves to the service of God. Allegations that widows took fraudulent vows in order to remain free to lead a life of sexual abandon leave no doubt that the cloistering of widows represented an integral part of the church's effort to enforce monogamy. As this program met with success and the conjugal family emerged as the basic unit of society, the function of sheltering unmarried ladies, formerly assumed by extended families, was taken over by the convents. As in other spheres of life, here too the royal family led the way. Louis the Pious not only sent his notorious sisters to nunneries but also installed his widowed mother-in-law as abbess at Chelles.

In earlier times, when the extended family was the dominant form of social organization, a woman could make herself useful in a variety of ways even if she were unmarried, divorced, or widowed. She could help her relatives with domestic activities and engage in religious pursuits. This wide range of options was not available to unmarried upper-class women in the ninth century. Those who were unwilling to or could not marry were confined to nunneries. No longer fulfilling a useful function, they were considered a threat to the stability of the conjugal unit or at best an anomaly in a society in which the center of economic activity was shifting from the extended family to the more restricted conjugal ménage.

The formalization of wifely duties in the ninth century, while enhancing the wife's influence in aristocratic families, strengthened male dominance in all other spheres and reinforced sexual stereotypes. The wife was occupied in a broad variety of domestic and nurturing roles and remained in the shadow of her husband. Should she try to exercise power in her own right, she met with criticism and was accused of unfeminine behavior. Women who were bold enough to petition assemblies were sternly rebuked by the Synod of Nantes in 895:

> It is astonishing that certain women, against both divine and human law, with barefaced impudence, plead in general assemblies and with abandon exhibit a burning passion for public meetings, and they disrupt, rather than assist, the business of the kingdom and the good of the commonweal. It is indecent and even reprehensible, even among barbarians, for women to discuss the cases of

men. Those who should be discussing their woolen work and weaving with the residents of women's quarters should not usurp the authority of senators in public meetings just as if they were palace officials.

The few known cases in which women, other than queens, appeared in public assemblies suggest that they were defending their honor or property rather than meddling in the affairs of men. Even queens, despite their public roles, merely acted as agents of their husbands, relieving them of the burdens of household and land management. The Carolingians acknowledged the importance of a wife, but they also perpetuated the notion that a woman's role was different from and auxiliary to that of a man. Women were to bear children and look after the spiritual and material welfare of their husbands and children, but their sphere of influence was to be restricted to family affairs. A woman could exercise public power only as an extension of her role as wife, mother, and property owner....

The impact of Carolingian marriage legislation may be ... measured by documents recording land transfers in a specific region. The Lorsch cartulary, which contains over 3,500 deeds dating from the mid-eighth to the end of the ninth century, lends itself to this type of analysis. The cartulary has been carefully edited, according to standards of modern scholarship. The monastery itself was located in the eastern part of the Carolingian heartland, the home of Charlemagne's biographer Einhard. Its properties extended from the valley of the Nahe and the Glan rivers on the left bank of the Rhine to Frankfurt along the valley of the Main, and southward into the valley of the Neckar along the west bank of the Saar. With a landowning aristocracy mainly of East Frankish descent, the social and economic organization of the area may be regarded as typical of the Frankish Kingdom.

The activities of women in the documents preserved in the cartulary were analyzed according to two major categories. The first includes women acting independently of men, transmitting property alone or acting jointly with other women in donating, selling, exchanging, or pledging property. The second comprises women appearing as coactors with their husbands, sons, brothers, or fathers, either as the equals of males in the transaction or in a secondary role by approving with their signatures the alienation of property by male relatives. Within each category the status of the actor or the relationship of the coactors and cosigners was also examined.

The tabulation of these documents reveals a close connection between women's economic activity and the history of the family in the region. The independent activity of women diminished between 814 and 840, during the reign of Louis the Pious.... Beginning with Louis's reign, women appear as sole actors or as coactors with other women in only 10.4 percent of the Lorsch documents. The level of women's activity as sole donors or joint donors with other women remains at the same level (10 percent) for the rest of the century. In contrast, the earlier Lorsch documents indicate a higher incidence of women's donations: 10.8 percent during Pepin's reign, 12.5 percent during Charlemagne's reign as king, with an increase to 14.4 percent during the years following his coronation as emperor.

The changes in the proportion of women acting alone or jointly with other women do not permit us to draw meaningful conclusions, but figures on women acting jointly with men clearly indicate that women were less prominent as donors of land after the reign of Louis the Pious than in the previous decades. Prior to the death of Louis the Pious, the incidence of joint donations by women and men is fairly steady, fluctuating between 16 and 17 percent in the reigns of Pepin, Charlemagne, and Louis. After 840, the incidence drops to 9.6 percent. These joint donations were issued mainly by married couples; the proportion of women appearing in the Lorsch documents as coactors with sons, fathers, or brothers was negligible, not exceeding more than 1 percent in any given period. If we combine the transactions in which women figure as donors and codonors, we find a significant drop in the visibility of women controlling land after 840. The fluctuations in the reigns of Pepin, Charlemagne, and Louis are between 26.8 percent and 30.3 percent, dropping to 19.6 percent after 840.

The drop in the proportion of women disposing of property with their husbands or alone after 840 cannot be attributed to changes in the form of landholding, because, with few exceptions, the transactions involved allodial land.[6] Nor is it enough to say that the higher proportion of donations in which women participated as donors and codonors before 840 reflected a desire by men to provide for the welfare of their souls before going off to war. The greatest military expansion of the Carolingian empire occurred under Charlemagne as king, when the proportion of donations in which women participated did not significantly increase. Moreover, these donations had as their purpose the salvation of the soul of parents and children and most frequently of the donors themselves, but not of a husband, brother, or son alone. Finally, because the laws of inheritance remained unchanged, we cannot assume that less land passed into the hands of women by means of inheritance after 840.

A more satisfactory explanation of the lesser prominence of women in the transactions after 840 is that the marriage regulations of Louis, albeit unintentionally, resulted in fewer marriages among the upper echelons of Frankish society. The strict punishment of divorce upheld by the Council of Mainz, one of the four great reforming councils held in 829, had important consequences for the control of land in the Lorsch region. Secular legislation against divorce began in 789, culminating in 802 with the instructions Charlemagne included in his *Capitulary to the Missi*. Cases reaching the courts after 802 were to be adjudicated according to the new laws. Ancient customs, however, could not be changed suddenly. Renewed legislation against divorce by Louis the Pious suggests the widespread failure of

---

[6] Land that is held by its owner absolutely, as an inalienable property.

Charlemagne's efforts. Finally, in 829, the four reforming councils, one of which met at Mainz in the vicinity of Lorsch, subjected husbands who had divorced their wives to public penance, the same punishment given a man who had killed his wife.

With the promulgation of this decree, Louis the Pious opened a new chapter not only in the history of marital relations but also in the history of the ownership of land by women. The threat of public penance was sufficient to discourage divorces. As escape from inconvenient unions became more difficult, if not impossible, and as the definition of a legitimate marriage became more precise, men of the nobility began to exercise greater caution in choosing a wife. The casual arrangements or quasi marriages of earlier times went on unabated. But in the ninth century... they came to be regarded as trial marriages that denied the woman any legal claim as a wife. Although these relationships were occasionally transformed into legitimate unions, normally they served only as a means for men to enjoy more than casual sexual relationships before settling down to marriage. With men of the aristocracy marrying somewhat later, marrying women who came from the same social class, and remarrying only after their wives died, fewer women had the opportunity to gain control of property through marriage. A mistress, even if she was of high birth with powerful connections and treasures at her disposal, did not qualify as a coactor in land transactions....

It is important to note that some of the transactions in which the wife appeared as a codonor of her husband's patrimony predate Charlemagne's legislation on the indissolubility of marriage. These deeds thus confirm the evidence provided by law codes and narrative sources that a wife had considerable economic rights under the pre-Carolingian marital system, even though in other respects the system favored men. The Carolingian legislation made the position of wives more secure, but did not augment female economic rights. The emphasis on the indissolubility of marriage increased the effective association of conjugal goods, but it did not improve the opportunities for women to acquire control over landed property through marriage. On the contrary, the elimination of divorce prevented the dispersal of a man's patrimony among a succession of wives. A woman in the Carolingian era could gain full legal control over her own property and a part of her husband's patrimony only if she became a widow. Indeed, under the new monogamous structure, the bridegift was gradually transformed into a widow's dower. Instead of giving the wife full ownership of a part of her husband's patrimony, a growing number of marriage contracts guaranteed her only the right of usufruct,[7] usually over a third of all his property....

Carolingian legislation probably had very little effect on the marriage customs of peasants. The economic interdependence of a peasant couple made divorce unlikely, even in the Merovingian period. There is no doubt

---

[7] A legal right to use and enjoy the fruits of something that is owned by another.

that, as the permanence of marriage and ecclesiastical distinctions between legitimate and illegitimate unions gained acceptance, women of low birth could no longer marry into the aristocracy. Only in the lower echelons of society did enterprising women continue to contribute to social mobility, bringing about the fusion of free and unfree elements. Not only individual lords but Charlemagne himself encouraged marriages between royal serfs and free women on the one hand and royal *fiscalines* [women in service to the court] and freemen on the other. By declaring that the free partner was to retain all the rights attendant to a person of free status, Charlemagne gave official blessing to a centuries-old practice that went against the letter of the law.

By the ninth century, legal principles and social customs that were to define women's role in the highest and lowest echelons of European society were clearly enunciated. Among peasants, comprising about four-fifths of the population, women worked hard and lived in poverty, but had the freedom to choose their husbands. Although they could no longer aspire to marry into the governing classes, they could marry peasants of a diversity of conditions and statuses, ranging from small proprietors through free, semifree and slave tenants and day laborers. As a member of the labor force, a woman could marry below her status and her status was not determined by that of her husband. If she was a slave or semifree, she could marry a freeman and give birth to children of intermediate status.

A woman of the aristocracy did not have these choices. In the ninth century, as the great families closed ranks against the dilution of their bloodlines by lower-class wives, they came to attach an even greater importance to the biological function of their daughters. Regarded as political and economic assets, women of the upper classes were carefully guarded in childhood and were married at a tender age. The high value assigned to aristocratic women's reproductive and domestic duties led to definitions that limited their role to the fulfillment of those duties....

The benefits of the Carolingians' efforts to impose lifelong monogamy on their subjects were reaped by women in the tenth and eleventh centuries. In the age of violence and political anarchy that followed the collapse of the Carolingian Empire, the family emerged as the most stable and efficient instrument of government. The effective association of conjugal goods under the monogamous structure enabled women to share sovereign rights with their husbands as political power came to be tied to the possession of land. Secure in their position as wives, women were equipped to act with authority as helpmates and *dominae* [rulers of households] in both economic and political affairs. Profiting from the consolidation of landed wealth by their fathers and husbands, a growing number of women appeared in this first feudal age as chatelaines, mistresses of land, and proprietesses of monasteries, exercising attendant rights of justice, military command, minting, and taxation.

Bibliography

C. ERICKSON and K. CASEY, "Women in the Middle Ages: A Working Bibliography," *Medieval Studies* 38 (1976):340–359.

HEINRICH FICHTENAU, *The Carolingian Empire: The Age of Charlemagne* (1964).

JACK GOODY, *The Development of the Family and Marriage in Europe* (1983).

JACQUES HEERS, *Family Clans in the Middle Ages: A Study of Political and Social Structures in Urban Areas* (1977).

DAVID HERLIHY, *The Social History of Italy and Western Europe, 700–1500* (1978).

R. T. MOREWEDGE, ed., *The Role of Woman in the Middle Ages* (1975).

PETER MUNZ, *The Age of Charlemagne* (1971).

EILEEN POWER, *Medieval Women* (1975).

PIERRE RICHE, *Daily Life in the Age of Charlemagne* (1978).

SUSAN MOSHER STUARD, ed., *Women in Medieval Society* (1976).

Townswomen

SHULAMITH SHAHAR

During the high and later Middle Ages, townswomen participated in a wide variety of professional activities beyond their basic housework. They were most evident in the cloth and food trades, where they often conducted business independently and held membership in established guilds and fraternities. Less frequently they engaged in the greater retail trades and merchant ventures, although many widows assumed responsibility for such businesses after their husband's death. Women engaged in a business had legal independence and, whether married or not, they could sue and be sued as individuals.

Despite the variety of their occupations and guild membership, however, professional women did not have the freedom of choice and movement that men had. Academic occupations such as law and medicine barred them outright, as men jealously guarded entrance into these higher professions. Some guilds and trades closed their doors to women (these varied from town to town), and where women were accepted, strict rules often governed their work. Women's wages tended to be 25 to 30 percent lower than men's for the same work. Women disproportionately filled the ranks of domestic servants, the lowest of the urban laboring classes. Many women found such work more attractive than life in the countryside, however, and migrated to the towns in search of it. Women also worked as prostitutes. Because towns recognized the social function of prostitution and carefully monitored it, the lot of prostitutes in the medieval town was actually better than in later periods of history.

Urban society was new in several senses and woman's role in it can be understood only against the background of its unique economic, social and cultural structure. But it is important to emphasize at the outset that

Reprinted with the permission of Methuen & Co., Ltd., from *The Fourth Estate: A History of Women in the Middle Ages* by Shulamith Shahar. Copyright © 1983 Shulamith Shahar.

women's rights continued to be restricted within the new structure of urban life, although this was no longer a warrior society like the nobility, or a partially unfree society like the peasantry. The town was a place of peace (*locus pacificus*). Peace was essential to its development and its economic activity, which was based on artisanship, commerce and money affairs. It evolved its own ethos, which differed from that of the feudal nobility. Though urban society was a class society from the outset, it abolished the distinctions between freemen and serfs and, legally speaking (in contrast to rural areas), all townspeople were free.

The town arose as a secular corporation, like the guilds which grew up within it and were also secular corporations (excluding the universities), and a stratum of lay officials, notaries and judges developed. A lay society which was not a society of warriors and whose members enjoyed free competition might have been expected to expand women's political rights, but this did not occur. This appears to substantiate the evaluation (based on comparative study of the history of women and their status in society) that woman's status in general and political status in particular in a specific society cannot always be explained on the basis of the economic structure of that society or the degree to which it is democratic. One need only recall democratic Athens in its heyday, where women's rights were restricted even according to the criteria of ancient Greece.

The restriction of the rights of urban women was reflected primarily in the fact that women played no part in running the town. Different forms of government evolved in different towns, some oligarchical, others aristocratic or semi-democratic. But in none, whatever their regimes, did women play a part in government. They were not elected to municipal councils, did not hold positions of authority, and only in exceptional cases did they take part in town assemblies. In this respect the townswoman's lot was no better than that of the peasant woman. However, though women could not fulfil functions in manors and village communities, spinsters and widows in rural areas did attend village assemblies, whereas in town no woman, whatever her marital status, attended such assemblies. The increase in the number of male officiaries and wielders of authority in towns did not bring about a corresponding increase in the number of women who played a part in government. The opposite is true, in fact, so much so that within the framework of the history of women in urban society there is no room for discussion of town government.

In contrast women played an important part in the urban economy. One could scarcely envisage production in the medieval town or its internal commerce without the activities of women. Their role in labour—and there are those who regard it as one of the manifestations of the new urban ethos—was particularly prominent, and won them some place in the guilds of artisans and petty merchants, despite the restrictions imposed on them....

Women's Work

In his *Utopia*, Thomas More wrote about the large number of idlers in various societies, in contrast to Utopia, where everyone worked. Among the idlers he includes priests, noblemen and their retainers, beggers and women: 'First there are almost all the women, who constitute half the whole; or where the women are busy, there as a rule the men are snoring in their stead.' But study of the history of women in the Middle Ages reveals that these remarks are in no way applicable to medieval urban society. The role of women in production in medieval towns was considerable, despite the restrictions imposed on them, and this is perhaps the most interesting chapter in the history of urban women. There were occupations in which women played a particularly important part, to the point where they were largely regarded as female occupations, yet they were also engaged in by men, who were never totally replaced in them. Nor was there any undermining of the status of those men who remained active in these occupations. One could not therefore claim that there was a clear division of occupations in towns by sex. Since the women who engaged in certain activities also worked in their own households, they were ruled by two separate rhythms of work: that accepted as 'feminine', characterized by the fact that the work was never-ending and was aimed at satisfying the needs of others, a husband and children, and the 'masculine' rhythm, consisting of alternate effort and rest.

Some women engaged in various occupations within the family workshop as the daughters and wives of craftsmen. It was common to teach girls and women various crafts, and the right of a craftsman to teach his trade to his wife and daughter and to utilize their help was recognized. Many widows continued to engage in their husbands' occupations, and this too was recognized, though various restrictions were imposed by the guild authorities. Had they not learned the trade from their fathers (they often married men who were in the same trade and had been their fathers' apprentices) or their husbands, they could not have engaged in it as widows, and certainly could not have taken their husbands' place in training apprentices. Even in those guilds which prohibited the hiring of women, members were permitted to utilize the services of their wives and daughters.

Women sometimes learned a trade in childhood as apprentices of craftswomen. Some later married men in the same trade and worked with them, some married men engaged in some other occupation and continued to work in their own trade, others never married and continued to follow their trade. Women who worked with their husbands were not usually members of a guild during the lifetime of their husbands, but, if they were widowed, they were permitted, with certain limitations, to continue their husbands' trade and to become members of the guild. Spinsters, and some of the married women who worked in trades other than those of their husbands, worked for wages. In some towns, particularly in the spinning and weaving industries, the women were given raw materials and worked at home. Some married women and spinsters were members of guilds. Then there were guilds composed exclusively of women, in which the statutes were drawn up by the women themselves. In the mixed guilds too, women sometimes participated in drawing up the statutes.

We learn of the role of women from the statutes and regulations of the various guilds, from royal and seigneurial decrees, court records and records of taxpayers. We can obtain a preliminary picture of the role of women in urban production by perusing the well-known *Livre des Métiers*, written by Etienne Boileau in the thirteenth century and containing the regulations of the guilds of Paris at that time. Of the one hundred occupations the author lists, six are occupations in which only female guilds engaged in Paris. In addition, women worked in another eighty of the listed occupations, that is to say in eighty-six of the hundred occupations listed. The occupations which were exclusively female were: spinning silk on a broad loom, production of elegant head-coverings decorated with jewels and gold thread (*chapeau d'orfroi*), and production of decorated purses (*aumonières sarrazinoises*). (A large number of the crafts practised in Paris were connected with fashionable garments.) Spinning on broad and narrow looms was done at home, and the women received the materials from the merchants. They were under the supervision of two male supervisors appointed by the *praepositus* [leader] of the merchants of the city, who enforced regulations as to quality, wage rates, conditions for acceptance of apprentices, fines for violations, acceptance of new workers and rest days. The purse makers, like the women who wove silk for head-coverings, were organized in women's guilds whose regulations were determined by the guild members and approved by the *praepositus*.

Many of the other occupations in which women engaged were also connected with clothing: the making of ribbons and bindings, sewing, fur production, hat- and scarf-making, wig-making, work with feathers for decoration and various stages of the textile industry: washing, dyeing, spinning and weaving wool and flax. Women also engaged in sharpening tools, and producing needles, pins, buckles, scissors and knives. They worked as goldsmiths, produced jewelry incorporating natural crystal, and made crystal vases—delicate work which demanded considerable skill. They also worked as barbers. The makers of ribbons, bindings and fringes were members of a mixed guild, where the rights of the widower of a guild member did not differ from those of a widow. If the surviving spouse was in the same trade, i.e. a ribbon and bindings maker, he or she could continue the trade of the deceased spouse as a guild member empowered to train apprentices. Both craftsmen and craftswomen trained boy and girl apprentices. The female crystal workers and makers of needles and pins and other tools used by seamstresses and goldsmiths were members of a joint guild. The wives of weavers who worked with their husbands were considered to be craftswomen like them, and the regulations stipulated that the wife of a craftsman could be responsible for apprentices of both sexes.

The registers of payment of tallage in Paris for the years 1296, 1297 and 1313 confirm and complete this picture of a wide range of female trades. The women mentioned in these records were all working independently in their trades and paid taxes separately. Married women who helped their husbands did not appear in the records, since their husbands paid for them. Among others, the records list the midwife Sara, who was unmarried (though we do not know if she was a spinster or a widow), and a retail trader whose husband Robert was a shoemaker. Note should be taken of the role of women in the guild of embroiderers in gold thread in Paris, who were classified as precious metal workers. Of the four guild officers, one was a married woman. They also played a part in the guild of leather-workers and workers in combinations of leather and metal and leather and wood. The right to work in part of this trade was granted in the days of Louis VII as a monopoly to a widow named Thecia and to her descendants. They processed the leather and made leather belts, straps, gloves, shoes and pouches in which seals, silver, documents, prayer missals and toilet articles were kept. In 1287 the monopoly was again granted to a woman, denoted as Marcelle. The caskets in whose manufacture women played a part were made of combinations of leather, wood and metal decorations. They also made various purses and scabbards for swords and knives. The registers of taxpayers list women as shoemakers and even as metal-workers, but with regard to the latter we do not know whether the denotations beside their names (*forcetière, favresse*) are meant to denote a trade or are merely family names.

Women followed a considerable proportion of the above-mentioned trades in other European towns as well: there were spinners and weavers in Sienna and Perugia; women members of the belt-makers guild in Florence, which was a mixed guild; and of the guild of the flax-weavers, women weavers in Toulouse; weavers and embroiderers with gold thread in Frankfurt, Cologne and most of the towns of Flanders.

In England the women who worked as silk-weavers in London sent a petition to the king in 1368 asking him to order the mayor to restrain a certain Nicholas, who for some time had been hoarding all the raw and coloured silk and other goods, causing a rise in prices and heavy financial damage to the king and to the petitioners whose profession and source of livelihood was silk-weaving. About one hundred years later, in the mid-fifteenth century, within the framework of the protectionist movements which developed in England to defend English production against the competition of imported goods, the London spinners, weavers and seamstresses in silk again appealed to Parliament. These women, who worked at home according to the putting-out system, and who were not registered in guilds, asked Parliament to pass a law forbidding the import of partly or fully processed silk goods into England. They stated in their request that this occupation had provided an honourable livelihood for many women who handed on their skills to others, and now some thousand women were learning the trade. The import of inferior goods from abroad made by foreigners eager for profit could ruin this honourable trade in which women worked, and cause numerous respectable women to be unemployed.

According to the taxpayers register of London in 1319, 4 per cent of all taxpayers were women. Some were rich widows who lived off rent, but they also included women both married and spinsters who worked independently. In York women were members of the hat-makers' guild alongside men, and the same was true in the tailors' guild in Lincoln. In England too, craftswomen, embroiderers and others trained girl apprentices. Sometimes the girl was registered in the contract as the apprentice of both husband and wife, but when a woman worked in a different trade to her husband, it was explicitly stated that it was she who would teach the trade. In York, as also in Paris, there were women members of the guild of leather processors, including women who prepared leather for parchment. In English towns and villages, brewing, which was also done at home, was mainly women's work. The court registers record many cases of women tried for violations of the Assize of Ale, and urban regulations on proper methods of production are often directed mainly at women. The registers of Colchester list a woman named Juliana Gray, who was fined several times not only for transgression of the Assize of Ale but also for selling wine illegally. Despite the charges, she apparently flourished, and on her death bequeathed landed property near the town to her second husband.

In some places, like England and southern France, women played a prominent role in the fraternities, those voluntary associations whose members banded together for joint religious and social reasons and which were sometimes affiliated, at least in part, to the guilds. They were not exclusively male clubs, and their membership included women. Women were also sometimes among the founders and the composers of the regulations. The founders of the fraternity of the Holy Virgin, established in 1351 at Kingston upon Hull, for example, included ten men and thirteen women. Ten of the women were the wives of the founders but three were not. The statutes stipulated identical entrance fees for bachelors or spinsters wishing to join the fraternity, and if they married the fee was not increased and the spouse was accepted as a brother or sister. The statutes were signed by the male founders on their own behalf and in the name of their wives, and by spinsters in their own right. This was a legal reflection of the differences we have already noted between the status of married women and that of spinsters. In these fraternities the female members usually enjoyed the same rights to welfare and aid as men. (The only thing forbidden them was to hold wake over a deceased male member of the fraternity...)

In all European towns women worked as washerwomen, gatekeepers and also as bathhouse attendants. And in conclusion let us note a bookbinder from Norwich, a female book illuminator who worked with a well-known illuminator at Avignon, and another female illuminator in Paris whose work, according to Christine de Pisan, surpassed in beauty anything done by men and whose wage was higher than theirs. Christine adds: 'This is known to me from experience since she did several illuminations for me.' Last but not least, there were women members of the guild of singers and players in Paris, who also took part in drawing up the statutes, led by the king's minstrel.

There were also many women who rented out houses, managed hotels and taverns, and in particular engaged in commerce in foodstuffs both in shops and stalls, in the markets and at weekly or seasonal fairs. Some of them worked alone while others helped their husbands. It seems to have been mainly the wives of petty merchants who helped their husbands in markets and at fairs. They often also came to their aid when brawls broke out with neighbouring stallkeepers at the fair. The records mention women selling poultry, fish and other sea and dairy foodstuffs. In Paris women engaged in trade in cloth and clothing, from old clothes to various garments and to textiles, as recorded in the statutes of the guilds and registers of taxpayers. The latter also list two female money-changers and one money-lender.

In Norwich there was a woman wheat merchant, a trade considered highly respectable, and there were several cases of widows of great overseas merchants who continued their husbands' businesses. The widow Alice demanded of the Guildhall court in London in 1370 half of the cargo of a certain boat which had been seized by the bailiff of Billingsgate as the property of some other person. She brought proof of her claim and the court ordered that the cargo be released and handed over to her. Margery Russell of Coventry, who was robbed of goods to the value of £800 by the Spaniards, obtained permission to seize the cargo of other Spaniards in order to compensate herself. She took a larger quantity than was due to her and the Spaniards lodged a complaint against her. Rose Burford, widow of a rich merchant who loaned a large sum to the king to finance his Scottish wars in 1318, continued her husband's business after his death. When the debt due to her husband was not repaid even after she had submitted several petitions, she proposed to the king that it be repaid in the form of exemption from the tax she was due to pay for wool she wished to export. She was summoned to court to submit her plea, the proposal was examined and her request was granted. There were others of her like, as can be seen from the hundred rolls of 1274, which list among the great wool merchants certain London widows engaged in large-scale trade in wool and other goods, like Isabella Buckerel and others. One woman is even mentioned as the Staple merchant in the days of Edward IV, that is to say the recognized exporter of wool from England to Calais.

As we have noted, these women were widows. Those women who traded independently, on the other hand, and were not continuing the work of deceased husbands, were active mainly in small local trade in garments or foodstuffs. An independent woman merchant who engaged in foreign trade, or even in domestic retail trade, whether a spinster or married woman, was the exception to the rule. It was also usually the wives of petty merchants who worked with their husbands in the markets and at fairs. The wife of a great merchant was more closely confined to the home, there was no economic need for her to work and her husband did not require her help. There were however scattered cases of women who worked without being in financial need. Margery Kempe, who later became a mystic (and whose history is therefore known), was the wife of one of the great merchants in Lynne. Nonetheless she worked, first at brewing and later at wheat-milling. She herself said that she worked because she had leisure time and could not bear for another woman to compare to her in elegance. In other words, her work was an outlet for a desire for activity and brought her an added income which enabled her to acquire the luxuries she wanted. Though she had fourteen children, she was bored and sought an occupation outside the home. This suggests that she did not devote too much time to bringing up her children. We also know of the wife of a London lawyer who owned a shop in Sopers Lane. The silk-making in London was carried out in part by the wives of merchants, who processed the raw material supplied by their husbands.

Some women engaged in retail commerce and were members of the guilds of petty merchants, like the poultry traders' guilds in Paris for example. On the other hand, we have found no record of women members of the great retail merchants' guilds, which in effect (though not always officially) constituted the central municipal authority in various towns. In some towns in which the merchants' guild acted as the town council in practice, the right of women to hand on guild membership to sons and husbands was sometimes abrogated, and it was determined that the right could only be inherited from a father or uncle. The right of women to hand on membership of merchants' guilds to husbands, sons and even grandsons was only recognized in towns in which the guild did not constitute the municipal institution. It is characteristic that in Paris women merchants are mentioned in the statutes of 1324 which relate to petty local merchants, but not in the 1408 statutes which deal with the great cloth merchants who were exporters and retail merchants.

The right of women to fulfil functions connected with economic activity varied from town to town. In Paris a woman could not hold the position of measurer of weights. In London, on the other hand, women sometimes held the office of weigher of silk. The assayer of oysters farmed his office to women, but this aroused opposition, 'since it is not fitting for the city because women are not capable of effectively preventing frauds in commerce.'

The female merchants, whether spinsters, widows or married women sued and were sued independently (as *femme sole*). This was to the advantage of the husband, who was thus exempted from responsibility for his wife's commercial activities and their possible outcome, and also bestowed complete independence on the woman merchant even if she was a married woman. This legal independence was recognized in all medieval European towns.

Here and there we find references by the authors of didactic works to women as an urban labour force. Francesco Barberino, for example, writes: 'Let not the woman who sells cheese wash it to make it appear fresh; the women weavers should use all the thread given them with the order and not take any of their own needs.' The author also refers to the professional ethics of servant girls, women barbers, women bakers, tavern-keepers, female haberdashers, and even women beggars. But generally speaking the authors of didactic works concentrated more on the sexual chastity of women and their duties towards their husbands than on their economic activities. The literature of the estates totally obscured the role of women in production in towns.

Women undoubtedly played a considerable part in crafts in town, in petty commerce and occasionally in great commerce. But they were not free to engage in whatever occupation they chose, as men were. Certain guilds were completely closed to them while in others they were restricted. In some guilds it was prohibited to employ women for wages, and in those occupations in which they worked for daily, weekly, monthly or annual wages, they were, almost without exception, discriminated against in comparison with men. In certain guilds unmarried or married women were not accepted, and only the widows of members were taken in, with certain restrictions, to continue the work of their husbands.

It is characteristic that according to a royal decree issued in England in 1364, craftsmen were permitted to engage only in their own crafts, excluding women who engaged in brewing, baking, various stages of production of wool, flax and silk, who were permitted to engage in several trades. The historian who quotes this decree adds that it was issued because medieval society already recognized the 'versatility' of woman, 'the eternal amateur'. But it is doubtful whether this dubious compliment is merited. The truth is that this regulation was issued because not all guilds accepted women and some of those which did take them in imposed certain restrictions. Therefore many women worked at home, the raw materials being provided by entrepreneurs, or worked for wages. They were not recognized as expert craftsmen with full rights in guilds and therefore engaged in several different crafts in order to earn what was needed to finance a household. The law confirmed their right to do so. They did not act out of free choice to answer the needs of their versatility or eternal amateurishness or for lack of the necessary qualifications to specialize in a certain trade.

The following are several examples of bans or restrictions on women from engaging in certain trades. In Paris women were prohibited from working on the carpets known as *tapis sarrazinois*, the argument being that the work was dangerous in general and for pregnant women in particular.

In Norwich women were banned from weaving with twine (that is to say weaving types of cloth which required dense weaving) on the pretext that they lacked the physical strength to carry out this work properly. In Ghent the wives of the makers of a certain type of men's hose were banned from working in the trade; they could only supervise the work of hired labourers. The daughters of the leather belt-makers in Paris were allowed to work as independent craftswomen in this craft even if they wed, but were not allowed to teach the craft to apprentices or to their husbands.

The ban against training apprentices often applied also to the widows of craftsmen who were allowed to continue their husbands' work. According to the statutes of several guilds, a widow could complete the training of an apprentice who had begun his service under her husband, but could not take on new apprentices. The widow of a maker of wax candles in Paris in 1399 was forbidden by the jurats to continue working in her husband's craft, the argument being that she was not an expert craftswoman. She appealed to the Châtelet court and the judges accepted her appeal and permitted her to continue working in the craft on condition that she did not work for someone else, did not send labourers to work for others and did not accept new apprentices. If she married a man from outside the trade, she could neither teach him nor their joint children her craft. The same rule applied to women who made prayer beads from shells and coral, and those who worked in crystal and precious stones. In the case of the latter, the pretext cited was that members of the craft could not believe that a woman could become expert in so delicate a craft to the extent where she could teach it to a child.

These are several examples of bans and restrictions on women in guilds. Nor were hired women workers allowed to work in all occupations. According to the statutes of the guild of wool fullers in Lincoln, members were forbidden to use female help in the various stages, apart from their own wives and the servant girls of their wives. The same was true in the guild of belt- and strap-makers in London and the weavers' guild in Bristol. In Bristol it was stated that the employment of hired female labour was responsible for the fact that many men in this trade could not find work and had become vagrants without sources of income. Women's wages were lower than men's, and there were undoubtedly craftsmen who preferred to hire women for this reason. According to G. d'Avenal, in 1326–50 the average wage of women was only 68 per cent of that of men doing the same work. In 1376–1400 their wage was 75 per cent of men's on the average, because after the Black Death there was a fall in the population and a rise in demand for hired labour. All wages rose despite legislation aimed at preventing this, and women's wages were included in the trend. But even in this marginal period, which in general was apparently kinder to surviving urban and rural workers than the period preceding the 1348 Plague, women's wages did not catch up with men's. The solution proposed by those of good intentions who wanted to prevent competition by cheap female labour was not to employ women. The idea of equalizing their wages to those of men occured to no one. In contrast to women who received daily, weekly, monthly or annual wages, those women who were paid by the piece for particular products (strips of woven cloth, embroidered cloth) were not deprived in comparison with men. This was particularly true in the spinning, weaving, embroidery and sewing trades, in which women specialized and where there was a demand for their labour.

Why were women excluded from some guilds? An important historian of the guilds, René de Lespinasse, has reiterated an argument also cited by historians to explain why women were burned at the stake rather than hanged, namely sexual modesty. According to him, attempts were made to keep women out of guilds mainly because the apprentices lived in the homes of artisans to mature age. For this reason a widow was forbidden to train apprentices even if she continued to work in her husband's trade. But the danger of adultery and fornication existed in the case of the artisan's wife and daughters as well, and not only that of his widow, and town craftsmen were well aware of this. An apprenticeship agreement drawn up in 1371 in the bow-makers' guild in York stipulated that if the apprentice committed adultery with the wife of the craftsman or fornicated with his daughter his years of service would be doubled. The punishment was imposed, but nobody contemplated abolishing apprenticeship. As we have already seen, the age did not always consider adultery and fornication to be the gravest of sins, and sexual modesty was neither the sole nor the dominant argument cited at the time for restricting women.

In addition to the claim that a woman was not likely to become an expert craftswoman, we also encounter the argument that certain jobs, like production of *sarrazinois* carpets for example, were too dangerous for women, and for pregnant women in particular. But it is unlikely that this was the true reason for denying the right of women to work in this trade. They often carried out arduous and very dirty tasks. The poultry slaughterers and sellers, for example, sometimes hired women to carry the innards to the walls of the town, a filthy task which involved carrying heavy weights, and no voice was raised against their employment in this work. A royal decree of Jean II of France in 1351 against idlers in Paris stated that all healthy idlers, whether male or female, who did not wish to work, should be expelled from the town. If they were caught again, they would be imprisoned; if a third time, placed in the stocks; and if a fourth time, branded on the forehead. Statutes issued in England after the Plague to establish maximum wages for workers stated that any hired worker, whether male or female, up to the age of 60 who was not working for some master must accept work offered for the wage specified in the decree. Any person of either sex who violated this decree would be punished by imprisonment. Court registers reveal that women were tried for contravening the decree, i.e. for refusing to work in return for the specified wage and taking other employment for higher wages. It seems that not only were there no objections to the work of women, not only were they obliged to work in order to support themselves or their families, but in the working classes this was in fact demanded of them by society and state. The objections to female labour arose only when their work competed with that of men and was likely to retrict male activity in that area, or when their occupation brought them status and prestige.

The well-known protectionism of the guilds intensified in the period of economic recession in the fourteenth century, although here the various regulations were not directed against women alone—for instance, the period of apprenticeship was extended. From the status of apprentice, a man rose to that of hired labourer and only after accumulating a considerable sum could he try to gain entry into a guild. Numerous regulations were passed aimed at combating foreign competition and safeguarding the rights of the sons of craftsmen; other regulations were aimed at preventing competition between craftsmen within the same guild....

But, generally speaking, women constituted a large marginal group among craftsmen; such a group, however large, could be cut, and in times of crisis it was the first to be affected. Many poor women joined Beguinages[8] in the fourteenth century precisely because the range of employment opportunities for women in the towns of Flanders and Germany was curtailed in this period. Pretexts were always found for the restrictions. Sometimes the argument was sanctimonious: women should be prevented from working too hard. Sometimes it was a new version of the classic argument of woman's incapacity, cited by jurists who wrote of feminine feebleness of mind and frivolousness. Sir John Fortescue wrote that women lacked the necessary power of concentration to conduct a business, and the authors of the guild statutes cited the inability of women to gain expertise in a craft. The factor of modesty was also sometimes mentioned.

Convincing proof that objections to female labour were voiced when it competed with specialized work which involved a respected status in society, and that the sight of a woman fulfilling a prestigious function was a thorn in their flesh, can be found in the few cases of women who practised medicine, in other words who refused to content themselves with the status of surgeon or midwife and adopted the methods of academic physicians. Throughout the Middle Ages women served as midwives both in towns and in rural areas. (In the period when witchcraft trials proliferated in the fourteenth and fifteenth centuries, some of the accused women were undoubtedly midwives and various kinds of healers who failed to cure their patients.) The daughters and widows of apothecaries and barbers often carried on the trade of their fathers and husbands. There were also female members of the guilds of surgeons, whose members were considered more respectable than barbers and who, apart from practising surgery, also healed skin ailments, swellings and sores. In order to become a surgeon, a

---

[8] A community of lay women who practiced asceticism and charitable works without taking religious vows.

man first served as an apprentice as in other guilds. They were experienced and dexterous and could almost certainly provide as much relief as academic physicians. They had their own professional pride and fought for a law to stipulate what types of injuries and sores barbers could treat, insisting that treatment of graver injuries be the monopoly of surgeons.

Royal decrees on the method of work for surgeons issued in Paris in the fourteenth century are addressed to both men and women. In some Italian towns where surgeons were under the supervision of the faculty of medicine, there were women who were licensed to practise surgery. In 1322, on the recommendation of the medical faculty of Salerno university, the court of Charles, duke of Calabria, ruled that Francesca, a married woman, was authorized to practise surgery after having been tested by the representatives of the faculty of medicine. According to the ruling not only did the law permit a woman to practise surgery, but it was even desirable, since for reasons of modesty it was preferable for women to treat women. The fact that women took their place among surgeons and apothecaries can also be learned from a document written in the thirteenth century to guide churchmen who tendered free treatment to poor patients who could not afford the services of academic physicians or even surgeons. The author of the book writes that he collected some of the prescriptions in his book from a woman surgeon and from a female apothecary, the daughter of an apothecary.

Nevertheless women were not permitted to practise as academic physicians. As the universities developed, medical knowledge became an academic subject, but universities remained closed to women, and their medical faculties jealously guarded their privileges. They issued regulations aimed at protecting the monopoly of their graduates and, on their initiative, various rulers forbade the practice of academic medicine by any person who had not studied at a medical faculty and been licensed by its teachers. These regulations and decrees were directed against all those who were likely to practise medicine; barbers, apothecaries and surgeons, both male and female.

It transpires that just as there were men who tried to evade the regulations and to practise medicine without being qualified, so there were women. Of particular interest is the story of a woman named Jacoba, who was tried in 1322 in Paris for practising medicine. According to the indictment she visited, examined and treated her patients in the manner of academic physicians: she took the pulse, tested the urine, let blood, prescribed medicines and purgatives and hot baths. All this she did without being qualified and without receiving a licence from the faculty of medicine. The gravest misdemeanour appears to have been the fact that she examined urine and measured the pulse—a method of diagnosis which was the source of pride and distinguishing feature of academic physicians. All the patients who were summoned to testify spoke in her defence: they praised her dedication and said that in contrast to prevailing custom, she did not demand payment in advance but only after having cured the patient; all of them emphasized that she succeeded where others had failed in curing them. The witnesses for the defence included both men and women.

Jacoba herself pleaded in her defence that the decree banning women from practising medicine had been issued only once, and that before she was born. The decree had been aimed at ignorant women, inexperienced in medicine, and she could not be considered as such since she was skilled in medical science. She also pleaded that it was desirable for women to treat women. Though it could be argued that by the same token it was wrong for a woman to treat men, as she had in fact done, since she had succeeded in healing them this could only be considered a secondary evil. It had prevented the greater evil of the death of patients whom other physicians had not succeeded in curing. But her plea fell on deaf ears. Jacoba was prohibited from continuing to practise medicine and was fined. It seems likely that she paid the fine and returned to her former practice, as she had done on a previous occasion.

Like Jacoba, several other women were tried for practising medicine without a permit: Clarice de Rotmago, a married woman; Johanna the convert; Marguerite of Ypres, the surgeon; and Belota the Jewess. They were excommunicated and fined. These women constituted interesting exceptions to the rule. In general, however, medicine like the other academic occupations which were practised by part of the new urban aristocracy—notaries, lawyers and judges—was closed to women. The criterion for granting the right to practise medicine was not skill or success in treatment but academic study and licensing by the faculty. In the indictment against Jacoba, her accusers did not confine themselves to accusing her of practising medicine without a licence (a crime of which men too could have been accused). They added that women, who were banned from becoming lawyers and giving evidence in criminal trials, should most certainly be banned from treating the sick and prescribing potions and medicines, since the hazards were much greater than those of losing a trial because of ignorance of the law. There can be no doubt that greater opportunities had been open to women in early periods, when certain activities were not yet defined and institutionalized, in marginal periods and even in periods of crisis. Those periods of institutionalization were detrimental to women, and the history of medicine is an example of this.

Maid-Servants

While women were deprived of the opportunity of engaging in more respected occupations, very many of them belonged to the servant class, the lowest of the urban labouring classes. The authors of the literature of the estates, who often glossed over the role of women in urban labour, thought it necessary to classify maid-servants as a separate subclass. Zita of Lucca, who went into service when she was 12 years old and had been a maid-servant in the same household all her life, became the patron saint of servant girls. She is usually depicted with a bunch of keys in her hand. Albert Memmi, in his book *L'Homme Dominé*, devoted a chapter to women and one to servants. Many women in the Middle Ages, as in later periods, were subjects twice over—as women and as servants.

The number of servants in towns was particularly great. Wages were relatively low, and hence even craftsmen kept servants. In the homes of the great burghers and the nobles there were often dozens of servants. Maid-servants did not appear in the lists of taxpayers because they were too poor to pay the poll-tax, and since they lived in the homes of their employers they were not liable to the payment imposed on the household (*festum*). There can be no doubt that one of the reasons for the large number of women in European towns in the later Middle Ages was the large number of girls who migrated to towns from nearby rural areas to work as servants. Sometimes a girl and a man would arrive in town together to seek their fortune. The Paris court register records such a case. Shortly after the couple arrived in town the girl was abandoned by the man and became a maid-servant. Some time later she married, was later tried for witchcraft, admitted having bewitched her husband and caused him to fall sick, and was executed. Did she really try to harm the man she had married, or was she tortured so cruelly that she was willing to admit to anything? We have no way of knowing the answer.

In his manual of guidance, the Goodman of Paris explains to his young wife in detail how to supervise her maid-servants in the execution of the various household chores. In the burgher household, as in the castle, numerous chores were carried out apart from cleaning, cooking and baking. The war against flies, lice and cockroaches was also no easy task (the Goodman goes into detail on this matter). Some maid-servants tended the domestic animals, cows and pigs. In large towns there was a special mediator (*recomandresse*) who mediated between the maid-servants and the employers and received payment from both parties for her services. In 1350, when the maximum wage for workers in various occupations was fixed in France, the list included the maximum sum to be paid to the *recomandresse* by both sides (1 sou (shilling) and 6 deniers (pence) for a maid-servant, 2 sous for a wet-nurse), and various maximum wages per annum for maid-servants and wet-nurses. The maximum annual wage for a maid-servant who worked only in the house was 30 sous; for a servant who also tended the cattle and pigs, 50 sous; for a wet-nurse 50 sous, and if she kept the child in her own home, 100 sous.

The wage of the servant woman was low compared to that of most urban workers but higher than that of most agricultural labourers. Since she ate at her master's table and lived in his house, she was probably able to save up a dowry within a few years. Withholding of payment was known in medieval towns as it was in later periods, and servants were sometimes forced to sue their employers. The wet-nurses of the children of great lords received higher wages than were stipulated in the regulations, as did some of the nurses in burgher families.

The authors of didactic works directed advice at servant women, stressing their obligation to work devotedly and to act properly (a servant woman should not ape her mistress etc.). Many servant women were young and the Paris Goodman writes of the frivolity and inexperience of servant girls aged 15-20. He also advises his young wife on how to choose a servant woman and how to supervise her work and conduct in general: before she hires a maid she should find out where the woman worked previously, and ascertain from her last mistress whether she was a drunkard or chatterer or had lost her virtue, for which reason she had been obliged to leave her last place of employment. She should clarify and write in the presence of the servant all details about her: name, place of birth, place of residence of her relatives. If the servant woman knew that all these facts were known, she would hesitate to commit a crime or to run away. The mistress should shun the impudent or servile maid but the shy and obedient one should be treated like a daughter.

The younger maid-servants should be housed near the room of the mistress, in a room which did not have a window facing the street. They should rise and retire at the same hour as their mistress as an additional means of keeping them out of mischief. If a serving man or woman fell sick, the mistress herself should nurse them with care and compassion. In good times they deserved good food and drink in sufficient quantities, but they should not be given expensive meat or intoxicating liquor. Some employers left bequests to the maid-servants who worked in their homes as well as to their men servants. Despite the simple and humane advice of the old Goodman, it may be assumed that some of the emotional distortions which characterized maid-mistress relations in later periods and which derived from excessive intimacy, dependence (sometimes mutual), humiliation and hostility were present in this period as well.

Prostitutes

Like maid-servants, prostitutes were also recognized as a separate 'socio-professional' class. This ancient occupation existed in the Middle Ages before the great expansion of the towns, and there was also prostitution in rural areas. In towns it became a profession like any other.

The attitude to prostitution in the Central and Later Middle Ages was undoubtedly determined to a large extent by the stand of the Church Fathers in the first centuries of Christianity. St Augustine wrote: 'If you expel prostitutes from society, prostitution will spread everywhere ... the prostitutes in town are like sewers in the palace. If you take away the sewers, the whole palace will be filthy.' Here we see the expression of the view that prostitution plays a certain part in Christian society and is preferable to the general spread of licentiousness. It is better for a man to make use of the services of a prostitute than to maintain relations outside wedlock with married women or to seduce virgins. Prostitution is a check on adultery and fornication, but its role is like that of a sewage pipe. The prostitute is a contemptible creature not because she poses as a loving woman and has sexual relations with men in return for financial reward, but because her entire life is devoted to the lusts of the flesh (*luxuria*), which are the prime sin. A thirteenth-century preacher adds: The sin of the prostitute is one of those sins which do not cause harm to the sinner herself alone but to others; not only to the property or the body of others but to their souls.

Essentially loyal to St Augustine's stand, medieval society permitted prostitution, but regarded it as a despicable and inferior occupation. Since it was permitted, it was official and legal. Since it was considered despicable and sinful, those who engaged in it were subjected to humiliating laws. This was clearly expressed in the legislation of Frederick II for Sicily. A woman who placed her body on sale should not be charged with fornication. We forbid any act of violence against her and forbid her to live among decent women.

The supply of and demand for prostitution were great. Apart from the married men who utilized the services of prostitutes, many men never married at all, or were forced to delay marriage for many years after attaining adulthood, while others lived in towns apart from their wives for lengthy periods. Secular churchmen who did not marry frequented prostitutes, as can be learned from the oft-reiterated regulations banning acceptance of churchmen as clients of brothels (and forbidding monks to bring prostitutes into monasteries). Students in university towns were among the most frequent customers of prostitutes.

The apprentices of artisans and the journeymen were obliged to postpone matrimony until they could open their own workshops. Many members of the prosperous burgher class also delayed marriage until they were financially settled or until they found a suitable match which could further their ambitions. Apart from these permanent town-dwellers who visited prostitutes, there were many men who visited towns for short periods: merchants, pilgrims, people who were sentenced to banishment from their own towns, wandering minstrels, jesters, vagabonds. The farmers who came to town to sell their produce would seize the opportunity to visit brothels. To the prostitutes who worked in towns and those who visited monasteries one should add the camp followers and those who flocked to places of assembly on special occasions, such as the markets, fairs and church councils!

As regards supply, women apparently turned to prostitution in the Central and Later Middle Ages for the selfsame reasons for which they have done so in other societies at other times: casual external circumstances, economic factors, emotional reasons deriving from childhood experience, and certainly natural proclivities. As regards the economic factor, it is interesting to note the comment of the Chevalier de La Tour Landry in his manual of guidance for his daughters. He wrote that noblewomen who had a source of income and who engaged in relations with a lover (either a married man, a priest, or a serving man) were several times worse than prostitutes. Many prostitutes had become what they were because of poverty or deprivation or the cunning of their pimps, while noblewomen sinned out of carnal lust alone. There are known cases of prostitutes who were connected with pimps who lured them into prostitution and sometimes also supplied their clients. A considerable part of their income was handed over to these pimps, who terrorized them. Apart from the professionals, unmarried women from the urban labouring class who did not reside with families also engaged in prostitution. Their virtue was suspect from the outset, sometimes justifiably and sometimes without cause. Some married women regarded prostitution as an additional source of income.

The economic recession in the fourteenth century reduced neither the supply of nor the demand for prostitutes in proportion to the size of the population. The opposite was probably true. Women were among the first to be affected by the exclusiveness of the guilds, and while this led many of them, as we have seen, to join Beguinages, others undoubtedly turned to prostitution. Many of those who survived the Plague were better off financially than before, and in the atmosphere of fear of death and 'eat, drink and be merry' which characterized the fourteenth century, the demand for prostitution increased. A woman became a prostitute of her own free will, and no person had the right to incarcerate her in a brothel against her wishes, at least not according to the law. And there were some women who found refuge in the special homes for repentant prostitutes or in the nunneries which cared for such women. (These homes were usually named after Mary Magdalene, the spiritual mother of all repentant sinners.)

In Italian and French towns there were official brothels in the twelfth century, and they are also recorded in England, Germany and Spain from the thirteenth century on. Since prostitution was not considered fornication or adultery in the accepted meaning of the terms, it was the concern, not of ecclesiastical courts but of urban tribunals. The desire to defend prostitutes is clearly evident in Frederick II's legislation, which laid down the death penalty for rape of a prostitute, as for any other type of rape. The urban authorities, through the supervision of brothels, kept a watch on prostitutes and extracted taxes from them for their own benefit or for the seigneur of the town. (These seigneurs included churchmen like the bishop of Mainz, who complained in 1422 that the citizens of the town were trying to rob him of this income which had always been due to the seigneur ...) They also determined which streets were permitted for their activity. The official brothels were run according to fixed and official regulations. The institutional and official character of prostitution found expression also in Church decrees which stated that it was forbidden to bar a prostitute from attending church on Sundays or Christian feast-days. Prostitutes had their own patron saints (usually repentant prostitutes who had become nuns and saints) like other fraternities organized for religious purposes. There is insufficient evidence in the sources to support the theory that the prostitutes were organized in guilds like other occupations, which had their own regulations, decrees and judges.

Together with recognition and defence of the rights of prostitutes, there were segregationist laws aimed at emphasizing their inferior and despised status. This was reflected first of all in the location of the brothels. The marginal groups and the inferior population groups lived on the outskirts of towns under the walls either inside or outside by the gates, and these areas were also earmarked for the brothels. But in most towns the municipal authorities were forced to recognize additional quarters as permissible areas for the activities of prostitutes. The charters granted by the lords of towns to citizens who wished to set up brothels, and the municipal regulations, reiterate the ban on establishing brothels and soliciting outside the permitted area.

The fact that prostitutes were confined to certain streets undoubtedly reflected the desire to set them apart from all other citizens, but it also expressed the view of prostitution as a profession. Other professions were also concentrated in special streets where artisans displayed their wares, and some authors went so far as to evaluate prostitution as a profession. Thomas Cobham, who composed a manual for confessors in the twelfth century, writes:

> Prostitutes should be counted among the wage-earners. They hire out their bodies and supply labour. It is wrong for a woman to be a prostitute but if she is such, it is not wrong for her to receive a wage. But if she prostitutes herself for pleasure and hires out her body for this purpose, then the wage is as evil as the act itself.

Successful prostitutes rented houses or even owned them. The poorer ones received their clients in the recognized brothels. But despite the regulations it was undoubtedly impossible to confine the prostitutes totally to the permitted houses in approved areas. They solicited customers in the taverns, the bathhouses and the town square, and received their clients in their own homes and in hotels, while the poorest and most degraded worked under the bridges and city walls. Sometimes men or women kept brothels under the guise of workshops, like the procuress in London who ran a brothel camouflaged as an embroidery workshop and supplied girls to all comers and particularly to churchmen. She was punished by being sentenced to the stocks and to banishment from the city.

In addition to being confined to special locations, the prostitutes were ordered to wear distinguishing clothing. They were required to wear eye-catching items of clothing such as red hats, ribbons on the sleeves or sleeves of contrasting colour to their robes. They were forbidden to wear quilted or fur-lined garments like those of noble ladies. The tightening of these regulations reflected a severe attitude, and prostitutes sometimes appealed for permission to tone down these distinguishing signs and to wear the latest fashions. The prostitutes' violations of the regulations were a source of income for the town coffers. Transgressors were fined and their garments confiscated. The costliness of the confiscated items indicates the income and high standard of living of the successful prostitutes. Among the items mentioned are silver jewels, precious stones worn as buttons, and fur garments. Their clothing was an outward expression not only of feminine love of adornment but also of their desire to compensate themselves by lavish display for their inferior status. Sometimes the municipal authorities did not confine themselves to restricting the locations for prostitution or forcing prostitutes to wear distinguishing garments. In Avignon in the mid-thirteenth century, for example, Jews and prostitutes were forbidden to touch bread and fruit set out on display. They were obliged to buy whatever they handled. The Church did not ban prostitutes from attending services, but allotted them special seats.

The most persecuted and humiliated element were the poorer prostitutes who did not work in recognized brothels and were often banished from towns. They formed part of the marginal groups of urban society, the vagabonds, beggars, and criminals, and as court registers show, they were often involved in assault and thievery. Like the other outcasts of medieval society, beggars, criminals and lepers, the prostitutes—probably the poorest and most unorganized among them—were often won over by the religious fervour of individuals or movements. They flocked to the sermons of Robert of Arbrissel in Anjou in the late eleventh century and repented their sins. But the periods of religious fervour, marked by zealous endeavour to reform the world in the spirit of Christianity, were also times of maximum pressure on the degradation of prostitutes. This was true of the activities of the Mendicants in the towns of Lombardy in 1233 and in the days of Louis IX in France, as well as under the Hussites in Prague. Prostitutes suffered, as did heretics, homosexuals and Jews. In general however the attitude to prostitutes in the Middle Ages was undoubtedly better than in the sixteenth and seventeenth centuries, when royal absolutism (which inherited some of the powers of the towns and corporations), the Reformation and the Catholic Counter-Reformation, and fear of venereal disease combined to intensify oppression of prostitutes and render attitudes towards them increasingly hypocritical.

Bibliography

GENE BRUCKER, ed., *The Society of Renaissance Florence* (1971).
JAMES A. BRUNDAGE, "Carnal Delight: Canonistic Theories of Sexuality," in *Proceedings of the Fifth International Congress of Medieval Canon Law, Salamanca, September 1976*, ed. STEPHAN KUTTNER and KENNETH PENNINGTON (1980), pp. 361–385.

J. HAJNAL, "European Marriage Patterns in Perspective," in D. V. GLASS and D. E. L. EVERSLEY, *Population in History: Essays in Historical Demography* (1965), pp. 101–146.

DAVID HERLIHY, *Medieval and Renaissance Pistoia* (1957).

ROBERT LERNER, *The Heresy of the Free Spirit in the Later Middle Ages* (1972).

E. W. MCDONNELL, *The Beguines and Beghards in Medieval Culture* (1969).

E. MCLEOD, *The Order of the Rose: The Life and Ideas of Christine de Pisan* (1975).

R. RAZI, *Life, Marriage and Death in a Medieval Parish: Economy, Society and Demography in Halesowen 1270–1400* (1980).

DONALD WEINSTEIN and RUDOLPH M. BELL, *Saints and Society: The Two Worlds of Western Christendom, 1000–17000* (1982).

Medieval Children

DAVID HERLIHY

Did medieval parents consider childhood a special, separate stage of life or did they treat their children as little adults? One thing is clear: attitudes toward children evolved during the Middle Ages. Among ancient Romans, family size was deliberately kept small by exposing unwanted children; however, special attention was bestowed upon surviving children. By contrast, the Germanic tribes that invaded the West in the fifth century had large families, but raised their children more casually, with little affection by modern standards. Low WERGILDS (fines levied for injury or death to a person) and the underreporting of children in censuses of manors suggest a low economic valuation of children. Wergilds rose dramatically between infancy and adulthood. A man's wergild, for example, increased five-fold between infancy and age thirty, a suggestion of the different worth to society of an able-bodied man and an infant. The wergild for a female child under fifteen was half as much as for a male child, but it increased eight-fold between infancy and a woman's child-bearing years.

Between the late eleventh and fifteenth centuries, the social and psychological investments in children increased markedly. They can be measured in large cities like Florence and Rome by increased vocational training for children, the growth of schools, orphanages, and hospitals, rising concern about health and hygiene, and even the new cult of the Christ-child. By the end of the Middle Ages childhood had become a clear and special stage of life.

In a fourteenth-century French poem, one of numerous surviving depictions of the danse macabre, the grim choreographer invites a baby to join his somber revels. "Ah, ah, ah," protests the infant, "I do not know how to speak; I am a baby, and my tongue is mute. Yesterday I was born, and today I must depart. I do no more than come and go."

Reprinted with the permission of the Webb Lecture Committee from "Medieval Children," by David Herlihy, in *Essays on Medieval Civilization*, B. K. Lackner and K. R. Phelp, eds. Copyright © 1978 by the University of Texas at Arlington.

Many, perhaps most, children in most traditional societies did no more than come and go. And most never acquired, or were given, a voice which might have recorded and preserved their impressions concerning themselves, their parents, and the world they had recently discovered. Of all social groups which formed the societies of the past, children, seldom seen and rarely heard in the documents, remain for historians the most elusive, the most obscure.

The difficulties of interviewing the mute have doubtlessly obstructed and delayed a systematic investigation of the history of childhood. But today, at least, historians are aware of the commonplace assumption of psychologists, that childhood plays a critical role in the formation of the adult personality. Perhaps they are awakening to an even older wisdom, the recognition that society, in the way it rears its children, shapes itself. "Childhood is the foundation of life," wrote Philippe of Navarre, the thirteenth-century lawyer and chronicler, "and on good foundations one can raise great and good buildings." This medieval man already sensed that the foundations of childhood help shape and support the structures of civilization.

Today, the literature devoted to the history of children in various places and epochs may be described, rather like children themselves, as small but growing daily. It remains, however, difficult to discern within that literature a clear consensus, an acceptable hypothesis, concerning the broad trends of children's history, even within Western societies. To be sure, there is frequent allusion within these recent publications to a particular interpretation which, for want of a better name, we shall call the "theory of discovered childhood." The principal formulator of this interpretation, at least in its most recent form, has been the French social historian Philippe Ariès. In a book published in 1960, called in its English translation *Centuries of Childhood*, Ariès entitled the second chapter "the discovery of childhood." In it he affirmed that the Middle Ages of Western history did not recognize childhood as a distinct phase in life. Medieval people allegedly viewed and treated their children as imperfectly formed adults. Once the infant was weaned, medieval parents supposedly made no concessions to its special and changing psychological needs and took little satisfaction in the distinctive traits of the young personality. The corollary to this assumption is that, at some point in the development of Western society and civilization, the young years of life were at last discovered: childhood needed a Columbus.

Proclamations of the alleged discovery of childhood have become commonplace in the growing literature, but wide differences in interpretation still separate the authors. When, for example, was childhood first recognized? On this important question, Ariès himself is indefinite, even evasive, and seems to place the discovery over three or four hundred years, from the fifteenth to the eighteenth centuries. A recent collection of essays, edited by Lloyd de Mause and published in 1974 under the title *The History of Childhood*, proposes several candidates, in several periods, for the honor of having first explored childhood in the Western world. M. J. Tucker, writing on English children between the years 1399 and 1603, begins his chapter with the now orthodox affirmation: "the medieval idea that children were not terribly important persists into the fifteenth century." In the conclusion of the chapter, adopting the interpretation of Ivy Pinchbek and Margaret Hewitt, he declares: "a new consciousness of childhood was beginning." Later in the same volume, Priscilla Robertson selects Jean Jacques Rousseau as the first advertiser of childhood: "special credit must go to Rousseau for calling attention to the needs of children. For the first time in history, he made a large group of people believe that childhood was worth the attention of adults, encouraging an interest in the process of growing up rather than just the product."

The editor of this collection of studies, Lloyd de Mause, presents still another view of the emerging consciousness of childhood. A devout believer in the idea of continuous and irreversible progress, De Mause traces the evolution in child-parent or child-mother relations through six styles of behavior, or psychogenic modes as he calls them: the infanticidal in the ancient world; abandonment in the Middle Ages; the ambivalent, intrusive, and socialization modes across the succeeding centuries; and now, at the term of this evolution, the helping mode. The helping mode "involves the proposition that the child knows better than the parent what it needs at each stage of its life." Parents who help the child attain what he wants will render him "gentle, sincere, never depressed, never imitative or group-oriented, strong-willed, and unintimidated by authority." According to De Mause, the full discovery of childhood and the full recognition across society of its special nature and distinctive needs are only now occurring.

If historians of the modern world do not agree concerning the date of childhood's discovery, their colleagues, working in more remote periods, show signs of restiveness with Ariès' postulate, that medieval people did not distinguish children from adults. A number of scholars—Christian Bec, Christiane Klapisch, Richard Goldthwaite, among others—have noted among the pedagogues, humanists, and even artists of fifteenth-century Italy a new orientation toward children, a new awareness of their problems, and an appreciation of their qualities. The fat and frolicksome babies, the *putti*, who cavort through many solemn paintings of the Italian Renaissance, leave little doubt that the artists of the epoch knew how to depict, and they or their patrons liked to contemplate, children. A still more radical departure from Ariès' views was proposed, in 1968, by the French medievalist Pierre Riché. Riché accepted Ariès' phrase, the "discovery of childhood," but radically changed his chronology. The initial explorers of childhood were, for Riché, the monastic pedagogues active in Western Europe between the sixth and eighth centuries. Their sensitivity toward the psychology of children allegedly transformed the harsh educational methods of classical antiquity and developed a new pedagogy which was finely attuned to the personality of the child-monk. Thus, over an extended period of time, from the early, Middle Ages until the present, one or another author would have us believe that a consciousness of childhood was at last emerging.

The lessons that I would draw from this confusion of learned opinions are the following. Historians would be well advised to avoid such categoric and dubious claims, that people in certain periods failed to distinguish children from adults, that childhood really did lie beyond the pale of collective consciousness. Attitudes toward children have certainly shifted, as has the willingness on the part of society to invest substantially in their welfare or education. But to describe these changes, we need terms more refined than metaphors of ignorance and discovery. I would propose that we seek to evaluate, and on occasion even to measure, the psychological and economic investment which families and societies in the past were willing to make in their children. However, we ought also to recognize that alternative and even competitive sets of child-related values can coexist in the same society, perhaps even in the same household. Different social groups and classes expect different things from their children; so do different epochs, in accordance with prevailing economic, social, and demographic conditions. In examining the ways in which children were regarded and reared in the past, we should not expect either rigorous consistency across society or lineal progress over time.

In the current, lively efforts to reconstruct the history of children in Western civilization, the long period of the Middle Ages has a special importance. The medieval child represents a kind of primordial form, an "eo-pais," a "dawn child" as it were, against whom Western children of subsequent epochs must be measured if we are to appreciate the changes they have experienced. To be sure, the difficulties of observing medieval children cannot be discounted. Medieval documentation is usually sparse, often inconsistent, and always difficult. The halls of medieval history, running across one thousand years, are filled with lights and shadows. The shadows are particularly murky when they enclose those who "do no more than come and go." We can hope to catch only fleeting glimpses of medieval children in their rush through, or out of, life. On the other hand, even glimpses may be enough to dispell some large misconceptions concerning medieval children and to aid us toward a sound reconstruction of the history of children in the Western world.

In surveying medieval children, it is first necessary to consider the two prior traditions which largely shaped the medieval appraisal of the very young—the classical and the barbarian. It is important also to reflect upon the influence exerted upon child rearing by a special component of the ancient Mediterranean heritage: the Christian church.

Classical society, or at least the elites within it, cultivated an impressive array of intellectual traditions, which were founded upon literacy and preserved over time through intensive, and expensive, educational methods. Classical civilization would be inconceivable in the absence of professional teachers, formal instruction, and numerous schools and academies. But as social historians of antiquity now emphasize, the resources that supported ancient society were in truth scant. "The classical Mediterranean has always been a world on the edge of starvation," one historian has recently written, with much justice if perhaps some exaggeration." Scarce resources and the high costs of rearing children helped form certain distinctive policies regarding the young. The nations which comprised the Roman Empire, with the exception only of the Jews, refused to support deformed, unpromising, or supernumerary babies. In Roman practice, for example, the new, born baby was at once laid before the feet of him who held the *patria potestas* [paternal power] over it, usually the natural father. Through a ritual gesture called *susceptio* [the taking in hand] the holder of paternal authority might raise up the infant and receive it into his family and household. But he could also reject the baby and order its exposure. Infanticide, or the exposure of infants, was a common and accepted social practice in classical society, shocking perhaps to modern sensibilities but rational for these ancient peoples who were seeking to achieve goals with limited means.

Here however is a paradox. Widespread infanticide in ancient society does not imply disinterest in or neglect of those children elected for survival. On the contrary, to assure a good return on the precious means invested in them, they were subject to close and often cruel attention and to frequent beatings. St. Augustine in his *Confessions* tells how his father, Patricius, and even his pious mother, Monica, urged him to high performance at school, "that I might get on in the world and excel in the handling of words, to gain honor among men and deceitful riches. "If I proved idle in learning," he says of his teachers, "I was soundly beaten. For this procedure seemed wise to our ancestors; and many, passing the same way in the days past, had built a sorrowful road, by which we too must go, with multiplication of grief and toil upon the sons of Adam. "The memories which the men of antiquity preserved of their childhood were understandably bleak. "Who would not shudder," Augustine exclaims in the *City of God*, "if he were given the choice of eternal death or life again as a child? Who would not choose to die?"

The barbarian child grew up under quite different circumstances. Moreover, barbarian practices of child rearing seem to have been particularly influential in the society of early medieval Europe, between the fifth and eleventh centuries. This is not surprising. Early in the Middle Ages, the cities which had dominated society and culture in antiquity lost importance, the literate social elites of classical society all but disappeared, and their educational institutions and ideals went down amid the debacle of the Western empire. On the other hand, barbarian practices were easily preserved within, and congenial to, the semibarbarized society of the early medieval West.

In a tract called *Germania*, written in A.D. 98, the Roman historian Tacitus has described for us the customs of the barbarian Germans, including their treatment of children. Tacitus, to be sure, likes to contrast barbarian virtues with Roman vices and doubtlessly exaggerates in his depictions of both, but his words are nonetheless worth our attention. The Germans, he claims, did not, like the Romans, kill their supernumerary children. Rather, the barbarians rejoiced in a numerous progeny. Moreover, the barbarian mother, unlike her Roman counterpart, nursed her own baby and did not hand it over for feeding to servants or a hired nurse. On the other hand, Tacitus notes, the barbarian parents paid little attention to their growing children. "In every household," he writes, "the children grow up naked and unkempt..." "The lord and slave," he continues, "are in no way to be distinguished by the delicacy of their bringing up. They live among the same flocks, they lie on the same ground..." Barbarian culture did not depend for its survival on the costly instruction of the young in complex skills and learned traditions; barbarian parents had no need to invest heavily in their children, either psychologically or materially. The cheap costs of child rearing precluded the adoption of infanticide as standard social policy but also reduced the attention which the growing child received from its parents. Only on the threshold of adulthood did the free German male re-establish close contacts with adult society. He typically joined the following of a mature warrior, accompanied him into battle, observed him, and gained some instruction in the arts of war, which, like the arts of rhetoric in the classical world, were the key to his social advance.

A casual attitude toward children seems embodied in the laws of the barbarian peoples—Franks, Lombards, Visigoths, Anglo-Saxons, and others—which were redacted into Latin largely between the sixth and the ninth centuries. The barbarian laws typically assigned to each member of society a sum of money—a fine, or wergeld—which would have to be paid to the relatives if he or she was injured or killed. The size of the wergeld thus provides a crude measure of social status or importance. One of the barbarian codes, the Visigothic, dating from the middle seventh century, gives a particularly detailed and instructive table of values which shows how the worth of a person varied according to age, sex, and status. A free male baby, in the first year of life, was assigned a wergeld of 60 solidi. Between age 1 and age 9, his social worth increased at an average rate of only 3.75 solidi per year, thus attaining the value of 90 solidi in the tenth year of life. Between ages 10 and 15, the rate of increase accelerated to 10 solidi per year; and between ages 15 and 20 it grew still more, to 30 solidi per year. In other words, the social worth of the free Visigothic male increased very slowly in the early years of childhood, accelerated in early adolescence, and grew most substantially in the years preceding full maturity. Considered mature at age 20, he enjoyed a wergeld of 300 solidi—five times the worth of the newborn male infant—and this he retained until age 50. In old age, his social worth declined, to 200 solidi between ages 50 and 65 and to 100 solidi from age 65 to death. The old man, beyond age 65, was worth the same as a child of ten years.

The contrast between the worth of the child and the worth of the adult is particularly striking in regard to women. Among the Visigoths, a female under age 15 was assigned only one-half the wergeld enjoyed by males—only 30 solidi during her first year of life. Her social worth, however, increased enormously when she entered the years of child-bearing, between ages 15 and 40 in the Visigothic codes. Her wergeld then leaped to 250 solidi, nearly equal to the 300 solidi assigned to the male and eight times the value of the newborn baby girl. The sterile years of old age brought a reduction of the fine, first to 200 solidi, which she retained to age 60, and then to 100 solidi. In old age, she was assigned the same worth as the male.

The contrasts in the social worth of the female child and the female adult are also sharp in the laws of Salian and Ripuarian Franks. The wergeld of the free woman was tripled during her years of childbearing, when she was also considered worth three times the free male.

The low values assigned to children in these barbarian codes is puzzling. Did the lawgivers not realize that the supply of adults, including the especially valued childbearing women, was critically dependent on the protection of children? This obvious truth seemingly escaped the notice of the barbarian lawgivers; children, and their relation to society, did not loom large in their consciousness.

Apart from laws, one other source offers some insight into the treatment of children in the early Middle Ages: surveys of the population settled on particular estates and manors. These sporadic surveys have survived from the Carolingian period of medieval history, the late eighth and ninth centuries. The largest of them, redacted in the first quarter of the ninth century, lists nearly 2,000 families settled on the lands of the abbey of Saint-Germain-des-Prés near Paris. The survey gives no exact ages, but of 8,457 persons included in it, 3,327 are explicitly identified as *infantes*, or children. Another 3,924 may be certainly regarded as adults, as they appear in the survey with a spouse or with offspring. Some 1,206 other persons cannot be classified by age: they are offspring not expressly called *infantes* or persons of uncertain age or status within the households.

The proportion of known children within the population is very low—only 85 children for every 100 adults. Even if all those of uncertain age are considered *infantes*, the ratio then becomes 116 children for every 100 adults. This peasant population was either singularly barren or it was not bothering to report all its children. Moreover, the sexual composition of the population across these age categories is perplexing. Among the known adults, men and women appear in nearly equal numbers. But among the known children, there are 143 boys for every 100 girls—a male-to-female ratio of nearly three to two. Among those of uncertain age, the sex ratio is even higher. The high sex ratio among the known children may indicate widespread female infanticide, but if this were so, we should expect to find a similarly skewed ratio among the known adults. The death of numerous baby girls inevitably would affect over time the proportions of adult women in this presumably closed population. But the proportions of males and females among the known adults were reasonably balanced. The more likely explanation is that the monastic surveyors, or the peasants who reported to them, were negligent in counting children and were particularly deficient in reporting the presence of little girls in the households. As the barbarian legal codes suggest, children, and especially girls, became of substantial interest to society, and presumably to their families, only as they aged.

The low monetary worth assigned to the very young, and the shadowy presence of children in the statistical documents of the early Middle Ages, should not, however, imply that parents did not love their children. Tacitus notes that the barbarian mother usually nursed her own babies. Kinship ties were strongly emphasized in barbarian society, and these were surely cemented by affection. The German epic fragment the *Song of Hildebrand* takes as its principal theme the love which should unite father and son. The warrior Hildebrand flees into exile to live among the Huns, leaving "a babe at the breast in the bower of the bride." Then, after sixty years of wandering, he confronts his son as his enemy on the field of battle. He recognizes his offspring and tries to avoid combat; he offers the young warrior gold and, as the poet tells us, his love besides. But Hadubrand refuses to believe that the old warrior he faces is truly his father. The conclusion of the poem is lost, but the mood portends tragedy. The poet plays upon the irony that Hildebrand dearly loves his son but has been absent from his life for sixty years. The German warrior might have had difficulty recognizing his children, but he still felt affection for them. If classical methods of child rearing can be called cruel but closely attentive, the barbarian child grew up within an atmosphere of affectionate neglect.

The Christian church also powerfully influenced the treatment of children in many complex ways. Christianity, like Judaism before it, unequivocally condemned infanticide or the exposure of infants. To be sure, infanticide and exposure remained common social practices in Western Europe across the entire length of the Middle Ages. Church councils, penitentials, sermons, and secular legal codes yield abundant and repeated references to those crimes. As late as the fifteenth century, if we are to believe the great popular preachers of the period, the streams and cesspools of Europe echoed with the cries of abandoned babies. But medieval infanticides still shows one great difference from the comparable practice in the ancient world. Our sources consistently attribute the practice to two motivations: the shame of seduced and abandoned women, who wished to conceal illegitimate births, and poverty—the inability of the mother, and often of both parents, to support an additional mouth. The killing or abandonment of babies in medieval society was the characteristic resort of the fallen, the poor, the desperate. In the ancient world, infanticide had been accepted practice, even among the social elites.

Christian teachings also informed and softened attitudes toward children. Christian scriptures held out several exmples of children who enjoyed or earned God's special favor: in the Old Testament, the young Samuel and the young Daniel; in the New, the Holy Innocents and the Christ child himself. According to the evangelists, Jesus himself welcomed the company of children, and he instructed his disciples in the famous words: "Unless you become as little children, you will never enter the Kingdom of Heaven."

This partiality toward children evoked many echoes among patristic and medieval writers. In a poem attributed to St. Clement of Alexandria, Christ is called the "king of children." Pope Leo the Great writes in the fourth century: "Christ loves childhood, for it is the teacher of humility, the rule of innocence, the model of sweetness." Christ's love for children seems to have given them occasional unexpected prominence even in the religious wars of the epoch. Already in the Merovingian period, an account of a saint's life tells the story of Lupus, Bishop of Troyes in northern France, and his efforts to defend his community against Attila the Hun. An angel instructs the bishop in a dream to recruit twelve little boys, baptize them, and march forth from the city, singing psalms, to confront the dread chieftain. The bishop and his youthful companions are martyred, but their sacrifice saves the city. It is easy to see, in this curious incident, the same sentiments which, later in the Middle Ages, at times made Crusaders out of children.

A favorable appraisal of childhood is also apparent in the monastic culture of the early Middle Ages. Western monasteries, from the sixth century, accepted as oblates to the monastic life children who were hardly more than toddlers, and the leaders of the monastic movement gave much attention to the proper methods of rearing and instructing these miniature monks. In his famous rule, St. Benedict of Nursia insisted that the advice of the children be sought in important matters, "for often the Lord reveals to the young what should be done." St. Columban in the seventh century, and the Venerable Bede in the eighth, praised four qualities of the monastic child: he does not persist in anger; he does not bear a grudge; he takes no delight in the beauty of women; and he expresses what he truly believes.

But alongside this positive assessment of the very young, Christian tradition supported a much harsher appraisal of the nature of the child. In Christian belief, the dire results of Adam's fall were visited upon all his descendants. All persons, when they entered the world, bore the stain of original sin and with it concupiscence, an irrepressible appetite for evil. Moreover, if God had predestined some persons to salvation and some to damnation, his judgments touched even the very young, even those who died before they knew their eternal options. The father of the Church who most forcefully and effectively explored the implications of predestination for children was again St. Augustine. Voluminous in his writings, clear in his logics, and ruthless in his conclusions, Augustine finally decided, after some early doubts, that the baby who died without baptism was damned to eternal fires. There were heaven and hell and no place in-between. If you admit that the little one cannot enter heaven," he argued, "then you concede that he will be in everlasting fire."

This cruel judgment of the great African theologian contrasts with the milder views of the Eastern fathers, who affirmed that unbaptized children suffer only the loss of the vision of God. The behavior of Augustine's God seems to mimic the posture of the Roman paterfamilias, who was similarly arbitrary and ruthless in the judgment of his own babies, who elected some for life and cast out others into the exterior darkness. And no one in his family dared question his decisions. Perhaps here as elsewhere, Augustine remains quintessentially the Roman.

Augustine was, moreover, impressed by the early dominion which evil establishes over the growing child. The suckling infant cries unreasonably for nourishment, wails and throws tantrums, and strikes with feeble but malicious blows those who care for him. "The innocence of children," Augustine concludes, "is in the helplessness of their bodies, rather than any quality of soul. "Who does not know," he elsewhere asks, "with what ignorance of the truth (already manifest in babies), with what plenitude of vain desire (initially apparent in children) man enters this life? If he is allowed to live as he wishes... he will fall into all or many kinds of crimes and atrocities."

The suppression of concupiscence thus becomes a central goal of Augustine's educational philosophy and justifies hard and frequent punishments inflicted on the child. While rejecting the values of pagan antiquity, he adheres to the classical methods of education. Augustine prepared the way for retaining under Christian auspices that "sorrowful road" of schooling which he, as a child at school, had so much hated.

Medieval society thus inherited and sustained a mix of sometimes inconsistent attitudes toward children. The social historian, by playing upon one or another of these attitudes, by judiciously screening his sources, could easily color as he pleases the history of medieval children. He could compile a list of the atrocities committed against them, dwell upon their neglect, or celebrate medieval views of the child's innocence and holiness. One must, however, strive to paint a more balanced picture, and for this we obviously need some means of testing the experiences of the medieval child. The tests we shall use here are two: the social investment, the wealth and resources which medieval society was apparently willing to invest in children; and the psychological investment, the attention they claimed and received from their elders. The thesis of this essay, simply stated, is that both the social and psychological investments in children were growing substantially from approximately the eleventh and twelfth centuries, through to the end of the Middle Ages, and doubtlessly beyond.

The basic economic and social changes which affected medieval society during this period seem to have required a heightened investment in children. From about the year 1000, the medieval community was growing in numbers and complexity. Commerical exchange intensified, and a vigorous urban life was reborn in the West. Even the shocking reduction in population size, coming with the plagues, famines, and wars of the fourteenth century, did not undo the importance of the commercial economy or of the towns and the urban classes dependent upon it. Medieval society, once a simple association of warriors, priests, and peasants, came to include such numerous and varied social types as merchants, lawyers, notaries, accountants, clerks, and artisans. A new world was born, based on the cultivation and preservation of specialized, sophisticated skills.

The emergence of specialized roles within society required in turn a social commitment to the training of children in the corresponding skills. Earlier educational reforms—notably those achieved under Charlemagne—had largely affected monks and, in less measure, clerics; they had little impact on the lay world. One novelty of the new medieval pedagogy, as it is developed from the twelfth century, is the attention now given to the training of laymen. Many writers now comment on the need and value of mastering a trade from early youth. Boys, notes Philippe of Navarre, should be taught a trade "as soon as possible." Those who early become and long remain apprentices ought to be the best masters. "Men from childhood," Thomas Aquinas observes, "apply themselves to those offices and skills in which they will spend their lives.... This is altogether necessary. To the extent that something is difficult, so much the more must a man grow accustomed to it from childhood."

Later in the thirteenth century, Raymond Lull, one of the most learned men of the epoch, compares society to a wheel upon which men ride ceaselessly, up and down, gaining and losing status; the force which drives the wheel is education, in particular the mastery of a marketable skill. Through the exercise of a trade, a man earns money, gains status, and ultimately enters the ranks of the rich. Frequently, however, he becomes arrogant in his new status, and he neglects to train his children in a trade. His unskilled offspring inevitably ride the wheel on its downward swing. And so the world turns. A marketable skill offers the only certain riches and the only security, and "there is no skill," Lull affirms, "which is not good."

One hundred and fifty years later, the Florentine Dominican Giovanni Dominici voices exactly the same sentiments. Neither wealth nor inherited status offers security. Only a marketable skill can assure that children "will not be forced, as are many, to beg, to steal, to enter household service, or to do demeaning things." Addressing a woman who belonged to one of Florence's patrician families, he still urged her to make sure that her child learned a useful trade.

Although statistics largely elude us, there can be little doubt that medieval society was making substantial investments in education from the twelfth century. Guibert of Nogent, a monk who recounted his personal memoirs in the middle twelfth century, observed that the number of professional teachers had multiplied in the course of his own lifetime. The chronicler Giovanni Villani gives us some rare figures on the school's functioning at Florence in the 1330's. The children, both boys and girls, who were attending the grammar schools of the city, presumably between 6 and 12 years of age, numbered between eight and ten thousand. From what we know of the population of the city, better than one out of two school-aged children were receiving formal instruction in reading. Florentine girls received no more formal instruction after grammar school, but of the boys, between 1,000 and 1,200 went on to six secondary schools, where they learned how to calculate on the abacus, in evident preparation for a business career. Another 550 to 600 attended four "large schools" where they studied "Latin and logic," the necessary preparation for entry into the universities and, eventually, for a career in law, medicine, or the Church. Florence, it might be argued, was hardly a typical medieval community. Still, the social investment that Florentines were making in the training of their children was substantial.

Another indicator of social investment in children is the number of orphanages or hospitals devoted to their care, and here the change across the Middle Ages is particularly impressive. The care of the abandoned or orphaned child was a traditional obligation of Christian charity, but it did not lead to the foundation and support of specialized orphanages until late in the Middle Ages. The oldest European orphanage of which we have notice was founded at Milan in 787, but we know nothing at all concerning its subsequent history or that of other orphanages sporadically mentioned in the early sources. The great hospital orders of the medieval Church, which sprang up from the twelfth century, cared for orphans and foundlings, but none initially chose that charity as its special mission.

The history of hospitals in the city of Florence gives striking illustration of a new concern for abandoned babies which emerged in Europe during the last two centuries of the Middle Ages. In his detailed description of his native city, written in the 1330's, Villani boasts that Florence contained thirty hospitals with more than a thousand beds. But the beds were intended for the "poor and infirm," and he mentions no special hospital for foundlings. A century later, probably in the 1420's, another chronicler, Gregorio Dati, in clear imitation of Villani, composed another description of the marvels of Florence. By then the city contained no fewer than three hospitals which received foundlings and supported them until an age when the girls could marry and the boys could be instructed in a trade. The charity was, in Dati's phrase, "an estimable thing," and the moneys expended by the hospitals were, he claims, worth a city.

At Rome, the history of the hospital of Santo Spirito in Sassia shows a comparable, growing sensitivity to the needs of foundlings in the late Middle Ages. The hospital, administered by the Order of the Holy Spirit, had been founded at Rome in 1201, with the blessing and support of Pope Innocent III. From its thirteenth-century rule, Santo Spirito indiscriminantly accepted pilgrims, the poor, the sick and crippled, and foundlings. After a period of disruption and decadence in the fourteenth and early fifteenth centuries, the hospital was re-formed, and, from about 1450, it devoted its principal resources to the care of foundlings. At the same time, a legend grew up concerning the hospital's early benefactor, Pope Innocent III: Instructed by a dream, Innocent one day ordered fishermen to cast their nets into the Tiber. The men hauled in from the waters the bodies of 87 drowned babies and, after a second effort, 340 more. The shocked pope thereupon endowed the hospital of Santo Spirito and commissioned it to receive the unwanted babies of Rome. The legend is today celebrated in fifteenth-century frescoes which adorn the still-standing hospital of Santo Spirito. The story is without historical foundation, but it illuminates the novel sentiments toward foundlings which came to prevail at Rome, not in the thirteenth but in the fifteenth century.

Even a rapid survey of the foundling hospitals of Europe shows a similar pattern. Bologna seems not to have had an orphanage until 1459, and Pavia not until 1449. At Paris, the first specialized hospital for children. Saint-Esprit en Grèves, was founded in 1363, but according to its charter it was supposed to receive only orphans of legitimate birth. Care of foundlings, it was feared, might encourage sexual license among adults. But the hospital in practice seems to have accepted abandoned babies, and several similar institutions were established in French cities in the fifteenth century.

This new concern for the survival of children, even foundlings, seems readily explicable. Amid the ravages of epidemics, the sheer numbers of orphans must have multiplied in society. Moreover, the plagues carried off the very young in disproportionate numbers. Parents feared for the survival of their lineages and their communities. About 1400, the French philosopher Jean Gerson denounced the inordinate concern for the survival of children which he detected among his contemporaries. The frequent creation of foundling hospitals and orphanages indicates that society as a whole shared this concern and was willing to invest in the survival of its young, even orphans and foundlings.

The medieval social investment in children thus seems to have grown from the twelfth century and to have passed through two phases: the first one, beginning from the twelfth century, largely involved a commitment, on the part of the urban communities, to the child's education and training; the second, from the late fourteenth century, reflected a concern for the child's survival and health under difficult hygienic conditions.

This social investment also presumes an equivalent psychological investment, as well as a heightened attention paid to the child and his development. This is evident, for example, in the rich tradition of pedagogical literature intended for a lay audience, which again dates from the twelfth century. One of the earliest authors to provide a comprehensive regimen of child care was Vincent of Beauvais, who died in 1264. Drawing on the learning of the Muslim physician Avicenna, he gives advice on the delivery of the baby; its care in the first hours, days, and months of life; nursing and weaning; the care of older children; and their formal education. Later in the century, Raymond Lull, in his *Doctrina pueril*, written in Catalan but soon translated into French and Latin, is similarly comprehensive, including passages not only on formal schooling but also on the care and nourishment of the child. "For every man," he explains, "must hold his child dear." In the following century, a Tuscan poet, Francesco da Barberino, who evidently had read Vincent of Beauvais, incorporated his advice on the care of infants in a long, vernacular poem intended for nurses. The learning of the scholars seems to have spread widely, even among the humble social classes.

These medieval pedagogues also developed a rudimentary but real psychology of children. Vincent of Beauvais recommends that the child who does not readily learn must be beaten, but he warns against the psychological damage which excessive severity may cause. "Children's minds," he explains, "break down under excessive severity of correction; they despair, and worry, and finally they hate. And this is the most injurious; where everything is feared, nothing is attempted." A few teachers, such as the Italian humanists Matteo Palmieri and Maffeo Vegio, wanted to prohibit all corporal punishment at school. For them, physical discipline was "contrary to nature"; it "induced servility and sowed resentment, which in later years might make the student hate the teacher and forget his lesson."

The teacher—and on this all writers agree—should be temperate in the use of force, and he should also observe the child, in order to identify his talents and capacities. For not all children are alike, and natural differences must be recognized and developed. Raymond Lull affirms that nature is more capable of rearing the child than the child's mother. The Florentine Giovanni Dominici stresses the necessity of choosing the proper profession for the child. Society, he notes, requires all sorts of occupations and skills, ranging from farmers to carpenters, to bankers, merchants, priests, and "a thousand others." The aptitudes and inclinations of the young had to be acutely observed, "since nature aids art, and a skill chosen against nature will not be learned well." The young man who wishes to become a wool merchant will make a poor barber. God in his infinite wisdom has distributed all needed talents among all the members of the body social. If all young persons developed and exercised the particular talent which they possess, then, in Dominici's view, "lands would be well governed, commerce would be justly conducted, and the arts would progress in orderly fashion; the commonwealth would rejoice in peace and fat abundance, happy in all its affairs."

To read these writers is inevitably to form the impression that medieval people, or some of them at least, were deeply concerned about children. Indeed, Jean Gerson expressly condemns his contemporaries, who, in his opinion, were excessively involved with their children's survival and success. In order to gain for them "the honors and pomp of this world," parents, he alleges, were expending "all their care and attention; they sleep neither day nor night and often become very miserly." In investing in their children, they neglected charitable works and the good of their own souls. Gerson tells of a rich married couple who wished for offspring and performed many good works, so that God would grant them a baby. God rewarded them with the birth of a beautiful infant. But the new parents began at once to consider how their baby might achieve success in this world. They gave up their pious thoughts and deeds and turned all their attention and wealth to the upbringing of their child. God, angered at their neglect of the Church and of the poor, took back what he had given; the splendid child died. God does this often, Gerson instructs us, in order to rescue parents from inordinate dedications to the welfare of their off-spring. Gerson, one suspects, would be surprised to learn of the opinion of recent historians, that medieval parents cared little for their offspring.

Medieval society, increasingly dependent upon the cultivation of sophisticated skills, had to invest in a supporting pedagogy; when later threatened by child-killing plagues, it had to show concern for the survival of the very young. But the medieval involvement with children cannot be totally described in these functional terms. Even as they were developing an effective pedagogy, medieval people were re-evaluating the place of childhood among the periods of life.

One indication of a new sympathy toward childhood is the revision in theological opinion concerning the salvation of the babies who died without baptism. Up until the twelfth century, the leading theologians of the Western church—Fulgentius of Ruspe, Pope Gregory the Great, Isidore of Seville, Anselm of Canterbury—reiterated the weighty opinion of St. Augustine, that such infants were surely damned. In the twelfth century, Peter Abelard and Peter Lombard, perhaps the two most influential theologians of the epoch, reversed the condemnation of unbaptized babies to eternal fires. A thorough examination of the question, however, awaited the work of Thomas Aquinas, the first to use in a technical theological sense the term *limbus puerorum*, the "limbo of children." The unbaptized baby, he taught, suffered only the deprivation of the Beatific Vision. As the poet Dante described their plight in a famous passage from the *Divine Comedy*, they were "only insofar afflicted, that without hope we live in desire."

Aquinas' mild judgment on babies dead without baptism became the accepted teaching of the medieval Church. Only one prominent theologian in the late Middle Ages, Gregory of Rimini, resisted it, and he became to be known as the *tortor puerorum*, the "torturer of children."

No less remarkable is the emergence, from the twelfth century, of a widespread devotion to the Child Jesus. The texts from the early Middle Ages which treat of the Christ Child—notably the "Book on the Origins of Mary and the Childhood of the Savior" falsely attributed to the evangelist St. Matthew—present Christ as a miniature wonder worker, who miraculously corrects Joseph's mistakes in carpentry, tames lions, divides rivers, and even strikes dead a teacher who dared reprimand him in class. All-knowing and all-powerful, he is the negation of the helpless, charming child. A new picture of the Child Jesus emerges, initially under Cistercian auspices, in the twelfth century. For example, between 1153 and 1157 the English Cistercian Aelred of Rievaulx composed a meditation, "Jesus at the Age of Twelve." Aelred expatiates on the joy which the presence of the young Christ brought to his elders and companions: "... the grace of heaven shone from that most beautiful face with such charm as to make everyone look at it, listen to him, and be moved to affection. See, I beg, how he is seized upon and led away by each and every one of them. Old men kiss him, young men embrace him, boys wait upon him.... How do the old women complain when he lingers a little longer with his father and his companions? Each of them, I think, declares in his inmost heart: 'Let him kiss me with the kiss of his mouth'".

Aelred goes on to speculate concerning the intimate details of the domestic life of the holy Child during the three days he was separated from his parents in Jerusalem: "Who provided you with food and drink? Who made up a bed for you? Who took off your shoes? Who tended your boyish limbs with oil and baths?" Passionate and sensuous, these meditations are the more remarkable as they come from a monk vowed to celibacy and asceticism.

Doubtlessly, the special characteristics of Cistercian monasticism were influential here. Like other reformed orders of the twelfth century, the Cistercians no longer admitted oblates, the boys placed in the monastery at tender ages, who grew up in the cloister with no experience of secular life. The typical Cistercians—St. Bernard of Clairvaux and his brothers, for example—were raised within a natural family, and many were familiar with the emotions of family life. Grown men when they entered the monastery, they carried with them a distinct mentality—a mentality formed in the secular world and open to secular values. Many doubtlessly had considered and some had pursued other careers before electing the monastic life; they presumably had reflected upon the emotional and spiritual rewards of the married state and the state of parenthood. While fleeing from the world, they still sought in their religious experiences analogues to secular and familial emotions. In numerous commentaries on the biblical Song of Songs, they examine the love which joins bridegroom and bride and the mystical parallels to it offered in religion. In celebrating the joys of contemplating a perfect child, they find in their religious experience an analogue to the love and satisfaction which parents feel in observing their growing children. The Cistercian cult of the Child Jesus suggests, in other words, that lay persons, too, were finding the contemplation of children emotionally rewarding.

In the thirteenth century, devotion to the Child Jesus spread well beyond the restricted circle of Cistercian monasticism. St. Francis of Assisi, according to the *Legenda Gregorii*, set up for the first time a Christmas crèche, so that the faithful might more easily envision the tenderness and humility of the new-born Jesus. St. Francis, the most popular saint of the late Middle Ages, was thus responsible, at least in legend, for one of the most popular devotional practices still associated with Christmas. St. Anthony of Padua, who died in 1231, was observed one day in the quiet of his room embracing and kissing an angelic child. This legend to be sure, appears more than a century after Anthony's death but gains wide popularity in the late Middle Ages.

Saints of lesser renown also sought and were favored with visitations from the Christ Child. A widow of Florence, Umiliana dei Cerchi, who died in 1246, prayed that she might see "the infant Jesus as he was at three or four years of age." She returned to her room one night to find a delightful child playing; simply from watching this child at play, she drew ineffable joy. A similar story, told of St. Agnes of Montepulciano, who died in 1317, ends with a bizarre twist. She too prayed for the special favor of holding and fondling the infant Jesus. One night in her convent cell, the Virgin gave her the sacred child: when Mary returned at dawn to reclaim the infant, Agnes, captivated by his charm, refused to give him back. The women argued, and their "loving and pious dispute", in the words of Agnes' biographer, aroused the convent.

This cult of the Christ Child implies an idealization of childhood itself. "O sweet and sacred childhood," another Cistercian, Guerric of Igny, writes of the early years of Christ, "which brought back man's true innocence, by which men of every age can return to blessed childhood and be conformed to you, not in physical weakness but in humility of heart and holiness of life."

How are we to explain this celebration of "sweet and sacred childhood"? It closely resembles other religious movements which acquire extraordinary appeal from the twelfth century—the cults of povery, of Christian simplicity, and of the apostolic life. These "movements of cultural primitivism," as George Boas might call them, point to a deepening psychological discontent with the demands of the new commercial economy. The inhabitants of towns in particular, living by trade, were forced into careers of getting and spending, in constant pursuit of what Augustine had called "deceitful riches." The psychological tensions inherent in the urban professions and the dubious value of the proferred material rewards seem to have generated a nostalgic longing for alternate systems of existence, for freedom from material concerns, for the simple Christian life as it was supposedly lived in the apostolic age. Another model for an alternate existence, the exact opposite of the tension-ridden urban experience, was the real or imagined life of the child, who was at once humble and content, poor and pure, joyous and giving joy.

The simple piety of childhood remained an ideal of religious reformers for the duration of the Middle Ages. At their close, both Girolamo Savonarola in the south of Europe and Desiderius Erasmus in the north urged their readers to look to pious children if they would find true models of the Christian life. Erasmus, in his *Colloquies*, after a pious child tells him of his religious practices, affirms his intent of following the child's example.

Moreover, the medieval cult of childhood extends beyond religious movements and informs secular attitudes as well. In the French allegorical poem of the thirteenth century, *The Romance of the Rose*, youth is presented as a young girl "not yet much more than twelve years old." The poet remarks on her innocence: she "did not yet suspect the existence of evil or trickery in the world." She smiles continuously, for "a young thing is troubled by nothing except play." She is also free from adult hypocrisy. Her sweetheart, described as a young boy of the same age, kisses her when he pleases. "They were never ashamed...," explains the poet, "rather you might see them kissing each other like two turtle doves." Later in the Middle Ages, a Florentine citizen and merchant named Giovanni Morelli, reflecting on his own life, calls childhood "nature's most pleasant age." In his *Praise of Folly*, Erasmus avers that the simplicity and unpretentiousness of childhood make it the happiest time of life. "Who does not know," Folly asks her audience, "that childhood is the happiest age and the most pleasant for all? What is there about children that makes us kiss and hug them and cuddle them as we do, so that even an enemy would help them, unless it is this charm of folly?" Clearly, we have come far from Augustine's opinion, that men would prefer eternal death to life again as a child.

The history of medieval children is as complex as the history of any social group, and even more elusive. This essay has attempted to describe in broad outline the cultural attitudes which influenced the experiences of medieval children, as well as the large social trends which touched their lives. The central movements which, in this reconstruction, affected their fate were the social and economic changes widely evident across Europe from the twelfth century, most especially the rise of a commercialized economy and the proliferation of special skills within society; and the worsening health conditions of the late Middle Ages, from the second half of the fourteenth century. The growth of a commercialized economy made essential an attentive pedagogy which could provide society with adequately trained adults. And the deteriorating conditions of hygiene across the late Middle Ages heightened the concern for, and investment in, the health and survival of the very young. Paradoxically, too, the growing complexities of social life engendered not truly a discovery but an idealization of childhood: the affirmation of the sentimental belief that childhood is, as Erasmus maintains, a blessed time and the happiest moment of human existence.

We have sought to identify patterns in the complex experiences of medieval children, but we recognize that the model we propose doubtlessly remains too simple. But this much can safely be affirmed: the Middle Ages developed and sustained a broad spectrum of prejudices and beliefs regarding children, some of them destined to influence the subsequent centuries of Western history, some of them living today.

Bibliography

PHILIPPE ARIÈS, *Centuries of Childhood: A Social History of Family Life* (1962).
LUKE DEMAITRE, "The Idea of Childhood and Child Care in Medical Writings of the Middle Ages," *Journal of Psychohistory* 4 (1977):462–490.

LLOYD DE MAUSE, ed., *The History of Childhood* (1974).
I. H. FORSYTH, "Children in Early Medieval Art: Ninth through Twelfth Centuries," *Journal of Psychohistory* 4 (1976):31–70.
DAVID HERLIHY and CHRISTIANE KLAPISCH, *The Toscans and Their Families* (1985).
JOHN T. NOONAN, Jr., *Contraception* (1965).
R. C. TREXLER, "Infanticide in Florence: New Sources and First Results," *History of Childhood Quarterly* 1 (1973):98–116.

Benedictine monks at choir. *The British Library*

PART THREE

The Late Middle Ages and Renaissance

Between the fourteenth and mid-sixteenth centuries lies a period of history distinguished by its extremes. On the one hand, there are unprecedented levels of disease, war, and religious persecution. This is the time of the Black Death and the Hundred Years' War, the heyday of the Inquisition, and the beginning of the infamous witch hunts. On the other hand, territories attained new levels of political stability during this period and representative institutions also flourished. Universities and colleges emerged and lay literacy expanded in the cities; a demand for books made the printing press a profitable venture. In both classrooms and royal courts a cultural reform movement known as humanism caught the imagination. Born in Italy the humanist movement rapidly spread northward.

Internal political consolidation advanced in both the nations and cities of Europe. Rulers developed sophisticated techniques to maintain and enhance their political authority. Edward Muir explains how the magistrates of Venice used art and pageantry for just this purpose during the late years of the Renaissance, when these techniques had been perfected.

Secular rulers also successfully established control over the church. Finding itself increasingly cut out of the political sphere, where it had moved with such authority in the twelfth and thirteenth centuries, the church enforced its authority fully in the spiritual sphere down through the Reformation. In consequence, minorities and dissenters found themselves under new pressures to conform to church teaching. Jeremy Cohen examines the effects on Jews when the new papal orders of Franciscans and Dominicans undertook a mission to unify the moral and religious life of Christendom.

If the church was on the march in the spiritual sphere, it was also on the defensive there. Royal propaganda and expanded lay education made the laity more critical of the church, and this fostered religious independence and dissent. The church found its most serious challengers within its own camp when the clergy and devout laity embraced the simple religious ideals of Jesus and the primitive Christian church. Scott Hendrix documents the often heretical and occasionally revolutionary quest for the "true" church during the last two centuries of the Middle Ages.

The pervasiveness of plague in the mid-fourteenth century, when perhaps two-fifths of Europe's population died, may leave the impression that normal life simply stopped in its tracks for decades thereafter. William J. Courtenay shows through the example of Oxford how the vitality of culture persisted throughout these years despite the plague, which left many areas and institutions largely unaffected.

Several vantage points from which the late Middle Ages and Renaissance can be evaluated suggest a physically whipped and politically subject age. The image of man cultivated by the scholastics in the universities also conveys this impression. They depicted human beings as creatures in whom the higher power of reason is constantly besieged by raw animal passion and a self-seeking will. But the humanist vision, which also became bright in this same period, rejected this image. Humanists portrayed the individual as a complex unity of intellect, will, and passion, a creature possessed of the talent and freedom to create even in the act of sinning. William Bouwsma defines the new humanist anthropology in distinction from the reigning scholastic view and also traces its checkered history.

Art, Pageantry, and Politics in Renaissance Venice

EDWARD MUIR

A government's self-image is defined not only in its chronicles and diplomatic papers, but also in its public art and pageantry, where it shows its face most self-consciously to the public. In its parades and processions, a government recounts traditional values, declares its authority, reaffirms internal order, and explains itself to non-native visitors. For the rulers who devise such ceremonies, art and pageantry are sophisticated political tools, serving both political self-expression and political control. Already by the fifteenth century Europe's rulers were becoming adept in the art of propaganda; by the sixteenth they were true experts.

In late Renaissance Venice rulers sent messages to friend and foe alike through public art and ceremony. Eloquent lip-service was given to republican virtues on the public stage, while actual political practice often contradicted these virtues. Sometimes the ceremony itself contradicted them. In lavish spectacles that must have baffled as well as entertained onlookers from the lower social classes, Venetian rulers compared themselves to Roman gods. Such elite myth-making directly served the political ambitions of rulers. It also promoted a unifying civic pride shared by all Venetians, regardless of social class. Official propaganda secured the government, but it also renewed the city.

The last three decades of the sixteenth century became the great age of Venetian pageantry. The magnificence of the antique style appealed to the ruling elite, who were concerned with projecting an image of strength and majesty both at home and abroad in the face of renewed external threats to Venice's imperial reputation, beginning with the loss of Cyprus to the Turks in 1573. This calamity was followed by a devastating plague in 1575–77 that killed over one-third of the population and by the fires of 1574 and 1577 that destroyed the council chambers of the Ducal Palace. All of these events brought into question the conception of Venice as a city favored by God.

Reprinted with the permission of the author from "Images of Power: Art and Pageantry in Renaissance Venice," *American Historical Review*, vol. 84 (1979), pp. 43–52.

The patricians in charge of planning responded by developing two artistic themes. In one, Venice's steadfast Catholic orthodoxy was contrasted to the machinations of the insidious heretics and powerful infidels who menaced Europe, and, in the other, Venice's situation was compared to Imperial Rome's struggle to rally forces against the barbarians. The themes were pointedly self-serving: without the Venetians would not all Europe fall to the sword of the Turk or to the perversions of the Protestants?

The 1570s had begun well enough. In October of 1571 the combined navies of the pope, Spain, Venice, and some minor Catholic powers defeated the Turkish fleet near Lepanto in the Gulf of Patras in Greece. At the joyous victory celebration in Venice, the traditions of depicting Venice in terms of religious virtues and through various personifications of the classical gods were combined with satirical portraits of the humiliated Turks. A tableau of one *scuola grande* [confraternity] compared Pius V, Philip II, and Doge Alvise Mocenigo (represented by Neptune) to the cardinal virtues—Faith, Hope, and Charity; on the same *solaro* [float] three youths stabbed a huge dragon with a crescent on its head, symbolizing the Grand Turk. On the other *solari* rode figures of Faith, Rome, Spain, the doge, and Victory as if in triumphal chariots, another classical allusion. At a celebration held later at the Rialto, an ingenious illuminated pyramid turned on its axis, bearing statues and paintings of Neptune, Jupiter, Saturn, and Mars.

Despite the loss of Cyprus, Venice's richest Eastern possession, in the peace negotiations with the Turks in 1573, the exultant tone of pageantry persisted. When Henry III of France visited Venice in 1574 on his way to be crowned 'Most Christian King' after spending an unhappy year as the king of Poland, the entertainments in his honor were the most expensive and spectacular of the Venetian Renaissance (see Figure 1). From the triumphal arch to the sugar sculptures served as dessert at the state banquets, the decorations had a consistent theme of courting French favor at the expense of the Spanish. A committee of nobles, including two already well known for their humanistic interests and their patronage of Palladio, planned the decorations, coordinating the diplomatic intentions of the state with the proper Neoclassical allusions. The major creation for the visit was a wooden triumphal arch built on the Lido by Palladio and decorated by Veronese and Tintoretto in imitation of the arch of Septimius Severus in Rome; on it the escutcheons of Venice and France were paired under statues of Victory and Peace, and around the arch were paintings of battles that Henry had won against the Huguenots. Classical images served an overall scheme that had strong military and religious tones: Venice was the natural partner of France because the city was the bulwark against the heathen Turk, just as the French kings were the stalwart protectors of the Catholic cause against the heretics.

The late sixteenth century's greater enthusiasm and appreciation for the dramatic as opposed to the merely spectacular was also marked in pageantry. The visit in 1585 of some Japanese nobles, newly converted to

Figure 1. Andrea Michieli, called il Vicentino, *The Ingress of Henry III*, engraving. Used by permission of Museo Civico Correr, Venice.

Christianity by Jesuit missionaries, offered a consummate opportunity for didactic drama. The Collegio postponed the procession scheduled for Saint Mark's Day (June 25) to coincide with the festival of Saints Peter and Paul three days later and ordered that the usual midsummer frolics and games be suspended so the city could prepare a properly spiritual and devout holiday for the guests. Built to tell "as in a theater" the sacred history of the Old and New Testaments and the trials of the saints and martyrs, three hundred *solari* were accompanied by an unprecedented display of reliquaries, and silver liturgical objects. The six *scuole grandi*, the Dominicans and Franciscans, and other religious orders created tableaux vivants instructing the Japanese about Christian truths and, inevitably, about Venice's special place in the divine plan. There were the usual personifications of Venice as a queen surrounded by the virtues and legions of saints, but there were also attempts to explain complex subjects, such as the local legend of Saint Mark's gift of his episcopal ring to a Venetian fisherman, Solomon's demonstration of his wisdom and wealth to the queen of Sheba, and the baptism of Constantine and his subsequent charity to the poor. Likewise, at the festivities following the league signed between Philip II and Henry IV in 1598, which ended years of hostilities between the two major Catholic powers, intricate presentations of religious and classical subjects dominated the tableaux. The Scuola Grande di San Rocco contributed a series of tableaux allegorizing the continents, including young girls riding on a bull, camel, crocodile, and rhinoceros representing respectively Europe, Asia, Africa, and America. In another series, the Scuola Grande di San Giovanni Evangelista created a timely exposition on the evils of war; one witness could not find the words to describe the "thousands of ingenious effects imitating the confusion war caused on earth." Neptune lamented anarchy on the seas; Death triumphed over corpses; castles burned; a company of soldiers abducted a young girl; and four "infernal furies" tied up a large globe. Pageantry had become political pedagogy of a high order.

Two final examples serve to illustrate the effectiveness of pageantry as a political tool. In one case late in the sixteenth century, it was used to leap republican barriers; in another it helped restore credibility in a time of diplomatic crisis. In 1597 Marino Grimani, elected doge two years before and wildly popular among the common people, announced his plans to revive the lapsed practice of having the doge's wife "crowned" in a formal entrance ceremony to the Ducal Palace. The Collegio of the Senate accordingly appointed a master of ceremonies to oversee the preparations, organized an *ad hoc* committee of young nobles to provide and pay for entertainments, and assigned to the guilds responsibility for building display booths for the Ducal Palace. The "coronation" of the dogaressa (see Figure 2) was almost a contradiction in terms, because she had never actually been crowned but was instead presented with a list of "promises" she swore to keep, in a rite that emphasized the formal restrictions on the behavior of the doge's family. The Grimani and Morosini families, however,

Figure 2. Andrea Michieli, called il Vicentino, *The Coronation of Dogaressa Morosina Grimani*, painting. Used by permission of Museo Civico Correr, Venice.

transformed the occasion of this solemn republican pledge into a ceremony of vaunting ambition. The company of young nobles hired Vicenzo Scamozzi, a student of Palladio, to design a grand barge (*gran macchina*) in which Dogaressa Morosina Morosini Grimani was rowed in a procession on the Grand Canal, accompanied by a large retinue of Venetian noble women and her two dwarfs. Decorations on the barge's columned loggia included a large Neptune riding the tail of a whale, a globe, and a scene in which Saint Mark himself crowned the kneeling doge and dogaressa. Here again the definition of ducal powers was a problem, for in this scene Saint Mark's coronation of the couple ignored the reality that electors had chosen Grimani for his office. Saint Mark was not just an aide to the doge, as in the revised version of the Veronese votive portrait of Doge Sebastiano Venier, nor was the doge representing the community in humble supplication to the saint; it was as if Saint Mark had personally chosen Marino and Morosina Grimani for "global" domination.

As she disembarked at the Piazzetta, Morosina Grimani walked through a triumphal arch that exalted the nobility of the two families. Surmounting the arch was a statue of a woman (Venice) holding a staff (authority) and bundles of wheat (prosperity), surrounded by paintings of the Venetian dominions. Symbols of the offices held by the Grimani and Morosini ancestors—royal and ducal crowns, cardinals' hats, episcopal staffs, a patriarchal cross, a legate's caduceus, and generals' batons—complemented the arms of the two families. There were specific references to Doge Grimani's eloquence as a legate to the Holy See, to his charity as a procurator, to his justice as a provincial governor, and to his popularity. Repetitions and variations of the same theme continued as the dogaressa proceded past the guilds' booths to her "arrival" in the private chambers of the Ducal Palace. Relying largely on pageantry, the Grimani turned upside down the tradition of the dogaressa's coronation, transforming the restrictive ritual, during which she swore to abide by the lengthy legal proscriptions on her conduct, into a court festival that taunted the republican traditions of patrician equality with the aristocratic pretensions of the oligarchy. Grimani could not at his own coronation legally claim to be as powerful as he hoped to be, but carefully directed pageantry made his ambition clear at the "coronation" of his wife.

The last illustration of particularly effective pageantry is drawn from the most famous event in the history of the "political reputation" of Venice. The very decline of the republican ideals in practice may have corresponded with a reassertion of them in theory, and it was this theoretical defense of republican values more than the realities of Venetian political life that garnered for *La Serenissima* its European reputation as the ideal living republic. Venice's reputation for the "defense of republican liberty," as William J. Bouwsma has called it, was immensely strengthened, particularly in Protestant countries, by its adamant resistance to papal interference in Venetian domestic affairs. The conflict between Venice and the papacy reached its highest pitch when Pope Paul V put Venice under interdict from 1606 to 1607, and Venice's most famous and long-lasting defense dates from this event, eloquently expressed in the writings of Paolo Sarpi, a Servite friar, who argued passionately against the supposed desire of the pope to establish a universal monarchy. The government, for its part, wanted to show the world that it had the complete loyalty of its subjects even on religious issues by carrying on the celebration of the liturgy in defiance of the interdict.

Thus, the Corpus Christi procession of 1606 provided the opportunity for a demonstration of popular resistance to the interdict and a display of antipapal propaganda through pageantry, a manifestation so wonderfully successful that the sympathetic English ambassador, Sir Henry Wotton, called it "the most sumptuous procession that ever had been seen here," and the Jesuit spy, Giacomo Lambertengo, derided it as a "spettacolo miserabile." The congregations of secular priests, most of the orders of the regulars, and the *scuole grandi* participated in the procession—the latter contributing numerous tableaux that, according to the official euphemism of the day, had "some scenes which alluded to the reasonable claims of the republic against the pope." In particular, the tableaux proclaimed the distinctions between sacred and secular authority on which the Venetians built their case. On one *solaro* an actor dressed as Christ stood above a Latin motto quoting Mark 12:17: "Render unto Caesar that which is Caesar's and unto God what is God's"; and, on another, Christ reminded his Apostles that their priesthood did not allow them to usurp the authority of kings who properly ruled over the temporal affairs of mankind. The most pointed reference to the follies of the pope was a collapsing church ("chiesa cadente") supported by the Venetian doge assisted by Saint Dominic and Saint Francis. On either side of the church, other friars held up broad swords, emblazoned with the motto, "VIVA IL DOSE."

The procession was a diplomatic coup. Some nine days earlier at Pentecost, when the Signoria had walked in the procession unaccompanied by any foreign ambassadors, rumors spread that Venice had been abandoned by its friends. To the delight of the crowds, both the French and the Imperial ambassadors made a belated appearance on Corpus Christi Day. Ambassador Wotton saw exactly what was going on: "The reasons of this extraordinary solemnity were two as I conceive it. First, to contain the people in good order with superstition, the foolish band of obedience. Secondly, to let the pope know (who wanteth not intelligencers) that notwithstanding his interdict, they had friars enough and other clergymen to furnish out the day." Apparently, the procession achieved these ends and helped to turn the diplomatic tide in Venice's favor.

In the course of the sixteenth century, pageantry had thus evolved into a signal art form and a public mirror meant to reflect images of political power. It had not superseded the other arts as a political device, but its pliable and adaptive form appealed to those trained to rule others. In pageantry the elite of Venice had a superior means of exploiting Machiavelli's dictum that to most men appearances mattered more than realities.

In all of the examples discussed, the arts disclosed political ideas by making analogies. Through symbolism and allegory the arts elevated a political idea—however self-serving, prevaricating, or mean—to a transcendent plane: doges resembled saints, the gods directed the fortune of war or diplomacy, and Venice itself was the epitome of the theological, political, and classical virtues. Although the images changed and pagan deities joined Christian saints in the city's pantheon, the analogical process remained the same. This form of reasoning was not unusual, for much Renaissance political thought, even when crafted by the finest minds, depended on metaphors—the "King's Two Bodies," the "Ship of State," or the "Marriage of the Sea," for example—to unveil in human terms the implications of a given principle or abstraction. It is certain that many people took these comparisons seriously, but it is much more difficult to tell to what degree such a habit of thought influenced ordinary political perceptions and decisions. In any historical period and for any one person, it is probably impossible to determine the exact balance of ideology, belief, and objectivity in motivating a particular action. In Venice, however, it seems that ideology always played a considerable role among supporters and opponents of the regime; in the major Renaissance protests against the dictatorial habits of the oligarchs, opposition was always phrased as "restoration" of a traditional balance of responsibilities and privileges to all patricians, and the most tired clichés of the established order were used by the protesters to argue against that very order.

Perhaps the most important attribute of political imagery in the arts was its persuasive power. Visual images cajoled belief by simplifying and distorting political issues, by ignoring objectionable facts, and by juxtaposing symbols that connected ideas that may not have had any relationship in logic or reality. Herbert M. Atherton has found a similar persuasive tendency in eighteenth-century political prints, and other instances of politics so translated into art can surely be traced to the present day. But for Renaissance Venetians, art was not just a gloss on public issues nor a mere reinforcement of status discriminations and hierarchical rank; rather, the arts provided a commentary upon the whole political and social order and specifically upon the nature of class distinctions, noble privilege, and sacred inherited institutions. If the art in Venice can be reduced to anything so simple as a "function," then its function was interpretive: it was a Venetian reading of Venetian experience, a story they told themselves about themselves.

The relationship between patronage of the arts and political power is a less elusive problem: the richest men in the highest ranks of power preserved exclusive control over all political ideas in the arts. Only nuances of disagreement about political images in the arts, such as how to depict the powers of the doge, ever emanated from within this tight circle of men who rotated the important offices among themselves. The poorer nobles, the few privileged *cittadini* [a lower-level hereditary elite] and the disenfranchised masses were mute. Art may have once been the common tongue of the people, as [Bernard] Berenson believed, but a small group of powerful men chose what was to be said, and in the sixteenth century they increasingly chose a language that only an educated few could fully understand: what did fishmongers and gondoliers know of Jupiter, Mars, and Latin epigrams?

This elitism is not surprising. Anthropologists have shown that in many traditional societies village strongmen dominate over the most popular and universally accepted phenomena. For Western society Morse Peckham has noted that the "high arts" have always been associated with and have validated the centers of power. The modern illusion that artists must be honest with themselves and only serve, to borrow a phrase from Danton, "Truth—truth in all her rugged harshness" ignores the harshest truth, that artists survive only at the will of their patrons, customers, and audiences, and the powerful who sponsor the high arts have seldom been interested in truth for its own sake. The bohemian individual had no place in Renaissance Venice, and, with the exceptions of a few doges, the arts did not extol the uniqueness of the self, supporting personal oppositions to an inherited social role, as believed by those who equate the Renaissance with individualism, but protected the claims of society on the individual and offered an explanation for the existing order.

There were, of course, some changes in the political use of art in sixteenth-century Venice. The rise of pageantry, the acceptance of the antique style and iconography, and the interest in ingenious allegories that followed in the century after the War of the League of Cambrai reveal, if not a direct correspondence to the elite's quest for *nobiltà* [nobility], at least the emergence of a culture less accessible to the common Venetians than the old Venetian world of religious myth and communal civic values preached from every pulpit and in every ceremony. It is also clear that the interest in classical culture did not correspond in any way to the triumph of "bourgeois capitalism" but more likely to its rejection as a dominant value. Lastly, these changes in Venetian state art may express a new sensitivity among the patricians to the notion that they could use the apparatus of the state to impose their own values and cultural proclivities on the entire society. This notion is, of course, a rudiment of what many historians call "modernization." What apparently governed the artistic transformation in Venice, then, was not so much an empirically verifiable change in economic or social conditions as it was the patricians' perceptions of a change. Had the world-view the patricians inherited so colored reality that they could see things in no other way? Very little of their heroic, mythic past was evident in the reality of sixteenth-century Venice. That they felt insecure as a consequence was only natural. From their ancestors, however, they had also inherited a remedy for insecurity—myth-making. For them the manipulation of ever more brilliant images of power remained part of the pursuit of power itself.

Bibliography

SYDNEY ANGLO, *Spectacle, Pageantry, and Early Tudor Policy* (1969).

D. S. CHAMBERS, *The Imperial Age of Venice, 1380–1580* (1970).

A. G. DICKENS, ed., *The Courts of Europe: Politics, Patronage, and Royalty: 1400–1800* (1977).

CLIFFORD, GEERTZ, "Centers, Kings, and Charisma: Reflections on the Symbolics of Power," in *Culture and its Creators*, ed. Joseph Ben-David and Terry Nichols Clark (1977), pp. 150–171.

RALPH E. GIESEY, *The Royal Funeral Ceremony in Renaissance France* (1960).

WERNER L. GUNDERSHEIMER, *Ferrara: The Style of a Renaissance Despotism* (1973).

JOHAN HUIZINGA, *Homo Ludens: A Study of the Play-Element in Culture* (1950).

WILLIAM H. MCNEILL, *Venice: The Hinge of Europe, 1081–1797* (1974).

EDWARD MUIR, *Civic Ritual in Renaissance Venice* (1981).

BRIAN PULLAN, *Rich and Poor in Renaissance Venice* (1971).

The Friars and the Jews

JEREMY COHEN

The early church, following St. Augustine, had tolerated Jews, and the papacy had traditionally protected them. But in the thirteenth century this changed. Pope Gregory IX condemned the Talmud and the Jews who adhered to it as deviating from the Bible. While the papacy declared its willingness to continue to protect "Biblical" Jews, this proved to be a specious guarantee, inasmuch as the papacy had now determined that no such Jews existed.

The attack on the Talmud as heresy reflected an ominous development in the church of the thirteenth century, led by the new orders of mendicant friars, and directed toward the elimination of Jews from Europe. Two factors inspired this crusade. One was the expectation of the second coming of Christ. Messianic belief, fueled especially by the prophecies of a Calabrian monk, Joachim of Fiore, fanned enthusiasm for the total conversion of Europe to Christianity and denounced all who resisted as allies of the Anti-Christ. More importantly, a new idea of the church emerged in the thirteenth century, according to which the Roman church was no mere papal see, but the "whole body of Christians." The friars aspired to transform Europe into a sacral corporation of Christians directly obedient to Rome. Herein lay a new theological perception of society as an organic unity. In such a vision no room existed for dissenters and infidels, now foreign bodies that had either to be conformed or cast out.

Condemning the Talmud in 1239 as a heretical deviation from the Jews' biblical heritage, Pope Gregory IX probably did not conceive of the important effects his pronouncements would have on the course of history. He could not have foreseen that he had sanctioned the commencement of an ideological trend that would justify attempts to eliminate the Jewish presence in Christendom, a radical shift from the Augustinian position that

Reprinted with the permission of Cornell University Press from *The Friars and the Jews: The Evolution of Medieval Anti-Judaism*, pp. 242–262. Copyright © 1982 by Cornell University Press.

the Jews occupied a rightful and necessary place in Christian society. Yet Gregory's awakening to the discrepancy between the religion of contemporary Jews and that of the "biblical" Jews whom Augustine had wished to tolerate, coupled with the pontiff's exclamation that belief in the Talmud "is said to be the chief cause that holds the Jews obstinate in their perfidy," laid important groundwork for those who came after him. In the generations that followed the Paris disputation of 1240 and the initial burning of the Talmud in 1242, mendicant inquisitors throughout Europe continued to persecute rabbinic literature, compelled the Jews to submit to their inflammatory sermons, and where possible often worked toward the complete destruction of specific Jewish communities. Early in the fourteenth century, Bernard Gui burned the Talmud even in the absence of Jews. Meanwhile, as the attack on rabbinic Judaism became an ever-increasing concern of the Inquisition, the Spanish Dominican school of Raymond de Peñaforte masterfully developed the charges of heresy against the Jews and their Talmud into an ideology that called for the elimination, by conversion, of all of European Jewry. Within several decades after Raymond Martini completed his *Pugio fidei* [*Dagger of Faith*], its arguments were being synthesized and disseminated at the University of Paris, in the theological discourses of Nicholas of Lyra. Finally, still other Dominicans and Franciscans proceeded to act upon the new ideology, trying to infuse into the European consciousness the desideratum of excluding the Jews: Raymond Lull [did so] in his elaborate campaigns to convert the Jews and in his call for the expulsion of those refusing baptism, Matfre Ermengaud in his illustrated book of romantic poetry, and Berthold von Regensburg and Giordano da Rivalto in their popular sermons.

Admittedly, these friars did not, in the mere span of a century, transform the way all Christians approached the question of the Jews. The medieval papacy never officially called for the expulsion or physical persecution of European Jewry. Some clerics still composed the old type of anti-Jewish polemic which had relatively little bearing upon the Jews and Judaism of their own day; even Dominicans and Franciscans occasionally produced polemical literature of this sort. But the continued presence of the old attitude toward the Jews could not stifle the increasing acceptance and influence of the new. Although the papacy officially protected the Jews, it was bound to protect only those who conformed to the classical Augustinian conception of the bearers of the Old Testament; and that sort of Jew no longer existed. Innocent III, for instance, added to his own version of the traditional bull *Sicut Iudeis*, which assured the Jews of their rights and liberties within Christian society, a noteworthy limitation: "We wish, however, to place under the protection of this decree only those who have not presumed to plot against the Christian faith." In view of the friars' estimation of rabbinic Judaism, such a stipulation might have excluded a large portion, if not all, of European Jewry. By the fourteenth century, the *Sicut Iudeis* bull in particular and papal protection of the Jews in general had all but lost their practical effectiveness. Or as Walter Pakter has recently shown, while the treatment of the Jews in the works of the canonists actually improved during the thirteenth century, it did so with regard to matters of little concern to contemporary Jews—for example, trading in non-Jewish slaves—and not in vital matters, such as the right to study and disseminate rabbinic literature.

Some historians have characterized these developments as manifesting a gap between theory and practice in the Jewish policy of the late medieval Church, a contradiction that confused the rank and file of Christian society and moved it toward a much more violent treatment of the Jews. My own findings, however, would lead to a redefinition of the contradiction as one between two differing ideological tendencies, that of Augustine and that of the friars. The late medieval attacks on contemporary Jewry did have their theological justification. Moreover, the mendicants stood in closer contact with the lay population of Europe than did the popes or the canonists. They had the opportunity not only to pursue their ideology in direct dealings with the Jews but also to transmit their sentiments to a wide and diversified audience.

From the thirteenth century onward, anti-Jewish violence increased throughout Europe. Only from this period were Jews portrayed as real, active agents of Satan, charged with innumerable forms of hostility toward Christianity, Christendom, and individual Christians. Blood libels (as distinct from the older accusation of ritual murder) and charges of host desecration first appeared in medieval Europe during the thirteenth century. In this century, the representation of Jews in Christian art became noticeably more hostile and demeaning, with the first examples of the infamous *Judensau* (portrayals of Jews sucking at the teats of a sow) and the frequent juxtaposition of the Jews and the devil. No longer were the Jews depicted like their Christian neighbors or as mere symbols in the drama of religious history; they had become pernicious enemies of Christians and the Church, and pictorially they often came to represent the archetypal heretics. Permanent expulsion of European Jewries began in 1290. By the middle of the next century, it was almost inevitable that Jews were blamed for the Black Death and many of their communities in Germany completely and permanently exterminated. And by the mid-1500s, most of Western Europe contained no Jews at all. In view of the great influence which religion wielded over the people of medieval Europe, it is difficult to believe that had the Church remained constantly committed to the Augustinian policy of tolerating the Jews, the Jewish presence in Western Europe could have been virtually eliminated. Surely, a change in Christian theological attitudes toward the Jews could not by itself exclude them from European society. The work of the friars was a vital prerequisite, one that eventually allowed other political, social, and economic trends to take their course.

Modern Jewish historiography has treated the plight of the Jews during the last centuries of the Middle Ages extensively, and a detailed account of the decline of the medieval European Jewish community would serve little constructive purpose here. Instead, I propose to...[consider] the new anti-Jewish ideology of the friars in a somewhat broader context: Whence did it arise? What led to the theological attack on rabbinic Judaism by the mendicants in the thirteenth century? [There is] the possibility that since the friars often stemmed from and responded to the needs of the Christian middle class, they would have harbored natural resentment against the Jews, who had long dominated much of the commerce and moneylending in Western Europe (and were infidels besides). The very state of the Church at the beginning of the thirteenth century, in which the friars played such a crucial role, lent itself to increased anti-Jewish hostility as well. Yet however near the truth these suggestions might be, they do not account for the ideational substance of the mendicant attack on the Jews. To be sure, the actual commencement of the confrontation between the friars and the Jews depended in large measure upon fortuitous circumstances: the rage of a single Jew who betrayed the works of Maimonides to the Inquisition in Provence or the vindictiveness of an apostate like Nicholas Donin. By the middle of the fourteenth century, however, the friars' attacks on the Jews were no longer fortuitous; they represented a deliberate effort on the part of groups of mendicants to rid Europe of contemporary Judaism. What in the religious and intellectual climate of the times both motivated and enabled the friars to break with the established Augustinian precedent and move in this direction? Or, if European Jews had always lived according to the teachings of the Talmud, as indeed they had, what suddenly led to the development and acceptance of the new attitude that rabbinic Judaism was heretical and had no place in Christendom?

One stimulus perhaps lay in a growing preoccupation with the notion of the imminence of the end of days and with different theories of successive ages in the salvific history of the world. Many important writers of the twelfth and thirteenth centuries revived the old patristic interest in the periodization of history. Undoubtedly the most significant of these, Joachim of Flora (ca. 1135–1202), infused much of Christian Europe with the expectation of an impending transition to the final, perfect age of the spirit. As Marjorie Reeves and others have shown, this sense of imminent change and crisis was inherited even by many of the chief opponents of Joachimite thought, including the Order of Preachers and those Franciscans who remained orthodox throughout the various doctrinal disputes of the period. The mild Roger Bacon and Nicholas of Lyra both reflected the influence of Joachim in their writings; Bonaventure, who himself defended the Franciscan Order against charges of Joachimism and attacked Joachim's views on many points, was, as Reeves notes, "a Joachite [in spite of himself]."

Descriptions of the end of days such as those of Joachim and those to which Joachim's legacy gave rise usually included the conversion of all infidels to Christianity. Messianic expectations, therefore, naturally contributed to the general conversionist spirit exhibited by the friars during the thirteenth century. Since of all the infidels the Jews were supposed to convert first, many probably viewed their conversion *en masse*—one means of ridding Christendom of Judaism—as a pressing task to be performed in order to pave the way for final redemption. Confuting the errors of the Jews thus took on a more aggressive character than it had had when intended chiefly for the internal consumption of the Christian community. Joachim himself, who ascribed especial significance to the conversion of the Jews in his own account of the end, explicitly drew this connection between polemic and eschatology. Introducing his own polemical *Adversus Iudeos*, he writes:

> Many have thought to act against the ancient stupidity of the Jews with texts from Scripture because, if there will not be one to resist those who assail our faith, opportunity will be given to the enemies of the cross of Christ to deride the simplicity of those believing in the Christian name. And these, who are weak in intelligence, will suffer the destruction of [their] faith. I, however, wish to oppose their [the Jews'] controversy and perfidy not only for this [reason], but also because I feel that the time for pitying them is at hand, the time of their consolation and conversion.

Some have speculated that Innocent III's attacks on the Jews may have derived from his own expectations of the apocalypse. In his commentary on the Apocalypse, the Franciscan Spiritual Peter Olivi called upon the members of his order to missionize among the Jews. And because the Jews had traditionally been labeled the devotees of Antichrist, the presumed imminence of the final battle between the latter and the forces of Christ may well have added to anti-Jewish hostilities still further.

The new attitude to the Jews, however, appears to have derived even more from a mounting trend in ecclesiastical circles to view the Church of Rome (*romana ecclesia*) not merely as the papal see or delimited jurisdiction of the pope in a Christendom governed jointly by spiritual and temporal swords, but rather as comprising the entire Christian *respublica* [commonwealth] or *congregatio fidelium* [congregation of the faithful]. The idea of the Church as a supranational entity had always held a prominent place in Catholic theology, but it began to have its greatest effect upon the European consciousness only with the Gregorian reform and investiture controversy of the eleventh century. As the Church endeavored to model European Christendom along the lines of Gregory's perfect *societas christiana*, it also claimed universal headship of that society, relegating secular princes to a level of secondary authority and importance. All of society came to be viewed as an organic unity, whose *raison d'être* consisted of striving for and ultimately realizing the perfect unity of Christ on earth. Within such a unity, every component or constituent unit had to be measured from a teleological perspective: not only did each component of the whole have to further the ideals of the whole, but it also had to embody on a microcosmic level the ideals of the macrocosm. The Christian nature of this unity accordingly determined the necessity for its governance by those who best reflected that nature, and the fact that the whole society far outweighed in value and importance the sum total of all its members precluded any allowance for individualism or deviation within the society at large. Otto Gierke thus describes

> those theocratic and spiritualistic traits which are manifested by the Medieval Doctrine of Society. On the one side, every ordering of a human community must appear as an organic member of that *Civitas Dei*, that God-State, which comprehends the heavens and the earth. Then, on the other hand, the eternal and other-worldly aim and objective of every individual man must, in a directer or an indirecter fashion, determine the aim and object of every group into which he enters.

This conception of Christendom, together with its hierocratic implications, came closest to being realized during the first half of the thirteenth century, beginning with the pontificate of Innocent III. Innocent's attempts at reform of the Church and his campaigns against its various enemies all served to further the higher unity of Christendom under papal direction, and many have singled out Innocent as the pope who in his relations with temporal rulers enunciated the most far-reaching claims of papal lordship over the world. Yet however one evaluates Innocent's claims to temporal power, the pope's desire to unite Christian society clearly emerges in the ecumenical Fourth Lateran Council that he convened in 1215. Inviting not only Catholic clerics but also laymen and representatives of the four Greek Orthodox patriarchs to this synod, Innocent intended that it truly represent the totality of Christendom. In his bull of indiction of the council, *Vineam Domini Sabaoth*, he consequently assigned to the gathering the most extensive of responsibilities: the reform of Christian life, the suppression of heresy, the regulation of the clergy, the waging of a crusade, and "other matters too many to enumerate." It is not surprising that Innocent's idealism and activities greatly strengthened the organic conception of Christian unity, allowing it to wield considerable influence over thirteenth-century Europe.

An overriding concern with the properly ordered wholeness and functional unity of Christendom manifested itself in multifarious ways in the spiritual and intellectual climate of the period. Numerous cultural historians have demonstrated how as an interest in a unifying synthesis overcame that in intellectual exploration and individualistic creativity, the humanism of the "renaissance" of the twelfth century gave way to the scholasticism of the thirteenth. The *summa*, the complete synthesis and clarification of a field of learning in accordance with accepted philosophical and logical principles, quickly came to constitute the crowning achievement of scholastic writers. Among theologians of the thirteenth century, there appears a trend of reinterpreting the traditional themes of nature and grace so as to place greater emphasis on life in this world. Whether one considers this phenomenon in terms of Francis of Assisi's attempt to live a life of evangelical piety without withdrawing from society, a way of life which laid great stress on the spirituality of nature, or of Thomas Aquinas's appreciation of the inherent goodness in nature, the new theological trend allowed for less bifurcation between the spiritual and mundane in daily life. It rather induced an attempt to unify every aspect of one's existence in the pursuit of the religious ideal. Even the architectural style of the period, epitomized by the Gothic cathedral, reflects the new interest in synthesizing the totality of the human experience. According to one writer, "The cathedral is perhaps best understood as a 'model' of the medieval universe. It is the theological transparency of this universe that transformed the model into a symbol."

As men in every discipline of human intellectual creativity thus came to concentrate on the functional unity of their world—based, as it was, in the notion of the universality of the Roman Church—many saw fit to liken the totality of Christian society to the *corpus mysticum Christi*, the mystical body of Christ. The use of this metaphor to denote the society of all the faithful, rather than the body of Christ as mystically contained in the Eucharist, commenced during the twelfth century, as a result of a new stress on the doctrine of transubstantiation which caused the body of Christ in the sacrament simply to be labeled *corpus Christi*. By the thirteenth century, philosophers, theologians, and lawyers alike appropriated the image of Christ's mystical body to express their conception of Christendom; many soon came to describe the state in the same way. The term effectively captured the end, the true nature, and the ideal constitution of Christian society, as they had to be reflected in the society as a whole and in the functioning of each of its constituent members. In its opening canon, the Fourth Lateran Council suggested that it too shared this outlook.

> There is one universal Church of the faithful, outside of which absolutely no one is saved, and in which Jesus Christ is himself at once both priest and sacrifice. His body and his blood are truly contained in the sacrament of the altar in the forms of the bread and the wine, the bread being transubstantiated into the body and the wine into the blood by the divine power, in order that to perfect the mystery of the unity [of Christ] we ourselves may receive from him what he received on our account. No one can perform this sacrament except a priest ritually ordained according to the [authority of the] keys of the Church, which Jesus Christ himself bestowed upon the apostles and their successors.

Introducing its legislative program, the council simultaneously declared the universality and unity of the Church, linked that unity to the mystery of Christ's transubstantiated body, and stressed the primary role of the clergy in perfecting that unity.

The view, as expressed by Thomas Aquinas, that "the holy Church is called one mystical body by analogy with the physical body of man," assumed particular significance because its period of prevalence coincided with the reentrance of the concept of the organic corporation—that is, of the corporation as a fictitious person—into Western political and legal theory. Inasmuch as anthropomorphic imagery befitted both the *corpus mysticum* and the corporation equally well, the former soon borrowed from the attributes of the latter, thus affecting more profoundly the particulars of conceptions of how Christendom should operate. Specifically, thirteenth-century decretalists, themselves also concerned with incorporating the proper order of the world into their legal system, used a concept of a corporate mystical body upon which to base their theory of papal monarchy: just as a body is governed by its head, so the universal *romana ecclesia* [Roman Church] must be governed by its head, or Christ, represented on earth by the pope. The logic of this power structure derived straightforwardly from the salvific goals of Christian society. The pope has the ultimate responsibility for the welfare of Christian souls; so to none other than his vicar should Christ have properly granted supreme authority on earth, in order that all Christian individuals and institutions might effectively contribute to the holy mission of the Church and the attainment of salvation for the faithful.

The theory of the pope's *plenitudo potestatis* [fulness of powers] enunciated by the decretalists [interpreters of Church law] thus translated current ideas on the unity of Christendom into law and political theory. During the thirteenth century, the internal organization of the Church did indeed come to resemble a monarchy. The administration of the papal curia was more centralized than the court of any European kingdom and assumed many of the trappings of royalty as well. Furthermore, the papacy demanded immediate submission from temporal rulers who thwarted its objectives; it did not hesitate repeatedly to depose and excommunicate the recalcitrant emperor Frederick II. Popes claimed supreme judicial authority not only over Christians but over infidels as well. And Pope Gregory IX in 1234 promulgated the first official code of canon law, the *Decretales*, to insure the smooth administration of his domains. Although the popes were by no means unopposed in these efforts, their monarchic tendencies demonstrate how the government, in addition to the self-consciousness, of Christendom during the period derived from an ideal of universal Christian society on earth. Boniface VIII, whose bull *Unam sanctam* of 1302 perhaps enunciates most explicitly the medieval papacy's claim to power, in that bull himself drew this connection.

> That there is one holy, Catholic and apostolic Church we are bound to believe and to hold, our faith urging us, and this we do firmly believe and simply confess; and that outside this Church there is no salvation or remission of sins, as her spouse proclaims in the Canticles, "One is my dove, my perfect one. She is the only one of her mother, the chosen of her that bore her"; which represents one mystical body whose head is Christ, while the head of Christ is God. In this Church there is one Lord, one faith, one baptism. At the time of the flood there was one ark, symbolizing one Church. It was finished in one

cubit and had one helmsman and captain, namely Noah, and we read that all things on earth outside of it were destroyed.... Therefore there is one body and one head of this one and only Church, not two heads as though it were a monster, namely Christ and Christ's vicar, Peter and Peter's successor.

At the time when Boniface VIII issued the bull *Unam sanctam*, the political realities of Western Europe did not comport with the ideal of a perfectly unified, papally dominated Christendom as described by the pontiff. The concept of distinct national states was rapidly on the ascendant. It has been argued, however, that during the previous century many had come to envision the "supremacy of unity over plurality" in Christian society as a polity. If that is correct, one could expect them to have expressed their devotion to the ideals of Christendom in terms of sentiments resembling nationalism and patriotism. It is precisely during the thirteenth century that scholars discern the first appearance of nationalism and patriotism in Western Europe, in the law and the propaganda of the period. By the end of the century, when the centralized, monarchic power of the papacy had already begun to decline, the term *patria* denoted specific national entities like England and France. Yet the notion of the *patria* and devotion thereto (patriotism) had always constituted important motifs in the theology of the Church; Ernst Kantorowicz accordingly urges that "one should at least consider the possibility whether—before the full impact of legal and humanistic doctrines became effective—the new territorial concept of *patria* did not perhaps develop as a resecularized offshoot of the Christian tradition and whether the new patriotism did not thrive also on ethical values transferred back from the *patria* in heaven to the polities on earth." More definitively, Kantorowicz has shown that like the theory of papal *plenitudo potestatis*, the emergence of feelings of patriotism on behalf of one's polity also derived from the current tendency to view Christendom as a corporate *corpus mysticum*. Patriotism too emanated at least to some extent from the conception of the world as the unity of a universal Christian society.

In a society which was committed to an ideal of organic unity, which demanded of all its members a functional contribution to the achievement of that unity, which defined both its ideal and its mode of organization in terms of the mystical body of Christ, which operated (at least in theory) as the centralized monarchy of the earthly vicar of Christ, and which gave rise to intense feelings of patriotism on its own behalf, no room existed for infidels. Such trends in the political and religious thought of the thirteenth century certainly made the climate ripe for the exclusion of the Jews, the infidels most deeply imbedded in the society, from Christendom. Still other developments, however, may have predisposed agents of the Church such as the friars to scrutinize the substance of contemporary Judaism and develop the theory of Jewish heresy which justified breaking with the Augustinian precedent of toleration. The power and unity of the *romana ecclesia* reached their peak during the first half of the thirteenth century; by the end of the century and throughout the following one, they proceeded along a course of rather steady decline. Sensing, as most empires do at their point of greatest expansion, the impending threat of centrifugal forces which would lead to contraction and decline, the Church attempted to protect the gains it had achieved. It strove to entrench itself at the summit of its power and exhibited in three significant ways the extreme sort of defensiveness characteristic of declining empires.

First, whereas the drive toward realizing the perfect unity of Christendom included the scholastic effort to produce intellectual syntheses which themselves mirrored that unity, the defensiveness of the thirteenth-century Church manifested itself in an attempt to rule and regulate human thought. Ideas or beliefs that did not accord strictly with those of the establishment were seen not only as undermining the Church's authority but as threatening to destroy the Christian unity that the Church struggled to maintain. And the ideal of an essentially totalistic society toward which the Church strove inevitably stimulated the rise of opposing intellectual and theological currents, which in turn only served to make the ecclesiastical reaction harsher. We have already considered the papacy's definition of heresy during this period as a crime of treason against Christendom and the subsequent founding of the Inquisition to combat it. As we have seen, heresy in general, and contemporary heresies in particular, opposed many of the basic pillars of medieval Christian society. We then need here only emphasize the underlying connection between the Inquisition and the earthly head of Christ's mystical body. As Walter Ullmann has observed,

> The papal Inquisition must be understood from the contemporary medieval standpoint which knew no freedom of expression or thought in regard to matters touching the substance of faith. Hence aberration from faith as papally fixed was not only (as it was said) a sign of intellectual arrogance, but also, and more so, an act of rebellion against constituted authority which claimed a monopoly in all matters relating to the religious foundations of society.

Nor did the papacy limit its expression of such monopolistic claims to the establishment of the Inquisition. The thirteenth century also saw a steady rise in the intervention of the papacy in the affairs of the University of Paris, an attempt to control the pursuits of the finest philosophical and theological minds in Europe; in the eyes of the Church, as F. M. Powicke has remarked, "the university was a function of Christian society, not a separate order." If ideas that did not conform to the established order of things had to be eradicated, one can appreciate the fervor with which the Church pursued the attack on the Talmud and the Judaism it maintained: Living according to the teachings of the Talmud, the Jews did not fulfill their proper function in Christian society; they and their doctrines accordingly detracted from the unity of Christ. And owing to the alleged hostility of rabbinic Judaism toward the proponents and fundamental beliefs of Christianity, the medieval Jew may well have presented an even greater threat to Latin Christendom than the typical heretic. It is perhaps appropriate that Pope Gregory IX issued his famous regulatory bull *Parens scientiarum* to the University of Paris, prohibited the study of unexpurgated texts of Aristotle, ordered that his *Decretales* be adopted at Paris and Bologna as the sole standard legal textbook, and founded the first permanent tribunals of the Inquisition, all only a few years before he received Nicholas Donin at the papal curia.

A second manifestation of defensiveness in the clerical establishment of the thirteenth century, and perhaps a corollary of the first, was a tendency to fear and attack all innovation in theology. Theoretically, the authentic teachings of Christianity all derived from Scripture, as it had been interpreted by the Church fathers, popes, and councils. What did not ultimately accord with the Bible and the teachings of the early Church had no proper place in the unifying religious synthesis of the period; the very fact of its novelty disqualified any claims to legitimacy and constituted prima facie evidence of heresy. The importance of this outlook in the friars' attack on contemporary Judaism should be evident. The Jews of medieval Europe espoused a new system of belief; they had lost the right to exist in Christendom previously accorded them because of their adherence to ancient, biblical Judaism. The appearance of such argumentation, however, was not limited to the exchanges between mendicants and Jews. One finds it in another controversy, which, like the first attacks on the Talmud, was centered at the University of Paris, but in which the friars themselves were depicted as guilty of *innovatio*. During the conflict between secular and mendicant clergy at the University of Paris, the secular masters expressed particular resentment at the mendicant doctrine of absolute poverty, portrayed by the friars as a necessary prerequisite for achieving the highest level of evangelical piety. The secular masters responded that the Bible did not portray Jesus and the apostles as living in absolute poverty, and that the friars, by maintaining the doctrine, cast aspersions on the piety of popes and prelates since the time of the earliest Church.

William of St. Amour, the first major spokesman for the secular masters, writes in one of his anti-mendicant works that a man is a false rather than a true preacher not only if he preaches against Scripture but even if he teaches what simply does not appear in or derive from the Bible. Turning to the friars, he then explains:

> Certain preachers, desiring to convert the people to their new way of life, introduce certain superstitious novelties not within the tradition of the Church but which bear the appearance of sanctity. It appears that they are seeking vain glory.... Of this sort seem to be those preachers who [perform] various

new and unheard of, simulated works of penitence, in order that it be believed by the multitude. They also practice certain new, unheard of, and superstitious traditions, and they display [them] and teach [that they should] be displayed publicly, contrary to divine Scripture, canonical institutes, and the custom of the Church.

William proceeds to charge that contravening the advice of Seneca against innovation, the friars have invented these new traditions to make themselves appear more perfect, humble, and pious than anyone else. Yet these traditions, dubbed *religiones* by the mendicants, are in fact the creations of men and not of God; one ought more suitably to call them superstition and sacrilege, since they actually violate the word of the divine author of the true religion. For instance, although these preachers conceal money like all other regular clergy and will accept a gift when offered one, they have invented the tradition of evangelical poverty to feign greater perfection, despite its opposition to the rules and teachings of the Church. They teach that one truly pious should not even engage in manual labor but should live entirely from alms, even though canonical tradition explicitly forbids unnecessary begging. Or they falsely state that they have the power of hearing confessions in parishes not specifically their own. In their departure from Scripture, William concludes, "those who under the guise of piety or *religio* contrive such or similar traditions opposed to divine and apostolic documents and the statutes of the holy fathers are similar to the hypocritical Pharisees, who, at the time of the teaching of Christ, on account of their own traditions which bore the appearance of piety, transgressed and caused the transgression of the precepts of God." Just as the traditions of the Pharisees, the first of the rabbis of the Talmud, departed from the authentic traditions of Judaism, so mendicant doctrines may, William wrote, be fairly labeled "superstition" because "they were not handed down to us by the Lord Jesus Christ nor by his apostles nor by the holy councils nor by the canonical writings of the holy doctors but were introduced by certain newcomers of their own will." So deviant were the friars' teachings that William finally dubs them *sectae* or sectarian; they have no place in the true faith and prove the falseness of the mendicant preachers. Gerard d'Abbeville, the next major propagandist for the secular masters, similarly accuses the friars of obscuring the divine teachings of Scripture with their own human traditions. According to Gerard, the mendicant doctrine of poverty challenges the legitimacy of various papal rights and powers, thereby causing the friars to detract from the unity of the body that is the Roman Church and to fall into the sin of heresy.

Admittedly, William and Gerard both wrote years after the first attack on the Talmud at the University of Paris; one could not argue that their campaign against the doctrinal innovation of the friars overflowed into a confrontation between the latter and the Jews. Nevertheless, the similarity between the accusations leveled during the two controversies appears marked, too much so to reflect mere coincidence. If the charges of one controversy did not directly lead to those of another—and the possibility does remain that the attack on the Talmud influenced that against the friars—they still manifest the same prevalent intellectual tendency among many clergy of the thirteenth century. All theological ideas required careful scrutiny to insure their conformity with the teachings of Scripture as interpreted in the tradition of the Church. Nonscriptural beliefs detracted from the unity of Christendom and could not be tolerated; they were novel and thus warranted eradication as sectarian or heretical. Given such a context, one can well appreciate the vehemence of the Church's attack on the hitherto unknown Talmud of the Jews.

Finally, a third by-product of the defensiveness of thirteenth-century Christendom emerged in the conversion of quasi-nationalistic sentiments of patriotism on behalf of the universal Church into expressions of nativism. The term "nativism" presently appears most often in the writings of American historians, but this should not impose any necessary limitation on the extent of its usefulness and applicability. Nativism denotes an outlook of a society in which anyone whose basic concerns, allegiances, and ideals lie outside those of the society cannot be a citizen in good standing and threatens the welfare of all other citizens. "Nativism is a state of mind, conscious or unconscious, intimately connected with nationalism. Its roots, like those of nationalism, spring from a sense of common associations, common history, common speech, common customs, common religion, etc." Many in the thirteenth century also seem to have taken this short leap from a sort of aggressive Christian nationalism or patriotism to a defensive nativism. If Europe comprised a wholly Christian unity, every non-Christian not only was alien to Christian society but very quickly became an enemy as well. The Spanish Council of Valladolid in 1322 reflected this mindset when it decreed that "the Church of God, in which the divine offices are celebrated and the sacrament of the Eucharist is consecrated, ought to be purged, in order that it might not be profaned by contact between infidels and the faithful." Foreigners in a homogenous society detracted from the society's unity and were therefore prone to antagonism from all good patriotic citizens. And as John Boswell has recently noted in the case of homosexuals, the purging of alien elements did not in itself suffice; even those Christians whose personal values openly differed from those of the majority faced persecution and social ostracism in thirteenth-century Europe. Like the extreme German nationalism of the late nineteenth century, which gave rise to anti-Semitic indictments of the satanic, talmudic culture of contemporary Jews and demanded their exclusion from the fatherland, or the great American reform movement earlier in the century, which denounced Catholics for deserting the truth of Christianity, opposing American ideals, and perpetrating grossly unethical and hostile crimes against society, the Church's scrutinizing and condemnation of medieval Judaism made perfect sense in the context of nativism. For the *romana ecclesia* was also a society which strove to achieve functional unity and root out foreign influences. It too attacked a religious group which detracted from that unity, charging it with the same basic crimes: heretical deviation from Scripture, blaspheming the ideals of the society, and immoral and unnatural hostility toward its citizens. Nativism may well have served as at least one catalyst in the development of the view that the Jews had no rightful place in Christendom. If so, one might further appreciate the fact that increased popular persecutions of medieval European Jewry, as well as the expulsion of Jews *en masse* from European countries at the end of the Middle Ages, characteristically accompanied the growth of nationalism and national representative governments.

The intellectual and spiritual climate of thirteenth-century Europe, ingrained with the notion of Christian unity, made the time ripe for a new exclusionist attitude toward the Jews. The monarchic papacy assumed the right of intervention in the internal doctrinal affairs of the Jewish community. Canonists began to claim direct ecclesiastical jurisdiction over the Jews. And as R. W. Southern has noted, the general religious enthusiasm of the time gave "specious justification" for the people of Europe to inflict violence upon the Jews. As we have seen, however, the major work for developing, refining, and justifying the new attitude was performed by the Dominicans and Franciscans. The friars' importance in this regard ought not to be deemed accidental, since the creation and character of the two mendicant orders derived from and responded to the same needs and the same climate of the European religious community of which we have spoken. Modern scholars have called the thirteenth century "the golden age of the friars," because, in the words of David Knowles,

> St Francis and St Dominic, in different but complementary ways, gave to the Church a new form of religious life, which had an immense and permanent appeal, and one which both attracted a new type of recruit and in its turn inspired an apostolate to the laity, to the heretic and to the heathen. Not only did the appearance of the friars rescue the western church from its drift toward heresy and schism, but the new warmth of devotional life, the preaching, the confessing and the daily counsel of the friars gave a new strength to the lower level of Christian society and indirectly acted as a powerful agent of spiritual growth and social union, thus inevitably compensating for the growing power of legalism and political motives at the higher levels of church life. In addition, the friars had a major share in the wonderful flowering of theological genius in the schools. They had a twofold influence in the realm of the spirit. They ... brought back to the Christian consciousness the earthly life of Christ in its love, its poverty and its suffering as an ideal to be followed to the end, while at the same time they presented the theological expression of Christ's message in the lecture-room and pulpit throughout Christendom.

The friars thus made a decisive impression on Christian society of the period, and in so doing, they contributed much to achieving and maintaining the unity of Christendom of which we have spoken. Established by the Church to teach and preach against heresy, the two mendicant orders actively combatted the centrifugal forces that threatened Christian unity. Pledged to rules which prescribed lives of evangelical piety, the friars exemplified the macrocosm of Christian universality in their own individual behavior. Owing to their own social origins, they added an entirely new dimension to Christian unity, by directing their own spiritual and religious life to meet the needs of the worldliest of middle-class types, the merchant and the financier. The mendicants thereby bridged some of the gap between the *religiosus* and the layman, enabling them to participate together in the same spiritual pursuits. And in disputing with and endeavoring to convert the infidel, the friars tried to expand and perfect the unity of the Christian society, both within and outside the physical domains of European Christendom. In the mystical body of Christ, the friars represented those cells charged with fighting off external enemies and combatting internal infection; or, in the image of Gregory IX's bull *Descendentes*, the friars were meant to set the ship of the Church aright and steer it from darkness into light, successfully catching the fish of the sea in its nets.

A significant number of the friars themselves expressed the prevalent conception of an ideally ordered and united Christian society. While serving as Gregory IX's chaplain during the 1230s, Raymond de Peñaforte compiled the *Decretales*, which Gregory proceeded to promulgate as the sole recognized code of canon law, to be studied and implemented universally —clearly a means of promoting Christian unity. Like the Franciscan author of the Bavarian *Schwabenspiegel*, Berthold von Regensburg consistently supported papal attempts to rule and unify Christendom. His two sermons in which he denied Jews access to the "field" of Christendom dealt specifically with the theme of Christian unity. In one of them, Berthold describes the three walls surrounding the field—the papacy, the temporal powers, and the angels—each of which must do its proper duty to protect Christendom or else suffer the punishment of damnation. In the other sermon, Berthold divides the population of Christendom into ten classes, corresponding to the ten orders of angels in heaven. The first three classes, comprising the pope and the secular clergy, the religious orders, and the temporal princes, again have the responsibility for protecting and administering the field, all under the direction of the papacy. Among the next six classes of laymen, every individual must strive to fulfill his own particular function for the sake of the entire society. Only in this way can Christendom preserve its unity. If one should not function properly and thus detract from Christian unity, he will fall into the tenth class of people, the apostates who have allied with the devil. Raymond Lull eagerly awaited the establishment of a universal and united Catholic world order, in the realization of which the conversion of the infidels constituted but one, albeit crucial, step. Bernard Gui's *Practica* was by its very nature committed to preserving and enforcing the unity of Christian faith. And recent research has shown how even Nicholas of Lyra concerned himself with the proper government of Christian society and ecclesiology of the Church; he too enunciated a belief in the unity of Christendom as comprising that of a single body. The attack of these friars on the Jews might well be understood, therefore, as deriving from the overriding concern for Christian unity during the thirteenth and early fourteenth centuries and from their active roles in trying to realize it—whether as inquisitor, missionary, Semitist, poet, or itinerant preacher.

Bibliography

BERNARD S. BACHRACH, *Early Medieval Jewish Policy in Western Europe* (1977).
JOHN BOSWELL, *Christianity, Social Tolerance, and Homosexuality* (1980).
ROBERT CHAZAN, *Medieval Jewry in Northern France* (1973).
NORMAN COHN, *The Pursuit of the Millennium* (1970).
JOHN B. FREED, *The Friars and German Society in the Thirteenth Century* (1977).
BERNARD MCGINN, *Visions of the End: Apocalyptic Traditions in the Middle Ages* (1979).
HEIKO A. OBERMAN, *The Roots of Anti-Semitism in the Age of Rennaissance and Reformation* (1984).
JAMES PARKES, *The Jew in the Medieval Community* (1976).
MARJORIE REEVES, *The Influence of Prophecy in the Later Middle Ages: A Study in Joachimism* (1969).
CECIL ROTH, *The Jews of Medieval Oxford* (1951).

The Quest for the True Church

SCOTT H. HENDRIX

Throughout the Middle Ages, when reform-minded churchmen and laity demanded a return to the "true church," they had in mind both personal and communal reform on the model of the "pure" church of the first apostles. After 1300, when the church had become an important temporal power, confidence in papal authority and church leadership was shaken because the papacy no longer embraced the apostolic model. This fueled a new, critical debate over the nature of the true church.

New authorities and models of the true church appeared. The Spiritual Franciscans, radical followers of St. Francis of Assisi, developed a "remnant" ecclesiology: the true church, they argued, was a small remnant of Christians who lived according to apostolic example. Marsilius of Padua, perhaps the most important political theorist of the fourteenth century, attacked papal claims to temporal power and declared Scripture to be the test of the true church. He also argued that the right to interpret Scripture authoritatively lay not with the pope but with a representative church council. The philosopher William of Ockham went still further. He depicted all institutional authority as fallible and argued that the church might exist in a remnant as small as a single individual, as he believed had happened at the time of Christ's crucifixion when only Mary remained faithful. Even the conservative chancellor of the University of Paris, Jean Gerson, deemed councils the truest medium of the Holy Spirit and superior to popes who manifestly abused their powers. The Hussites of Bohemia, whom Gerson persecuted at the Council of Constance, attempted to recover the true church by implementing such apostolic practices as *utraquism*, that is, lay communion in both bread and wine (the Roman church traditionally reserved the Eucharistic wine to the clergy).

At the end of these many debates, and as something of a synthesis

---

From "In Quest of the *Vera Ecclesia*: The Crises of Late Medieval Ecclesiology" by Scott H. Hendrix. Copyright © 1976 by The Regents of the University of California. Reprinted from *Viator*, vol. 7, 1976, pp. 347–378, by permission of the author and The Regents.

of them, stands the Protestant Reformation, which declared the true church to exist wherever the Word of God is truly preached and believed.

The quest for the true church is almost as old as the church itself. Prior to the year 1300 this search manifested itself most frequently in the call for personal and communal reform and renewal. The predominant model for this reform was the *ecclesia primitiva* [primitive church] an idealized picture of the earliest Christian community. This picture was a composite of the simple life and teachings of Jesus and his disciples, the allegedly unadulterated gospel of the apostles and, finally, the unselfish communal life shared by the earliest Christians as portrayed in such New Testament passages as Acts 4:32ff. The last-named element served as the most important basis for the exemplary form of the quest, monasticism, which in the West became the vehicle for the Christian idea of reform. The monastic renewal movement of the tenth and eleventh centuries, spearheaded by such monasteries as Cluny and Hirsau, resulted in the stringent clerical reform of Gregory VII and in the proliferation of stricter orders such as the Cistercians of the twelfth century.

Reform on the model of the apostolic ideal was also the mother of dissent in the early Middle Ages. This dissent was sparked by the failure of the Roman Church to live up to the standards of simplicity and poverty set by the ideal picture of the primitive church. As the Roman hierarchy became more and more unwilling and unable to fulfill the demands for reform imposed by dissenters such as the Humiliati and the Waldensians, it excluded them from the church, labeled them heretical, and sought to repress them by means of the Inquisition.

Beginning with the fourteenth century, however, the quest for the true church assumed a multifaceted form which resulted in a much more complex ecclesiological landscape than had hitherto existed. The ideal of the primitive church was not discarded, but it was supplemented by a variety of ecclesiological theories which went beyond the simple call for a return to the apostolic ideal. These theories were embodied in treatises which were devoted primarily to ecclesiological questions. Whereas prior to 1300 ecclesiological issues seldom received exclusive attention except in the writings of the canonists, the next two centuries were punctuated by the appearance of tracts *De ecclesia* ["On the Church"], which sought to define the locus of the true church and to spell out the foundation of its authority. These screeds were written by papalists, conciliarists and advocates of views which can be classified as neither of the above. Studies of the church and its authority were composed by orthodox and heterodox alike, from the

Augustinian James of Viterbo at the turn of the fourteenth century to the ex-Augustinian Martin Luther at the end of the Middle Ages.

The variety and sophistication of these ecclesiological works transposed the late medieval quest for the true church into a higher key. The new intensity which marked this quest was sparked by a crisis of confidence in the papal hierarchy which began in the thirteenth century with the challenge of the Waldensians and the Franciscan Spirituals. It received added fuel in the conflict between the papacy and the French and imperial rulers and burned brightest during the conflict between pope and pope, and pope and council, during the Great Schism (1378–1417). In the aftermath of the schism the quest appeared to die down, only to flame up again, at first a mere flicker, in the reluctant resistance of Martin Luther which finally ignited the Protestant Reformation. In all stages of the crisis, critics of the established church and especially of the papal hierarchy proposed ecclesiological alternatives which substantially limited (and occasionally eliminated) the authority of the papacy in their views of the church. Dissident groups and thinkers constructed models of the church which in many cases were far removed from the existing ecclesial reality.

The new quest for the church thus resulted in a broad spectrum of ecclesiological options being made available to late medieval men. Consequently, to a number of historians who have taken note of the complexity of late medieval ecclesiology, the late Middle Ages have appeared to be a period of ecclesiological confusion and uncertainty. A few have even used this disagreement on the nature and authority of the church to discredit the later Middle Ages in contrast to the preceding centuries and to explain how the Reformers of the sixteenth century were able so easily to captivate late medieval people. Just as crisis does not equal decline, however, neither is variety equivalent to confusion and decadence. Crisis periods do, to be sure, tear down old securities and ideals. However, they also produce new solutions and new certainties. Instead of disparaging the diversified late medieval quest for the true church as a sign of theological and ecclesiastical degeneration, it is historically more productive to look for its provenance and significance in the context of its times.

The heightened sense of urgency which characterized the quest both distinguishes it from its early medieval manifestations and identifies it as part and parcel of the crisis atmosphere of the late Middle Ages in general. This crisis went deeper than a crisis of confidence in the papacy. It presented many faces—social, political, economic, and ecclesiastical—and historians are by no means agreed on which factors ought to be weighed most heavily in assessing the crisis. Recently, however, F. Graus has offered a tentative explanation for the ecclesiological crisis of the later Middle Ages which deserves attention for its ability to interrelate economic, social, political and religious factors. According to Graus, the description of a crisis includes all the phenomena which result in the breaking up of a way of life in a society. Most important is the feeling of the people that the basic values of their society have been menaced to such an extent that they appear on the verge of disintegrating. Late medieval society manifested this heightened sense of insecurity in several domains: economic instability, social unrest, urban tension, national feeling. For Graus, however, spiritual values are more crucial than socio-economic factors to any analysis of the causes of crisis in a society. These spiritual values were particularly threatened by the religious perplexity provoked by the Great Schism of the Western church. Thus Graus regards the crisis of the late Middle Ages as coming to a head in the crisis of confidence in the identity and authority of the church.

The insights of Graus suggest why a crisis of confidence in the papacy could provoke such an intense quest for the true church in the later Middle Ages. The purpose of the present essay is to examine selected expressions of this quest from the perspective of Graus, that is, to view the ecclesiologies which arose out of this quest as responses of late medieval people to the uncertainty surrounding the church's nature and authority. Since it is impossible to deal with the whole of the late medieval ecclesiology in one essay, this discussion is limited to representative samples of the quest which display both the nuances of ecclesiological answers and the continuity of ecclesiological themes which have been recognized with ever finer discrimination in recent research. From this perspective, the crisis-marred landscape of late medieval ecclesiology appears much less confused and disarrayed, since the varied contours of the quest for the true church are seen as attempts to establish a sure ecclesiological foothold in the midst of an unsure social and ecclesiastical order. Furthermore, as the concluding section will propose, the Reformation of the sixteenth century may be appropriately regarded as the concluding phase of the late medieval quest in which again a variety of ecclesiological responses are made to the last medieval crisis of papal authority.

I

In the transition from the early medieval call for reform to the late medieval quest for the true church, many critics who railed against the wealth and power of the thirteenth-century church continued to measure that church by the standard of the *ecclesia primitiva*. In fact, this ideal persisted so strongly in the late Middle Ages that Gordon Leff was led to call the ideal of an apostolic church "the great new ecclesiological fact of the later Middle Ages." For centuries, however, the apostolic ideal had been cherished and invoked in countless cloisters of western Europe without questioning the legitimacy of the church hierarchy. Why, beginning with regularity in the twelfth and thirteenth centuries, were existing monastic structures no longer able to embody and nourish this ancient and revered ideal? Why did dissenting groups, such as the Waldensians and Franciscan Spirituals, give to this ideal an ever sharper polemical edge in their quest for the true church? Although the employment of the apostolic ideal *per se* was by no means a new ecclesiological strategy in the later Middle Ages, the peculiar critical intensity with which it was applied marked the first stage in the later medieval quest for the true church.

According to Leff, this intensity could be attributed to the revolutionary way in which late medieval dissenters harnessed the Bible into an historical justification for demanding a church modeled on the early Christian community. This use of the Bible assumed two forms. On the one hand, Christ's words and deeds were taken as real historical events and, where necessary, were used to counter the allegedly false claims and laws of the existing hierarchy. On the other hand, the Bible became a vehicle of prophecy in which real events took on eschatological significance.

The Waldensians illustrate the first type of usage. At first, their purpose was merely to embody and proclaim the apostolic ideal of poverty and simplicity. In spite of the papal prohibition against their preaching without clerical sanction. [Peter] Valdes considered it more necessary to obey the biblical injunction to preach (Mark 16:15) than the injunction to be subject to authority (Romans 13:1). As a result, in 1184 the "Poor Men of Lyon" were declared heretical. The Waldensians then developed their own hierarchy and employed the Bible as a blueprint for their common life together apart from the Roman Church. Indulgences, oaths, intercession of the saints and many other non-biblical practices were rejected as ecclesiastical innovations. They believed that they alone constituted the true church and that their priests alone deserved to perform sacramental functions because they were faithful to the *vita apostolica* [apostolic life].

Since the Waldensians were early ejected from the church, they never posed as serious a threat to the hierarchy as did the Franciscan Spirituals of the later thirteenth century. The more polemical Spirituals struck at the hierarchy from within what had quickly become one of the most significant orders of the church. They read Scripture through the bifocal lens of Saint Francis's Rule and Joachim of Fiore's prophecy. Hence, they illustrate the second usage of the Bible which Leff delineates: the Bible as a vehicle of prophecy. For example, the prophetic exegesis of the Apocalypse by Peter John Olivi (†1298) gave added urgency to the Spirituals' criticism of the pope. Olivi's followers, the Fraticelli, were quick to identify the carnal church of the Antichrist with the Roman Church which would soon be superseded by the true spiritual church composed of themselves. Such eschatological interpretation of current events turned the debate over apostolic poverty into a confrontation between the true and false churches....

...Although the apostolic ideal formed the core of the Spirituals' concern, the scriptural basis of this concern assumed a secondary role. The primary issues became, as in the case of the Waldensians, the nature of the church and the authority to interpret Scripture. The Spirituals, like the Waldensians, eventually came to believe that they composed the true spiritual church because they alone faithfully adhered to the rule of apostolic poverty. Since this belief placed both groups in minority positions, they were forced to develop remnant ecclesiologies which located the *vera ecclesia* [true church] in the faithful few opposed to the apostate many. On the question of authority, the Spirituals were even willing to endow both an extrascriptural document and an extrascriptural office with divine authority —all, of course, in the name of a scriptural ideal.

Granted that the reading of the Bible imparted new seriousness to the apostolic ideal in the twelfth and thirteenth centuries, the question still remains: why at this particular juncture in the Middle Ages did medieval *viatores* [earnest Christians] become so serious about the apostolic ideal that... they attempted to apply it to the entire clergy and laity? After all, the Bible had always been the source of the apostolic ideal. Cultural, social and economic factors figure significantly in the answer to this question, but to an extent as yet unclarified. Additional guidance in answering the question can be gained by analyzing the crucial ecclesiological shift in the medieval landscape which occurred in the late twelfth and thirteenth centuries. The shift involved the transition from an ecclesiological stance which sought to reform the church on the model of the *ecclesia primitiva* to a remnant ecclesiology which limited the true church to a minority either outside (the Waldensians) or within (the Spiritual Franciscans)... the Roman Church. What made this transition necessary? On the surface, the Roman Church was unwilling to allow such expressions of the apostolic ideal to persist unsupervised and unchecked in the church. At a more profound level, however, the transition was made necessary for the same reason that the apostolic ideal was treated with new seriousness and breadth in the first place: a heightened degree of uncertainty as to the locus of the true church.

The concept of the *ecclesia primitiva* itself can provide helpful insights into the reason why this uncertainly developed. G. Olsen has shown that the twelfth-century canonists used the term *ecclesia primitiva* to refer primarily to the pre-Constantinian church; such usage "suggested that the great divide in early church history was the reign of the first Christian emperor Constantine." The canonists themselves, while not explicitly expressing distaste for the success of Christianity after Constantine, at least implicitly were concerned about the integrity of Christianity in a world which made the church materially prosperous. Moralists like Bernard of Clairvaux had no qualms about making this implicit concern explicit and bewailing the worldliness of the post-Constantinian church in which the apostolic ideal had been betrayed. In a passage well known throughout the Middle Ages and quoted approvingly even by Martin Luther, Bernard noted the manifold persecutions which the pre-Constantinian church had to suffer. Consequently, he warned against the easy security which the prosperous church of his time enjoyed; this security constituted a far greater threat to the peace of the church than open persecution, for the church's worst enemies were those who posed as her friends.

A stark contrast with the worldliness of the post-Constantinian church therefore colored the concept of the *ecclesia primitiva*. It is not difficult to understand why, then, certain groups within the church invoked the ideal of apostolic poverty for everyone in order to restore the medieval church to its pre-Constantinian integrity. The Gregorian reform attempted to impress marks of the *vita apostolica* upon the clergy. Amidst the growing involvement of the medieval church in the economically and intellectually awakening world of the twelfth-century renaissance, it was only natural that this ideal would be extended by some groups to the entire church. In the case of the Franciscans, the situation was somewhat different. Here the concern was to restore their order, which had received special revelation of the divine sanction of this ideal, to its original state of strict poverty. Nevertheless, the result of both remarkably earnest applications of the ideal was the same. The concept of the *ecclesia primitiva* was transformed into a remnant ecclesiology when the demand for broader communication and stricter application of the apostolic ideal was not granted. Thus, in contrast to their status as the only true church, the Waldensians portrayed the Roman Church as having embodied the *congregatio peccatorum* [the gathering of sinners] from the time of Sylvester I. And the Spirituals claimed to represent the spiritual church over against the *ecclesia carnalis* [carnal church] which refused to attribute due significance to the ideal of poverty.

The concept of an *ecclesia primitiva* served these groups well as long as they fostered realistic hopes of reforming the Roman Church on the basis of apostolic poverty. When these hopes were dashed, however, the first in a series of spiritual crises which rocked the later Middle Ages occurred—a crisis of confidence in the church hierarchy serious enough to stimulate a quest for the true church apart from that hierarchy. This crisis was fundamentally ecclesiological in nature. In its first phase, uncertainty as to whether or not the Roman Church was living up to the ideal of the primitive church caused the biblical source of this ideal to be taken with renewed seriousness. When it became clear that the Roman Church would not allow this ideal to be expressed to the extent to which these groups desired, the crisis then moved into its next phase in which a decisive shift of emphasis was made: the concept of the *ecclesia primitiva* was applied to a remnant. Without delay, this remnant began to manifest one of the essential criteria for claiming equality with the primitive church—persecution. Persecution haunted the Waldensians in the Inquisition and the Spirituals before and after their condemnation. In this radically new ecclesiological application of an old ideal, the late medieval quest for the true church was underway.

II

The ecclesiological crisis atmosphere became increasingly tense during the first half of the fourteenth century. The controversy between Boniface VIII and Philip the Fair ended in a debacle for the papacy. Strong measures had to be taken to shore up its authority and prestige. That became clear already during the course of the controversy when the curial publicists, led by Giles of Rome, articulated the hitherto most radical claims to papal sovereignty. As the ecclesiastical conflict shifted from the confrontation between the papacy and the king of France to that between the papacy and the emperor (Louis of Bavaria), other champions of papal sovereignty arose to tighten the bond between membership in the true church and obedience to papal rulings. Some curialists... used the target of thirteenth-century papal critics, the Donation of Constantine, to support the pope's authority over the emperor, while others... adopted Olivi's concept of infallibility to preserve that papal sovereignty which it was originally intended to restrict.

The radical nature of the curialist claims betrays the gravity of the situation which threatened the papacy. The seriousness of the crisis during the conflict with Louis of Bavaria was also revealed by the earnestness and intensity with which the two most significant critics of the papacy undertook their task: Marsilius of Padua and William of Ockham. Both men employed ecclesiological tools forged already in the preceding century in order to gauge the approximation of the Roman hierarchy to their conception of the true church. Both found the amount of deviation too great for their liking and proposed ecclesiological adjustments which would correct for the inordinate authority attributed to the papacy. For both writers, albeit in slightly differing respects, the abuse of this authority accounted for the crisis which afflicted the church.

In the case of Marsilius, the very title of his work, *Defensor pacis* [Defender of Peace] (condemned in 1327), indicates that he considered himself to be the guardian of social tranquillity and peace against a "singular and very obscure cause [of strife] by which the Roman Empire has long been troubled." At the end of the first discourse, Marsilius finally reveals that this singular cause is the wrong opinion of certain Roman bishops that they have coercive temporal jurisdiction over the Roman ruler and also, perhaps, their perverted desire for rulership allegedly owed to them because of the plenitude of power bestowed by Christ. The source of this papal claim to authority over all other bishops and even over temporal rulers is "a certain edict and gift which certain men say that Constantine made to Saint Sylvester, Roman pontiff."

Marsilius's reference to the Donation of Constantine suggests that Gordon Leff may be correct when he contends that Marsilius stood in the tradition of those seekers of the true church who invoked the pre-Constantinian apostolic ideal as the model of church reform. Although, of course, he was not the first to employ that ideal, Leff claims that Marsilius "wrought it into the most devastating weapon of political criticism in later medieval ecclesiology." According to Leff, this reaffirmation of the apostolic way of life is much more crucial to Marsilius's criticism of the Roman hierarchy than his use of Aristotelian political philosophy to formulate a theory of popular sovereignty. Although Leff has not conclusively demonstrated what he calls the "bypassing" of Aristotle by late medieval critics of church and society, he has once again pointed to the central ecclesiological issue at stake in the crisis of the later Middle Ages. The issue is the locus of the true church and its authority, and it is discussed by Marsilius in the important chapter which follows his treatment of the early Christian church.

Marsilius raises the question, which beliefs are necessary for salvation and by whose authority are these beliefs determined. He answers that it is necessary for Christians to believe as irrevocably true no writings except the canonical scriptures or those interpretations of doubtful meanings of Scripture which have been made by a general council of faithful or catholic Christians. Why is this the case? Because in order to be certain of the faith, one cannot trust in writings produced by the human spirit, but only in the canonical scriptures. The latter do not include "the decretals or decrees of the Roman pontiff and his college of clergymen who are called 'cardinals,' nor any other human ordinances, contrived by the human mind, about human acts or disputes." A case in point is the bull *Cum inter nonnullos* of John XXII denying that Christ practiced absolute poverty. If such a papal decision were to be accepted, Marsilius says, "then the whole body of the faithful would lie in danger of shipwreck with respect to the faith." Only Scripture is certain and only a general council representing all faithful Christians can claim certain revelation of the Spirit when interpreting ambiguous points of Scripture like the extent of poverty required of Christ's followers.

Marsilius found his appeal to a general council to be quite compatible with the apostolic ideal by which he measured the papacy. It is well known, however, that his contemporary, William of Ockham, did not think highly enough of a general council to endow it with infallible authority. In fact, it is questionable to what extent Ockham appealed to the apostolic ideal at all, although he certainly favored the principle of absolute poverty. Rather than employing the *ecclesia primitiva* as a model for reform of the Roman Church, Ockham chose the more radical solution of locating the true church in a remnant of faithful Christians which theoretically could continue to exist apart from the Roman hierarchy if it were thought to have fallen into error.... In fact, this remnant ecclesiology assumed existential proportions for Ockham when he found himself defending the true church against precisely the kind of heretical pope which Olivi had envisaged—John XXII, the censurer of the Franciscan *usus pauper*.[9] ... As a true successor of Olivi, Ockham sought to uphold against John XXII the claim of those Franciscans who espoused absolute poverty. To carry out his purpose, he adopted and elaborated upon Olivi's theory of the irreformability of papal decrees....

... It is Ockham's remnant ecclesiology which appears to substantiate the charge [by his critics] of total subjectivity. Indeed, it does seem as if Ockham drops the responsibility of discerning truth from error into the lap

---

[9] The Franciscan ideal of owning nothing and leading a life of total, literal proverty.

of each individual Christian to an extent that would justify such a charge....

... It is possible nonetheless to put a more charitable construction upon Ockham's remnant ecclesiology which does not presume him guilty of the basest self-interest. For example, J. Miethke has recently argued that the possible survival of the church *in uno solo* [in a single individual] was not the reflection of a radical individualism arising out of Ockham's nominalist metaphysics. On the contrary, Ockham was appealing both to a venerable ecclesiological-liturgical tradition centered around Mary's lonely vigil at the Cross and to a theory of the canonists which has come down to us as the "corporation sole" [lodging authority in one person alone]....

Recently, S. Ozment has pointed to one ecclesiological implication of the Ockhamist emphasis upon God's free commitment to his covenant. If God has ordained that knowledge of himself and of the way of salvation reach man through his church, then the church is just as safely ensconced in the Ockhamist soteriological plan as it is in a Thomistically arranged hierarchy of being—and just as immune to attack. Over against Thomism, the church for the Ockhamists receives its unique mediatorial role as the result of a covenant and not because of its position within a supposed metaphysical hierarchy. Compared with mysticism, however, and its emphasis upon the unmediated relationship between God and man, the covenantal foundation of the church would classify as conservative and hardly subversive of the existing ecclesiastical order. In this context it appears not at all contrived for Ockham to appeal to the universal church in time as the standard of truth; such an appeal, in fact, fits naturally into a dynamic, covenantal understanding of God's historical activity. The church, although no longer confined to a static institutional representation of an eternal ecclesial ideal, remains the reliable custodian and interpreter of God's revelation.

Furthermore, for the Ockhamists God's covenant is two-sided. In the realm of soteriology man's part is defined by the *facere quod in se est* [doing the best that is in one], the expectation that man would make optimal use of his own natural powers to prepare himself for grace. A certain ecclesiological parallel to this idea may inhere in Ockham's assertion that every Christian has the right, and even the duty, to ascertain catholic truth for himself in light of the historical consensus of the faithful. This is anything but the blind fideism of which Ockhamist ecclesiology has been accused. On this basis, Ockham's argument for papal infallibility—as an attempt to check the sovereignty of a reigning pope—can be interpreted as an appeal to God's consistent and reliable revelation to his covenant people in the past in the face of apparent infidelity to this covenant by the contemporary ecclesiastical hierarchy.

In summary, it appears that neither total subjectivity nor a complete divorce between his philosophical-theological and his political-ecclesiological writings can be said to characterize Ockham's ecclesiology. In contrast to Marsilius, who relied on the *ecclesia primitiva* to serve as a model of a church to be reformed under the aegis of a general council, Ockham proposed a highly original form of Olivi's remnant ecclesiology as a theoretical solution to the crisis of the papacy in his day. This "ecclesiology of cognitive expertise," which placed understanding above institutions, was a unique contribution to the late medieval quest for the true church.

III

Ockham's contribution did not, however, become the preferred solution to the most devastating of the late medieval ecclesiological crises: the disorientation with regard to the nature and authority of the church wrought by the Great Schism (1378–1417). Those men who sought reform of the church at the turn of the fifteenth century turned instead to the ecclesiological solution proposed by Marsilius—a general council. In reality, conciliar theory was much older than Marsilius and represents a response to the crisis of the late fourteenth century which has its own ecclesiological integrity and deep roots in the earlier Middle Ages....

The necessity for some basic ecclesiological homework was especially clear to Jean Gerson [leader of the Council of Constance (1414–1417)], the author to whom conciliar thinkers at the beginning of the sixteenth century were most indebted. Gerson's career effectively combined his active life as an ecclesiastical reformer with his contemplative life as a mystical theologian and ecclesiological thinker. Our awareness of this interrelation has been enhanced by a recent study which points out a common pattern of reform in Gerson's mystical theology and in his ecclesiology. The key to the *via mystica* [mystical way] for Gerson is the *synderesis* [an inextinguishable spark of goodness] which has been naturally implanted in the soul. As the innate point of contact between God and man, the *synderesis* becomes the home of the Holy Spirit where Christ is spiritually born into the soul. The reform of the soul takes the *synderesis* as its intrinsic point of departure. In an analogous way, the reform of the church takes as its intrinsic point of departure the *semen Dei* [seed of God] which is "deeply and inseparably placed within and diffused throughout the ecclesiastical body as lifegiving blood." A general council may derive from this innate divine power authority to reform the church when its head, the pope, proves incapable of governing the church. The legitimacy of the ecclesiastical hierarchy is not based on the papacy itself but on the "seed of God," a resource intrinsic to the body of Christ. On the other hand, the power which accrues to a council from the seed of God does not establish absolute conciliar supremacy over the see of Peter; it applies only in cases where papal power is abused.

Thus, in addition to the remnant ecclesiology present, for example, in Olivi and the "ecclesiology of cognitive expertise" in Ockham, it is permissible to speak of a "seed-ecclesiology" in Gerson. In one respect, namely in its appeal to the *ecclesia primitiva*, this seed-ecclesiology is related to the conciliarism of Marsilius. As the Holy Spirit itself, the reformative power of the seed is especially operative whenever the church is gathered in council; according to Gerson, the primitive church provides an authoritative precedent for this. In quite another respect, however, Gerson's conciliar ecclesiology is considerably more sophisticated than that of Marsilius. The seed, received by the church in its primitive stage, establishes the hierarchy much closer to the center of his ecclesiology than is the case with Marsilius. This sanction given to the hierarchy also distinguishes Gerson's ecclesiology from that of Ockham, which identified the true essence of the church more with belief than with hierarchical structure....

... It is ... clear that conciliarism itself can be most appropriately understood as covering a variety of ecclesiological responses in which a general council served as the agent of reform. Although the ideal of the *ecclesia primitiva* certainly played a role in these conciliar ideas of reform, the ecclesiological options developed in response to the Schism were considerably more varied and sophisticated than a naive call for return to the uncomplicated apostolic life. Searchers for the true church during the later Middle Ages traveled along roads much better graded than the dusty paths of the apostles and much more diverse than the main highways of papalism and conciliarism.

IV

One of these roads was the ecclesiological path along which John Hus and his followers pursued their opposition to the Roman Church.... In his discussion of the spiritual crisis provoked by the Great Schism, F. Graus portrays the Hussite movement as a response to the threat which the Great Schism posed to the religious values of the Czech people. Exposed to the constant criticism of a church racked by schism and moral abuse, the Czech people became uncertain about the locus of the true church and the efficacy of its sacramental channels. In Graus's opinion, the Hussite movement captured the enthusiasm and fantasy of the previously indifferent Czech masses because it offered to them a new concept of the church which assured them of their status as true Christians and (in the symbol of the chalice) of the validity of their Eucharist.

Although the Hussite doctrine of the church, backed by a strong emphasis on the Eucharist, was able temporarily to restore confidence and security to a disoriented Czech people, Graus maintains that this concentration on the church and the chalice was not able in the long run to satisfy the needs of late medieval people beset by spiritual and socioeconomic uncertainty. It remained for the new humanist emphasis on man and the religious shift from the church to personal faith to lay the groundwork for a solution. "They were the means by which the intellectual crisis of the late Middle Ages was overcome and a new system built upon its ruins."

From the perspective of the late medieval quest for the true church, two aspects of Graus's thesis deserve comment: first, his evaluation of the causes behind the failure of the Hussite movement and, secondly, his brief estimate of the solution provided by the sixteenth century to the late medieval crisis of the church. The first point will be dealt with in the remainder of this section. The second aspect will serve as the springboard for concluding remarks on the sixteenth century in the last section.

First, why was this emphasis on the church and the Eucharist not able to satisfy the religious needs of the Czech people and serve as the foundation for a lasting reformation? Graus implies that the cause of the failure lay in the appeal of the Hussite reformers to the past, "the attempt to form a new society on a primitive Christian model." Insofar as the Hussites employed the *ecclesia primitiva* as the model of church reform, they were simply following in the footsteps of many another medieval reform movement. Furthermore, the primitive church continued to be used throughout the sixteenth century as a criterion of reform. The employment of this model was too extensive both before and after the Hussites to isolate it as the cause of their apparent failure to solve the crisis of the Middle Ages. More importantly, in what sense can they even be said to have failed? True, Bohemia did not become the launching pad for the sixteenth-century Reformation; but this does not necessarily mean that Hussite ecclesiology did not provide a viable answer to Czech people in search of the true church for the period in which they needed it. It is sufficient to regard Hussite ecclesiology as a solution to their crisis, which was only one in a series of late medieval ecclesiological crises, without blaming the Hussite doctrine of the church for not solving the crisis of the late Middle Ages viewed as a whole.

The fact remains, however, that the mainline Hussites, the Utraquists, did not establish and maintain a church completely independent of the Roman hierarchy. This was attained only after 1467 in sectarian form by the *Unitas fratrum* [the Unity of the Brethren], who, much like the Waldensians, strictly implemented the ideal of the *ecclesia primitiva*. In contrast to these Brethren, the moderate outcome of the Utraquist revolt may be explained by the intimate relation between the church and the sacraments which existed for Hus and his followers.

One way of stating the issue is this: Was the Hussite doctrine of the church subversive to the extent of constituting a theoretical basis for breaking with Rome and establishing an independent church? H. Kaminsky argues forcefully that the Utraquist revolt of 1414–1417, both as theory and as practice, imposed a duty to construct an alternative church composed of those true Christians who obeyed Christ's law, which included communion in both kinds. Kaminsky also contends that the ecclesiology of Hus, following Wyclif, constituted a real threat to the authority and institutional sacrosanctity of the Roman Church....

It is questionable, however, whether this subversive potential was ever present in Hussite ecclesiology to the same degree in which it was present in some sixteenth-century Reformers, for example, in the theology of Luther. In spite of their peculiar emphasis on the Eucharist, the Hussites and the late medieval church shared belief in the necessity of sacramental grace.... The ecclesiology of Hus himself (who never conceded that the lay chalice was necessary for salvation) was not subversive, because even his church of the predestined was dependent on sacramental grace administered through the legitimately ordained hierarchy.

The Hussite movement did not fail to solve the crisis of the later Middle Ages because it offered an outdated model of reform based on an unrealistic appeal to the primitive church.... There was more to Hussite ecclesiology than that. In their attention to the necessity of sacramental grace, even for the church of the predestined, the Hussites remained theologically profound and firmly rooted in medieval ground. Compared with the sixteenth-century Reformers, however, Hus and his mainstream Prague successors were ecclesiologically superficial—not in terms of a doctrinal comparison, but in an historical sense. That is, Hussite ecclesiology, except in its extreme sectarian form, did not supply an adequate conceptual framework within which to build a new church independent of the Roman hierarchy. The reconciliation with the Council of Basel tamed the mainstream Hussite movement into peaceful coexistence with the Roman Church and relegated its ecclesiology to one among many options in the late medieval quest for the true church.

V

Did the quest die with the dawn of the sixteenth century? Graus implies a positive answer to this question in his assertion that the humanist emphasis on man and the Reformers' concept of personal faith succeeded where Hussite ecclesiology failed. They allegedly rescued gasping man from the polluted late medieval crisis atmosphere and thrust him into the liberating air of the modern era where he could breathe with confidence again. Since a series of ecclesiological crises was to a great degree responsible for the predicament of late medieval man, it seems only fitting to look for his savior in non-ecclesial or anti-ecclesial concepts and forces. This emphasis on the rebirth of individualism and subjectivity has been a favorite way of defining the *novum* ["new"] which the sixteenth century offered to late medieval men. Nowhere is this better illustrated than in the work of Joseph Lortz, who regards the Reformation as "[replacing] the basic medieval attitudes of objectivism, traditionalism and clericalism with those of subjectivism, spiritualism and laicism."

It is now known that the fifteenth century, in Germany at least, was an era of exceptional piety and religious devotion. According to B. Moeller, it was also a time of greater fidelity to the church than in any other medieval epoch. Moeller interprets this churchliness as the result of a spiritual and intellectual crisis similar to that which Graus has described.... Men sought peace and solace in what was traditional, time-proven and holy, that is, in the laws of the church. But, claims Moeller, this search was not for the church as such; rather, men yearned for the salvation which the church possessed.

While this statement may pinpoint the attraction of the church for some medieval people, it is questionable whether one can distinguish so neatly between the church *per se* and its treasure of salvation. The church and salvation were bound together inseparably in the minds of late medieval people. In the exegetical tradition of medieval scholarship, for example, soteriology was intimately linked to ecclesiology. The same passages of Scripture were often applied to the church and to the individual soul. If many non-scholars in late medieval Germany were searching for certitude and meaning within the established ecclesiastical structure, it was also because they felt that the Roman Church was the true church and could provide them with the salvation for which they were yearning. The ecclesiastical fidelity of the late fifteenth century in Germany does not necessarily lead one to conclude a lapse of interest in the quest for the true church. In fact, it can be read as a last attempt on the part of many *viatores* to find their earthly home in that ecclesiastical environment which they knew best—the bosom of mother Rome.

Moeller notes that devotion to the church did not by any means preclude criticism of the clergy and other church leaders. He refers particularly to the views of theologians associated with the *Devotio moderna* and to the German humanists.... The non-revolutionary nature of the criticism voiced by all these men does not mean that they had given up hope in the church and begun to turn toward deviant, non-ecclesial forms of spiritual satisfaction. On the contrary, by remaining within the church, they may have helped to foster a climate in which the quest for the true church could be taken up anew by the Protestant Reformers. The way in which the second generation of humanists swelled the ranks of the Reformers is indicative of their interest in the re-establishment of the church at the center of men's lives.

Thus, there is as yet inadequate support for the opinion... that the sixteenth-century Reformation, including the humanists, dealt with the crisis of the later Middle Ages by appealing to individualistic and subjective values and abandoning the church as the objective framework for the means of grace. The most damaging evidence against this view is the attention which the Reformers themselves paid to the nature of the church and its authority. This point cannot be fully developed within the limits of this essay. It can be pointed out, however, that the theology of Luther, for example, was anything but subjectively oriented and did not overshift to the side of individual faith. Ecclesiological concerns were at the center of his theological development and a correlative concept of the church grew up together with his new soteriology. Luther was not interested in how the individual Christian could survive apart from the church, but in how the church properly conceived could feed the Christian faithful with the word of life in the midst of crisis and uncertainty.

Essential to Luther's reforming motivation was his conviction that the Roman Church was not performing this indispensable function of the true church. In the account of his pivotal encounter with Cajetan at Augsburg in 1518, Luther is concerned, but not overly surprised, at what he labeled Cajetan's "distortion of the Bible," because "it has long been believed that whatever the Roman Church says, damns or wants, all people must eventually say, damn or want, and that no other reason need be given than that the Apostolic See and the Roman Church hold that opinion. Therefore, since the sacred scriptures are abandoned and the traditions and words of men accepted, it happens that the church of Christ is not nourished by its own measure of wheat, that is, by the word of Christ, but is usually misled by the indiscretion and rash will of an unlearned flatterer. We have come to this in our great misfortune that these people begin to force us to renounce the Christian faith and deny Holy Scripture." Luther's mature ecclesiology continued to stress the dependence of the church on the word of Scripture and the definition of the church by that word. This definition meant that the locus of the true church could in no way be circumscribed by any particular city or by obedience to any one hierarchy (especially Rome); the true church could exist wherever the word of Scripture was truly proclaimed and was nourishing the church.

Luther's Reformation, and indeed the entire withdrawal from the papacy in the sixteenth century, is not correctly understood if it is read as the result of the personal spiritual crisis of an overzealous Augustinian monk. Quite the contrary is true: Luther's Reformation is best explained as an ecclesiological response to the last great medieval crisis of the church's identity and authority. Other factors played important roles in the popular support and political breathing room which the nascent Reformation churches received. Nevertheless, the crucial factor was their own ecclesiological support base, the ability of the Reformers to maintain confidence in their churches as new manifestations of the true church over against the papacy and the Roman hierarchy. This crucial role played by ecclesiology is illustrated by the failure of Protestant and papal negotiators at the Colloquy of Regensburg (1541) to agree on the nature of the church and its authority after they had reached a consensus on justification. In the dissenting Protestant statement submitted to the emperor, Philip Melanchthon based the authority of the true church on the genuine understanding and interpretation of Scripture which was not bound to any persons or places but belonged to the "living members of the church."

Not all sixteenth-century men were convinced that the churches of the magisterial Reformers were in fact distinct enough from Rome to claim the title of the true church. Thus, additional ecclesiological options were offered by Anabaptists and other radical Reformers who drew more directly on medieval patterns of reform like the *ecclesia primitiva*. One desideratum of

Reformation research is a detailed investigation into the ecclesiologies of both major and minor Reformers which would trace the interaction between their concepts of the church and the way in which their reforming activity met the needs of men still affected by the crises of their late medieval environment. As this data is more fully evaluated in light of the variety in late medieval ecclesiology, it will become increasingly difficult to contrast "Reformation" and "medieval" ecclesiology as if they were two relatively homogeneous entities. Rather, the development of various ecclesiologies during the Reformation period will be more suitably viewed as the continuation of the late medieval quest for the *vera ecclesia*. As in the case of the Anabaptists, some sixteenth-century ecclesiologies will appear to have medieval counterparts. Upon investigation, other ecclesiological responses to the last great medieval crisis of the papacy may reveal features sufficiently unique to help explain why this crisis would no longer be called medieval at all, but would mark the beginning of a new era. With the advent of the Reformation, the crises of medieval ecclesiology may have ceased, but the quest for the true church continued.

Bibliography

FRANTISEK GRAUS, "The Crisis of the Middle Ages and the Hussites," in Steven Ozment, ed., *The Reformation in Medieval Perspective* (1971), pp. 76–103.

JOHANN HUIZINGA, *The Waning of the Middle Ages* (1962).

GERHART B. LADNER, *The Idea of Reform* (1959).

GORDON LEFF, *Heresy in the Later Middle Ages*, 2 vols. (1967).

GORDON LEFF, "The Making of the Myth of a True Church in the Later Middle Ages," *Journal of Medieval and Renaissance Studies* 1 (1971): 1–15.

JOHN O'MALLEY, *Giles of Viterbo on Church and Reform* (1968).

STEVEN OZMENT, *The Age of Reform, 1250–1550* (1980).

LOUIS B. PASCOE, S. J., *Jean Gerson: Principles of Church Reform* (1973).

BRIAN TIERNEY, *Origins of Papal Infallibility 1150–1350* (1972).

CHARLES TRINKAUS and HEIKO A. OBERMAN, eds. *The Pursuit of Holiness in Late Medieval and Renaissance Religion* (1974).

The Black Death and English Higher Education

WILLIAM J. COURTENAY

By keying on the great demographic crisis of mid-century, when plague killed an estimated two-fifths of Europe's total population, scholars have been tempted to interpret the fourteenth century as a time of near-universal death and decline. This perspective, however, can distort the cultural life of the period, which in many places remained strong and vibrant, virtually unaffected by the death and dying. Oxford University is a case in point.

The mortality from the Black Death was much lower at Oxford than in England at large. University youths, who had better diets and living conditions than most, seem to have been better able to resist disease, and many also had the opportunity to escape to the protective isolation of country homes when the plague hit. The Black Death also had little effect on the number of great university teachers living at the time. It may, however, have lowered the quality of incoming students by killing off many of the skilled masters of grammar and members of the clergy who taught in the town and parish schools that supplied students to Oxford. A lack of preparation in Latin and critical thinking may have put profound scholastic learning out of the reach of a new generation of students and may help explain the lessening of scholastic rigor by the end of the fourteenth century. However, there was already a general shift away from the more speculative forms of philosophy and theology before the plague.

If the quality of students may have been affected by the plague, the numbers of matriculating students definitely were not. Indeed, in the theological faculty enrollments steadily increased in the decades after the plague. Climbing enrollments reflected the need to replenish lost parish clergy and chantry priests (who said masses for the dead), posts filled by university men who now found the clerical market even more open and attractive than before the plague. Also, some youths came into early inheritances because of the plague and, finding themselves

---

Reprinted with the permission of the Medieval Academy of America from "The Effect of the Black Death on English Higher Education" by William J. Courtenay, in *Speculum*, vol. 55 (1980), pp. 696–714. Copyright © The Medieval Academy of America.

in a stronger financial position, happily took advantage of a university education.

The effect of plague on fourteenth-century education is not a neglected topic. While there may be no recent thesis on the relationship similar to the provocative but controversial work by Millard Meiss on the effect of the Black Death on Florentine and Sienese art, many scholars have noted a decline or at least a period of quiescence at various medieval universities in the decades immediately after 1348, a change often attributed to the Black Death. The only general work devoted to this important subject remains Anna Campbell's *The Black Death and Men of Learning*, which surveys most of the information available a half century ago. Since then, some work has been done on the relation of plague to elementary and secondary education, but despite the appearance of additional quantitative evidence on medieval universities, little that is new has appeared on the relation of plague and higher education either in England or on the Continent.

The lack of any useful or extensive quantitative data in the earlier part of this century led to widely differing opinions and a tendency to base conclusions on subjective or vague contemporary statements that at best gave an impressionistic assessment of the situation. In the absence of other types of evidence, Campbell placed considerable emphasis on statements by contemporary scholars, or similar pronouncements culled from foundation charters of universities and colleges established between 1350 and 1380, bemoaning the contemporary decline in education, either numerically or qualitatively, and sometimes both. Notwithstanding the fact that many of these statements have a formulaic ring, especially those in foundation charters, and the fact that the supposed decline was as frequently blamed on warfare, the mendicants, the monks, or some other cause as on plague and population decline, Campbell felt that most of this material was evidence for the severity of the Black Death on education. Even where Campbell used statistical data, such as the figures gleaned from the rolls submitted by universities for papal provision, or the number of deaths among professors at Padua before, during, and after 1348, or the decline in university documentation in the decade following the Black Death, or the closing of several universities, the evidence is either too slight for significant quantitative evaluation or can be explained in other ways.

Recognizing that the death rate and its educational impact differed from university to university, Campbell avoided giving precise mortality percentages or even a European average. Still, with the exception of Paris, it was her assumption that the death rate among scholars was high. Other opinions have been asserted. H. E. Salter, who edited several of the cartularies and registers of Oxford foundations, placed Oxford mortality at five percent. In his estimation masters and students fled at the first signs of plague, returning when its virulence had abated. Most historians who have touched on the effect of plague on medieval education have adopted Campbell's conclusions. Some have admitted our ignorance. As Guy Lytle summed up the situation for Oxford: "The town of Oxford, situated on the London-Gloucester-Bristol trade route, was certainly hit by plague, but its impact on the university remains an open question."

In the past few decades evidence has become available that can make our understanding of the effect of the Black Death on education less conjectural. We now have large bodies of statistical evidence for universities of sufficient size and age to permit a significant comparison of the situation before and after 1348. For example, we have published records for some of the nations in the arts faculty at the University of Paris, recording those paying examination fees and being promoted. The biographical registers compiled by A. B. Emden for medieval Oxford and Cambridge are a different but no less useful type of evidence. Each source must be used with discretion, since none contains total figures for a university population or evidence that is not skewed in some direction. When used properly, however, these sources together represent one of the largest bodies of statistical evidence for the years immediately preceding and following 1348 and permit a quantitative answer to questions that was not possible two generations ago.

Unfortunately, university sources will never yield the kind of statistical evidence through which one could determine the percentage of overall population decline resulting from the Black Death. In the first place, the medieval scholar was not geographically stable. While he might be resident at the university for a decade or two, shorter stays were more common, and he could leave on short notice. One is looking, therefore, at a migratory, not a fixed, segment of the population. Secondly, the medieval university never contained a cross section of the entire society. It was by its very nature an elitist institution, although the selection of that elite group in the fourteenth century was generally not based on family ties or social class but on preparatory training in Latin grammar (available in a variety of ways, including tuitionless town schools) and access to financial support. While the fee structure of the medieval university was not high, the costs of living in Oxford, Paris, or Bologna did require some income, usually from outside the university. Thirdly, the university did not always constitute the same percentage of the total population. In contrast to many of its modern counterparts, the medieval university had no set enrollment policy or ceiling. It did not exclude willing and qualified candidates. With the exception of the colleges and religious houses, whose endowments or facilities set maximum limits but which were still in a minority in mid-fourteenth century Oxford and Paris, the university could theoretically take all those who had the desire, the resources, and the educational preparation to attend. Consequently a sharp decline in the general population might appear far less severe in the university documentation, since the university could to some degree replenish its ranks from among the survivors of a major epidemic by accepting students who for one reason or another might not have been attracted or acceptable in an earlier generation. While there are some ways the quantitative data can be used to give us glimpses into the effect of the Black Death on the university population itself, one must rely on other evidence to assess the severity of the plague for the society in general.

England forms a particularly interesting case study in the possible relation of plague and learning. In the first half of the fourteenth century English masters led the way in the development of logic, mathematics, and science, while Paris lagged behind and by 1340 began concentrating its attention on analyzing and building upon the English achievements in philosophy and theology. At mid century, however, that picture changed radically. As Mullinger stated the problem over a century ago:

> How is it, that from the middle of the fourteenth century up to the revival of classical learning, the very period wherein the munificence of royal and noble founders is most conspicuous in connection with our university history, such a lull comes over the mental life of both Oxford and Cambridge, and so few names of eminence, Wyclif and Reginald Pecock being the most notable exceptions, invite our attention?

We are in a good position to assess what role the Black Death may have played in that intellectual change. Some of the most detailed studies on the effect of the Black Death and on late medieval population decline have been done for England. On the other side, we possess for Oxford and Cambridge what we have for no other medieval university: biographical registers, providing sketches of all scholars *known* to have attended those institutions before 1500. We also have information on a number of *studia particularia*, centers of higher education that were not recognized as universities.

Among these educational sources *The Biographical Register of the University of Oxford* is the richest, containing some 15,000 biographical sketches of students, teachers, and others who were resident at Oxford and connected with the University in the high and late Middle Ages. It is the principal source upon which the following study is based, and its contents have become more usable through the recent creation of a computerized index. The *Register*, however, has some characteristics that affect its use as a source of quantitative data. Among these characteristics we are concerned just with those that affect the number of masters and scholars resident at Oxford in the fourteenth century.

As was already mentioned, the names included in the *Register* represent only a portion, probably a minority, of the total university population for any period in the high and late Middle Ages. The *Register* was not compiled from a sequence of similar records, such as matriculation lists or bursars' accounts that purportedly would include all those entering or resident in any one year. In the absence of such documentation Emden drew his material from a variety of sources, particularly college records, the Calendars of Patent and Close Rolls, episcopal registers, and papal registers. One is faced, therefore, not simply with a problem of under-reporting but rather with a mixed collection of names that is subject to further growth and revision as more research is done. Estimates for the total university population at any one time in the late fourteenth or early fifteenth century range between 1,000 and 1,700. When those conjectured totals are placed alongside the evidence from Emden's *Register*, arranged according to academic generations, it appears that at various points in the fourteenth century we probably know the names of fifteen to forty percent.

For our purposes the total figure need not concern us. If all other factors remained constant, any increase or decline in the total number (whatever it might have been) should be reflected in the known number. However, the situation is not so ideal. As one moves from 1200 to 1500 and the amount of surviving documentation increases, one would expect the proportion of unreported students to decline. Consequently, any increase in the size of the reported group would not necessarily reflect the percentage of increase in the total university population. Similarly, any dip in the number of documentary sources available in any generation, for whatever reason, would result in a lowering of the number of students reported to have been there in that generation. Fortunately, the data base from which Emden compiled his *Register* does not alter much in the fourteenth century. Therefore, when adjustments are made for artificial statistical changes caused by the appearance of a new source, the raw figures for the fourteenth century derived from Emden probably reflect real changes in the university population.

I. Oxford University Population Before and After 1348: The Quantitative Effect

In assessing the effect of the Black Death on the university population, two separate questions must be addressed. First, what percentage of students and masters at Oxford actually died in the plague of 1348–49? Second, was Oxford able to recover quantitatively or did the rapid drop in the English population cause a numerical decline in the decades immediately following the Black Death?

The first question is difficult to answer with any precision. For those scholars whose connection with a college, diocesan administration, or a judicial proceeding placed them in a position to be "recorded" *while* they were students, a large proportion drops out of sight in all periods and is not mentioned in later documentation. Some scholars surely died, but for most one cannot assume death to be the cause of their post-Oxford anonymity.

On the other hand, those scholars whose presence at Oxford is known *because* of the visibility of their later careers, survival is a contributing factor in their being known. Thus one has to examine a sub-group within the university for whom there is sufficient documentation produced before 1348 (in which the surviving group should not be significantly better reported than the non-surviving) and yet a group whose field of study is more likely to make them visible in later life if they do survive. To meet those criteria I have chosen the theological faculty. As the most numerous higher faculty in the fourteenth century, with close ties to the largest document-producing institution of that age, the church, it provides us with a large sample and one that has a higher percentage of reporting than for any other group. Furthermore, only those whose presence at Oxford is attested to in documentation before the Black Death are considered, so that visibility "by means of survival" will not affect the percentage. It should be kept in mind, however, that the statistical results only represent trends and cannot have any absolute standing.

Of the 87 theologians known to have been in residence in the decade before the Black Death, 61 are known to have survived beyond 1350, 1 is known to have died before the Black Death, and only 5 are known to have died in 1348–49. Since the percentage of those for whom we have no subsequent information (28.7 percent) is not substantially higher than for earlier decades, and since the normal ten-year mortality rate in the fourteenth century for those in the age range of 20 to 30 would probably have been around ten percent, there is no evidence that the Black Death took any more than an additional five to ten percent.

There is also no reason to assume that the faculties of arts or law would have been harder hit than theology. This can be seen for arts if we examine the number of students continuing on into a higher faculty, such as theology. Unlike the arts faculty, which drew its students from among the numerous grammar schools and those privately educated outside the university, the theological faculty drew its students either from among those who had been arts students in the previous decade or, in the case of the religious orders, from among a limited number of preparatory teaching convents. Excluding the mendicant orders, which usually imposed limits on the number of students in residence at Oxford and which could, despite a major epidemic, draw qualified candidates from among the survivors within their order, the number of secular theologians, whose program was open and self-selective, should reflect any substantial reduction in the population of the arts faculty as a result of the events of 1348–49. We find, however, that the reported number of secular theological students increases after the Black Death, from 33 to 46, an increase of slightly over 28 per cent.

The apparently low mortality rate among university scholars is in striking contrast to the percentages often given for the country at large. Although estimates vary from region to region and between urban and rural, the general mortality rate for England in 1348–49 has been placed between twenty and forty percent, with the majority of recent historians favoring the higher figure. As a group, the mortality rate among the clergy is the best documented, being placed between thirty-five and forty percent. However, for the higher clergy, whose living conditions were less crowded and healthier than those of the parish priest, the mortality rate was lower. For example, of the twenty-three bishops in England and Wales holding office on the eve of the Black Death, only six died in 1348–49 (twenty-six percent), three of them in London.

We can only conjecture why the Black Death had only a slight effect on the Oxford University population. First of all, considering the epidemiology of the plague, the university age group, 15 to 35, was more resistant to disease, and their diet and living conditions were probably above average. Although no one was immune from the plague by reason of age or social background, the epidemic was more severe among those who lived in crowded conditions, in buildings or districts that easily housed a sizable rat population, among children, the elderly, and those of fragile health, and among those who ministered to the poor, sick, and dying. Secondly, unlike townspeople, the students and masters could leave Oxford quickly, for few were permanent residents. By the fifteenth century these "escape plans" were well worked out, with countryside manors designated as places of retreat for continuing education. Thirdly, there was some advance warning. The plague entered the port of Bristol (one of the first places hit) late in the summer of 1348, and it moved to Oxford that fall. Since the fleas that carry the plague bacillus breed best in warm, wet weather, the plague was more severe in the summer in Bristol and the following summer in Norwich and London than in the winter at Oxford. Assuming that we are not dealing in Oxford with the pneumonic form, and the mortality statistics would bear that out, plague in winter was less virulent. Summer was its high period, and summer was the long vacation at Oxford. The students did not return until mid-October, and in 1348 some may have chosen not to return. Finally, the Oxford student body was not drawn from large population areas. There were surprisingly few students from London, Norwich, or other large centers. Rather, they came from small towns and from families of modest means. Those who left the university, who took positions in urban parishes and settled down, may well have died in high numbers. Many returning to isolated manors or small towns may have been spared. But one needs to keep in mind that death after one leaves the university does not alter what is happening in Oxford.

For the second question, namely the level of the university population before and after the Black Death, we have more dependable and revealing statistics. Since the average period of university residence was about eight years, we are, for the decade 1350–1360, looking not at the survival rate but at the replacement rate. If we look at the total reported university population, there was no substantial decline in the scholarly population at Oxford in or around 1348, certainly not what one would expect in view of the conjectured drop in the English population. Moreover, a general decline in the fourteenth century, as suggested by Salter, cannot be supported by the biographical data in Emden's *Register*. The computerized index lists 1,112 persons for the period 1300–1319, 1,192 for 1320–1339 (a reported growth of seven percent), 1,086 for 1340–1359 (a reported decline of almost nine percent), 1,100 for 1360–1379 (a reported growth of slightly over one percent beyond the previous generation but still more than seven percent below the previous high), and 1,547 for 1380–1399 (a reported growth of over forty percent beyond the previous generation). These figures must be adjusted to reflect changes in the amount of documentation on which they are based. The period 1320–1339 probably does not represent a growth as large as seven percent over the previous period, since it includes a temporary improvement in documentation for Merton College. Similarly, the figures for the periods after 1340 include records of newly founded colleges, some of which, like Queen's, rented rooms to scholars outside college who may have been resident but unrecorded in the previous period. The figures for those periods should be reduced slightly. Finally, the rapid growth at the end of the century is due in part to matriculation lists of New College, founded in 1379. Even after these adjustments, however, it would appear that the fourteenth century was a period of growth, which was halted only slightly in the period from 1350 to 1375.

Putting the evidence together, one can conclude that the Black Death had only a marginal impact on the population of the University of Oxford, either for those in residence or for those who replaced them in the next student generation. The quantitative data now available to us, therefore, supports Salter's impressions and makes those of Campbell unlikely, at least for Oxford.

II. The Issue of Qualitative Decline

Despite a low mortality rate and the ability of the University of Oxford to maintain its enrollment levels in the face of the Black Death, it is still possible that the plague could have exercised a negative effect on the quality of education by removing a number of important masters, by hurting parts of the university community that contributed most prominently to its intellectual life, or by a general lowering of the quality of incoming students. Each of these areas needs to be examined.

One often encounters the assertion that the Black Death killed the leading writers and thinkers of the English universities, which in turn precipitated a qualitative decline. It is true that in the period 1348–49 we know that a number of major intellectuals died: John Baconthorp, William of Ockham, Robert Holcot, Thomas Bradwardine, John of Rodington, Richard Rolle, and probably John Dumbleton and John Went. But none of these was at Oxford at the time (their teaching careers having been completed earlier), and Ockham had been living outside England since 1324. Had they all survived the Black Death, it is difficult to see how the quality of education at Oxford after the Black Death would have been any different. One must contrast that group with those who we know survived the Black Death, some of whom were living at Oxford at the time and who continued to teach there. To this surviving group belong Richard Fitzralph, Adam Wodeham, Thomas Buckingham, William Heytisbury, Richard Swineshead, Nicholas Aston, Osbert Pickingham, Richard Billingham, Ralph Strode, and John Wyclif. If the Black Death was a factor here, it was not in removing the great minds of that generation but in removing those who might have been the great minds of the next generation.

The possible failure to replenish one's ranks with equal talent may have been a factor for certain colleges such as Merton and Grey Friars, who together had established much of the intellectual reputation of Oxford in the early fourteenth century. A sharp decline in the general population, if it were to be reflected in the enrollment level of any individual unit within the university, might not appear immediately, but after a period of ten or fifteen years. The Franciscans had a reported increase in the decade immediately after 1349, helped in part by additional scholars from abroad—mostly Italians but also Germans, Czechs, and one Frenchman—but there is a drop in their numbers reported in Emden's *Register* after 1360 until the end of that century. Similar drops can be noted in some of the other mendicant and religious houses. However, the destruction of documents for the religious orders in England has left us only a fraction of the names of mendicant scholars, and one cannot place much credence in the accuracy of the picture formed from these modest statistics.

The evidence from Merton College is more reliable. If one discounts the sharp rise in reported figures in the period 1320–1340 because it includes the presence of abnormally detailed documentation, the reported enrollment levels for Merton are roughly the same throughout the fourteenth century with the exception of the period 1360–1380. Since there is no particular change in the documentation that would explain this decline (from a reported 170 to 136), one can assume that Merton probably experienced a quantitative decline in that period that may have had qualitative implications.

Finally, we must consider the possible effects of the Black Death on the quality of preparation among incoming students. The type of philosophy and theology that was pursued at Oxford in the 1330s was highly sophisticated, requiring very advanced knowledge of Latin, logic, and mathematics. The minds of the Oxford scholars of the 1360s and 1370s may have been capable, but their skills and understanding were only as good as their early training made them, particularly their training in Latin grammar. If we assume the death rate in 1348–49 among masters of grammar in the town schools and the clergy teaching in parish schools was equivalent to that cited earlier for the parish clergy, then the quality of basic education in the decade 1350–1360 would be impaired. We have many references after 1348 to vacancies and the appointment of less qualified candidates. For a period of time primary education would have been less available and in many places less rigorous. We should not assume too gloomy a picture, since throughout the second half of the fourteenth century there remained highly qualified grammarians in some town schools. But, unlike the university, primary education usually depended on one teacher whose presence and training determined the educational future of most boys in that town. It was probably rare for a family to seek out a good teacher in another town: the usual pattern was to be educated locally.

The effects of this situation would not become visible at the university level for some time. The decay of the educational system moved from the bottom upward, and it was a gradual process that took several decades. If significant at all, one would expect to see it in evidence among the arts students in the period 1360–1375 and among the students and masters in the higher faculties in the period 1370–1385. Under these circumstances it is not difficult to imagine students whose skills in Latin and critical thinking were not sufficient for the subtleties of speculative grammar, who found Aristotle opaque, and who ceased to read Ockham, Wodeham, Bradwardine, or Kilvington. No matter how gifted and accomplished the university masters of the 1360s may have been, they could not repair the damage done by a poor elementary and secondary education, and gradually the task of teaching at all levels of the university was fulfilled by those who learned their letters after the Black Death.

The degree to which this last factor affected or altered the quality of learning at Oxford must remain hypothetical. We know that after 1365 the arts faculty moved away from supposition logic to an earlier, more elementary logic. We also know that the theological faculty in the same period moved away from complex metalinguistic concerns to problems of practical theology. There is no question that the philosophical and theological studies at Oxford after 1360 were easier to grasp and did not require as extensive a technical training in logic and mathematics. It is another thing, however, to prove that this change was precipitated by an inability to comprehend the former learning. What may appear to the modern scholar to be a drop in quality may in context be largely a shift in interest. There is little evidence in the university documents that those studying theology after 1350 were any less literate in Latin than their predecessors. The amount of publication by Oxford graduates after 1350 confirms this. Moreover, the University of Paris, which admittedly drew its students from a far larger geographical area, shows few signs of qualitative decline among those whose primary education was subsequent to the Black Death. The achievements of early fourteenth-century Oxford were continued at Paris in the writings of Henry Totting of Oyta, Henry of Langenstein, Marsilius of Inghen, Pierre d'Ailly, Peter of Candia, and John Capreolus. One must assume, therefore, that there were other forces at work beyond any decay in linguistic skills that formed the intellectual milieu of Oxford in the age of Richard II.

A more immediate effect of the Black Death on qualitative change may have come through changes in the "feeder" institutions of the religious orders. The mendicants, who did not have their students prepare philosophy in the arts faculty of the university, maintained their own schools within each province. Many priories and convents provided training in the liberal arts and logic. For the more advanced study of natural philosophy and theology each province maintained several schools (*studia particularia*), usually one for each major subdivision of the province, known in the Franciscan Order as "custodies" and in the Dominican Order as "visitations" or "nations." From these schools mendicant scholars were sent to the *studium generale* at the university for further study in theology and canon law, and to these schools and local convents many of the best graduates returned for a time to teach. In England the mendicant *studia particularia* were often located in large centers of population, such as London, Norwich, and York, and in the crowded, poorer parts of the city, in contrast to the *studia generalia*, which, with the exception of the Carmelites, were located in the smaller university towns of Oxford and Cambridge. If the mortality rate in London, Norwich, and York was higher than at Oxford, which it seems to have been, one could expect that the mendicant educational system might have been crippled, although such a fact might be less evident quantitatively in the Oxford data. We know of entire mendicant communities that died, and we can assume that if the quotas for the university convents were filled with a higher percentage of marginal students, the subsequent quality of education when they returned to these schools would be lower. For the Franciscans, on whom much of the intellectual quality of Oxford depended, the presence of a number of great minds in the Oxford and London convents in the first half of the fourteenth century probably created an atmosphere that stimulated others and helped recruit talented young minds. The absence of their equivalent in 1360 may have precipitated a downward spiral that increasingly impoverished Franciscan education. To what extent the Black Death was a major factor here is uncertain. However, the decline in the number of Franciscans significant enough to be noted in contemporary documents (and therefore to be included in Emden's *Register*) is a reflection of an important change.

III. The University and Society: The Response to The Black Death

The Black Death was an important stage in a steady population decline across the fourteenth century that was accentuated but not begun or fully explained by incidence of plague. By the second quarter of the fifteenth century the English population was only thirty to fifty percent of what it had been in 1300; that is, the decline was possibly as high as seventy percent. And yet, as we have seen, the scholarly community at Oxford did not decline but probably grew in the course of the century. More surprising perhaps, the number of reported theological students in the decade after 1349 increased twenty-eight percent, and it continued to grow throughout the second half of the fourteenth century. If language skills of the average student did not meet the task or if the problems and approaches of earlier scholastic thought were no longer appealing, what magnetic attraction did the university have?

Several studies have shown a growth after 1348 in the number of elementary and secondary schools in England. Most of the growth was in the form of reading and song schools, but some grammar schools were founded as well. Jo Ann Hoeppner Moran has linked this development in the York diocese with an increasing demand after the Black Death for priests and teachers at the local level, although the rise in the number of ordinations lagged behind the rise in the number of schools. One reason for this renewed educational and ecclesiastical commitment was, no doubt, the depletion of the local clergy by plague. Another reason seems to have been the uses to which money was put after the Black Death. With a declining population, money was concentrated in fewer hands, through inheritance and other means. Much of this increased spending power seems to have been devoted to various forms of late medieval piety, in particular the endowment of chantries throughout England.

Guy Lytle has suggested a somewhat different picture at the university level. He sees the period from 1325 to 1430 as one of crisis for the university as a result of the shrinkage of the traditional sources of patronage, and consequently of benefices, income, and job opportunities within the church for university graduates. His assumed decline in university enrollments is, therefore, not simply part of a decline in population but an indication of a growing realization that university study did not necessarily improve one's chances for a comfortable living, and that a young man was better advised after his early education to seek advancement through the crown or some powerful family that could control church positions and other careers. The future lay with the bureaucrat of the royal *familia* or its aristocratic equivalent. This crisis in scholarly patronage was solved only through the development of new forms of patronage. The transition by which Oxford became a university of colleges was part of that solution. While the thesis about a decline in university enrollment in the fourteenth century is questionable, the statistics that Lytle has gathered on the shift in patronage are impressive. They affect both the sources of funding among advanced students at the university and the expectations for a career after the university.

When examining motivations for education in terms of post-university opportunities, one must keep in mind not only the realistic expectations of a position in the parochial clergy or of income from one or more benefices that did not entail the care of souls, but the more distant model of former graduates whose administrative careers, often in royal service, had been rewarded with a bishopric. A crisis in the ability of university graduates to obtain high ecclesiastical office is far less visible, although it may at times have been a factor. No student in theology or canon law was so naive as to hope for appointment to an episcopal see on the grounds of a distinguished academic career. The examples were too few. But the university connection was thought to be an advantage. In the thirteenth century several major scholastic thinkers had occupied important sees: Robert Grosseteste at Lincoln and Stephen Langton, Robert Kilwardby, and John Pecham at Canterbury. The zeal among some leaders in the English church toward the end of the thirteenth century to increase the proportion of candidates with notable academic careers was part of a wider movement in that period toward a learned episcopate and a learned church, paralleled at the parish level by the papal constitution *Cum ex eo* [which called for a more able priesthood]. In addition to those scholar-bishops who were known through their scholastic writings, there were also a number, for example, Robert Winchelsey at Canterbury, Simon of Ghent at Salisbury, and John Dalderby at Lincoln, whose high reputations at the university were based more on personality and service than on outstanding scholastic achievement.

W. A. Pantin has argued that the relationship of university and episcopate altered in the course of the fourteenth century. Although the proportion of university-trained bishops remained stable throughout the century, roughly two-thirds of the total appointed to episcopal office, distinguished scholars (a category in which Pantin places men of distinguished university service, e.g., chancellors of the university, as well as men of distinguished scholastic writing) "were gradually edged out of the greater sees like Canterbury, and confined to lesser or distant sees like Rochester or Chichester or Armagh." The pattern that Pantin saw was a gradual shift in emphasis from the scholar-bishop at the beginning of the century, to the civil servant at mid-century, to the aristocratic bishop by 1400. These categories, of course, were not mutually exclusive, but they probably do reflect the predominant reason for appointment. "Thus whereas in the reign of Edward III bishoprics had been given as administrative salaries or rewards, in the reign of Richard II we find them given as political rewards or retainers."

This, of course, is how it looks from our modern perspective. When it is a question of career goals and models, however, the issue is whether and to what extent these shifts were apparent in the period, how they were perceived, and what effect those perceptions might have had on university careers.

Under Edward II there is a marked absence of distinguished scholars among appointments to episcopal office, and in the second decade of the century even university-trained men of the stature of Winchelsey and Simon of Ghent were not being appointed. Pantin noted the difficulties of the Canterbury Chapter in attempting to elect the scholar Thomas Cobham, whose candidacy was rejected in favor of Walter Reynolds, a civil servant. But this movement away from the great scholar may not have been viewed as such, since many of the civil servants who were appointed in their place were at least university graduates.

Throughout the first half of the fourteenth century the tie between university and high church office remained in evidence. Although few scholars whose ideas and writings had made them "household" names at the university were given bishoprics, Edward III did appoint Richard Fitzralph to Armagh and Thomas Bradwardine to Canterbury. The fact that the latter died within a few weeks of his investiture in no way negates Edward's willingness to appoint one of the most brilliant scholars of that time to the highest ecclesiastical office in England. Moreover, some of the civil service appointees were strong supporters of the university and scholarship, most of them university graduates as well. This is true of John Grandison at Exeter, Richard de Bury at Durham, William Wykeham at Winchester, and William Courtenay at Canterbury. The change that would have been most visible would have been the increasing prominence of aristocratic background and of legal training in the appointments in the last quarter of the fourteenth century.

What does the Oxford evidence we have been examining suggest about the role of the university in society in the second half of the fourteenth century? We can perceive a leveling off and even a slight decline in enrollment in the theological faculty during the second quarter of the fourteenth century. Although the qualitative work in theology being done at Oxford at that time was outstanding, and Oxford had many figures of international reputation, that reputation depended largely on the Franciscans, whose education was not dependent on outside patronage and for whom church offices were rarely a principal goal, and the Mertonians, whose needs were cared for on a modest level through the endowment of the college. Beneath that elite level the enrollment in theology slipped from its high in the opening years of the fourteenth century and was declining at a time when the general enrollment of the university was still increasing. Some of this decline may have been in response to the shifts in patronage and the worsening picture for career opportunities for theological graduates in the church. Much of it, I suspect, was a result of the shifting pattern of patronage, which had reduced one of the major sources of funding *at the university* for students in the theological program. When viewed against the total enrollments the number of benefices given to students while at the university was small, but within the category of those to whom benefices were given, namely advanced students in theology and canon law who were not in religious orders, these benefices represented a major and necessary part of university finance. In fact, in the second quarter of the fourteenth century we also find enrollments in canon law declining while enrollments in civil law were rising, suggesting the same pattern. In the university's desire to improve sources of income for its graduates, the issue of present funding may have figured as heavily as future expectation.

It would appear that the Black Death altered that trend. The pattern of distributing ecclesiastical livings did not alter, in fact worsened for university graduates, but something happened to cause the theological enrollment among the reported group to increase sharply in the decade after the Black Death. One has to keep in mind here that the university did not suddenly *permit* more students to attend, for there was no enrollment level. The increase must be seen in terms of attracting students rather than taking students. Suddenly theology, or the careers to which it led, became a more attractive possibility for qualified students seeking careers.

One possibility seems obvious. The high death rate among the parish clergy, which in some areas appears to have run as high as forty percent, produced an immediate need for educated clergy at all levels and, viewed less altruistically, an immediate opportunity for the qualified to receive important positions with handsome incomes. Considering the large number of vacant livings and the small number of university graduates, it is no wonder that the majority of these positions were filled with non-university men. But in the quest for fatter livings many may have felt that a few years at the university might well produce greater rewards in the future. In this crisis the theological program at Oxford may have accepted those less qualified than in earlier years, but they also were now probably able to attract other qualified students who, in the face of a long program with limited financial aid and limited career possibilities, might not have been as attracted before. The slow but steady growth in elementary and secondary schools from the mid-fourteenth century on, at a time of population decline, is further evidence of the growing respect for and uses of education.

A second factor that may explain this shift lies in the chantry endowments, the masses for the dead, and the annual obits that grew rapidly in England in the wake of the Black Death, a reflection of the inherited wealth that could be spent in non-productive activity (viewed from the economic perspective) but grim testimony to the societal need for prayers for the souls of family members whom death may have caught in less than a state of grace. Chantries provided jobs, and many of these went to priests with university backgrounds.

Finally, we cannot ignore the possibility that a university training, particularly in theology, lived on in the social aspirations of many families who before 1348 could not afford the luxury of higher education. It may well be that sudden and unexpected inheritance provided a means of realizing a long cherished dream, quite apart from the issue of whether in the long run the university was the best or most direct route to royal service or a comfortable ecclesiastical living. Either through the attraction of available positions or through the sudden realization of financial support, the enrollments in the theological faculty in the second half of the fourteenth century continued to climb—despite no apparent change in the pattern of ecclesiastical patronage in favor of the university.

To the degree that Emden's *Register* is an adequate reflection of what is going on at Oxford in the fourteenth century, the Black Death did not have the effect on higher education in England often ascribed to it. The mortality rate was not particularly high, either of the brilliant or of marginal scholars and masters. The enrollment levels across the next few decades do not seem to have been seriously affected. It did coincide with a change in interests and possibly a change in quality—certainly within the areas of philosophy, science, and theology on which the reputation of the university had depended. If the Black Death helped catalyze this change, it was by initially impairing the quality of primary education, and only subsequently higher education.

Bibliography

ANNA CAMPBELL, *The Black Death and Men of Learning* (1931).
CHARLES CREIGHTON, *A History of Epidemics in Britain* (1965).
ROBERT S. GOTTFRIED, *Epidemic Disease in 15th Century England* (1978).
JOHN HATCHER, *Plague, Population, and the English Economy* (1977).
GORDON LEFF, *Paris and Oxford Universities in the Thirteenth and Fourteenth Centuries* (1968).
HEIKO A. OBERMAN, *Forerunners of the Reformation: The Shape of Late Medieval Thought* (1966).
NICHOLAS ORME, *English Schools in the Middle Ages* (1973).
C. H. TALBOT, *Medicine in Medieval England* (1967).
PHILIP ZIEGLER, *The Black Death* (1969).

The Image of Man in Renaissance Culture

WILLIAM J. BOUWSMA

Humanists of the early Italian Renaissance, men like Petrarch, Salutati, Bruni, and Valla, distinguished themselves by their skill in rhetoric, that is, correct, intelligent, eloquent speaking and writing. For them, form and content, style and substance, were one; thought, speech, and action formed a complex unity. This belief reflected a view of human nature. In distinction from the scholastics of the thirteenth and fourteenth centuries, the humanists did not envision human beings to be creatures possessed of neatly ordered hierarchical powers of the soul peaking in reason. A person was rather a complex bundle of will, passion, and intellect, each of which was vital and active at any one moment of life. Humanists did not address people merely as rational beings requiring only a statement of abstract truth; people also possessed passions and feelings and a will with a mind of its own. Humanist rhetoric attempted to deal with the whole person and with society at large. Humanists made thinking concrete and directed the mind toward reality.

    Later Renaissance thinkers began to lose faith in the power of rhetoric to influence human behavior. Form and content can be seen separating in the thought of men such as Castiglione, Pico, Ficino, even Erasmus. Rhetoric became mere verbal embellishment, even a distraction from reality. As this occurred, abstract thinking came back into vogue among humanists. Riddles, aphorisms, and allegories reappeared as indirect intellectual forms of communication. The life of the mind pulled away from the active life; humanism became academic and confined to intellectual elites. As with the scholastics of the high Middle Ages, the later humanists deemed reason to be the essence of the individual; the will and passions were again inferior parts requiring subordination and control.

    Why did such a shift in the conception of human nature occur? Perhaps the French invasions of Italy in 1494 were a cause. They created such social and political disruption in Italian life that order

From "Changing Assumptions in Later Renaissance Culture" by William Bouwsma. Copyright © 1976 by The Regents of the University of California. Reprinted from *Viator*, vol. 7, 1976, pp. 421–440, by permission of the author and The Regents.

gained a higher value than freedom. The widespread desire for social order and political control found intellectual expression in the revival of the hierarchical image of man, whose lower nature required domination by his higher. But, Bouwsma also insists, the changing image of man in the Renaissance remains something of a mystery.

The familiar notion of a "later" Renaissance immediately presents itself as an innocent effort at chronological arrangement, as a convenience for determining relationships in time. But of course it is much more. It calls upon us to distinguish the differing characteristics of successive moments, to trace a process of development from inception to maturity and possibly on to decline; and it introduces the complicated problem of the relations between Italy and the Northern Renaissance. It is thus closely connected with one of the most fruitful tendencies in all aspects of modern Renaissance scholarship: the effort to distinguish stages in a larger movement which, without such analysis, is filled with an ambiguity that makes useful discussion almost impossible. This tendency is perhaps nowhere more apparent than in the study of Renaissance humanism, a subject which, though by no means their only significant expression, brings into unusually clear relief the assumptions underlying what was most novel and creative in Renaissance culture. By the same token concentration on humanism is a convenient way to deal with the inner development of Renaissance culture.

The most persuasive attempts to work out the stages in the evolution of Renaissance humanism have concentrated on particular places, as, for example, the work of Baron on Florence, of Branca on Venice, or of Spitz on Germany. Such efforts have proved remarkably useful, but by their very nature they can be no more than suggestive about the development of humanism as a general phenomenon of Renaissance Italy or even of Renaissance Europe, responsive to more than local influences. In addition, what has so far been said on this subject is not very helpful for the problem of the later Renaissance. Students of humanism have been concerned chiefly with its earlier, formative stages, as though, once the movement were well established, its full story had been told. Here, as elsewhere in Renaissance scholarship, we can perhaps sense a reluctance to deal with the notions of maturation and then of decay, decline, and end. Back of this may lurk the old idea of the Renaissance as the beginning of the modern age—which, by definition, must still be with us.

I should like to approach the problem of the later Renaissance, then, by calling attention first to changing attitudes towards rhetoric, now generally recognized as the core of Renaissance humanism. The Renaissance humanist was first of all a rhetorician, concerned to perfect in himself and others the art of speaking and writing well. From this standpoint his interest in the classics was secondary and at any rate hardly a novelty; we are now fully aware of the deep classicism of medieval culture. What was significant in the Renaissance humanist was not his classical interests but the novelty of his preferences within the classical heritage. For him the most important classical writers were the Latin orators, the supreme teachers, by both precept and example, of the rhetorical art. It is now clear, therefore, that humanism must be understood initially as a movement in the history of education which proposed to substitute, for the philosophers beloved by the dialecticians, a new group of classical authors, the orators, and then their allies, the ancient poets, historians, and moralists, as the center of a new curriculum, the *studia humanitatis* [the liberal arts].

For some scholars this conception of humanism makes it appear less serious. The reason is, perhaps, that in our own culture rhetoric is popularly regarded as an ambiguous art, and we try to protect ourselves from those who abuse it by attaching to it the adjective "mere," though the need for such protection suggests a fear hardly consistent with the adjective itself. The phrase "mere rhetoric" implies that a rhetorician is at best only a frivolous and minor artist who does no more than decorate serious content with ultimately superfluous adornments; at worst he is a seducer. Back of the phrase "mere rhetoric" also lies, perhaps, a quasi-metaphysical assumption that form is distinguishable from substance, a conception that betrays the persistent influence of one important strand of ancient thought on the Western mind. But it seems to me the very essence of Renaissance humanism, insofar as it differed from the humanism of the Middle Ages, that it rejected this distinction. It took rhetoric seriously because it recognized that the forms of thought are part of thought itself, that verbal meaning is a complex entity, like the human organism, which also cannot survive dissection. This, I think, is the significance of Lorenzo Valla's translation of *logos* [word] not as *ratio* [reason] but *oratio* [discourse], a conception which not only suggests the dynamism and the substantive importance of rhetoric but is also significantly closer to the biblical than to the philosophical world of thought. It is in this light that we must understand Valla's praise for the eloquence of Saint Paul. Rhetoric, rhetoric alone, seemed able to address man, every man, at the vital center of his being.

And there is a further profound implication of this position, which Valla, the deepest mind among the earlier humanists, did much to elucidate. Since the forms of thought can at any rate be perceived as historically determined, the indivisibility of form and content suggests that all intellectual activity is relative to its times. So Renaissance rhetoric opened the way to a denial of absolutes in favor of a novel cultural relativism. Man, for the rhetorician, not man as a species but man in a particular time and place, becomes the measure of all things, a conception that suggests a further element in the lineage of rhetoric, and also brings out the irony in the familiar humanist designation of the Schoolmen as "sophists."

Thus there was nothing frivolous in the cult of rhetoric in the Renaissance, or at least in the early Renaissance in Italy. Nor was there anything trivial about its practical uses. As the art of effective communication, rhetoric was not only the instrument of divine revelation but also the essential bond of human community, and therefore of supreme value for an increasingly complex society struggling to develop more effective patterns of communal life. Enthusiam for rhetoric was most intense among townsmen responsible for welding the inchoate mass of individuals thrown together within the urban walls into a genuine community. Rhetoric thus provided a natural foundation for the new urban culture of the Renaissance, and it operated at every level of human interaction, both private and public. Businessmen had to communicate persuasively with their customers, suppliers, and associates; lawyers had to argue conflicts of interest in the courts; citizens conversed and corresponded with their friends on personal matters or sought the agreement of their peers on questions of public policy; rulers had to maintain the support of their subjects; governments corresponded with each other, sent out embassies, courted foreign opinion.

Rhetoric therefore, because it gave form to every subject of human concern and made it communicable, was not on the periphery but at the very center of human existence. Accordingly a rhetorician could only be a generalist, and a rhetorical education became, in the Renaissance, the first truly general education in European history. A Florentine statute at the end of the fourteenth century, even before Poggio's discovery of Quintilian, justified the appointment of a public teacher of rhetoric on the ground that "the art of rhetoric is not only the instrument of persuasion for all the sciences but also the greatest ornament of public life," and that it "embraces the precepts for advocating or opposing anything we wish." Rhetoric brought into focus all knowledge and all experience.

This elevation of rhetoric also had other major ideological implications; thus if, as Kristeller has shown, it had no explicit philosophical substance, it had considerable significance, as he also recognized, for philosophy in a larger sense. Above all, the new rhetorical culture rested on a novel conception of man. Rejecting the abstract man of classical anthropology with its separate, hierarchically distinguished faculties, rhetoric accepted and appealed to man as it encountered him in the individual moments of his existence. Man was no longer merely a rational animal but an infinitely complex being, a dynamic and unpredictable bundle of psychic energies, simultaneously sensual, passionate, intellectual, and spiritual; like the rhetoric he used, a mysterious unity. If his nature could be defined at all, he was a social and verbal animal who needed to share with others the whole range of his experience. As Leon Battista Alberti's Uncle Lionardo remarked, "Nature, the best of builders, not only made man to live exposed in the midst of others, but also seems to have imposed on him a certain necessity to communicate and reveal to his fellows by speech and other means all his passions and feelings."

But this position not only subverted the old hierarchy of the human personality; it also eroded the gradations of status in society corresponding to it. The broader function of speech meant that communication should not primarily serve the intellectual needs of the few but the general needs of many. The first requirement of speech was that it be commonly understood. Petrarch, himself no lover of crowds, pointed to this perception early in the history of the movement. "The strongest argument for genius and learning is clarity," he declared. "What a man understands clearly he can clearly express, and thus he can pour over into the mind of a hearer what he has in the innermost chamber of his mind." Castiglione's Court Lodovico was only repeating an old humanist cliché when he urged the Courtier to employ "words which are still used by the common people." Language was the common property of men.

The tendency in rhetoric to break down the old barriers and divisions previously seen as inherent in the nature of man, society, and the cosmos itself, points to a further aspect of its deeper significance. Rhetoric was uniquely suited to reflect a world whose order was tending to escape objective comprehension. Its malleability, its adaptability to the nuances of experience, allowed it to mold itself flexibly around the infinitely varied and constantly shifting particularities of life, and at the same time it encouraged the conviction that reality could not be grasped by the fixed and general categories of rational and systematic thought. Rhetoric was agnostic in regard to general propositions; from its standpoint man could not hope to penetrate to the ultimate order of things but only make particular sense of his immediate experience. But the result was that rhetorical expression could be supremely creative, as language could not be if it aimed only to reflect an absolute and static reality. Language itself was a human creation, a point on which Valla rebuked the Schoolmen, who, as though forgetting Genesis 2:19, seemed to believe that God himself had invented words.

The apparently neutral rhetorical doctrine of decorum concealed another set of striking implications. Decorum meant simply that effective communication required the adaptation of a speaker's discourse to his subject and above all to his audience: to its special characteristics, its immediate circumstances of time and place, its mood, and the purpose of the speaker. It too suggests that language seeks man out as he is from moment to moment and addresses him not as the representative of a species, in the timeless language of absolute truth, but as an individual. When Petrarch declared, "I am an individual and would like to be wholly and completely an individual," he was thus expressing one of the deepest impulses underlying Renaissance rhetoric. At the same time, decorum pointed to an attitude of complete flexibility in confronting the infinite variety of life.

Step by step, then, the humanists of earlier Renaissance Italy developed this new vision of man who, with all the resources of his personality, engages fully with the total range of experience. We can trace their progress most vividly in their growing recognition of the role of the passions and the will in the human personality, which advanced into prominence as the intellect receded. Petrarch was still ambivalent and allowed Augustine, improbably disguised as a Stoic sage, to rebuke him for his attachment to love and glory, which Petrarch nevertheless insisted on regarding as "the finest passions" of his nature. But by the next generation Salutati was prepared to acknowledge that, however desirable, the suppression of feeling was impossible. "Indeed," he wrote, "I know not if any mortal ever attained to such perfection besides Christ." And by 1434 Alberti's Uncle Gianozzo was locating the essence of man precisely in his emotions. The first gift of nature to each of us, he declared, is "that moving spirit within us by which we feel desire and anger." Valla brought this motif to its climax in his *De vero bono* [*On True Good*], which argued that even man's moral and spiritual life cannot be advanced by deliberate intellectual activity but only by surrender to the supreme pleasure of divine love.

Closely associated with the passions was the will, which translates the impulses of the passions into action. For in this new vision of man the will was no longer merely the servant of reason; it had replaced reason, in Nancy Struever's phrase, as the "executive power" of the personality. The quality of man's existence thus depended now not on the adequacy of his reason but on the strength and freedom of his will. For Salutati the will was a faculty "whose force ... is so great and its hegemony over the other powers of the soul so large that even though the instruments of the senses receive the images of sensible things, the effect of such reception scarcely proceeds further without the commands of the will." The will represented the active power of the soul.

Thus its primacy pointed, finally, to a revised conception of the existence best suited to man in this life. Since man was no longer an intellectual being, he could no longer hope to fulfill himself through contemplation but only through active engagement with the demands of life, especially in society. Even the ambivalent Petrarch, though frequently lamenting the interruption of his repose, sometimes admitted that a life free from choice and struggle is unsuited to human nature, and his successors were steadily clearer on this issue. Alberti's dying father emphasized the point in his parting message to his sons. "Adversities are the material of which character is built," he declared. "Whose unshakeable spirit, constant mind, energetic intelligence, indefatigable industry and art can show its full merit in favorable and quiet situations?" Uncle Lionardo said this less solemnly: "Young men should not be allowed to remain inactive. Let girls sit and grow lazy."

I do not mean to offer the line of thought I have traced here as a balanced description of earlier Renaissance humanism; Petrarch's equivocations are also significant, and they were never fully overcome by his successors. I have simply tried to offer a brief sketch of the radical novelties implicit in the movement, in the hope that they may help us to assess the quality of the later Renaissance. For, beginning about the middle of the fifteenth century, humanism began subtly to change. The impulses we have just reviewed were still at work and capable of further development, as we are reminded by such figures as Machiavelli, Pomponazzi, and Guicciardini. Yet even in writers in whom we can still discern the earlier attitudes, the novelties of the earlier Renaissance were often being modified.

Once again we may conveniently begin with the problem of rhetoric, towards which attitudes were changing. We still can find, to be sure, enthusiastic celebrations of the power of words. Vives, for example, could describe language as more important for society than justice itself. "Words," he declared, "win the approval of others and control their passions and emotions.... I see nothing more relevant to society than the ability to speak properly and eloquently. Emotions can be set ablaze by the spark of words; reason is aroused and directed by language. There is no occasion in public or private life, at home or outside, where words can be left out. Words can be the cause of great evils and the beginning of incomparable blessings. It is very important, therefore, always to use a decent language adapted to the circumstances of time, place, and people ... which will prove that eloquence is a most important part of prudence."

Yet even among the champions of eloquence one is aware of a growing sense of its limits. This is evident in a tendency, once again, to see eloquence as the mere embellishment of truth. Rhetoric no longer seemed to give access to the solid realities of life, which once more appeared to have some absolute and independent existence; and the relationship between eloquence and knowledge, form and content, once thought an indissoluble marriage, began to look like a passing affair.

This is particularly evident in the attitude of later humanists to the Gospel, which for Valla had been, in the fullest sense, rhetorical communication. Now such a view hardly seemed serious; as ultimate truth, the Gospel could not be dependent on the contingencies of eloquence, and rhetoric could only be of incidental help for its communication. Thus the French scholar Gaguin commended eloquence in preaching to the young Erasmus only on the ground that "the memory of those who have an old-womanish, hesitating and stuttering style will truly last only a few days," and that "only those who have combined eloquence and knowledge are respected and renowned among men of letters," a position that reduces rhetoric to a memory aid or an element in personal reputation. Erasmus agreed. "Religious matters," he responded, "can be made to shine more brightly with the aid of the classics, provided that only purity of style is sought." For Erasmus eloquence could not itself convey the Gospel into the heart; it merely put the reader into a hospitable mood. And Vives denied the universal competence of rhetoric. "Everyone can see clearly," he wrote against Quintilian, "that to speak of the heavens, the elements, and the angels is not the orator's concern."

A natural accompaniment of this separation of the form from the content of verbal expression was a growing emphasis on the value of literary refinement for its own sake, or at most for the esthetic satisfaction it could provide. Thus Castiglione's discussion of language in the *Courtier* suggests more concern with the propriety of language than with its deeper powers of communication. He devotes much attention to this subject, indeed, but the effect is largely to trivialize what had earlier been of profound human importance. There is no concern with virtue or duty in Count Lodovico's vision of the Courtier's literary education. He reviews the old curriculum; the Courtier is to acquaint himself with both the Greek and Latin classics "because of the abundance and variety of things that are so divinely written therein," and he is to pay particular attention to the poets, orators and historians. But the count's explanation lacks the old high seriousness: "besides the personal satisfaction he [the Courtier] will take in this, in this way he will never want for pleasant entertainment with the ladies, who are usually fond of such things." The humanities will, to be sure, also "make him fluent, and ... bold and self-confident in speaking with everyone." But this contribution to the personal effectiveness of the Courtier seems something of an afterthought; after all, as the count remarks, arms are the chief profession of the Courtier, and all his other accomplishments are only "ornaments thereto." The Courtier is a specialist. Another of Castiglione's interlocutors drives the point deeper. For Federico Fregoso the Courtier "should be one who is never at a loss for things to say that are good and well-suited to those with whom he is speaking, he should know how to sweeten and refresh the minds of his hearers, and move them discreetly to gaiety and laughter with amusing witticisms and pleasantries, so that, without ever producing tedium or satiety, he may continually give pleasure."

One can observe of this ideal that at least it does not discriminate against women. Indeed it seems particularly suited to women; the old curriculum of the rhetoricians here provides a culture for aristocratic ladies, but for men chiefly when they are in the company of ladies. By sixteenth-century standards nothing better illustrates the low estate to which the *studia humanitatis* had fallen. And decorum, which in the earlier Renaissance meant primarily the appropriateness of language to its audience or the intentions of the speaker, tended now to mean appropriateness to the speaker's status in life, and eventually what was appropriate to the upper classes. It was no longer the vehicle of a flexible attitude to existence but simply a virtue of the drawing-room. Ficino, to be sure, defined decorum more grandly, but only to elevate it altogether above ordinary human life. "Decorum," he declared, "is God Himself, from whom and through whom all decorous things come to being."

But Ficino's conception was exceptional and perhaps only inadvertently applicable to rhetoric. In general rhetoric tended now to be seen as little more than embellishment and thus relatively frivolous; and so it became in some circles, a kind of play, a source of pleasure and a form of self-display, but therefore for serious men an object of suspicion, as a distraction from the naked apprehension of truth. This concern seems to have some bearing on the Ciceronian controversy in the generation of Erasmus, who himself attacked a Ciceronian floridity in favor of the plain style. His preference, at least in principle, for "the sententious density of matter" over "the cadency and chiming of words" suggests a long step back from rhetoric to philosophy. "Farfetched conceits may please others," he wrote, but "to me the chief concern seems to be that we draw our speech from the matter itself and apply ourselves less to showing off our invention than to present the thing." Form and content have apparently become separable.

This divorce between eloquence and wisdom was, of course, nowhere more pronounced than among the Florentine Platonists. Ficino, concerned with truth, was troubled by the rhetorical enterprise. Pico distinguished sharply between truth and eloquence, which he thought likely only to obscure, distort, and taint truth. From their perspective the authentic task of language is simply to describe objective reality, and the fact that the majority of men lack the capacity to understand philosophical discourse suggested not the limitations but the distinction of philosophy. "What if," Pico wrote in defense of philosophers, "we are commonly held to be dull, rude, uncultured? To us this is a glory and no cause for contempt. We have not written for the many.... We are not unlike the ancients who by their riddles and by the masks of their fables made the uninitiate shun the mysteries; and we have been wont by fright to drive them from our feasts, which they could not but pollute with their far more repulsive verbal inventions."

One result of this sentiment was a return to abstraction; another, more widespread but perhaps equally remote from daily life, was a new type of communication, both verbally and in the plastic arts, through a variety of cryptic devices: riddles, allegory, hints. This notion of communication was as applicable to reading as to writing; and it meant, among other things, a recovery of medieval ways of studying the classics, the discovery in ancient texts not simply of a noble but human communication from the past but hidden insights into a perennial and ultimate truth. Landino made the point in his commentary on Horace's *Art of Poetry*: "When [poetry] most appears to be narrating something most humble and ignoble or to be singing a little fable to delight idle ears, at that very time it is writing in a secret way the most excellent things of all, which are drawn forth from the fountain of the gods." Erasmus, for all his evangelical impulses, preferred the allegorical to the literal meaning of the Scriptures.

But the familiar classics, already too widely known, were insufficiently esoteric to satisfy the longing for an exclusive wisdom by which aristocrats of the spirit could raise themselves above the corrupt and vulgar masses. The result was a turn to less accessible writings in Greek, Hebrew, and eventually other Semitic languages, to the Orphic hymns, the Hermetic corpus, the cabala. As Pico observed, the canonical scriptures could only meet the needs of "tailors, cooks, butchers, shepherds, servants, maids," persons whose "dim and owlish eyes could not bear the light." For superior souls some further revelation was required. Nor were such conceptions confined to a fringe of intellectual extremists. The eminently respectable General of the Augustinian Friars, Giles of Viterbo, one of the most influential figures at the Curia, shared Pico's conviction that the Gospel of Christ required cabalistic explication. We may also note in these interests the disappearance of the incipient cultural relativism of the earlier Renaissance.

In this new atmosphere classicism itself became increasingly academic. No longer an inspiration for the active life, it developed into a new and often less serious form of the contemplative life; a humanist was now less likely to be an orator than a philologist or a man of letters. The leading humanists of the later fifteenth century were men like Poliziano, who discovered the esthetic virtues of the Latin silver age; Merula, who edited texts and standardized spelling; and Ermolao Barbaro, who restored the Greek text of Aristotle. We continue to call these men humanists, but it is sometimes hard to see them as more than superficially like Petrarch, Salutati, Bruni, or Valla. They loved the classics, they knew them better than their predecessors, and they wrote better Latin. But earlier humanism, with its high seriousness about the tasks of rhetoric, had rebelled against the detachment of literature from life, the style from the substance of communication. Barbaro, Pico, and sometimes even Poliziano and Erasmus look increasingly like professional intellectuals.

But, as this account of the fate of rhetoric in the later Renaissance has at various points already suggested, these changing attitudes to language and communication were accompanied by, and gave expression to, a deeper set of cultural changes. If rhetoric in the earlier sense of the art of touching men in their hearts and so stimulating them to action was now declining, the reason was that man himself was increasingly perceived, once again, as essentially an intellectual being. Since intellect is a faculty man shares with other men, man was also beginning to lose some of his passionate individuality. And since the object of intellect is the general and rational order of reality itself, the decline of rhetoric signified too the recovery, albeit under somewhat new forms, of the old sense of the cosmos as a unity organized according to fixed patterns, accessible to the mind, which dictate the norms of man's individual and social existence. The attitudes of the earlier Renaissance, it is well to repeat, by no means disappeared. But a major shift in the intellectual climate seems to me unmistakable.

At the center of the change was a decline of the secular principle underlying the culture of the earlier Renaissance: the sense, to cite the typically Renaissance sentiment of a seventeenth-century Englishman, that man lives in divided and distinguished worlds, each of which operates in accordance with principles of its own. The movement of thought was now towards synthesis rather than analysis; men preferred the One to the many, simplicity to complexity. Thus if, in describing the assumptions of earlier Renaissance culture, we must begin with its anthropology, in dealing with those of the later Renaissance we must start with its cosmic vision. We are back in a world of thought in which the imagery of divine activity and human existence is once again cosmological. Colet recalls Dante in his description of "the uniting and all-powerful rays of Christ ... streaming as it were from the Sun of Truth, which gather and draw together towards themselves and towards unity, those who are in a state of multiplicity." The aged Erasmus hinted at something very like the naturalism repudiated by earlier humanists in his explanation of man's yearning for rest:

> Why is it that even in inanimate things you may see that each and every one is drawn to its own peculiar abode? As soon as a rock dropped from a height hits the earth, it comes to rest. How eagerly a flame is attracted to its own place! What is this which sometimes rocks the earth so hard it dislodges mountains and stones except the north wind struggling to break through to the place where it was born? Thus it is that a bladder full of air, when forcibly pressed down into water, springs back up. Now the human spirit is a flammable thing which, though hindered by this absurd little body of clay, still does not rest until it mounts up to the seat of its beginning. By nature, indeed, all men hunt for repose; they seek something in which the spirit can rest.

This impulse to imbed man once again in the objective order of the cosmos, from which earlier humanism had freed him, explains the popularity now of the notion of man as microcosm, a conception whose prominence in the later Renaissance hardly requires illustration. It is also closely related to the revival of various forms of occultism, both esoteric and popular, which sought, in Pico's words, to "wed earth to heaven." It nourished too the ideal of harmony (though this could be expressed in human as well as absolute terms) and above all the revival of the conception of hierarchy, which was, for Ficino, almost synonymous with order itself. Valla's doubts about the authenticity of the writings attributed to Dionysius the Areopagite were now forgotten; a new group of readers craved to believe in it. For Ficino Dionysius rivaled Saint Paul as "the wisest of the Christian theologians"; Giles of Viterbo called him "the unique light of Greek theology"; Colet devoted a major part of his life to the study of his works; and Lefèvre d'Étaples edited his *Celestial Hierarchies* and described his writing as "most sacred" and "so eminent in dignity and excellence that no word of praise is adequate to describe them. Even Erasmus, though less enthusiastic, did not hesitate to apply the Dionysian hierarchical vision to both the ecclesiastical and political order. Thus we are once again back in a single holy order of reality whose principles are mandatory in every aspect of existence. It is true, of course, that something of the earlier Renaissance persists in the uses of hierarchy by the Neoplatonists. Ficino's hierarchy is not simply a static structure but a system for the transmission of vital influences; and Pico sought to protect human freedom by allowing man the liberty to ascend or descend "the universal chain of Being" and so freely to shape himself. But what is most significant here, it seems to me, is not the impulses retained from the earlier Renaissance but the overwhelming presence of the hierarchy itself. For Pico man ought clearly to rise rather than to descend on the ladder of being; its existence prescribes the uses of human freedom.

But it is above all in the application of these conceptions to the understanding of man that we can best see the difference from the earlier Renaissance. Once again the human personality was conceived not as a dynamic unity but, reflecting the structure of the cosmos, as a set of distinct and graded faculties, properly ruled by reason, the soul, or the spirit; the terminology varied from thinker to thinker, depending somewhat on whether he wrote under Aristotelian, Stoic, or Platonic influence. Vives attached the idea directly to the larger order of things. "This is the order of Nature," he declared, "that Wisdom be the rule of the whole, that all creatures obey man; that in man, the body abides by the orders of the soul, and that the soul itself comply with the will of God. Whoever violates this order, sins." Men played changes on the general conception. In the *Courtier*, Ottaviano Fregoso noted that "even as our mind and body are two things, so likewise the soul is divided into two parts, one of which has reason in it, and the other has appetite." For Erasmus "the body or flesh is our lowest part.... The spirit represents in us the likeness of the divine nature.... Lastly, God founded the soul as the third and middle faculty between the other two, to hold the natural senses and impulses."

But the sovereignty of the highest part of man meant that the essence of man was once again seen to reside in his intellect, or, as sometimes in Ficino, something above the intellect, but always a high and separate faculty. Thus for Castiglione's Bembo (we may compare him with Petrarch or Valla on the point) knowledge is prior to love, for, "according to the definition of ancient sages, love is nothing but a certain desire to enjoy beauty; and, as our desire is only for things that are known, knowledge must precede desire, which by nature turns to the good but in itself is blind and does not know the good." This intellectual vision of man was also accompanied by a remarkable optimism; it agreed with the classical traditions by which it was nourished that to know the good is to do the good. Thus Erasmus remarked that it is fitting "for all to recognize the motion of the mind, then to know none of them to be so violent but that they can either be restrained by reason or redirected to virtue." This, he continued, "is the sole way to happiness: first, know yourself; second, do not submit anything to the passions, but all things to the judgment of reason." In his colloquy *The Wooer and the Maiden*, the maiden Maria tells her lover, a bit pompously, "What emotions decide is temporary; rational choices generally please forever"; and her young man rather surprisingly agrees in what might be taken also, however, as a bit of Erasmian irony: "Indeed you philosophize very well, so I'm resolved to take your advice." Obviously the will remains an important element in this conception; every exhortation to choose the way of reason implies both its existence and its power. But the will is no longer at the center of the human personality; it has been reduced to servitude: if virtuous, to reason; if vicious, to the passions. Much of the educational thought of the later Renaissance rests on this conception.

Inevitably now the passions, identified either with the body or the lowest part of the soul, once again presented themselves rather as a problem than as a resource for good as well as evil. Even Erasmus, although a bit ambivalent, did not give them much praise. Indeed he applauded his own poems for their *lack* of passion: "There is not a single storm in them," he wrote, "no mountain torrent overflowing its banks, no exaggeration whatever." He preferred the poetry that seemed most like prose and disliked the choruses in Greek drama because of their violent emotionality. Vives similarly distrusted the passions, though technically admitting their ethical neutrality. "The more pure and lofty a judgment is," he declared, "the less passion it tolerates; such a judgment examines with much care the possible good aspects of each object and does not accept any excitement, except on rare occasions and with serene moderation." "Whenever a passion crops up with all its natural power," he wrote again, "the wise man represses it with the control of reason and forces it to withdraw in the face of a prudent judgment."

Nor is there much question, for the later Renaissance, of the vileness of the body, which was once again, as with Ficino, an "earthly prison" and the "dark dwelling" of the soul. Ficino excluded the body from his definition of man. "Man," he asserted, "is the soul itself.... Everything that a man is said to do, his soul does itself; the body merely suffers it to be done; wherefore man is soul alone, and the body of man must be its instrument." Erasmus could make the point lightly, as when his lovers agree that the soul is a willing prisoner of the body, "like a little bird in a cage." But at times he was in deadly earnest. "If there is any evil in the mind," he wrote in his *Education of a Christian Prince*, "it springs from infection and contact with the body, which is subject to the passions. Any good that the body possesses is drawn from the mind as from a fountain. How unbelievable it would be and *how contrary to nature*, if ills should spread from the mind down into the body, and the health of the body be corrupted by the vicious habits of the mind." Again we are reminded of the dependence of human existence on the larger order of nature. Vives was more violent: "Our souls carry the heavy burden of bodies with great misery and pain; because of bodies, souls are confined to the narrow limits of this earth, where all filth and smut seem to converge." In this insistence on the separation and even antagonism between the higher and lower parts of man, between the rational soul or the spirit and the body and its passions, we can discern a significant counterpart to the distinction between the substance and form of verbal discourse, or between its rational content and its rhetorical embellishment, the soul and body of thought.

This attitude of the body had its positive corollary in a peculiar emphasis on the immortality of the soul, a doctrine sometimes denounced by the Fathers because it appeared to contradict Christian belief in the resurrection of the body. The typical representatives of the later Renaissance occasionally defended the resurrection, and Ficino spoke of the natural desire of the soul to be reunited with the body, a desire that had in the nature of things eventually to be satisfied. But the true interests of the later humanists lay in another direction; and even when they discussed the subject, they emphasized not so much the glorification of the resurrection body as its transformation into something less bodily and more spiritual. They were preoccupied with the immortality of the soul. Ficino devoted most of his *Platonic Theology* to proving it; and there are echoes of the idea, on a more earthly level, in Gargantua's letter exhorting Pantagruel to virtue: "If, beside my bodily image, my soul did not likewise shine in you, you would not be accounted worthy of guarding the precious immortality of my name. In that case, the least part of me (my body) would endure. Scant satisfaction *that*, when the best part (my soul which should keep my name blessed among men) had degenerated and been bastardized." The proclamation of the immortality of the soul as an official dogma of the Church at the Fifth Lateran Council in 1513 can perhaps be attributed to this interest of the later Renaissance.

This new tendency in the idea of man also helps to explain the revival of the contemplative ideal, and the recovery of interest in philosophy. Pico was typical. "I have always been so desirous, so enamored of [philosophy]," he wrote, "that I have relinquished all interest in affairs private and public, and given myself over entirely to leisure for contemplation." Giles of Viterbo oddly thought of Jesus as a man who avoided cities, market places, and the company of men; "the happy man," he wrote a friend, "is he who, conscious of how short life is, lives for himself, apart from the tumult of human affairs." Even Castiglione's Ottaviano, confronted with the stock problem whether the active or contemplative life is to be preferred by a prince, could only offer the unlikely suggestion that "princes ought to lead both kinds of life, but more especially the contemplative," which ought to be "the goal of the active as peace is of war and as repose is of toil." The persistent longing of Erasmus for peace devoted to study is not only a personal taste but the ideal of a generation, and the peace movement among the intellectuals of his time was no more simply a response to the political situation than was Dante's *De monarchia*.

In this atmosphere Scholasticism no longer appeared so distasteful. We have learned to take more seriously Erasmus's protestations that he attacked not the Schools but their abuses; and if he could not bring himself to praise the Schoolmen, he sufficiently venerated the idea of philosophy to reunite it with theology in his *philosophia Christi*. Pico saw his mission in life as the renewal of philosophy after decades of attack, and Ficino, Lefèvre, and Vives were all eager to bring philosophy once again into the service of faith. Aristotle, Plato, the Stoics, now no longer merely names to conjure with, all found ardent admirers and increasingly serious students. And even Thomas Aquinas began to develop a prestige he had never before enjoyed outside the Dominican Order. Erasmus himself admitted that Thomas had "a certain unction in his writings." Thus two cultural worlds, largely kept apart in the earlier Renaissance, were now converging. Raphael's great *Stanza della Segnatura*, with its effort to combine all culture, human and divine, under the parallel auspices of theology and philosophy, was a product of this movement.

Again, I must emphasize, there was here no absolute change, no total repudiation of the ideals of the earlier Renaissance. Yet it seems clear that a profound shift was under way, which calls for some explanation. Part of the explanation is probably to be found in a kind of dynamic within humanism itself. When men first sought to enlarge their powers of verbal expression by imitating the classics, they discovered not only the principles of classical expression but also new and undreamt of potentialities within themselves. But as classical philology was more and more fully explored and objectively mastered, it could be submitted to general rules; and classicism became no longer liberating but confining. The feeling for propriety in the use of language was also nourished by the printing press, another major development of this period, which standardized every aspect of verbal expression and, as printed books poured off the presses by the millions, imposed its norms on a growing literate public. Yet, even if we do not look beyond humanism itself, I think we can see a deeper impulse at work, pushing the movement in the same direction. For implicit in the culture of the rhetoricians, with its rejection of an objective cosmic order by which man could take his bearings, was not only liberation but also the danger of total anarchy and disorientation. From the beginning the more sensitive among the humanists had been aware of this problem and had tried to solve it by calling for the union of eloquence with wisdom. But there was no necessary reason, in the absence of an objective order accessible to philosophy, or of spiritual guidance supplied by faith, for such an alliance; and in fact the earlier humanists were themselves not only exuberant about the newly-discovered freedom and creativity of the individual but also increasingly anxious about the uses men were likely to make of these gifts. Petrarch allowed Augustine to reproach Franciscus for glorying in his eloquence; Salutati was troubled by the fact that many orators were not good men; Poggio was increasingly depressed that rhetoric seemed rather a tool for the abuse than for the strengthening of human community. Thus, in spite of its attacks on philosophy, even early humanism recognized the need for something more than the power of rhetoric. From this standpoint the later Renaissance seems to have been seeking to supply a defect in the culture of the earlier Renaissance. At the same time we must ask whether this defect was not in fact a necessary element in its identity.

Yet I think that we must finally look beyond humanism itself to developments in the larger social and political world. We may point immediately to the deterioration of conditions in Italy. Centuries of internal conflict within the towns of Italy had produced, by the middle decades of the fifteenth century, a climate of intolerable insecurity; and this was aggravated by the long period of large-scale warfare and destruction initiated by the French invasion of 1494, which effectively destroyed the freedom of the Italian states. Order, not freedom, was the most urgent need of this new age; society became more rigidly stratified and governments more authoritarian; all change appeared increasingly terrifying. And in the same period too the papacy, at last fully recovered from the conciliar ordeal, was reasserting the authority of the medieval vision of reality. The general proposition that all things are part of a single holy order of reality at once objective, intelligible, hierarchically organized, and ruled from above was, under these conditions, not entirely anachronistic. It provided relief from the immediate and pressing dangers of the times. Its conception of government also bolstered the authority of princes, with whom the papacy was now prepared to come to terms by concordats. In Italy, with the exception of Venice, princes were everywhere in the ascendancy; and, whatever their particular differences with the pope, princes found the new hierarchical vision of order congenial. Under these conditions rhetoric lost much of its public utility; social solidarity and social order were no longer created from below, by persuasion, but imposed from above, by force; and intellectuals, their own social roles reduced, were increasingly contemptuous of the masses, who corresponded socially to the doubtful passions of the body politic. By the same token the art of speaking well became a badge of social distinction, the peculiar property of a social and political aristocracy gathered in princely courts. And the image of man, which at least since Plato had been closely correlated with the image of society, once again reflected the perception of the general order of things.

This account of the changing assumptions of later Renaissance culture is obviously not a sufficient or balanced description of the later Renaissance. Just as, along with its novelties, the culture of the earlier Renaissance preserved some residues of medieval culture, itself not entirely homogeneous, much from the earlier Renaissance survived in the later fifteenth and sixteenth centuries, often in uneasy tension with the tendencies I have described. And it is at this point in the argument that we must take cognizance of the relationship between the Italian Renaissance and cultural developments in other areas. The fact that Germans, Frenchmen, Spaniards, and Englishmen were nourished by Italian movements of thought largely in the period of this retreat from earlier novelties is worth some reflection. Thus it may be that the regressive tendencies in later Renaissance culture made Italian modes of thought more congenial than they would otherwise have been to Europeans elsewhere, who might have been put off by the less veiled novelties of earlier humanism. The modification of earlier Renaissance culture, as it was transposed from the urban republics of its birth into the milieu of the princely courts, doubtless also assisted its adaptation to the aristocratic circles of the northern monarchies, though these changes had a more ambiguous meaning for the free cities of the Empire, now under growing pressure from territorial princes.

But, as I have from time to time emphasized, the more vital impulses of the earlier Renaissance had not altogether disappeared from the culture of the later Renaissance even in Italy, however much they had been compromised; and these too were known beyond the Alps, where they nourished, if they did not precisely cause, the novelties in what, for all the ambiguities in the term, is conventionally described as the "Northern Renaissance." Northern Europeans, however equivocal their feelings about Italy, regularly admired her Renaissance achievement as a break with the medieval past; and the deepest assumptions of earlier humanist culture found theological expression in the Protestant Reformation. Thus if the earlier Renaissance was an Italian affair, and the attitudes of the later Renaissance found expression, as the examples cited here reveal, in both Italy and the North, the later Renaissance seems to have had a very different significance outside of Italy, where it presents itself rather as the beginning of a new phase in cultural history than as the decline of a movement already well established. In the North, therefore, and perhaps most conspicuously in England, we can discern with increasing clarity much the same sense of the potentialities of human freedom, the same restless and creative exploration of the possibilities of individual existence as in earlier Renaissance Italy. And this too requires explanation.

The major cause for the continuation of the vital impulses of the Renaissance in Northern Europe after the first decades of the sixteenth century is to be found, I think, in its political pluralism. This, together with geographical and spiritual distance from Rome, the symbol and champion of universalism, posed an insuperable obstacle to the full recovery of any conception of a single, holy, and cosmic order. On this point the distinction between Catholicism and Protestantism is largely irrelevant. France and Spain, the piety of Philip II notwithstanding, resisted papal influence as successfully as England or the Elector of Saxony; all together represented the secular principle of divided and distinguished realms that made any conception of a unified hierarchy embedded in an objective structure of reality ultimately implausible. And political particularity provided a foundation for the development of national cultures which, because of their secularity, also gave room for the same kind of personal individuality that had characterized the earlier Renaissance in Italy. Nowhere is this development more apparent than in the emergence of the great vernacular literatures, in which Northern Europeans discovered for themselves the creative and liberating power of language, much as the rhetoricians of Italy had begun to do two centuries before.

Bibliography

HANS BARON, *The Crisis of the Early Italian Renaissance* (1966).
JOHANN HUIZINGA, *Erasmus and the Age of the Reformation* (1953).
PAUL OSKAR KRISTELLER, *Renaissance Thought: The Classic, Scholastic, and Humanist Strains* (1961).

James K. McConica, *English Humanists and Reformation Politics Under Henry VIII and Edward VI* (1965).

James H. Overfield, *Humanism and Scholasticism in Late Medieval Germany* (1984).

Gerald Strauss, *Luther's House of Learning: Indoctrination of the Young in the German Reformation* (1978).

Nancy S. Struever, *The Language of History in the Renaissance: Rhetoric and Historical Consciousness* (1970).

Charles Trinkaus, *In Our Image and Likeness: Humanity and Divinity in Italian Humanist Thought* (1970).

Luther and the Wittenburg reformers.   *The Toledo Museum of Art; gift of Edward Drummond Libbey*

PART FOUR

The Age of Reformation

The Reformation is the first of the great revolutions that have shaped the modern world. Although it did not directly create new systems of government or overturn the reigning class structure of society, its impact on contemporary politics and society was deep and lasting. In many territories the Reformation brought to a conclusion the long struggle between secular and ecclesiastic governments for local political control. Robert M. Kingdon shows how Protestants aided and abetted the transition from episcopal to lay government in Geneva, ending the clergy's political, economic, and ideological power over that city.

In the struggle for the hearts and minds of the laity, Protestants employed a new and powerful weapon: the printing press. The Reformation is the first historical example of successful mass propaganda through print. Vernacular pamphlets appeared by the tens of thousands in the 1520s and 1530s. Because the vast majority of people could not read, such propaganda was often designed to be read aloud to them; sermons were turned into pamphlets and pamphlets often contained pictures. In propagandizing the masses, Protestants also made wide use of single-leaf broadsheets. These were one-page pictures, rich in symbols, accompanied by a simple text that was often rhymed to better catch the imagination. The shrewd use and abuse of traditional images for purposes of propaganda is the subject of Robert Scribner's essay.

The Age of Reformation was an age of great rulers, a time when determined individuals could shape the direction of history within their immediate sphere of influence. Such an individual was the English king Henry VIII, whose single-minded political ambition transformed English politics and religion, and not necessarily for the better, according to J. J. Scarisbrick. Scarisbrick critically examines the character of the king and the achievements of his reign.

Wherever the Reformation succeeded, it ended or severely restricted monasteries and nunneries. This was one of the most visible changes brought about in contemporary institutions by the Reformation. Protestants universally rejected the celibate life of the religious on the grounds that it created an elite body of Christians allegedly superior to ordinary laity and, further, demeaned the estate of marriage. Displaced monks and nuns in Protestant territories were encouraged to marry and did so in large numbers. Marriage was presented as the most God-pleasing of human institutions. The consequences for women of this new Protestant exaltation of marriage and family life are the subject of Jane Dempsey Douglass's essay.

Was the Reformation a Revolution? The Example of Geneva

ROBERT M. KINGDON

Was the Reformation a true social and political revolt or an upheaval only in theological doctrine and religious practice? In most cities and territories where it succeeded, the Reformation does not appear to have had a profound effect on the composition of secular ruling elites nor to have radically rearranged the social structure. Those who were powerful or poor before the Reformation tended to remain so after it. When, however, one remembers that the Roman clergy were also a powerful ruling class, the revolutionary nature of the Reformation becomes clearer.

In Geneva the clergy wielded significant political power. They also controlled vast properties and ran their own courts. In addition, they defined the prevailing social myth by which society was ordered, a myth that placed the clergy at the pinnacle of a godly society. Genevan temporal and ecclesiastic government had long been centralized under the bishop of Constance, the city's traditional overlord. By successfully attacking Rome, the Reformation helped bring about sweeping change in political organization, social structure, the economic control of property, and the dominant social myth. In doing so, Protestants allied themselves with independent secular efforts to limit the power of the church over civil life and to put the laity firmly in control. In these regards the Reformation was a true revolution.

Was the Protestant reformation a revolution? The question should be of interest to a number of different students. It should interest those who are attracted to the period of the Reformation, who want to understand as fully

Reprinted with the permission of the author from *Transition and Revolution: Problems and Issues of European Renaissance and Reformation History*, Robert M. Kingdon, ed. Copyright © Robert M. Kingdon.

as possible just what happened in that movement and what its full significance was. It should interest those who are curious about the nature of violent social change and who want to know more about the origins of the revolutions which have been such an important part of recent world history. It may even interest those who regard themselves as spiritual descendants of the Protestant Reformers and who want a clearer idea of the precise nature of their heritage.

Before we can answer the question, however, we must establish a definition of the term "revolution." This is not an easy task. The word has been used in many ways and much of this use has been by men passionately committed either to the glorious triumph or the complete eradication of a revolution. The term has thus come to carry strong emotional connotations. It is not easy to discuss it objectively and to define it in a way most people can accept. Nevertheless we must try.

Very few men at the time of the Protestant Reformation would have called it a revolution. In those days the term did not have a political or social meaning. It was basically a scientific term, used primarily by astronomers. Its best known usage was in the title of the famous treatise in which the Polish astronomer Nicolaus Copernicus advanced his radical new theory that the sun, not the earth, was center of the solar system. This treatise was titled *On the Revolutions of the Heavenly Bodies* and was first published in 1543. In this context the term "revolution" referred to the motions of heavenly bodies in orbits around either the earth or sun. There are two aspects of these motions which we should note. They involved constant return, as each heavenly body, in describing its orbit, returns again to each place it has been before. They also involved inevitability, as each heavenly body moves without interruption or distraction along a path which can be predicted with complete confidence by a trained astronomer.

There are obvious ways in which this astronomers' term can be applied, by analogy, to certain political and social changes. One can find a few examples of such an application during the sixteenth century. For example, one observer in 1525 called the rebellion of the Communeros in Spain a "revolution of the people." But this usage is rare and its precise meaning is often uncertain. One can find more examples of this application in the seventeenth century. For example, a prominent English historian in 1674 called the overthrow of the ruling Rump Parliament and the restoration of the Stuart monarchy in 1660 "the revolution." This particular application of the term is quite close to the original astronomers' meaning of the term. For 1660 witnessed a return to a form of government the English had challenged in 1640, with the meeting of the Puritan Long Parliament, and had abolished a few years later, following the English Civil War. This application, however, is quite far from modern usage.

Only in the eighteenth century did the term "revolution" come to be used commonly in a way we would recognize. It was applied then to the two great upheavals which we know as the American and French Revolutions. It still contained some resonance of its original astronomers' meaning. Both American and French revolutionaries thought they were returning their governments to earlier and purer forms, found in a historic state of nature or in some government of classical antiquity. Their knowledge of classical political thought was impressively detailed. And their respect for classical political institutions, particularly those of republican Rome, is striking. It is reflected, for example, by the adoption of the Roman name "Senate" for the upper house of the American legislature. Both groups of revolutionaries also thought these returns to be inevitable and irresistible, part of an inexorable historical process, of which they were the destined leaders.

These men also conceived of their revolutions as being primarily political. The fundamental problem they saw facing their societies was the behavior of a form of government, monarchy, which they felt had become obsolete and tyrannical. They felt they could solve most of society's problems by creating a new form of government, a republic, which would be more sensitive to the needs and aspirations of the general population. Some later analysts, however, saw these same revolutions as fundamentally social. They involved the triumph of a rising new ruling class, the bourgeoisie, over a decadent old ruling class, the feudal nobility. In this view the political changes which are so obvious were relatively superficial. The two types of government, monarchic and republican, were institutions created by the two ruling classes to perpetuate their control. The best known and most influential of these analysts was Karl Marx. It is his view of revolution, involving explosive conflict between social classes and a consequent restructuring of economic as well as political institutions, which tends to prevail in the twentieth century. And the revolutions he forecast, in which another rising new class, the proletariat, would overthrow and replace the victors of the eighteenth-century upheavals, the bourgeoisie, have come to dominate modern thinking on the subject. In particular the Marxist revolutions which succeeded in reshaping Russia and China supply the type to which most modern usage of the term "revolution" refers.

Many contemporary thinkers have analyzed this modern view of revolution at length. Some have reduced their analysis to succinct definitions. One particularly useful definition is provided by Sigmund Neumann, and eminent political scientist who died not long ago. He defined revolution as involving "a sweeping, fundamental change in political organization, social structure, economic property control, and the predominant myth of a social order, thus indicating a major break in the continuity of development." It seems to me that this formula sums up modern opinion successfully enough so that we can use it. Armed with Neumann's definition, we can now return to our orginal question.

Was the Protestant Reformation a revolution, in Neumann's sense of the word? At this point some scholars would object that to use the term "revolution" in speaking of the Reformation era is to adopt an anachronism. It forces phenomena from one period into a concept drawn from another period. Such forcing distorts both the phenomena and the concept and is thus the greatest sin any historian can commit. It seems to me that this objection is specious. In order to understand a period one need not restrict oneself to the language of that period. Indeed it is often possible to understand some aspects of a period in history even better than the men who lived through it, by use of concepts developed and refined since they died. Modern economic historians, for example, understand far more about the development of the European economy during the fifteenth and sixteenth centuries than did businessmen who participated in that development. Their superior understanding is based in part on the use of concepts derived from modern economics and mathematics, unknown to the Renaissance and Reformation. Modern scholars, for example, can construct price indexes which show exactly what prices increased or decreased during the fifteenth and sixteenth centuries and where and how. These indexes are most frequently derived from the accounts kept by convents, hospitals, and other institutions housing groups of people, of the prices these institutions paid for grain, wine, and other essentials they had to buy continuously year after year. Men of that period often complained bitterly of rising prices but not even the best educated of them would have been able to construct a price index. That does not prevent modern scholars from creating price indexes and then using them to explain many facets of the economic and social development of the period only imperfectly understood by contemporaries. These indexes, for example, help us to explain more fully than ever before many of the food riots of the fifteenth and sixteenth centuries. I would argue that the concept of revolution is like the concept of a price index. If it is used with care, by someone who knows both what it means and what happened in the earlier period, it can be enormously illuminating.

A far more weighty objection to the suggestion that the Protestant Reformation was a revolution comes from specialists in the period itself. Many of them would argue that the Reformation did not involve changes in political organization, social structure, economic property control, and social myths which were fundamental enough to be fairly labeled revolutionary. It was thus not a revolution in Neumann's sense. One thoughtful expression of this point of view can be found in the writing of Professor J. H. Elliott. He sums up his argument in these words:

> The sixteenth and seventeenth centuries did indeed see significant changes in the texture of European life, but these changes occurred inside the resilient framework of the aristocratic-monarchical state. Violent attempts were made at times to disrupt this framework from below, but without any lasting degree of success. The only effective challenge to state power and to the manner of its exercise, could come from within the political nation—from within a governing class whose vision scarcely reached beyond the idea of a traditional community possessed of traditional liberties.

Professor Elliott, to be sure, advanced this argument in the course of a debate on the meaning of early seventeenth-century political uprisings. He is a great authority on uprisings in Spain, particularly the revolt of the Catalans from the Spanish government between 1598 and 1640. He has not considered with equal care the uprisings which accompanied the beginnings of the Protestant Reformation, early in the sixteenth century. Still, he seems to believe that his conclusions apply to the entire early modern period in European history.

I would argue that the conclusion of Professor Elliott and others who share his point of view is defective as an explanation of Reformation changes because it overlooks one crucial fact: it ignores the role of the clergy in pre-Reformation European society. A revolution does not need to be aimed at the power of kings and aristocrats to be a true revolution. It can also be aimed at other ruling classes. The class against which the Protestant Reformation was aimed was the Roman Catholic clergy. In most of Europe before the Reformation, the Catholic clergy did constitute an important element in most political organization and in social structure, did control a good deal of the property, and were custodians of the predominant social myth. A challenge to the clergy thus had to be a radical challenge, calling for a revolutionary change in European society. It is my contention that the Protestant Reformation was such a challenge.

The power of the Catholic clergy in pre-Reformation Europe was revealed in many ways. One way was in politics. A significant number of clergymen exercised direct political power. The pope was the prince of a large state in central Italy, the capital of which was Rome. This state was one of the five largest and most powerful in the peninsula. To maintain and protect this state, the pope controlled all the mechanisms used by any of the leading princes of the period. He directed an army and navy. He supervised one of the largest and best diplomatic services in Europe. He collected taxes and administered justice. In other parts of Europe prince-bishops exercised similar powers. This was particularly true in Germany. There the three prince-archbishops of the Rhineland not only governed their own principalities but also sat in the upper chamber of the imperial Reichstag, the legislature which assisted the Emperor in ruling all of Germany. Other prince-bishops possessed similar if less extensive powers in other parts of Germany. In addition, many clergymen exercised considerable indirect power. There were powerful bishops and cardinals in the councils of practically every king in Western Europe. At times these clergymen gained a significant share of sovereign power in these monarchies. Thus Cardinal Ximenes de Cisneros served as regent of Spain during the minority of Charles V; Charles de Guise, the Cardinal of Lorraine, was a leading figure in the governments of Francis II, Charles IX, and Henry III in France; Cardinal Wolsey dominated the government of Henry VIII in England on the eve of the Reformation.

Another way in which clerical power was revealed in pre-Reformation Europe was in legal systems. Over the centuries the Roman Catholic Church had created a large body of law, called canon law. This law was enforced in a Europe-wide court system, reaching into every community and climaxing in the papal appellate courts in Rome itself. Much of this law was designed to control the internal operations of the Church. But much of it reached out to touch the lives of men who were not clergymen. Most cases involving marital problems, for example, were handled in church courts since marriage was a sacrament of the Church. And even many problems that we would never expect to see handled by clergymen were in fact controlled by church courts in this period. In the province of Franche-Comté, for example, many of the loan contracts were enforceable in church courts. Debtors who had defaulted were hauled before the courts of the archbishop, not the courts of the king, and could be punished with spiritual penalties like excommunication as well as by fines and imprisonment.

These extensive political and legal powers were sustained by formidable economic power. The economy of Europe was still basically agrarian and the fundamental means of production was arable land. A substantial percentage of all the land in Europe was owned directly by clergymen. Parish priests in villages would control land which provided income for their support and for the maintenance of church buildings. Monasteries and other church corporations would control large estates which supported the work of their communities. Bishops and their more important assistants would also typically control a good deal of land.

This considerable economic power was justified in part by extensive social services. Education tended to be a monopoly of the clergy. In much of Europe all of the schools, from elementary grammar schools to universities, were controlled and largely staffed by clergymen. Charity also tended to be a monopoly of the clergy. In cities it was usually administered in "hospitals," all-purpose charitable institutions, staffed by clergymen, with priests or monks in actual residence. These hospitals did much more than take care of the sick. Indeed, those who came down with contagious diseases were more likely to be treated at home or segregated in special pestilential hospitals. The normal hospital took care of orphans and foundlings, of people too old to care for themselves, and of the chronically sick and handicapped. They often also provided hotel services for newcomers and visitors, as did certain other ecclesiastical establishments.

All of this power was justified by a widely accepted social myth, rooted in a version of Christian theology. Every man was held to possess an eternal soul, which could escape damnation and enter into eternal bliss only with the active assistance of the clergy. This assistance could be provided only by clergymen who had been properly trained and ordained and who accepted the direction of the pope and his appointees within the hierarchy of the Roman Catholic Church. Even the myth itself was monopolized by the clergy. Only clerical intellectuals could refine its meaning. Only clerical preachers could proclaim its essential message.

Of course, Protestants were not the only enemies to clerical power. In fact, much of the power of the clergy had been attacked and eroded in many parts of Europe well before the Reformation, during the Renaissance and even earlier. Emperors and kings had challenged the plenary powers claimed by popes; powerful aristocrats had challenged the less sweeping powers claimed by bishops; petty noblemen had even challenged the local powers claimed by priests; cities had often secularized services previously supplied by the clergy. Furthermore, clerical power survived the Reformation in many areas and in many ways. In some instances it even grew in strength. However, Protestants, wherever they were active, invariably opposed the Catholic clergy, often with considerable vehemence and insistence. The Protestant Reformation can fairly be called, I believe, an anticlerical revolution.

To document this conclusion fully would require massive empirical studies of the growth and nature of anticlericalism all over Western Europe during the Reformation. That is clearly beyond the capacity of any one scholar or group of scholars. Some indication of the plausibility of this conclusion can be given, however, by case studies. I would like to present here one such case study. The case I have selected is of a European community in which I have lived and whose history I know particularly well, the canton of Geneva.

Before the Reformation Geneva was an episcopal city, part of an episcopal principality. Her temporal and spiritual ruler was a bishop. Occasionally, especially in the early Middle Ages, she had claimed to be a part of the Holy Empire, centered in Germany, but as an ecclesiastical principality rather than as a free imperial city. More important by the sixteenth century was the fact that she was then lodged securely in an orbit of the duchy of Savoy. This duchy, which straddled the Alps and included parts of modern Italy, France, and Switzerland, was the most powerful principality in the area. Almost all of the rural areas and villages surrounding Geneva belonged directly to Savoy. Many of them were controlled in the usual feudal manner, by noblemen who maintained fortified castles or houses for the defense of the area, and conceded allegiance to the duke of Savoy. For several decades before the Reformation the bishop of Geneva had always been closely connected to the court of Savoy. Often he had been a younger son or brother of the duke. Sometimes he had been consecrated in his office while still a child, and a vicar had to exercise all of his power. This arrangement had the advantage for Geneva of securing Savoyard support for the city. She could call on the ducal army for defense and her merchants could trade more freely throughout the duchy. It also meant, however, that the bishop was seldom in actual residence within the city. He had to spend a good deal of time in following the ducal court, in superintending other properties, or in handling yet other types of secular and ecclesiastical responsibilities within the duchy. Some of the bishops also acquired charges outside of Savoy. A few of them were called to Rome to work for the central administration of the Catholic Church. Many of them acquired ecclesiastical property with attendant responsibilities in neighboring France. Still, the power of the bishop was always felt within Geneva. That power was symbolized graphically by the large cathedral church on the top of the hill in the center of the old city. It had been splendidly rebuilt and redecorated in the course of the fifteenth century, when the commercial fairs for which the city was famous in that part of Europe were particularly flourishing. It was visible for miles around, even from the high mountains which enclose three sides of the city from a distance. It easily dominated the city physically.

Within Geneva, the bishop's power was exercised by an episcopal council. The most important members of this council carried the titles of vicar and "official." The vicar was the bishop's chief representative in the city and presided over the council in the bishop's absence. The "official" was a judicial officer, responsible for supervising the administration of all ecclesiastical justice, both civil and criminal. There were also certain other agents of the bishop who sat in the episcopal council. This council acted as both an administrative body and an ecclesiastical court. The bishop was further assisted in his rule of Geneva by a cathedral chapter of thiry-two canons. Almost all of them came from prominent Savoyard noble families. The chapter was thus a microcosm of the Savoyard ruling class, technically presided over by a member of its most prominent family, filled out by members of many of its lesser noble families. Each of the canons was assigned a luxurious house near the cathedral of Geneva. Vacancies in the chapter were filled by the canons themselves, through co-optation. Their most important single function was to elect a new bishop on the death or resignation of an incumbent. However, they often saw their choice set aside by the pope. He retained the right to confirm any election of a bishop, and in the case of Geneva he reserved to himself the right to make his own final selection. Both the chapter elections and the final papal selections reflected very heavy political pressure from neighboring secular authorities. This pressure came primarily from the dukes of Savoy but it could also come from the French royal house and the Swiss cantons.

For the exercise of his spiritual responsibilities, the bishop depended upon ordained clergymen. There were several hundred of them in pre-Reformation Geneva, out of a total population of about ten thousand. They included secular priests, most of whom were attached to one or another of seven city parishes. They also included regular clergy, mostly of the mendicant orders, housed in some seven convents. The newest of these convents had been built in the century before the Reformation for communities of Augustinian hermits and Poor Clare sisters.

For the exercise of his temporal responsibilities, the bishop delegated some of his powers to laymen. Justice for laymen, in both civil and criminal cases, was supervised by an officer with the unusual title of *vidomne*. Some time before the Reformation, the bishops of Geneva had ceded the right to choose this officer to the ducal government of Savoy. The *vidomne* and his staff lived in a castle on an island in the middle of the Rhone river which cuts Geneva in half. That castle symbolized graphically the power of Savoy within the city. The bishop further allowed the lay population of Geneva to elect certain other officers to share in local government. The most important of these elected officers were four syndics, chosen once a year by the entire body of male citizens in an assembly called the General Council. These syndics had the right to act as judges in the more important criminal trials initiated by the *vidomne*. That right, along with many others, had been spelled out in writing in a charter of liberties of the citizens of Geneva promulgated by a bishop in 1387. Every subsequent bishop was expected to swear to uphold these liberties at the time of his installation. The syndics also chose a Small or Ordinary Council, of twelve to twenty-five men, who met at least once a week to handle local civic problems. Both syndics and Council members were normally relatively well-to-do Genevan merchants. Some of them were professional men. They were often older men, well enough established so that younger members of the family or assistants could keep their businesses going. To these men were assigned a variety of matters of purely local concern. They had to see to it that the walls and moats which fortified the city were maintained in good condition, that adequate food supplies were regularly brought into the city and stored with care, that the streets were kept clean. They also had to direct the collection and expenditure of much of the city's money. And they supervised a variety of educational and charitable institutions.

At this last point ecclesiastical and temporal authority overlapped again, for most of the educational and charitable institutions were staffed by clergymen. The education of clergymen had been handled within the cathedral establishment for a long time. In the fifteenth century, an independent school for laymen had been established. It was financed and supervised by the city Council, but normally staffed by clergymen. The city had been awarded the right to establish a university, but had never done so. Charity was handled primarily by seven "hospitals." Most of them had been founded by the gifts or legacies of wealthy individuals, to provide for both the repose of their own souls and assistance to the poor. A typical "hospital" would be located in a converted house, perhaps itself part of the original bequest. Resident in it would be a priest, who would be in charge and would say masses for the souls of the founder and his family. He would be assisted by a "hospitallier" or administrator, who would assist the poor. Usually there would be a dozen or so poor people also in residence, a mixture of orphans, the handicapped, and the very old. From the middle of the fifteenth century, many of these hospitals were supervised by a municipal foundation, controlled by the Council, which also had supplementary funds to assist the poor who could remain in their own homes. In addition, the city maintained a pestilential hospital, outside the walls and near the cemetery, for people with serious contagious diseases. It was staffed by a priest, a doctor, and several, servants. The city also maintained two small leprosaria outside its walls for victims of leprosy.

The control of public morals should have been the responsibility of the bishop, but he was seldom interested. There were always a good number of prostitutes in pre-Reformation Geneva, to service both visiting merchants and clergymen unable to keep their vows of chastity. Seldom was any effort made to drive prostitutes from the city. Instead they were regulated by the city Council. At one point they were asked to organize themselves into a kind of guild and elect from their number a "queen" who would represent them in dealings with the government. The prostitutes were also expected to live within an assigned quarter of the city, wear distinctive kinds of clothing, and limit their solicitation to specified times and places. If a sexual or marital problem required legal intervention, of course, the courts were prepared to act. Most cases of this sort were handled by the court of the bishop.

Geneva's ecclesiastical establishment was supported materially from a variety of sources. Church property and taxes within the city provided some income. A great deal of additional income came from a patchwork of rural properties scattered over the countryside around Geneva and belonging directly to the bishop. These were superintended by episcopal officers who saw to it that order was maintained in each rural village, that local priests served the spiritual needs of the peasants, and that all the rents and taxes due the bishop were regularly paid.

After the Reformation Geneva was a secular city-state. The bishop and all his officers had been evicted, including the ones appointed with his permission by the dukes of Savoy. The clergy had all been forced either to leave the city or to convert to Protestantism and abandon clerical careers. Almost all of the ecclesiastical property, both within the city and in the countryside, had been confiscated by the new government. Many of the social services provided by clergymen had been secularized. A new Reformed Church had been created to minister to the spiritual needs of the population, but it was completely under the control of the city government. All of this had been engineered by the lay merchants and professional men of Geneva, led by their elected syndics and Council members. These changes began in the 1520s, with the whittling away of the bishop's powers. They reached a climax in 1536, with a formal vote by the entire male population to adopt the Protestant Reformation. They were not fully consolidated until 1555, when John Calvin, the new director of Geneva's spiritual life, finally won a definitive triumph over all local opposition.

The Reformation in Geneva began as a rebellion against the government of the bishop and his Savoyard allies. Step by step the syndics and the city Council seized powers that had heretofore been held by the episcopal government as parts of its sovereign prerogatives, until finally nothing remained for the bishop. The first powers to go were those of control over foreign affairs. This crucial attribute of sovereignty had naturally been claimed by the bishop. As sovereign lord of Geneva he had traditionally directed its relations with other governments. When he became allied to the House of Savoy, its government could help speak for Geneva. Now, however, the syndics and city Council, on their own initiative, opened formal negotiations with other governments, particularly with those of the free city-states of the Swiss Confederation. These were states with which Genevans had long had commercial relations. Merchants who dealt with the Swiss tended to have interests different from those who dealt with Savoy. That fact helped split the population into pro-Savoyard and pro-Swiss factions. These two factions began struggling for control of the Council. When the pro-Swiss faction won the upper hand, it tried to consolidate its power by negotiating formal alliances with two of the more powerful neighboring Swiss city-states, Fribourg and Berne. After several false starts, an alliance which persisted was finally signed in 1526. Fribourg withdrew from the alliance several years later, after Berne turned Protestant and Geneva began considering Protestantism. But Berne remained as Geneva's staunchest ally and that alliance was important, for Berne was one of the greatest military powers in the area. This was the period of the zenith of Swiss military might. Crack troops of Swiss mercenary infantrymen were hired by royal governments all over Europe to fill in their own armies when really major military campaigns were planned. And Berne was an important recruiting point for the formation of these armies. That meant Berne could recruit for her own purposes a powerful army, powerful enough to defeat the ducal armies of Savoy, if that became necessary.

The Savoyards protested vehemently against this alliance, arguing that it amounted to usurpation by the Council of a sovereign power really belonging to the bishop. Pierre de la Baume, the incumbent bishop, however, did not back up this Savoyard protest. He had become alienated from the duke at that point, despite the years he had spent in the ducal entourage, and was trying to play an independent game. In the course of personal negotiations with city Council, he fatefully conceded to that body the right to sign alliances. That occurred in 1527. He also tried to make himself a party to this particular alliance. The Bernese refused to admit the bishop to the alliance and the bishop tried to revoke his concession to the Geneva Council. But it was too late.

The next episcopal powers to be seized by the city Council were the rights to control justice, another crucial attribute of sovereignty. The syndics had already won much earlier, under the terms of the 1387 charter, the right to sit as judges in certain criminal trials. But the arrest and execution of lay criminals remained in the hands of the *vidomne* and his staff. Clergymen accused of crimes were tried by the "official" and tried in the bishop's court. All civil cases were handled by either the *vidomne* or the "official." And all decisions could be appealed to the bishop. The first of these powers to go was jurisdiction over civil cases. The Council persuaded the bishop to surrender it voluntarily in 1527, when he was eagerly trying to placate the city and win the Council's support. This meant that the bishop had surrendered some of the powers previously exercised by the *vidomne* and the "official." The concession of the *vidomne's* powers made the Savoyards furious, since he was appointed by their government. Again the bishop changed his mind and tried to retract his concession, but again he was too late. Instead the city Council proceeded to take over more judicial powers. It blocked all appeals to superior courts outside of Geneva. It transferred to the syndics the right to execute criminal sentences. Finally a new elective magistracy was created, the office of the lieutenant, charged with supervising all criminal justice. By 1530 all the judicial powers once belonging to the bishop and his agents had been transferred over to the elective government of the city. Pierre de la Baume may have been trying to win these powers back in 1533, when he returned to the city in person, after a nasty religious riot in which a prominent canon named Werli had been killed. The council was quite prepared to bring the murderer to justice but unwilling to discipline certain others whom the bishop thought deserving of punishment. And it refused to grant the bishop any role in the judicial proceedings. He then left the city for good. Before long he transferred his entire court to the small neighboring town of Gex. A number of canons also left Geneva during these years of turmoil over judicial jurisdictions.

Meanwhile Protestantism had begun to penetrate Geneva. It was introduced with powerful encouragement from Berne, which had itself formally adopted Zwinglian Protestantism in 1528. The leader of the campaign to convert Geneva to Protestantism was an inflammatory French preacher named Guillaume Farel, who repeatedly visited Geneva during these years in spite of fierce opposition from the leading local clerics. Farel's impassioned semons and public appeals plunged the city into further turmoil. Iconoclastic riots began, in which mobs of boys and young men pulled down altars, smashed religious statues, desecrated relics, destroyed stained glass windows. Catholic religious services were repeatedly disrupted, with preachers being publicly challenged on points of Bible interpretation in the middle of their homilies. Protestants seized certain of the church buildings, most notably the Franciscan convent, and began holding services and administering sacraments in them, in competition with the local priests. Finally in 1535 a public debate was held between a group of Protestant pastors and a few local priests. (Many of the Catholic clergy boycotted it.) The Protestants claimed that the debate had resulted in a decisive victory for them, and that the population was now generally convinced of the truth of their point of view. They demanded that the city adopt legislation to establish firmly a truly Reformed service of worship. Many members of the Council seemed inclined to accept this claim, but the Council as a whole did not want to proceed too abruptly. It ordered a temporary suspension of the Catholic mass, until the problem could be fully resolved.

That step convinced most of the Catholic clergy who were still in the city that they could no longer remain. A number had already left Geneva, because of the constant popular turmoil and harassment or because they had been caught in intrigues involving the bishop. A few had abandoned their religious vocation, had publicly converted to Protestantism, had turned to secular occupations, and had even married. In 1535, after the great debate, practically all the remaining Catholic clergy left Geneva. This included the bishop's vicar, the remaining canons, most of the parish priests, and most of the friars and sisters. A handful of priests who tried to stick it out were ordered by the Council either to leave or to conform to the Protestant settlement and regularly listen to Protestant sermons. The few who remained were relieved of all clerical duties.

Once most of the clergy had left the city, the Council seized control over all church property, both within the city and in the country districts heretofore controlled by the bishop's officers. Some of this property was used to pay off a substantial debt contracted to Berne for armed defense against Savoy. The rest was allocated to charity. All the hospitals created during the Middle Ages to minister to the poor were closed down. A new Hospital-General was established in the building which had been the convent of the Poor Clare sisters. A civilian staff, including a "hospitallier" or administrator, a teacher, a doctor, and servants, was assembled and housed in the building. A special committee of the government was created to supervise the activity of this staff. The administration of charity was thus thoroughly laicized and rationalized in Geneva. Later Calvin was to give these laymen responsible for the Hospital-General, both on the supervisory committee and in the office of "hospitallier," the additional ecclesiastical title of deacon. But they remained laymen without any clerical ordination or special clerical training for their jobs.

As a final assertion of sovereignty, the city Council authorized and supervised the coining of money. The new coins carried a slogan, somewhat modified from an earlier slogan used by the episcopal government, which was to become a rallying cry of the Reformation. It was: *Post tenebras lux,* "after darkness light."

Naturally all of these changes increasingly alarmed the bishop, the ducal government of Savoy, and the Savoyard noble families of the area surrounding Geneva. The bishop could see his power and wealth evaporating, the duke could see his claim on the city withering away, the nobles could see their relatives among the canons insulted and exiled. Considerable military pressure was brought to bear upon Geneva to stop this course of events. Armed bands of Savoyard noblemen, encouraged by the duke and the bishop, ravaged the countryside, interdicting much of the trade so vital to the city's economy and making it hard for the city to gather in essential food on a regular basis. By 1535 the city was virtually under siege. Geneva appealed for help in several directions and finally persuaded its Bernese ally to act. A sizable Swiss army came pouring down from the great plain to the north. There was little the Savoyards could do to withstand it. The army commanded by the Bernese effectively conquered all the Savoyard and independent territory surrounding Geneva. It even tried to take over the city itself, but the Genevans were able to resist that pressure.

With a ring of Bernese dependencies around her, Geneva was now free to go all the way to Reformation. In a special meeting of the General Council held in May of 1536, the final step was taken. It was voted that the city would henceforth live by the Gospel and the Word of God as it had been preached in Geneva since the suspension of the mass. It was further voted that "masses, images, idols, and other papal abuses" would no longer be permitted in the city.

That decision ended the power of Catholic clergy in Geneva. But it did not immediately create a Reformed Church. It really only left a vacuum, which was unstable and dangerous in an age when almost all Europeans felt it necessary to build their lives and their communities around some form of religious ideology. Farel, the most prominent of the preachers who had persuaded Geneva to abandon Catholicism, desperately tried to fill this void. He had the great good luck to recruit as his principal assistant a brilliant young French humanist lawyer who happened to be passing through Geneva only a few months after its fateful decision to become Protestant. This was John Calvin. He had only recently converted to Protestantism and fled from religious persecution in his native country to Basel. There he had composed and published the *Institutes of the Christian Religion*, a book which was to become, in its later and expanded versions, the most important single summary of Protestant doctrine produced in the century. Calvin had not planned to settle in Geneva, but Farel managed to persuade him that it was God's will that he should stay and help build a Reformed Church in this place. Calvin was appointed a public lecturer in theology. Even with this help, Farel found it very difficult to organize a Reformed Church. For two years they worked together to announce the Christian truth as they saw it and to give it reality in the community by developing Reformed services and ecclesiastical institutions. They found it harder to control behavior than to persuade men to their belief. Calvin himself later reported that when he first arrived in Geneva, "the Gospel was preached... [but] things were very disorderly... the Gospel consisted mostly of having broken idols... there were many wicked people." They were frustrated at every turn by the Genevans, who did not want to trade what they regarded as Catholic clerical tyranny for a new Protestant yoke. Finally Farel and Calvin were both rather unceremoniously ejected from the city.

Now Geneva was really drifting, without any clerical leadership it could respect. Some thought the city might return to Catholicism. The liberal Cardinal Sadoleto of the Roman curia wrote from his diocese in southern France to urge the Genevans to consider this possibility carefully. Others thought the city might drift into some wild and eccentric religious experiment. This period of indecision finally ended when Calvin, alone, was invited back to take charge. He had settled in German Strasbourg, where he had been named pastor of the French refugees' congregation, and he was reluctant to return to Geneva. He posed strict conditions, and they were accepted. Finally, in 1541, he came back. He remained in Geneva until his death in 1564, and created there a Reformed Church which proved to be a model for Protestants in much of Europe and America.

Calvin accomplished this feat solely by moral suasion. He never possessed even a fraction of the legal power of the deposed Catholic bishop. He never commanded even a fraction of the material resources owned by the bishop, or for that matter by any one of the Catholic cathedral canons. Political power remained solely within the hands of the elected Council and syndics. Calvin and the other pastors were only employees of the municipal government, living on salaries paid by the city, most of them in houses owned by the city. They were far fewer in number than the Catholic clergy whose places they took. Altogether there were only nine pastors in 1542. The number had risen to only nineteen by 1564, the year of Calvin's death. In addition, a few men with Protestant theological training secured positions as chaplains, teachers, or tutors. But the total of all these men was far short of the hundreds of Catholic religious who had served Geneva under the bishop. Furthermore, none of these Protestant clergymen was allowed to become a full citizen of Geneva. The city had become so suspicious of foreign pressures that it granted citizenship, with full rights to vote and hold office, only to certain native-born residents. All the pastors were immigrants, most of them from France, like Calvin. No native Genevan had been able to secure the type of advanced education the Council now decided was essential for this position. A few of the pastors became "bourgeois" of Geneva, an intermediate status which gave a man many political and legal rights, but not full citizenship. Calvin was granted the status of "bourgeois," but only toward the end of his life, in 1559.

This does not mean that Calvin and the other pastors did not exercise considerable political power in Geneva. But it always had to be exercised indirectly, usually through preaching or consulting. Calvin used both means to win great power for himself. He became an eloquent preacher, who clearly commanded the respect, if not always the affection, of his audience. This was in marked contrast to many of his predecessors both in the Catholic clergy and among the earliest Protestant preachers. He also became an active and useful consultant to the city government. The Council found his skill as a trained lawyer and his first-hand knowledge of the greater world of international politics to be extremely useful. He was often called in for consultation and his advice was usually accepted.

One of the first things Calvin did on returning to Geneva in 1541 was to draft a set of ecclesiastical ordinances, to give institutional shape and legal standing to the newly Reformed Church. His right to do this had been part of the bargain that led to his return. After some discussion and a few minor amendments, these ordinances were enacted into law by the government.

They organized the Genevan Church by creating four categories of ministers and then building institutions through which the work of each could be channelled. The categories were: (1) the pastors who were to preach the Word of God and administer the sacraments, (2) the doctors who were to study the Word of God and teach, (3) the elders who were to maintain discipline within the community, and (4) the deacons who were to supervise the administration of charity.

The pastors were distributed among the parishes created before the Reformation both within the city and in the country villages it controlled. There were seldom enough men and resources to staff all of these parishes fully, but arrangements were made so that everyone had access of some sort to a pastor. The pastors' job was to proclaim the Word of God, as it had been discovered by Calvin, from the parish pulpits. They also had to administer the two remaining sacraments which the Reformed Church acknowledged as genuine, baptism and communion. For organizational purposes the pastors were grouped into a Company, which met once a week to handle routine church business, to discuss theology, and to engage in criticism of themselves and their colleagues. Calvin served as Moderator, or presiding officer, of this Company until his death. That was his only position of preeminence in Geneva. He also served as one of the pastors in the cathedral parish of St. Pierre, and occasionally also preached in the nearby church of the Madeleine, where many of the city's merchants attended services. The pastors were all chosen by co-optation, with the existing Company deciding on any new appointment. No choice could become final, however, until the candidate had also been approved by the city Council and presented to the parish in which he was to serve. The Council reserved to itself the right to dismiss without notice any pastor who displeased its members. Over the years a number were in fact dismissed, most commonly because they had offended Council members by things they said in sermons.

In the beginning, Calvin was really the only doctor. In addition to his pastoral duties, he spent a good deal of time in writing and lecturing on the Bible. His lectures attracted hundreds of eager young intellectuals from all over Europe. This teaching did not get formal institutional shape, however, until 1559, fairly late in Calvin's life. In that year Geneva created a new Academy, providing both secondary and university-level training in theology. Calvin, of course, was the star of this faculty. He was joined by a number of his disciples who had been teaching in neighboring Lausanne but who had recently been driven out by Berne. The Bernese, who controlled Lausanne directly, had come to object to some of the disciplinary and dogmatic ideas taught by these men. Material support for Geneva's Academy was provided primarily from property confiscated by the Council from native Genevans who had been driven out of the city in a number of internal upheavals ending in 1555. These ejections had had the net effect of eliminating all opposition within Geneva to Calvin and fully consolidating his authority.

The other two orders of ministers, elders and deacons, were laymen most of whom served in this capacity only on a part-time basis. They were drawn from the same pool of wealthy merchants and professional men who served in the city Council and on the city's various governing committees. Near the beginning of every year, a meeting of the General Council was called to elect the syndics and Council members for the coming twelve months. At the same time members of a number of governmental committees were elected, from slates prepared by the outgoing government. These committees included ones to maintain the city's fortifications, control its grain supply, keep the streets clean, act as courts to judge certain legal cases. Calvin's ecclesiastical ordinances added two new committees to the list: a committee to maintain Christian discipline, staffed partly by elders; a committee to assist the poor, staffed by deacons.

The committee upon which the elders sat was called the Consistory. The pastors were also members of this body. It acted as a kind of ecclesiastical court and met once a week. One of the Syndics served as its presiding officer. The elders were chosen so as to represent all of the "dizaine" districts into which the city was divided. They reported to the Consistory names of residents whose religious ideas were suspect, who still clung to Catholic practices, and who did not behave properly. A high percentage of their cases were of people accused of sex crimes—prostitution, fornication, adultery, sodomy, rape. They examined each case. If the fault was minor and the accused penitent, he might be let off with a scolding. If the fault was more serious and the accused stubborn, he could be excommunicated. This was a serious penalty in a population which took its sacraments seriously, and could cause great distress. If the accused had done something of a criminal nature that required further punishment, he would be referred to the city Council.

This was the most controversial single institution established by the Reformation in Geneva. Calvin insisted on its creation when he returned in 1541, and threatened to resign when its power to excommunicate was threatened in later years. Few Protestant governments elsewhere in Europe were willing to grant judicial powers of this kind to an ecclesiastical body of this type. But Calvin ultimately had his way, the opponents of the Consistory were discredited and driven out, and a moral "reign of terror" followed. All of this helped to create that particularly austere pattern of behavior which has come to be labeled "Puritan."

The deacons worked with the Hospital-General. Their positions had actually been created before Calvin's arrival, in the series of events which led up to the final break with Catholicism. Calvin simply made room for them in the Ecclesiastical Ordinances and found Biblical warrant for their assignments. In effect he sanctified this office, gave it a special religious character, and in so doing made it a more highly valued and respected feature of Genevan society.

The Ecclesiastical Ordinances required the Council to consult the pastors when it drew up its slates of nominations for elders and deacons before the annual elections. However, this rule was not followed invariably. It was followed more often in the choice of elders than of deacons, and was followed quite scrupulously in the selection of both after Calvin's power had been fully consolidated toward the end of his life.

This ecclesiastical structure was an outstanding success in consolidating the Reformation in Geneva. Much of it persists in that city down to the present. It helped win for the city the international reputation as a center of Reformed Protestantism which has accounted for much of Geneva's distinctive character over the centuries.

Taken all together, it seems obvious to me that the changes in Geneva between 1526 and 1559 constitute a genuine revolution. They meet every requirement of the definition of a revolution laid down by Neumann which we adopted earlier. There was a fundamental change in political organization: a government run by a bishop assisted by canons, chosen according to Church law, was overthrown; a new government run by a Council of local laymen elected by the people took its place. There was a fundamental change in social structure: several hundred Catholic clergymen, a number of Savoyard noblemen, and ordinary laymen hesitant to go all the way to Calvinism were all driven out of the city; their places were taken by hundreds of immigrants, most of whom were artisans and merchants and most of whom came from France, as had Calvin. There was a fundamental change in economic property control: large amounts of property were confiscated from the old Church and its supporters and in effect socialized, put at the disposition of the entire community as represented by its government, rather than being distributed to private individuals. All of these changes were justified and sanctified by the most obvious change of all, in the predominant myth of social order. Roman Catholic theology was brutally rejected and a new variety of Protestant theology was created to take its place.

There remains one final problem that must be explored, however, before we can answer our initial question satisfactorily. We must consider the extent to which the Reformation in Geneva was typical. Even if the Reformation clearly meant revolution in this particular city-state, it may not have had the same meaning elsewhere. Geneva may have been unique, and thus not a case upon which generalizations should be built.

To resolve this problem would require extensive comparative studies. Even some tentative and preliminary studies of this sort do make one thing clear: the Reformation in Geneva was obviously more radical than in many communities. In few places had the power of the Catholic clergy remained as strong and as pervasive as it was in pre-Reformation Geneva. Cities all over Europe had once been controlled directly by bishops. For example, in

Germany most cities had been ruled by bishops back in the tenth century. Since that period, however, new secular cities had been founded and many old cities had broken loose from episcopal control. By the time of the Reformation only a few German cities remained under the effective direct control of bishops. Most of the cities of importance had become free imperial cities, acknowledging allegiance to only one sovereign—the Holy Roman Emperor. Remnants of episcopal power remained in most of these cities, but most temporal power was concentrated in elected city councils like those of Geneva.

Furthermore, in many cities services that had previously been performed by the clergy had been turned over to secular institutions well before the Reformation. This was particularly true of educational and charitable services. The move to secularization of these services was especially pronounced in the great Italian city-states of the late Middle Ages. In fact it can be argued that the celebrated culture of the Italian Renaissance was made possible by the creation of secular schools and academies supported by municipal governments and wealthy laymen in communities like Florence. Similarly the administration of charity had been laicized and rationalized in communities like Milan which built and endowed large municipal hospitals for this purpose. Clergymen still staffed some of these institutions. But clerical control was gone and clerical participation was reduced if not ended. It can thus be argued that Geneva in the sixteenth century was socially retarded and that she used the Reformation to catch up, to introduce changes which had already occurred in other communities.

It is also clear that in few places did the Reformation go as far as it did in Geneva. It was not common for the entire body of the clergy in a community to be deposed or ejected. More often Catholic parish priests were simply converted to Protestantism, with a greater or lesser appreciation of what that meant, and allowed to remain at their work. Only slowly was a body of clergymen fully trained in Protestant doctrine developed. This seems to have happened in most of the Lutheran principalities in Germany and in the kingdom of England. In England the changes must have been particularly bewildering. For there priests were expected to renounce the pope yet remain Catholic in doctrine under Henry VIII, become Protestant with permission to marry under Edward VI, return to Rome and put aside their wives under Mary, become Protestant again and remarry under Elizabeth I. A remarkable number of priests in England seemed to be able to make many of those changes.

However even if the changes accompanying the Reformation were seldom as abrupt and as far-reaching as in Geneva, there were always some changes. In every single instance, for one thing, a community adopting Protestantism rejected the authority of the pope and broke all ties with Rome. And this was not a trivial move. The papacy had long symbolized in a concrete institutional way the unity of all Western European civilization. Rejection of its power meant a move to some sort of particularism, often to some type of nationalism. This marked an extremely important shift in the most fundamental values held by Europeans, from one basic assumption about society to another. It was a shift which was to have tremendous consequences for the history of Europe for at least another four hundred years, until the middle of the twentieth century.

Another change that almost always came with the Reformation was the closing of all monastic communities and the confiscation of their often considerable property. On rare occasions convents or monasteries were simply walled up and not allowed to recruit new members, thus going out of existence when all existing members died. But more commonly all the monks and nuns, friars and sisters, were required either to leave or find new occupations. And they lost all of their community property. There is a good deal of debate as to how significant were the resulting massive transfers of property. In many areas wealthy noblemen who already controlled much of a monastery's activities no doubt were able now simply to control this property more directly. But changes of some sort had to occur. And often they were brutal and of far-reaching consequences.

Yet another change that almost always came with the Reformation was the collapse of the system of church law and church courts. Appeals to Rome, of course, were always stopped. So at least that element in the Catholic legal system invariably disappeared. But a good many further changes usually followed. Church courts were either abandoned completely or their powers and the range of their jurisdiction were sharply reduced. New Protestant ecclesiastical bodies were seldom given many legal functions. In at least one aspect of legal practice, most Protestant communities went further than Geneva. Before the Reformation cases involving marital and sexual problems were normally tried before church courts. Geneva assigned these cases to a semi-ecclesiastic court, the Consistory. This court did not, to be sure, use Catholic canon law to settle these cases, turning instead to civil law and the relevant parts of the Bible as interpreted by Calvin. But clergymen were at least involved in this part of the judicial process in Geneva. In most Protestant communities they were not granted this right, and jurisdiction over marital and sexual offenses was jealously reserved to secular courts. Both Catholic law and the Catholic type of court were abandoned.

Taken together, the renunciation of papal authority, the closing of the monasteries, and the dismantling of the Catholic legal system were significant changes. They required some modifications in political organization, in the social structure, and in the economic control of property. They reflected a profound change in the predominant myth of the community. It seems to me that these changes can fairly be called revolutionary. Their full implications, to be sure, become obvious only when one examines an extreme case like Geneva. But they were always present. I would therefore conclude that the Protestant Reformation was indeed a revolution.

Bibliography

LORNA JANE ABRAY, *The People's Reformation: Magistrates Clergy, and Commons in Strasbourg, 1500–1598* (1985).
L. P. BUCK and J. W. ZOPHY, eds., *The Social History of the Reformation* (1972).
MIRIAM CHRISMAN, *Strasbourg and the Reform* (1967).
JOHN T. MCNEILL, *The History and Character of Calvinism* (1957).
WOLFGANG J. MOMMSEN, et al., eds., *The Urban Classes, the Nobility and the Reformation* (1979).
E. W. MONTER, *Calvin's Geneva* (1967).
RONNIE PO-CHIA HSIA, *Society and Religion in Münster 1535–1618* (1984).
FRANCOIS WENDEL, *Calvin: The Origins and Development of His Religious Thought* (1963).

Print and Propaganda in the German Reformation

R. W. SCRIBNER

In the early sixteenth century the vast majority of Germans could not read. Although literacy rates in the large cities ran as high as 25 percent, perhaps 95 percent of the total population were illiterate. This did not mean that printed sources were unavailable to these people. Protestant pamphlets, for example, could be read aloud to others as well as privately by oneself. The culture of the early sixteenth century remained an oral one.

The Reformation directed special sermons and visual propaganda at the masses of illiterate people. Protestant polemic was artfully cast in language and images that meant something to simple folk. Protestants drew on popular beliefs and played on popular fears and prejudices to disseminate their message. They also reshaped traditional images to this end, often outrageously so. Woodcuts employed well-known images, like the religious procession, the passion of Christ, and the ship of the church, to expose the excesses of the Roman church and to advance the evangelical alternative.

Such images proved effective because people, generally, worried about their eternal destiny. Protestant spokesmen touched in the common folk deeply ingrained feelings they also shared. They too were fatalistic, believed in astrological portents and other omens, and trusted traditional prophecies to interpret such signs. Protestant visual propaganda made use of all of these. Although the reformers attacked "superstition," their propaganda also exploited popular belief in order to win over the simple folk. Credulity was used to fight credulity. In the process the Reformation confirmed and extended certain features of popular belief, while exposing and overcoming others.

Popular belief may, in general, be regarded as the belief held by the mass of the people, by contrast to that held by the religious elite who make up the

Reprinted from *For the Sake of the Simple Folk* by R. W. Scribner, by permission of Cambridge University Press. Copyright © Cambridge University Press 1981.

clerical hierarchy of the Church, the 'professional men of religion'. But this distinction should not be too rigidly drawn. The rural parson or the wandering friar, for example, may well have shared the belief of the masses, or at least have adopted some of their attitudes, rather than those officially approved by the Church. This concept of popular belief is expressed clearly enough in the medieval saint and miracle cults. Such a definition, however, tells us only where popular belief is to be found, but little about its nature. One of the most persistent dilemmas in the study of religion is whether to approach it as a set of held beliefs or as a set of practices. The dilemma is the more acute in the case of popular belief, where the ideas behind religious practices are rarely formulated clearly and concisely in any formal conceptual structure. Often they appear only through the practices, yet they also give meaning to them. The two must be studied as inextricably linked....

Because it is less structured and more fluid, popular devotion is a kind of liminal area where beliefs are volatile and susceptible to new suggestions and influences. It also involves individual and collective expressions of faith at the same time, best exemplified in the pilgrimage. This made it an ideal ground for propaganda that sought to influence opinion and behaviour. This [essay] will examine how popular belief and its codes were drawn upon to disseminate the Reformation message, and especially how popular devotional imagery was reshaped to this end.

One of the most common forms of communal devotion was the religious procession, which occurred with such regularity throughout the year that it was almost a defining characteristic of the sixteenth-century small community. Besides the processions on major feasts, such as Corpus Christi or Whitsun, there were those of the church fairs held even in small villages. At times of exceptional distress—war, plague or famine—the community held a religious procession to beseech the intervention of God to alleviate their suffering. Such occasions were an expression of communal solidarity, and a manifestation of social and spiritual relations within the community. For evangelical belief, these events epitomised Catholicism in its most superstitious form, the notion that God's intervention was at the disposal of man's behest. It was the more offensive because processions involved the display of the Sacrament, the chanting of litanies invoking the saints and display of the Church hierarchy.

It is hardly surprising that the religious procession should have featured in evangelical propaganda.... The best example is a satirical church fair procession by Peter Fletner. A procession of monks, nuns and priests passes across an open space between two churches, a reminder that religious processions usually wound their way from church to church, making a halt for prayer at each in turn. This procession seems to have little of religion in it: it is bacchic and carnivalesque. It is led by a swine and a very fat priest swinging an incense burner. Behind him a curate sprinkles holy water from a kettle held by a woman in secular clothes, doubtless a priest's concubine. Here any resemblance to a religious procession ceases. Next in the parade come two friars, vomiting copiously and behind them two canons drinking from huge beer steins, thus indicating the cause of discomfort of the two ahead.

The central place in the procession is taken up by a very fat abbot being borne on a litter. He is preceded by two child monks, bearing candleholders in which the flame is represented by spirals of excrement. The abbot is carried by two fools, the foremost of whom has a profusely running nose. Behind the litter, a nun carries a spit packed with sausages, behind her are two nuns with hay-forks, from which hang cod-pieces in parody of the banners carried in religious processions and making a jibe at clerical sexual licence. Two other nuns sing from a gaming-board instead of from a hymn book, and yet another holds aloft a large roast goose. The procession is closed by two nuns, one holding a wine decanter and glass, the other a swaddled baby, a nun's illegitimate child.

This procession is a brilliant carnivalesque parody of the immoral excesses of the clergy.... The work ... embodies the anticlericalism through which evangelical propaganda sought to discredit the opponents of the Gospel. To this end it uses themes drawn from popular culture: excessive eating and drinking, folly, grotesque realism and carnival parody....

So far the example highlights the influence of popular culture, and the church fair was certainly as much an occasion for communal feasting and festivity as it was a religious event. However, several features direct our attention to elements of popular belief.... First, there is the parody of the religious objects themselves, by which hymn books, candleholders, banners and possibly the relics often carried in processions have been replaced by objects of gluttony. There is also the retention of the incense and holy water at the beginning of the procession, thus associating these items with the irreligious. Second, there is an association of folly with vice, a familiar theme of popular moralists of the later Middle Ages, such as [Sebastian] Brant and Geiler von Kaisersberg. Folly here is no longer laughable stupidity or mere brutishness: it is sinful excess....

If we turn from the visual to the written text, we find that the religious theme is more fully stressed. Come to the church fair, the first verse entreats, where indulgences are earned by monastic life. One can be 'holily impure', but if one honours the abbot one's sins can be swept away. This refers to one of the great religious attractions of church fairs, the indulgences attached to the performance of the religious activities which took place there. The second verse alludes to the excessive bulk of the abbot, but the third returns to the theme of Catholic belief. Written as a parody of a litany, it invokes the clergy as those who give an example of religious life. They are the light of the world, the Nazarenes, true followers of Christ .... Thanks to papal bulls, the verse concludes, all things are free to the clergy, and they carry around holiness. The fourth verse also refers to the visual text. The monks sing so that 'the notes rise up in our throats', exemplified no doubt by the two vomiting monks, but this can be relieved with holy water and other things mixed with indulgences.

Perhaps the most important feature of this procession is what is omitted, for it includes only clergy. The only lay figure is the concubine holding the holy-water kettle. The religious procession is thus identified with both vice and with the clergy....

A work known as *The Seven-headed Papal Beast* (Figure 1) ... appeared ... in 1543. It shows the arms of Christ: the instruments of the Passion, the cross, the nails, the scourges and the crown of thorns grouped at the head of the cross, and the spear and sponge on a staff placed on the crossbeam. In parody of the inscription INRI commonly found on the crucifix, an indulgence letter has been attached to the cross, with the motto: 'For cash a sack of indulgences'. The altar usually found in the devotional pictures has been replaced by a cash chest, the repository of proceeds from the sale of indulgences. It was thus an altar of mammon, and upon it, in the place usually taken by Christ, is seated a seven-headed monster, flanked by flags bearing the papal arms, crossed keys and a papal tiara. The arms of Christ are thus mocked by the arms of the pope. The seven heads of the monster are those of a pope, two cardinals, two bishops and two monks. From beneath the cash chest appears a demon, and to underline the message, the artist has placed the title *Regnum diaboli*, the kingdom of the Devil, at the sides of the chest.

The printed text equates the monster with the beast of the Apocalypse, although the description does not quite match the illustration. Just like the papal beast, the apocalyptic beast has seven unequal heads. All are crowned, signifying the tonsures of the clergy; it has ten horns, signifying spiritual power; it bears a blasphemous name, which the text interprets as the seductive tongue of the papacy. The beast is like a leopard, that is, the tyranny of papal rule. It has feet like a bear's, to tread the Gospel underfoot. It has a lion's mouth, which signifies the papal gullet never full with all that its great maw swallows—indulgences, palliums, annates, offerings, foundations, the proceeds of the ban. The beast bears on one of its heads a mortal wound, which signifies the deadly harm done to the papacy by Luther and his writings....

Another motif frequently used in popular devotion was the image of the ship. This was no doubt based on Luke 5.3, in which Christ teaches from a boat, works the miracle of the prodigious shoal of fish and promises the apostles that they will be fishers of men. The ark of Noah, as a prefiguration of the Church, would also have contributed to the connotations of this image, and by the late fifteenth century it was a standard topos for the Church .... The perils of sea travel in that age added another connotation, the precarious and dangerous nature of ship voyages, which could be adapted for devotional exhortation. A woodcut from around 1512, *The Ship of Salvation*, gives an elaborate exposition of the motif .... The ship sails over the sea of life to the places of salvation, such as Jerusalem. This suggests a

Figure 1. *The Seven-headed Papal Beast.*

further influence on this metaphor, the perilous sea voyages undertaken by those on pilgrimage to the Holy Land. The first ship of life was made by God, but the first sailors, Adam and Eve, ran it onto the rock of disobedience. Baptism provided a second ship, but this is all too easily breached and sinks through sin. Penance is the third ship, which each man can make for himself with the aid of Christ the carpenter. This ship sails the sea of the world, in which lurk the numerous monsters of vice. These often overturn or swamp the ship, but the sailor can bail out the water with confession. Faith, with the infallible needle of belief, is the compass; the rudder is God's commands and precepts; the mast is Christ's cross; the sails are laid on with free will, but not in every wind, only in the fair wind of piety. There is the anchor of hope, and the ship's hands are the holy angels who take good care for the barque.

These two images, the ship of the Church and the ship of the individual believer, are joined by the third common ship image of the early sixteenth century, the ship of fools. In his brilliant image of an overloaded ship entrusted to the folly of its becapped crew, Sebastian Brant skilfully combined both of these images. In chapter 103 of *The Ship of Fools* he contrasts St Peter's barque with the ship of the Antichrist. The latter is frail and easily wrecked, endangering those foolish enough to board it.... Brant's pessimism led him to express ... the fear that even St Peter's ship might founder: 'St Peter's ship is swaying madly. It may be wrecked or damaged badly'.... The ship image was firmly established as a popular devotional sign by the eve of the Reformation, and it is not surprising that it should have been adapted for evangelical propaganda....

The ship of the papal Church was used with brilliant inventiveness in an engraving from the latter half of the sixteenth century (Figure 2). Here we see a papal ship setting sail from land, the body of the ship formed by a grasshopper-like creature lying on its back. Six of its legs support a church, whose steeple forms the mast for the sail. The comb and spike on the creature's forehead provide a rudder with which the pope steers his barque, which is rowed by seven sets of clergy. The rowlocks for these clerical oarsmen are supplied by row of teeth along the side of this 'boat', and give it the appearance of the jaws of some great monster. It thus has iconographical links to depictions of the pope enthroned in the jaws of hell. Clearly the papal ship is a diabolical craft, confirmed by the winged demons who assist its passage by pulling it forward and driving it through the water by means of a fan, a pair of bellows and a trumpet.

This ship is not, however, just a ship of papal clergy. It is as much the ship of Catholic practice. The church, supported by the legs of the monster, has three idols and the papal arms above its entrance. A pilgrimage church is perhaps intended, for votives can be seen through the windows on the side. In the prow of the ship there is a procession, with the host exposed in a monstrance. On the shore behind the departing ship stands a nun holding a cloth stuffed full of the items of Catholic belief. She also carries under her

Figure 2. *The Ship of the Papal Church.* Photograph courtesy of Staatliche Graphische Sammlung, Munich.

arm a swaddled child, the result of illicit sexual activity. Finally, two owls perch on the sail of the ship, birds of ill-omen, doubtless signifying the fate of the Catholic Church.

In contrast to this polemical use of the ship image, we can also find the later Reformation adopting it again as a pious image. *The Ship of the Apostles* by Matthias Zundt from 1570 provides an example (Figure 3). Here we have a ship of the Church or ship of faith, not dissimilar to the version of 1512. On the prow are the four Evangelists, on the stern the other apostles. Peter and Paul are the steersmen, John the Baptist the lookout in the prow. On a raised deck is Christ with the cross, beside him the Protestant sacraments—baptism, the Lord's Supper, confession and absolution. Four archangels bear the instruments of the Passion, recalling Christ's salvific death. The ship is rowed forward by the Christian emperors since Constantine, an appropriate theme for the age of the territorial Protestant Church. In the sea encircling the ship, swimming or riding on sea-horses, are the hostile and heretical powers: Nero, Caiphas, Pilate, Sergius, Nestorius, Pelagius, Arius and Mahomet (all swimming), Antiochus, Attila, Genser-

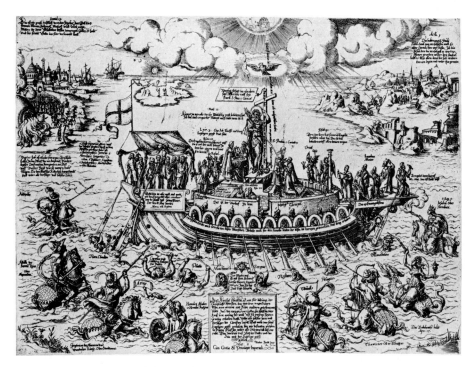

Figure 3. Matthias Zundt, *The Ship of the Apostles*. Photograph courtesy of Staatliche Museen Kuperfstichkabinett, Berlin.

ich, Herod, the Turk, the Tartar, Jezebel and the whore of Babylon (all on horses). These are all persecutors or opponents of the Church, a theme continued by two scenes on land. On the left, the three children in the fiery furnace, saved from persecution by the intervention of the Lord; on the right, St Paul another persecutor of the Church, struck down on the road to Damascus. Thus the Protestant Church is depicted as the true Church, whose enemies will not prevail against it.

The role of the visual image in popular devotion was to call the mind of the pious believer to spiritual truths, and to concentrate his attention on them. The examples of evangelical propaganda we have discussed above all depend on this principle. Often working through satire or parody, they nonetheless serve to call attention to the truth about the old and new belief, and to concentrate the reader's attention on it. The process involved is one in which familiar images are set in new surroundings or given new connotations. The viewer is thus led from the familiar to the unfamiliar and is asked to ponder the implications of this revelation. Its content is that the Catholic clergy and the papacy are sinful and vicious, opposed to Christ and inimical to salvation. This is a pious message, but it depends heavily on anticlerical feeling, which makes the reader the more susceptible to its argument. Yet one may question whether such a process of itself would be capable of arousing any deep and passionate religious feeling which might dispose the reader to shun Catholicism and embrace the new belief. How far did Reformation propaganda seek to touch stronger religious emotions, the impulses which led men of that age to turn to popular devotion of whatever kind?

One of the major preoccupations of the Christian believer of that time was the salvation of his soul and the time when this was adjudged. For this reason, eschatology was a dominant theme of sixteenth-century religion, the reminder of the last things of life and the last days. This took two forms, the general judgment of all men at the end of the world, and the judgment of the individual soul. Eschatology is a persistent motif in evangelical propaganda....

The judgment of the individual soul was often represented by a weighing in a pair of scales. The saved soul is weighed against personified evil in the other tray—either the Devil, wicked souls or personified sins or vices. Until the sixteenth century this weighing up of souls was a component part of depictions of the Last Judgment. Our titlepage (Figure 4) shows a pair of scales suspended from the heavens, held by the invisible hand of God. On one tray sits Christ, so much outweighing the combined bulk of a pope and cardinal in the other tray that they are flung high into the air. The pope clutches a bull of indulgence, affixed with the papal seal, but this is of no

Figure 4. Titlepage to *Ein schöns tractetlein von dem Götlichen und römischen Ablas* [J. Schmidt, Speyer, 1525].

weight compared to the true remission of sin provided by Christ, shown handing such a remission to three simple laymen. Christ's letter of indulgence is sealed with a true token of forgiveness, the image of the Saviour. Beneath the pope, two devils examine the indulgences presented to them by a naked soul, one of whom makes a gesture of rejection—papal forgiveness will not save one from hell, for the second devil places a possessive arm around the suppliant figure. On a near-by tree two animals, perhaps a cat and a squirrel, thus possibly signifying [Thomas] Murner and [Eucharius] Henner, leap up to catch bulls dropped by the pope... This woodcut cleverly combines the notion of the Last Judgment, through the weighing up of papal and Christian belief, with the idea of personal judgment, through the plight of the single soul. For the believer concerned about salvation, its message was direct and simple.

The emotive force of such eschatological references for a sixteenth-century reader can be understood only by examining the greater sense of immediacy about the last days which prevailed at the beginning of the sixteenth century.... [T]he Reformation occurred in an apocalyptic age, an age which expected a great change in the world.... A number of different elements went into the making of this apocalyptic fervour, each reinforcing the others in their cumulative effects. Taken together, they form the most characteristic elements of popular belief during the age of the Reformation. First, there was a strong sense of pessimism and fatalism; second, there was the powerful influence of astrology; third, there was a deep-rooted belief in signs and omens; fourth, there was a tradition of mystical prophecy which offered a cogent spiritual interpretation of these events; finally, there was a broad stream of one particular kind of prophecy, Joachimism, which enabled men to locate this great change historically and to link it to hopes for spiritual and secular improvement. In the context of our present discussion, such elements can best be understood through their iconographical representation.

Fatalism was embodied in the wheel of fortune, a motif of classical origins which the middle ages struggled to reconcile with the Christian idea of providence. One feature of the wheel of fortune was its warning against pride and haughtiness on the part of the mighty. The wheel of fate turns inevitably, and brings down those who believe themselves invincible. Thus most fifteenth-century depictions of the wheel of fortune show a king riding high on the wheel while another topples from the pride of place, and a third rises on the turning wheel, soon to take his position of honour for a time. This concept of fate was essentially non-Christian, but was reconciled in the iconography with Christian belief by showing a rein or scarf attached to the wheel handle or to the figure of Fortune who turned it. This rein was held by the hand of God, so that ultimately it was he who set the wheel in motion, and his providence which decided men's fortunes....

Thus a woodcut from the 1530s (Figure 5) ... combines the theme of the fatalism of the wheel with that of hope for the underdog. A king and two princes sit atop the wheel, the prince on the left clutching two wine glasses to

Figure 5. The Wheel of Fortune.

signify luxurious living. Two artisans clamber onto the wheel, while a noble on the right has reached a point where he must fall from it. The wheel is turned by the blindfolded figure of Fortune, guided by a rein around her neck, held by the hand of God in the clouds. Two ragged figures, representing the poor, respectively pray for and greet the turn of the wheel. To the left, a crowd of well-dressed burghers and clergy are engaged in discussion in apparent ignorance of the scene being acted out behind them. One figure alone, bearded and holding a stick, perhaps a peasant, draws the reader's attention to the scene with a hand gesture. It is a warning to the complacent and well-to-do of the way in which fate would sooner or later turn against them.

The wheel of fortune could be linked to pessimism in two ways, by showing the wheel as the ages of man, depicting his inevitable decay and the unavoidability of death. Thus, in one version of the theme, death in the form of a mockingly laughing corpse turns the wheel. In another it is linked to the idea that death comes to all men by an accompanying depiction of a corpse in a grave. If it was pessimistic, this motif was also intended to provide consolation: death is the great equaliser, reducing all men to the same level. However, the motif was also capable of bitter social comment, shown by a woodcut from around 1480. At the top of the wheel sits Reinecke Fuchs[10]

---

[10] Reynard the fox, the hero of the most popular late medieval animal epic, a cunning, self-seeking, and uncompromising figure, who knows how to get his way.

crowned with a triple tiara to signify the pope. On each side of him is a monk, a Franciscan on his right in the form of a bear, signifying Begging and Greed; on his left, a Dominican in the form of a wolf, representing Avarice. On each side of these are two mounted figures, on the left Pride, on the right Hatred. Seated on the horizontal spokes of the wheel are a man with a sickle representing Falsehood and a priest with a host and chalice representing Self-conceit. At the bottom of the wheel lies Constancy, broken by the fall and naked but for a loin-cloth. Behind the wheel is the giant figure of Patience, who will turn it in due course, aided by the figures seated bottom left and right, a Samaritan monk representing Love and a beguine representing Humility.

This sheet is remarkable for several features. It adapts [well-known] animal allegories ... to attack the financial and political pretensions of the papacy and the monastic Orders. The nobility and the priesthood are also targets of attack, while the author is clearly sympathetic to the sufferings of the common man, crushed at the bottom of the wheel. It is anticlerical and anti-papal, and indeed the written text castigates the pope's pretensions to rule all lands, an anticipation of the more virulent Reformation attack on the papacy. For the common man it is consolatory: if he is patient, the wheel will turn and his time on top will come....

Fatalism may well have been one result of the widespread interest in astrology which dominated the age. This involved the belief that man's fate was influenced by the heavenly bodies and consequently that future events could be read from their movement. Two kinds of heavenly event were of particular interest. The first was the regular and predictable course of the planets, the second the extraordinary occurrence, such as a comet or meteorite. Among the regular movements of the planets, eclipses and conjunctions attracted most attention....

Popularisation of Arabic astrological tracts in western Europe at the end of the fifteenth century stimulated the overwhelming interest in conjunctions. From around 1470 these formed the subject-matter of the small printed works, *Praktiken* or prognostics, which foretold events for the coming year or years, based on the anticipated movements of the planets and their conjunctions. From the beginning of the sixteenth century, this belief was concentrated on the year 1524, when no fewer than twenty planetary conjunctions were expected, sixteen of them in the sign of the fish. The first prediction concerning these conjunctions dated from 1499, by the Tübingen astronomer Johann Stoeffler. He called attention both to the large number of conjunctions and to the momentous effects these would have on world affairs.

By 1517 oral tradition had embroidered this prediction, directing attention to the influence of the sign of the fish to foretell a great deluge caused by the conjunctions. This in itself occasioned a flood of literature about the conjunctions, in total some fifty-six authors taking up the discussion in 133 works in six languages. The high point was reached, naturally enough, in 1523–4 with fifty-one works published in 1523 and sixteen up to February 1524. German interest was strongly aroused in 1521, when the first work in German was published. The conjunctions were much discussed at the Reichstag of Worms, where large illustrated broadsheets were put on sale. In fact the peak of interest was reached in Germany, where the effects of the conjunction were linked both to social unrest and to the emergence of the evangelical movement. In foretelling imminent disaster for the clergy, and in particular for the papal hierarchy, prognostics dealing with this conjunction provided progaganda for the new religious movement. Vivid titlepages and illustrations made these points visually....

Comets or meteors, as extraordinary events in the heavens, were held to presage some momentous occasion, even to exercise some influence causing it. Thus the fall of a giant meteorite at Ensisheim in Alsace in 1492 was taken to prefigure great changes in the politics of the Holy Roman Empire, ranging from the death of the Emperor Frederick III to the inauguration of a new golden age. Sebastian Brant, in particular, took it as a sign that the time was propitious for Maximilian of Austria to act boldly against his foes: fate now favoured him, and he should seize the spokes of the wheel of fortune and arrest its course to his own advantage. Heavenly lights seen in Vienna for five days during the first week of January 1520 prompted Pamphilus Gengenbach, an able evangelical polemicist, to issue a broadsheet interpreting their significance. Gengenbach called attention to the fact that similar lights seen in 1514 were followed by several disasters—epidemic, floods and a great battle in Milan. The Vienna lights were a warning to Charles V that the Church was in danger; but Luther was on the right path, and one should follow him gladly. Gengenbach especially pointed out the dangers expected for 1524, and warned the monastic Orders to prepare for reformation. There was a danger of a new Hussite movement....

Monsters and misbirths were accorded special significance in the canon of signs and omens. They were usually taken to signify misfortune, although they could also be regarded as political allegories. Sebastian Brant in 1496 published two broadsheets dealing with misbirths, one on Siamese twins born near Worms, the other on the birth of a sow at Landser in the Sundgau with two bodies, but one head. Brant interpreted both events as political omens. On the other hand, a much-publicised misbirth to a nun in Florence in 1512 was interpreted as a divine punishment for her denial of her pregnancy. A broadsheet by Lorenz Fries on a misbirth near Rome in 1513 cast the net more widely, seeing it as signifying God's wrath, expressed in plague, disunity of Christians, advances of the Turk and loss of money from the land. But God also looked on man with pity, and had given them a pious, wise and learned pope, who would turn all to good. The 1513 misbirth thus becomes a sign of hope, associated with the accession of Leo X in March that year.

Skilled publicists...knew how to make the most of misbirths, and it is not surprising that Reformation propaganda should have seized eagerly such opportunities. Two monsters, one a real misbirth, the other half legendary, provided ammunition for evangelical propaganda in 1523, a year when popular opinion was especially susceptible to ominous portents. The first was a calf born near Freiberg in Saxony on 8 December 1522, the second a fabulous monster allegedly found in the Tiber near Rome in 1496. The calf misbirth had a large bald patch on the head, with two horny knobs on it. It was covered with blotches or bald patches on its body, and had a long lolling tongue and only one eye. A large flap of skin on its back resembled a cowl, and from this and the bald patch on the head resembling a tonsure it was known as the Monk Calf (see Figure 6). It was first interpreted by someone around the court of Margrave George of Brandenburg as applying to Luther, although the sign was seen as directed against the Catholic clergy. One pamphlet treated it as a misbirth which might symbolise the clergy, but did not mention Luther. Rather it was a warning to the Catholic clergy about their greed and high living. The author admonished them to live according to evangelical principles. This is not exceptional for treatment of a misbirth, and in its moral point is not too dissimilar from the sheet on the Florence misbirth of 1512.

Figure 6. The Monk Calf of Freiberg.

A second work was a broadsheet published before September 1523, which applied the calf to Luther. This depicts the monster being shown to the pope by a number of clerics, although the explanation is contained wholly within the printed rhymed text. Two interpretations are offered, one by the clergy, the other by the pope's fool. First, the clergy interpret the omen. The calf is identified as Luther. The two warts on its head are the two swords of the papacy, which Luther would have taken away from the pope. That the beast cannot see signifies that Luther has blinded the whole world with his teaching, the long tongue the great trouble brought to the papacy by his slanders. The 'cowl' can be nothing other than what was foretold long ago by Reinhard, that a monk would bring a great heresy. The monster is thus linked to the popular prophetic literature of the fifteenth century. Indeed, the text continues, this prophecy is attested by the beast and by Luther. The pope should beware lest his great power be lost, for such births also marked the coming of Mahomet, who robbed Christendom of two empires and twenty-four kingdoms.

The fool then steps forward to contradict this interpretation. He reminds them that great disturbance has arisen from the monastic Orders, indeed that all evil flows from them. The beast is indeed a figure of Luther, but must be seen in a different light. The two warts signify the pride and avarice characteristic of the monks, against which Luther has written continuously. The beast has but one eye, signifying the sole evangelical doctrine which Luther teaches. The long tongue signifies how far his godly teaching has spread throughout Christendom. The cowl indicates the monks and nuns, whose abuses he castigates. That the beast resembles an ox is a sign of Luther's robustness, for he charges forth like a bull. The fool concludes his interpretation by bidding Pope Adrian to do the Christian thing and to release all monks from their Orders, so that a reform may be possible. The fool's interpretation, although favourable to the new religious movement, is far from Lutheran. Like the pamphlet mentioned above, it sees the calf as a warning to the Catholic clergy, and uses it to express anti-monastic feeling. However, it stands closer to a reforming Catholicism, reflecting the optimism for internal reform aroused by the accession of Adrian VI in 1522. Although it is sympathetic to the aims of the Lutheran movement, it shows no sign of the latter's implacable hostility towards the papacy as a whole.

The Monk Calf was also taken up by Luther and Melanchthon in a pamphlet of 1523. Melanchthon had first published an interpretation of the 1496 monster, the so-called Papal Ass, and then at Luther's instigation it was republished alongside Luther's interpretation of the Monk Calf. This pamphlet depicts first the Papal Ass (see Figure 7), then the Monk Calf, followed by the two interpretations. Luther's explanation stressed the multiplicity of signs to be found at that time. Although he explicitly avoided a prophetic explanation, he was convinced that such signs foreshadowed some great change in the affairs of the world. He mentions specifically a

Figure 7. The Papal Ass of Rome.

similar misbirth at Landsberg, which he dubbed the Parson Calf because of its resemblance to a priest. This was a sign appropriate to the priestly estate, he argued, which he would not attempt to explain; he would be content, rather, to stick to that appertaining to his own, the monastic estate. As he saw it, the misbirth revealed what kind of folk the monks were, and he proceeded to give a detailed allegorical interpretation, taking each feature of the misbirth in turn.

First, the monster was no joke, but revealed the false appearance of spiritual and godly life found in monkery. The Monk Calf is 'the false idol in their deceitful hearts'. The calf is depicted in anthropomorphic fashion, standing on its hind legs, one front leg hanging at its side, the other stretched out like a hand. This feature Luther interprets as the gestures of a preacher, with his head thrown back, his tongue out and his hand gesturing. The Monk Calf thus depicted what kind of preacher the world had hitherto had to hear, the apostle and pupil of the pope. Is it not fitting that the ass-headed pope should have a calf-headed apostle? The calf is also blind, recalling the warning of Matthew 23.16: 'Woe to you blind guides.' The ear-like shapes of the 'cowl' signify the tyranny of confession, the tongue that monkish teaching is nothing more than idle, useless gossip.

The two knobs on the head are a sign that the monks have only the appearance of the Gospel: horns signify the Gospel and its preaching, but the calf has only the merest hint of them. That the knobs are on the 'tonsure' shows that the Gospel must conform to the tonsure, that is, to the will of the monks. That the cowl is wound so tightly around the neck signifies stubborn, stiff-necked monkery; that it is closed behind but open at the front shows that monks are only spiritual for the world, which stands behind them. The lower jaw is like that of a human being, the upper that of a calf's snout. This shows the nature of their preaching of divine law, for the two lips should signify the two kinds of preaching, the lower the divine law, the upper the Gospel. But instead of God's Word they preach the calf's snout, that is, their own good. The calf is smooth all over, signifying their hypocrisy. Finally, that it has now come forth from the cow means that they are revealed to the whole world, and can no longer hide themselves.

Taken by itself, Luther's interpretation of the Monk Calf could be seen as the application of spiritual allegory to a natural phenomenon, and so as a careful avoidance of appeals to popular superstition. However, it was published alongside Melanchthon's interpretation of the Papal Ass, a creature more lurid both in its appearance and in the interpretations which could be extracted from it. This curious monster was composed of an ass's head, a female torso with one human hand and the other an animal limb. One leg ended in a hoof, the other in a claw. It was covered in scales, with a dragon-like tail. This fantastic assembly of animal and human parts seems to have been invented in Italy at the end of the fifteenth century as part of a campaign to exploit signs and omens for political polemic. In particular, the original depiction of the monster seems to have been directed against Alexander VI. The building flying the papal flag in the background is the Castel Santangelo, built as a fortification by Alexander VI. The square tower on the right has been identified as the Tor di nona, a tower across the Tiber used by Alexander VI as a papal prison. Both were taken over unchanged in sixteenth-century copies of an Italian original. There was also a series of omens or portents throughout most of the years of Alexander's reign which were interpreted in connection with his rule. The alleged discovery of the monster in the Tiber after a flood in 1496 seems also to have been intended as an omen directed at him. The monster was used to attack papal power, and may have been part of a pasquillade mocking Rome's pretensions as 'head of the world' at a time when the papacy had suffered defeat by invading French forces....

Melanchthon interpreted the Papal Ass along lines similar to those used by Luther for the Monk Calf. The whole stood for the papacy, the ass head for the pope. The Church should have no bodily head, and the ass head on the human torso was as fitting as the pope as head of the Church. The right hand is an elephant's foot, signifying the spiritual power of the pope, with which he treads all consciences underfoot, for the right hand usually signifies the inward, the soul and the conscience, which should be ruled by the gentle rule of Christ, not that of the ass head. The human left hand signifies the secular power of the pope, something acquired only by human means. The right foot is an ox foot, signifying the servants of the spiritual power who oppress the soul. These are the papal teachers, preachers, parsons, confessors and especially Scholastic theologians. The left foot resembles a griffin's claw, signifying the servants of the secular power of the pope, the canonists who repress the whole world. The female belly and breasts signify the papal body, cardinals, bishops, priests, monks and like whorish folk who lead unashamed lives, just as the Papal Ass shows its naked female belly.

The scales on the arms, legs and neck signify the secular princes. These cling to each other, and although they do not dare to protect open lusts and desires, signified by the parts they do not cover, they nonetheless tolerate them, and hang the more firmly on the arms, legs and neck of the monster, the papacy. Moreover they protect it, both as spiritual and secular power. The old man's head on the rear of the beast signifies the decline and end of the papacy, that it will grow old and pass away. The dragon spewing out fire behind it is nothing other than the poisonous bulls and abusive books of the papacy. Finally, that the beast was found dead in the Tiber indicates that the papacy's end has come, that it was found in Rome is confirmation of all the foregoing interpretation. Throughout his explanation Melanchthon also relates the beast to descriptions of the Antichrist in Daniel 8, the beast which Daniel saw in a vision, and to Job 41, the vision of Behemoth and Leviathan. The Papal Ass, Melanchthon argues, confirms and extends identification of the papacy with the antichristian beasts described there....

[The] widespread interest in this kind of propaganda was probably a result as much of the appearance of the monsters themselves as of the allegorical interpretation attached to them. However, this interest was not just idle curiosity or thirst for sensation. It came, rather, from the conviction that nature reflected the rule of God. Monsters were an infringement of nature and so a perversion of God's creation. God permitted them as signs of disorder, although their essence was contrary to him. In this sense, there was a close relationship between monsters and sin. Sin was a disfigurement of God's image in man which transformed him into a monster. The monster thus stood close to the very origin of sin, the Devil, and the monster could itself become a visible expression of evil. The monster motif could then be used to associate the papacy and its supporters with the Devil....

We can see this concept expressed in the depiction known as *The Devil's Bagpipe* (Figure 8). This shows a devil playing his tune through the ears and nose of a monk, identified by his broad tonsure. But the basis of this illustration is not a devil perched on a monk's shoulders. It is the monk as two-headed monster, for the devil has grown into one creature with the

Figure 8. Erhard Schoen, *The Devil's Bagpipe*.

monk whom he uses as his instrument. The identity of the Devil with the monk as monster became a commonplace of Reformation propaganda. It could be indicated as simply as in the titlepage of a work by Pamphilus Gengenbach from 1522, showing a monk with large claws beneath his monastic habit. This kind of depiction itself probably went back to a popular pre-Reformation proverb linking monks with the Devil. 'Misfortune has broad feet, said the peasant, as he saw the monk coming.' The representation of monks as the Devil in disguise leads us to another feature of monsters in propaganda. The notion of a mask could be turned around, and the humanity of the opponent regarded as a mask hiding a monster underneath. This is the thought involved in a famous broadsheet depicting Alexander VI, which had a flap that could be lifted up to reveal who the pope really was (Figures 9 and 10)....

... One of the most interesting [polemical works bearing the apocalyptic outlook of the time is] the small booklet published in 1527 by the Nuremberg pastor Andreas Osiander, the *Wondrous Prophecy of the Papacy*. This was based on a pseudo-Joachimist work, the *Vaticinia de summis pontificibus*, two copies of which Osiander discovered in Nuremberg libraries. The work consists of two sets of illustrated prophecies. Each set contains fifteen pictures, each picture representing a pope, accompanied by a key phrase and an enigmatic description. These prophecies mentioned holy and

Figure 9. Broadsheet on Pope Alexander VI.

Figure 10. Alexander VI revealed as Devil.

unholy popes, and referred also to future popes, intended to represent the Antichrist....

Osiander seems to have paid little heed to the commentary in the edition he discovered. He interpreted it according to Lutheran views, reshaping the prophecy completely to fit the needs of evangelical propaganda. As the basis of his edition he retained only the thirty pictures, added a new, brief commentary for each, with an accompanying verse by Hans Sachs. This raises the question of how seriously Osiander took the prophetic nature of the original. His preface to his 1527 edition certainly sounds a sceptical note. Christians should be adequately informed from holy Scripture of things that are to come, but in the strange times in which they now live men look more to human words and prophecies than to those of God....

Osiander explicitly envisages the work as a pictorial prophecy, one expressed 'not in words, but in pictures alone'. He ... dispensed with the written text because the pictures are older than it and, as has often been the case, the prophecy has thereby been misunderstood. To aid the simple, an interpretation had been supplied, but all people of reason will see plainly what it means without any exposition. In sum, it shows the progress of the papacy from the time it became a tyranny until the end of the world....

Osiander's pamphlet is ... a remarkable attempt to shape the pseudo-Joachimist original into a prophecy of the evangelical movement, in the process providing it with prophetic legitimation. This legitimation is twofold: the old prophecy is fulfilled to date in the appearance of Luther and subsequent events of the 1520s, and the evangelical movement is a promise of the apocalyptic fulness of all things, leading to the last age before the coming of Christ.... The *Wondrous Prophecy* shares the characteristics of other works of propaganda seeking to invoke the apocalyptic mood of the time. Whether dealing with comets, conjunctions, omens, monsters, visions or prophecies they were ambiguous about the amount of credence to be given to such phenomena. Reformation aversion to superstition led to attempts at spiritual interpretation, but these depended enough on literal belief in such signs for the matter to remain ambivalent. Thus, evangelical propaganda did not break with pre-Reformation apocalyptic feeling, but rather exploited it. In terms of the religious emotions it aroused, the propaganda confirmed and extended these elements of popular belief.

Bibliography

PETER BLICKLE, *The Revolution of 1525: The German Peasants' War from a New Perspective* (1981).
PETER BURKE, *Popular Culture in Early Modern Europe* (1978).
NATALIEZ DAVIS, *Society and Culture in Early Modern France* (1978).
RONALD C. FINUCANE, *Miracles and Pilgrims: Popular Beliefs in Medieval England* (1977).
A. N. GALPERN, *The Religions of the People in Sixteenth Century Champagne* (1976).
CARLO GINZBURG, *The Cheese and the Worms: The Cosmos of a Sixteenth Century Miller* (1980).
EMMANUEL LE ROY LADURIE, *The Peasants of Languedoc* (1974).
JAMES OBELKEVICH, ed., *Religion and the People, 800–1700* (1979).
STEVEN OZMENT, *The Reformation in the Cities: The Appeal of Protestantism to Sixteenth Century Germany and Switzerland* (1975).

The Reign of Henry VIII

J. J. SCARISBRICK

The reign of Henry VIII changed the face of England more than any event between the Norman Conquest and the Industrial Revolution. Henry initiated a profound and lasting transformation of English foreign policy, domestic government, justice, and religion. Beloved by his people, he did not always consider their best interests. His brilliant advisers, to whom he owed so much of his success, proved more loyal to him than he to them. His achievements, like his person, turn out upon examination to be ambivalent. He promised more than he gave, and he destroyed as much as he built. His religious policy divided the nation, seriously reduced the resources available for education and charity, cost England the lives of many great men and women, devastated magnificient treasures of art and architecture, and ultimately benefited primarily the royal purse. The dissolution of English monasteries had considerable negative effects on the incomes of colleges, churches, cathedrals, and universities. Henry turned too much of his confiscated treasure to the purpose of making war with France and promoting his own glory, increasing further the suffering of the English people. The Protestant princes on the continent appear by comparison to have been far more generous and constructive in their disbursement of confiscated religious lands and endowments.

He was in his fifty-sixth year when he died, and had reigned for thirty-seven years and eight months. He had survived pretenders, excommunication, rebellion and threats of invasion, died in his bed and passed his throne peacefully to his heir. He had won a title, Defender of the Faith, which English monarchs still boast, written a book which is still, occasionally, read, composed some music which is still sung. He had made war on England's ancient enemies and himself led two assaults on France. For nearly four decades he had cut an imposing figure in Europe, mattering to its affairs, bestriding its high diplomacy as few of his predecessors, if any,

Reprinted with the permission of the University of California Press from *Henry VIII* by J. J. Scarisbrick. Copyright © 1968 by J. J. Scarisbrick.

had done. He had defied pope and emperor, brought into being in England and Ireland a national Church subject to his authority, wiped about a thousand religious houses off the face of his native land and of those areas of Ireland under his influence, and bestowed on English kingship a profound new dignity. He who had broken the secular Church in England, hammered monks and friars, and, recently, laid his hand on the chantries, had brought the Scriptures in the vernacular to his people, hesitantly and perhaps partly unwittingly, but none the less decisively, allowed his country to be directed towards the Continental Reformation into which it was to enter fully in his son's and second daughter's reigns, and given to his people a new sense of unity—the unity of 'entire Englishmen' rather than that of 'Englishmen papisticate' or of those who were 'scarce our subjects'. The England which he had led back into European affairs and exposed to the immense creative energies of continental Protestantism and which, at the same time, had disowned allegiance to any external authority, indisputably emerged from his reign with a new political 'wholeness', thanks to the destruction of the independent Church, the final incorporation of Wales, the pruning of many liberties and refurbishing of local Councils in the North and West, which lay under the surveillance of a Privy Council that, at least by the 1540s, had established itself as the supreme, omnicompetent executive body. Thanks above all to Thomas Cromwell, his reign had given England much 'good governance'. The administrative machine was more efficient and capacious than it had ever been—as was the legal (and this was largely to Wolsey's credit). A good deal probably had been done to discipline a society in which violence abounded and, in particular, to curb the peoples and their dangerous overlords in the remoter parts of the land— the Marcher lordships in the North and West. Henry's own commanding presence, the prestige and evident significance of his Court, and the growing authority of his servants in central and local government greatly strengthened the 'lines of force' which ran between king and subject, often (probably) swamping, always overlaying and, where necessary, checking, local loyalties. Again, never before had England felt the power of the 'state' so widely and deeply as in the 1530s and '40s. The compilation of the *Valor Ecclesiasticus* (a work cast on the scale of *Domesday Book*), the imposition of the oaths of Succession and Supremacy, the immense operation of dissolving the religious houses and distributing their property, the heavy taxation of the lay and clerical estates, the marshalling of large forces by sea and land, all this over and above the achievement of an ecclesiastical and doctrinal revolution, was a concentrated display of the power and ubiquity of central authority the like of which had not been seen hitherto; and if the major administrative developments of the years of Cromwell's dominance (and after) may be better described as a return to the medieval practice of building professional, bureaucratic government outside the royal household—after decades of intense concentration upon the latter—rather than a 'modern' event, it remains true that the consolidation of the Council and the foundation of four new financial courts gave the central government a new, firm grip on the realm. Finally, never before had Parliament been called upon to carry out so vast and consequential a programme of legislation as that which came onto the statute book between 1529 and 1545—a programme which ranged from the acts of Appeals and Supremacy, of Dissolution of Monasteries and Chantries, of Succession and Treason to the act of Six Articles and the first Poor Law. Henry's reign in many ways left a deeper mark on the mind, heart and face of England than did any event in English history between the coming of the Normans and the coming of the factory.

Henry was a huge, consequential and majestic figure. At least for some, he was everything that a people could wish him to be—a bluff, confident patriot king who was master of his kingdom and feared no one. By the end of his long reign, despite everything, he was indisputably revered, indeed, in some strange way, loved. He had raised monarchy to near-idolatry. He had become the quintessence of Englishry and the focus of swelling national pride. Nothing would ever be quite the same after he had gone.

Yet, for all his power to dazzle, for all the charm and bonhomie which he could undoubtedly sometimes show, and for all the affection which he could certainly give and receive, it is difficult to think of any truly generous or selfless action performed by him and difficult not to suppose that, even those who enjoyed his apparently secure esteem, like Jane Seymour or Thomas Cranmer, would not have been thrown aside if it had been expedient to do so, along with the many others who had entwined their lives around his, given him so much, and yet been cast away. He has sometimes been portrayed as one who, despite all that he was and all that he did to those who were close to him, retained a fundamental sense of the mood and mind of his people which, in the last resort, he would never transgress and with which he was always instinctively in accord. But it is not easy to substantiate this benevolent image. That Henry could be held back by his subjects' feelings is true. [T]his happened in the years 1530 to about 1532. But that he felt beholden to the mind of the political nation or would ever have expected it to thwart his will either seriously or for long may be doubted. He may indeed have declared to Parliament in 1543 'we at no time stand so highly in our estate royal as in the time of Parliament, wherein we as head and you as members are conjoined and knit together into one body politic', but the simile of head and members was an ambivalent one and in his scheme of things, probably, the former commanded, the latter merely obeyed. The sting, like many good stings, was in the head. He used Parliament, of course, to legalize his momentous programme and would never have thought of not doing so, but he probably never expected Parliament, however difficult it might prove on occasion, to deny him what he seriously desired any more than the judiciary would refuse to condemn an important political personage.

Three times he led England back into war with France, wars that brought him little more than 'ungracious dogholes' and ephemeral international prestige. He left England's relations with Scotland, with which he had not dealt dexterously—recently, at least—in bloody confusion. For much of his reign he so completely ignored the new worlds across the seas, preferring instead to pursue antique ambitions across the Channel, that for over a generation English maritime expansion languished. Certainly he had once tried (in 1521) to stir his people to follow up the pioneer voyages of the Cabots and been rebuffed. It was no fault of his that English foreign commerce had concentrated upon the export of unfinished cloth to Antwerp and that this trade expanded so fast during the reign that his merchants had little incentive to venture elsewhere. But the English voyages of 1517, 1527 and 1536, as well as Robert Thorne's pleas, suggest that the memory of the Cabots was not dead. Had Henry been so minded, he could surely have roused it successfully.

It has been suggested that he seriously mishandled his divorce suit. It is also arguable that, though the need for a son was obvious, as things turned out, Henry placed England in at least as great political jeopardy by repudiating his first marriage as he would have done if he had accepted his lot and resigned himself to leaving behind a mature heiress. Had he died during the ten years which ran from 1527 to 1537, that is, between the time when the divorce became public and Edward was born, there might well have been an ugly crisis, with Mary, perhaps the duke of Richmond and (after 1533) Elizabeth, and maybe others, all finding their supporters and opponents. Had he died some time between Anne Boleyn's death and Edward's birth, that is, at a moment when he had no legitimate offspring, he would have left a yet more perilous situation. For ten years the succession was desperately insecure; and, of course, despite everything, he still left behind a minor heir. The grim upsets of his son's reign and the evident political success of his younger daughter's both made something of a mockery of his own matrimonial scramblings. Had Mary been the only child, and had she ascended the throne in 1547 after a normal youth and young womanhood—happily married, perhaps to Pole—Henry might not have provided badly for the nation. It is easy to appreciate that, by 1527, the king was sincerely beset by a dynastic problem. The point is that his attempt to solve it was dangerously unsuccessful for ten years, and not notably happy thereafter.

A reign which accomplished an evident political integration of the kingdom at the same time saw the nation acquire a religious discord of a kind which it had not known before and which would soon become bitter and complex, sending fissures down English society to its lowest strata and setting neighbour against neighbour, father against son in a disunity from which that society has not yet fully recovered. Of course, this would have happened in some form or another anyway. Nothing could have insulated England permanently against continental Protestantism. But the fact remains that this disunity first took root in Henry's reign—despite his efforts to create a new national unity around the Supreme Headship. He who had been made the richest king in Christendom and seemed to have rescued the crown for ever from any recurrence of those financial worries which had beset it in the previous century left it in debt. He who was always ready to parade his paternal care for the commonwealth was guilty of tampering seriously with that most delicate sinew of society, the currency, and embarking on a wholesale debasement of English coin, without parallel in English history, in order to raise quick money to feed his wars. It is true that the pollution of her silver coinage stimulated trade with Antwerp, and it is also true that the celebrated price rise of the sixteenth century—a European phenomenon—was due fundamentally to the growth of population and the increased velocity of money, itself a consequence of such things as heavy taxation and government spending, the quickened activity of the land-market and the expansion of trade. None the less, the sudden increase in the total volume of specie in circulation which debasement brought about inevitably hastened England into galloping inflation; and, in the long run, to tamper with the currency was a dangerous expedient.

He had proclaimed himself as one who would lead the English Church from bondage, but his overlordship was a good deal more stern than that of the popes had ever been. The acts in Restraint of Annates had spoken of the 'intolerable and importable' burden of papal taxation, but the act of First Fruits and Tenths of 1534 would bring to him perhaps as much as ten times the amount per annum which English churchmen had paid to Rome before he liberated them and multiplied about threefold the total amount which they had hitherto paid, as they had long since paid, to king and pope combined. Popery, as it happened, was cheaper, if nothing else.

He had struck down incomparable men and women like Catherine of Aragon, More, Aske, Cromwell; he had sent the first cardinal to martyrdom, namely, Fisher, and would like to have done the same to another, namely, Pole. In a few years, hundreds of glorious buildings, 'one of the great beauties of this realm', as Aske said, the fruit of generations of piety and architectural accomplishment, and the many fellows of those few survivors, like Fountains, Rievaulx, Wimborne or Tewkesbury, which still stand glorious and defiant, disappeared off the face of the land which they had so long dominated and adorned. Nor was this the full toll of destruction which Henry unleashed; for, with the soaring stone, the vaults, towers and spires, went glass and statue, choirstalls and rood-screens, plate and vestments—the flower of a dozen minor arts. How much of the fair and precious almost every town of England and every corner of the countryside lost in three or four years from 1536 onwards, what it must have felt like to see and hear workmen set about their emptied, echoing spoil and reduce a great abbey to piles of lead and dusty stone, we shall never know. Nor can we know what marvels once awaited the pilgrim to St Thomas's shrine at Canterbury, or St Swithin's at Winchester, St Richard's at Chichester, or

St Cuthbert's at Durham; for Henry bade them go. He who built more than any other Tudor (though little of his work survives) was responsible for more destruction of beautiful buildings and other works of art than the Puritans. Not since the coming of the Danes, and then on a much smaller scale, had so many sacred fanes been despoiled and so much treasure smashed.

Doubtless many rejoiced to witness all this and to see a nation walk out of so much of its past. The Erasmian had much to commend, as also did those who had so eagerly acquired ex-monastic land. Some lamented that England's steps towards true religion had so far been so hesitant and erratic, that so many of the old evils had scarcely begun to be rooted out. Clerical pluralism and non-residence had been lightly scotched, far from killed; the dumb-dogs, that is, ignorant clerks who neglected preaching, abounded; the paraphernalia, the lumber, the man-made superstructure of deans and archdeacons, commissaries and apparitors, bishops' courts and (to quote a later aphorism) 'filthy canon law' were yet to be hacked down, together with those 'popish dregs', like tithes, excommunications and the holy clutter of trentals, dirges, god-parents, holy oils, blessings, candles and the rest. For some the true reformation had scarcely begun. The vineyard cried out for labourers, but the honest labourers were few and the Supreme Head showed little sense of urgency for the godly work which had to be undertaken. Generations of Romish aberration had to be undone. An ignorant, hungry people had at last to be fed.

But there was another, and, for some, yet more serious charge to be brought against the king. Undoubtedly Henry roused hopes that, when he turned an avenging hand against the English Church and, in particular, against English monasticism, he would use the wealth that had been locked up therein to serious purpose, that is, for educational and social ends. Never before had any Englishman had the power to bestow such obvious and long-lasting benefit on the nation as did this king when the vast landed wealth of English monasticism came into his hands for him to dispose as he willed. Out of the Dissolution could have come scores of schools, hospitals and generous endowment of the universities, new highways, almshouses, and perhaps a major attack on poverty. Wolsey himself, John Fisher, Richard Fox, to name only Henry's contemporaries, had converted monastic endowments to educational ends and, had Henry wanted to follow them, these were precedents enough to guide him. Again, Renaissance humanism was above all concerned with education (at all levels) and social justice. Henry lived in a world whose prophets, like Erasmus and More and their successors, cried out for educational reform and protested indignantly against the suffering of the poor at the hands of the grasping rich. For all its alleged materialism, Tudor society often showed a remarkable zeal for 'good works'; and the sixteenth century is only rivalled by the late nineteenth and twentieth in its importance in the history of English schooling. Moreover, it seems clear that the continental Reformation preserved a considerably higher proportion of monastic wealth for charitable purposes—schools, hospitals and the like—than the Henrician.

In 1533, Thomas Starkey had urged that clerical first fruits and tenths should be used for poor relief and proposed that some monastic revenues also be used to this end, as well as to support learning. Three years later he urged to Cromwell that the monasteries which still stood should be turned into little universities. With the income from the secular church and from lands of suppressed monasteries let 'some notable charitable works be undertaken', an anonymous writer proposed. Wriothesley had drawn up a paper listing what his king could do with the monastic wealth, including setting aside 10,000 marks *p.a.* to found new hospitals and re-furbish old, 20,000 marks to support the army, 5,000 to build highways and the like, and thus provide employment for poor folk. Indeed, Henry himself appeared to subscribe to these lofty aims. After the dissolution of the smaller monasteries in 1536, it had evidently been assumed by some that this was the end of the matter, that the remaining houses would stand unscathed—especially as the first act of Dissolution had declared that there were 'divers and great solemn monasteries of this realm wherein, thanks be to God, religion is right well kept and observed'. It may well be that, at this time, Henry sincerely intended to go no further. In January 1538 Richard Layton crushed as 'vain babbling' and slanderous misrepresentation of the king a rumour which he had heard in Cambridge that all monasteries would fall; and that rumour was solemnly disavowed in an official paper produced some months later. In July 1537 Henry himself refounded Chertsey Abbey as Bisham and a nunnery at Stixwold in Lincolnshire to pray for him and his queen; while as late as May 1538 a house for Cistercian nuns was refounded 'in perpetuity' at Kirkless. Though Layton's disavowal must have been disingenuous, for, even as he spoke it, he was about the business of bullying superiors of houses in Norfolk into surrender, Henry's curious refoundations may well have been further evidence of how untidy and, in the long term, often unpremeditated his campaign was. Anyway, by early 1538 the last phase was under way of the giant operation of abolishing the remaining monastic houses, together with the suppression of the friaries, a class of institution which had hitherto escaped attention; and in May 1539 Parliament passed the second act of Dissolution, which bestowed on the crown all monastic possessions surrendered since 1536 or to be surrendered in the future.

Thus was solemnly sanctioned what Henry's own actions and his own servants had recently argued would never happen. Parliament, however, had not yielded easily. On 20 May Marillac reported to Francis that the dissolution of the remaining monasteries was being discussed and that the members wanted to use 'certain abbeys' to provide for bishoprics and the foundation of schools and hospitals. Parliament itself, therefore, was uttering concern that the wealth of English monasticism should not be wasted. It was almost certainly to placate (and to stifle) these dangerous ideas that, on the very day when the bill for the dissolution of the greater monasteries completed its journey through the two houses of Parliament, there should have been rushed through in a single day a further piece of legislation whose grandiloquent preamble seemed to promise exactly those things which, according to Marillac, the king's own subjects desired; and interestingly enough, that preamble was written by Henry himself, in his own hand.

The enacting clause of the bill which had thus suddenly made its appearance empowered the king to create as many new bishoprics as he might judge necessary—on obvious and long-overdue reform, which Wolsey had been preparing to effect shortly before his fall—and to endow them with ex-monastic revenue. In the preamble of the act, the Supreme Head wrote of his desire that, by this conversion of monastic wealth, 'God's word might be the better set forth, children brought up in learning, clerks nourished in the universities, old servants decayed to have living, alms-houses for poor folk to be sustained in, readers of Greek, Hebrew and Latin to have good stipend, daily alms to be ministered, mending of highways, exhibition for ministers of the Church'. That out of the Dissolution should come some lasting benefit to the community was not, therefore, the cry of a mere handful of day-dreamers. The king himself publicly proclaimed numerous good causes to which monastic revenue was to be turned, and publicly promised to endow them.

Shortly after the bill became law, a group of bishops, which included Stephen Gardiner and Richard Sampson of Chichester, set about elaborate plans for erecting a large crop of new bishoprics. Henry himself drew up his own design for endowing thirteen new sees with the revenues of some twenty large abbeys and so redrawing the diocesan map of England that every major county or, in the case of the smaller counties, neighbouring pairs thereof should be the seat of a bishopric. Thus Waltham Cross would provide for the see of Essex, St Alban's for that of Hertford, Bury St Edmund's for that of Suffolk, Fountains for that of Lancaster, Peterborough for that of Northants and Huntingdon. Three houses were to be given to the new diocese of Cornwall, three to that of Nottingham and Derby; three to that of Bedford and Buckingham, etc. But this plan was not to be implemented. Eventually only six new dioceses were set up and endowed with one abbey apiece, viz. Westminster, Gloucester, Bristol, Oseney, Peterborough, and Chester. Eight pre-Reformation cathedrals had been served by monks or canons—a practice almost peculiar to England—and though the monastic establishments were dissolved the new chapters of what now became secular cathedrals inherited the endowments of their monastic predecessors. Finally, the two abbeys of Thornton and Burton were converted into secular colleges. In all, therefore, sixteen former religious houses, having undergone a change of one form or another, either remained with, or were gained by, the secular Church. These sixteen included some of the wealthiest houses of all, with a total net income amounting to 'almost 15 per cent of the total income of all houses'. But

Henry's largesse was not as bounteous as this figure suggests. The new chapters of the ex-monastic cathedrals received only a small proportion of the revenues of the convents which they had supplanted; and, thanks to careful cheese-paring, the six new cathedrals were 'considerably more modest than . . . even the smallest and poorest of the old secular cathedrals'. As a result, less than a quarter of the total wealth of these sixteen houses was restored by the crown to the Church. Henry's re-endowments were niggardly; and time was to make them more niggardly yet. By forcing bishops to sell and exchange land, a tactic which seems usually to have given the crown the better of the bargain, Henry was able to begin a programme of fleecing the secular Church which his successors would elaborate, and to take back with one hand some of the little which he had given with the other. Furthermore, in 1544 and 1546 respectively the two colleges which he had re-founded, Burton and Thornton, were judged 'superfluous' and joined the many other colleges which were then being sacrificed.

Six new bishoprics, meanly endowed, and eight secularized cathedral chapters to whom but a fraction of previous revenue had been restored—this was all that Henry spared for the Church of which, under God, he was Supreme Head. In some places canons' churches which had hitherto been either wholly or partly parochial survived the Dissolution and continued to serve the neighbourhood. Elsewhere, as at Bolton, Malmesbury and Malvern, the disappearance of the local religious house could cause sufficient hardship for the townsfolk to buy back the church for use as a parish church; and at Tewkesbury, too, the monks' church was saved thus. But there may have been many other places, less enterprising than these, where the religious life of local layfolk was seriously upset by the disappearance of monastic churches in which they had hitherto worshipped.

The religious houses were certainly not the generous homes of refuge and succour of legend, but it is indisputable that they supported, directly or indirectly, a large number of those institutions which are collectively styled 'hospitals'—hospices and hostels, almshouses, hospitals in the modern sense, leper-houses and asylums, etc. A considerable number of these, especially almshouses attached to houses of the old orders, survived. Bristol kept perhaps as many as nine out of its eleven houses for the old and sick; Exeter four out of seven; Newcastle thirteen; Norwich perhaps fourteen; Winchester three out of five; Worcester two out of three. But alongside the survivals there was undoubtedly widespread, patchy destruction. Sometimes the houses suppressed may have been the least flourishing institutions; sometimes, as at St Nicholas's in Pontefract, the inmates received pensions. But elsewhere the suppressions must have been a serious affliction. The hospitals belonging to Bermondsey abbey, Bury St Edmunds, Hexham priory, Peterborough and Whitby, and the large hospice at Walsingham were swept away; York lost its St Leonard's, the greatest of all English hospitals, as well as the house of St Nicholas; Worcester its St Wulstan's. If York was sorely hit, so too was London. The hospitals of

St Thomas (of Acon), St Bartholomew, St Mary within Cripplegate (Elsing Spital, a house for the blind), St Mary without Bishopsgate (which had some 180 beds for the sick), St Giles in the Fields and St Thomas at Southwark—all were suppressed, despite the petition of the lord mayor that the houses which had been closed should be restored and the survivors spared. At the end of his life Henry yielded to entreaty and, as his letters patent claimed, 'divine mercy inspiring us', restored St Bartholomew's and endowed it with an income of 500 marks per annum, a sum which the citizens, 'thinking it for their parts rather too little than enough', promptly doubled. Two years later the citizens bought back and reopened St Mary's. The story of English hospitals and their fate at the time of the Reformation awaits definitive study. When it is made, the king who is honoured as the founder of the College of Physicians in 1518, whose reign (in 1540) saw the incorporation of the united companies of Barbers and Surgeons in London, and who had so keen a personal interest in medical lore and his own health, will probably not occupy an exalted place in it.

Nor can he in the history of education. Early in his reign, John Fisher had struggled hard to secure sufficient revenues from the lands of the late Lady Margaret Beaufort to complete the building and equipping of her college of St John at Cambridge, but had found himself so 'straitly handled and so long delayed and wearied and fatigate' that he gave up the fight and allowed the king, as Lady Margaret's heir at law, to enter his inheritance. Thereupon Henry apparently promised Fisher £2,800 to complete the foundation, but less than half, about £1,200 to be precise, even came from the king into the building fund, with the result that Fisher had to embark on the dissolution of three small, largely derelict monasteries to make good the deficit; an inauspicious beginning, this, both to Henry's dealings with the cause of learning and to his relations with Fisher. Moreover, despite the praise which Erasmus and others lavished upon this golden prince, despite the proximity of educational zealots such as Catherine of Aragon, Richard Fox and More, and despite the example of Wolsey, the king showed little interest in the academic life. He gave no more than conventional patronage to any scholar (and, indeed, presided over a Court in many ways less open, less cosmopolitan and interesting than his father's); he inherited none of his grandmother's interest in higher education; until he turned to the universities for support in the divorce he had little care for them and, in the whole of his reign, seems to have visited only one, namely Oxford, once. Within a few days of Wolsey's fall he was threatening the two educational establishments which the cardinal had founded, that is Cardinal's College at Oxford and the grammar school in his native Ipswich. By 22 November 1529 royal agents had sped to the last-named and, under the pretence of searching for hidden treasure, had stripped the school of its plate, vestments and sacred vessels, and set to work on its suppression. Thus perished a grammar school upon which its founder had lavished much imaginative and enlightened care; a school which, had it not been snuffed out, might well have rivalled

St Paul's as a landmark in Tudor educational history. Instead, its stone was carried to London to supply the royal building at Whitehall. However, after many anxious months, the college at Oxford was saved. From his exile, Wolsey wrote to Henry beseeching him to remember his 'painful and long-continued service' and spare his foundation; and he wrote to More, Norfolk, Arundel and others, begging them lend their voice to his. In August 1530 a deputation came from the college, headed by the dean, to plead with the king. 'Surely we purpose to have an honourable college there,' said Henry to his visitors with something less than complete honesty, 'but not so great and of such magnificence as my lord cardinal intended to have.' Norfolk had reported that the king would dissolve the college and allow its inmates no more than the lands of St Frideswide's, the core of its endowments. But at length, thanks, it was said, to the duke's advocacy, the college survived—though with its establishment reduced and its offensive name changed.

The monasteries had not provided a large-scale network of schools throughout the kingdom, but many of them were useful places of education. Evesham, Reading and Glastonbury, for example, supported schools of some considerable size, St Mary's, Winchester took in twenty-six daughters of the local squirearchy, some nunneries taught small boys, many other houses provided schooling on varying scales to outsiders, as well as to the boarders in almonry and song-schools. When the crash came a good deal lived on in one form or another. Thus many of the secularized cathedrals, for example Canterbury, Worcester and Ely, received their 'King's Schools', nearly all of them refoundations rather than the fruit of royal bounty, and smaller than originally planned. Elsewhere schools survived or appeared as the result of local, private enterprise. At Sherborne the town not only bought the abbey church from the royal grantee, but rented the schoolhouse and retained the former master to teach there. Likewise the townsfolk of Abingdon kept a former monastic school alive, and Cirencester, having lost ('to the great discommodity' of the town) a school dependent on Winchcombe abbey, resuscitated it a few years later by turning a chantry endowment to new purpose; and, at least for a while, schools continued at Reading and Bruton. At Warwick and Ottery St Mary townsfolk bought back some lands hitherto held by suppressed colleges in order to endow and re-found parish schools. The worst damage to schooling was, therefore, often avoided or made good. None the less the Dissolution brought losses and upsets. Similarly the passing of English monasticism and all that went with it brought tempestuous times to the universities. Queens' College Cambridge joined in the scramble and successfully petitioned Cromwell for the neighbouring Carmelite friary; in 1546 Henry founded Trinity College, rolling together three existing establishments, Michaelhouse, King's Hall and Physwick Hostel, and endowing the new college with the revenues of no less than twenty-six dissolved religious houses. Buckingham College was re-founded and re-named Magdalene College in 1542; much later Sir

Walter Mildmay gave the site of the Dominican friary to his new college, Emmanuel, and part of the Greyfriars convent (which had been quarried for stone for Henry's Trinity College) passed into the possession of Sidney Sussex. Likewise Oxford acquired, directly or indirectly, a few pickings, such as the Cistercian hall of residence, St Bernard's, which went to King's, formerly Cardinal's College (and eventually Christ Church). Finally, in 1540 Henry endowed five regius professorships at Cambridge—out of the revenues of Westminster Cathedral, however—in Greek, Hebrew, civil law, divinity and medicine. Yet all this was probably small recompense for the buffeting which higher learning had suffered at his hands. Heads of colleges had been purged and two chancellors of Cambridge (Fisher and Cromwell) beheaded, royal injunctions had upset curricula by banning the teaching of scholastic theology and canon law, Richard Layton and his fellow royal visitors had unleashed gross vandalism when they visited Oxford to 'set Duns Scotus in Bocardo [the local prison] and ... utterly banished him for ever', leaving him and 'all his blind glosses ... a common servant to every man, fast nailed up upon posts in all common houses of easement'. A little later, so Layton reported delightedly to his master, he had seen the quad of New College bestrewn with leaves ripped from the works of Scotus and doubtless others, and watched 'the wind blowing them into every corner'. Both universities lost their friaries and monastic halls of residence, of which there had been twelve in Oxford, and both suffered decline in numbers when the supply of students from the religious orders was halted. Though Cromwell's *Injunctions* were seriously aimed at amending university life and teaching, and Dr Leigh's visitation of Cambridge fruitful of much sound advice, the 1530s on the whole brought upsets and dislocation to the universities—so much so that, in 1539, Cambridge reported to Cromwell that the number of students had been halved. Moreover, scarcely had the colleges emerged from the stormy years of the Dissolution of the religious houses proper than they had to face the Chantries act of 1545 which gave the king the power to dissolve any institution at either University and seize its possessions. As Matthew Parker, then vice-chancellor, said later, the real threat probably came from folk about the king who were 'importunately suing to him to have the lands and possessions of both universities surveyed, they meaning afterwards to enjoy the best of their lands and possessions by exchange of impropriated benefices and such other improved lands'. Ravening 'wolves' who stood near the king and who, so the high-minded Dr Cox would soon warn Paget, would devour the endowments of colleges, chantries, cathedrals, churches and universities—these were the real predators.

The university lands were surveyed, but surveyed by commissions headed by university men. Fearful of what the recent act might bring them, Parker and the University of Cambridge wrote urgently to Henry and Paget for protection, and turned also for help to Catherine Parr, who not long before had looked to them to supply the chief luminaries of her school for the royal children. Catherine proved a good friend. She 'attempted the king's majesty' and reported her consort inclined rather to 'advance learning and erect new occasion thereof, than to confound those your ancient and godly institutions'. When the commissioners presented their report to Henry at Hampton Court in the spring of 1546, the king was struck by the good husbandry of the colleges and the leanness of their endowments, adding 'that pity it were these lands should be altered to make them worse'. Thus were '*lupos quosdam hiantes*' [some wolves with gaping mouths] disappointed and thus did a king who may only have been finally dissuaded from pruning Cambridge's colleges by the appeal of Sir Thomas Smith, the first Regius professor of civil law, deliver the Universities from spoliation.

It is impossible to believe that Henry ever intended to inflict any serious damage on the universities. Indeed, his lavish endowment of Trinity College and his foundation of the Regius professorships mark him as one of the most generous royal patrons in Cambridge's history; and all in all he could claim to have given more to education than any other king of England. Yet though this is true, though many medieval hospitals survived, though he restored a few others, though some monastic schools were re-founded by him and others redeemed by private individuals and enterprising townsfolk, and though, sooner or later, a good deal of ex-monastic wealth found its way back into educational, civic and charitable undertakings, the fact remains that Henry destroyed, damaged or dislocated scores of institutions which were actually or potentially of great value to the community. Furthermore, the most grievous charge which some were to raise against him was concerned not with what he did, but with what he failed to do. Six new episcopal sees, five Regius professorships, a college at Cambridge and a handful of other endowments — though impressive in themselves — were not much to show for the immense fortune which had flowed into his hands and with which he could have created a unique monument to enlightened kingship.

At the time, a number of voices cried out to him to do so. No less a person than Dr John London, himself one of the royal visitors to the religious houses, pleaded in vain that the church of the Franciscan friary at Reading be given to the township for use as a guildhall and a little later begged that the revenue of the houses of Northampton should succour the poor and unemployed of that town, which was passing through a period of economic distress. Bishop Latimer asked Cromwell unsuccessfully that the income of the two friaries of Worcester be given to the upkeep of the city's school, bridge and wall, and pleaded (also unsuccessfully) that the priory of Great Malvern be allowed to survive, 'not in monkery, God forbid', but to serve the cause of 'learning, preaching, study, and hospitality'. The mayor and aldermen of Coventry asked that the two friars' churches to allowed to stand as 'isolation' churches, for use of the sick in time of plague. The reformer Robert Ferrar interceded in vain for the house of which he had been made prior, St Oswald's, near Pontefract, that it should stand as a college 'for the nourishment of youth in virtue and learning'; and the abbot and community of Evesham likewise begged to be allowed to stand as a college providing much-needed education and hospitality to their neighbourhood—and likewise met no success. Similarly the University of Cambridge besought Henry that monasteries hitherto given over to superstition be turned into colleges of learning. Meanwhile, no less a person than Lord Audley, who himself acquired a fortune in monastic spoils, had appealed to Cromwell to save two great abbeys in Essex, St Osyth's and St John's Colchester, not as monasteries, but as colleges where poor folk could continue to have 'daily relief' and hospitality. Despite his offer of £200 to Cromwell if the latter would press his suit, the plea went unanswered. Colchester Abbey fell (and its abbot went to the gallows); St Osyth's became one of Cromwell's many ex-monastic trophies.

'Our posterity will wonder at us', the illustrious Dr Cox would later write to Paget, as he saw all about him nothing but unconcern for learning and good works, and watched the 'wolves' devour their prey. Henry himself set them a telling example. He had built St James's Palace on the site of a lazar house; he used the chapel of the London Charterhouse, whose inmates he had purged so bloodily, as a store for tents and garden equipment; Chertsey Abbey and Merton Priory supplied stone for Nonsuch Palace, which itself stood on the site of a parish church; God's House, Portsmouth, became an armoury; Maison Dieu, Dover, a victualling yard. Small wonder if his subjects fell upon the booty with zeal.

The 'wolves' were no doubt a large, influential number and no doubt, by responding to their clamour and shedding the great wealth of medieval English monasticism among them by gift, lease and sale, Henry not only yielded to widespread appetitiveness, but created an invaluable vested interest in the new regime. If, however, he had chosen to heed the cry of that positive, creative anti-clericalism, if he had wanted to follow English precedent, if, indeed, he had honoured his own high-flown promises, then at least a large proportion of the monastic wealth would have been used as such as Fisher and Wolsey had used it, and men like Starkey, Dr London and Bishop Latimer had begged him to use it. Had the king given his weight to the cause of righteousness, a nation to which the humanists and 'Commonwealth men' made such urgent appeal and which, for all its greed, showed itself ready to endow good causes with remarkable generosity, would have applauded him. But Henry virtually ignored that cause. He was not one of the enlightened. He had taken hold of little of what Tudor humanism stood for and was a stranger to the fire that consumed an Erasmus or a Latimer. The disposal of the monastic lands, particularly the sales thereof, was skilfully enough done. Grantees paid a fairly high price, the land they received was subject to the annual tenth due from all ecclesiastical possessions and was held by knight service in chief—and therefore exposed the whole of the recipient's lands to feudal incidents levied by the Court of Wards. The avalanche of sales during the 1540s which had carried away about two-thirds of the monastic lands by Henry's death guaranteed, therefore, some income for the crown, despite the fact that the need for quick money had driven it to apparently reckless alienation of its capital asserts. But the tactics of the operation were one thing; the strategy another. Not only did Henry fail to use the wealth that came to him in generous service to the cause of education, social justice or religion; worse, he squandered it to pay for the very cause which an Erasmus or a More most hated, namely, the fruitless war of prestige and amour-propre waged by vainglorious monarchy. Like so much else that was precious to England, the wealth of centuries of piety (or much of it) was poured out on the fields of northern France. It was a shrewd, bold subject who had written, probably in the 1530s, that it would be better to convert monastic revenue to building towns and providing better justice than ever to allow the king to take hold of them.

It was not long before bitter cries of disappointment rose from the lips of those who had expected too much. The freer pulpit and the freer press in the first years of Edward's reign finally released the angry voice of the so-called 'Commonwealth men'—men like the tireless Hugh Latimer, the ex-friar Henry Brinkelow (alias Roderyck Mors), the social critic Robert Crowley, preachers and divines like Thomas Lever and Thomas Becon, and John Hales, a mere clerk of the Hanaper. As these men flailed the ungodliness and inhumanity of their fellow-men, trouncing every iniquity from merciless landlordism which oppressed the poor with fines, rack-rents, evictions and enclosures, to the tyranny of bishops and the bizarre, costly mysteries of the law (and much in between), so did they indignantly lament the betrayal of the Reformation from which they had hoped for so much. In the past, writers from Langland onwards had denounced worldly prelates, grasping clerks, ''abbey-lubbers' and above all the friars, so many of whom had manifestly fallen away from their founders' ideal of humble poverty; but it was now beginning to seem that the active greed of the new 'possessioners', the laymen who had taken over from the clergy, was more disgraceful than the parasitism of those whom they had supplanted. The critics of the old order were to lay about the new with yet greater violence and even to begin to speak about the monasteries with the same regret that Robert Aske had once voiced. As Becon lamented in his *The Jewel of Joy*, the Dissolution allowed the rich to oppress the poor on a larger scale than hitherto. The new 'Caterpillars of the Commonweal', *i.e.* those who had entered the monastic lands, 'abhor the name of monks, friars, canons, nuns, etc., but their goods they greedily gripe. And yet, where the cloisters kept hospitality, let out their farms at a reasonable price, nourished schools, brought up youth in good letters, they did none of these things.' 'The state of England,' he cried, 'was never so miserable as it is at present.' Said Thomas Lever, taunting the recipients of the monastic booty with bitter indignation, 'in the great abundance of lands and goods taken from abbeys, colleges and chantries for to serve the king in all necessaries and charges, especially in provision of relief for the poor and maintenance of learning, the king is so disappointed that both be spoiled, all maintenance for learning decayed and you only enriched'. The poor commons, another savage broadside exclaimed, had expected to be delivered from their suffering, but 'alas they failed of their expectation and are now in more penury than ever they were.... Then they had hospitals and almshouses to be lodged in, but now they lie and starve in the streets.' These outpourings are certainly not to be taken as well-informed, scientific analyses either of prevailing conditions or of their causes. Becon, Lever and the others exaggerated (probably wildly) the decay of learning and the collapse of relief for the poor. What they denounced as mere greed and heartlessness was probably more often than not a legitimate desire of landlords struggling to hold their own against inflation to improve their circumstances by raising rents, enclosing, etc. Becon's rosy picture of the kindly monks of yore made good pamphleteering, but, alas, was quite misleading; and there is no reason to suppose that, if the religious had survived, they would not have been as oppressive as their lay successors. Nonetheless, they voiced a just, bitter disappointment at finding that a dream had become damnably like a nightmare.

Some years before, Henry Brinkelow had uttered that most interesting diatribe *The Complaynt of Roderyck Mors*, in the course of which he called on Parliament, among other things, to complete the destruction of the wealth of the Church that had been begun with the attack on the religious. 'Ye must first down with all your vain chantries, all your proud colleges of canons and specially your forked wolves of bishops,' he declaimed. But he then quickly remembered what had happened to the monastic property. 'For the goods of these chantries, colleges and bishops,' he therefore added, 'for the Lord's sake take no example at the distribution of the abbey goods and lands; but look for your erudition to the godly Christian Germans in this case, which divided not such goods and lands among the princes, lords and rich people, that had not need thereof, but they put them into the use of the commonwealth and unto the provision of the poor according to the doctrine of the Scripture.'[3] If Brinkelow overestimated the virtue of the continental Reformation, he had a sound suspicion that it had been a good deal more godly than Henry's. And what was it that that great Lutheran Robert Barnes, wanted to say as he addressed the crowd which had come to see him burn at Smithfield, and was prevented from saying by the Sheriff? He had begged to be allowed to make five requests of the king. The first began: 'whereas his grace hath received into his hands all the goods and substance of the abbeys'—but then the sheriff stopped him and, in the confusion, Barnes was not able to do more than exclaim, 'Would to God it might please his grace to bestow the said goods, or some of them, to the comfort of his poor subjects, who surely have great need of them.' He was able to continue with the remaining items of his appeal—that Henry would strike down adultery and fornication, punish swearing and 'set forth Christ's true religion'. But his first plea, concerning the monastic lands, was stifled by a nervous sheriff. Had Barnes prepared for his prince some clarion-call to enlightened benefaction?

Perhaps Crowley might speak last—Crowley, a man of burning compassion from whose pen came pages of remorseless denunciation of greed and covetousness, and who deserves to stand with Langland, More, the Diggers and Marx is one of the great apostles of social justice. It is appropriate to end, not with some thunderous passage from a major work setting forth the familiar theme of Christian stewardship and calling upon the rich to 'repent the oppression wherewith they vex the poor commons and show themselves, through love, to be brothers of one father and members of one body with them'; but, rather, with a so-called 'epigram'—a quiet, mediatative piece of execrable verse:

> As I walked alone
> and mused on things,
> That have in my time
> been done by great kings,
> I bethought me of abbeys
> that sometime I saw,
> Which are now suppressed
> all by a law.
>
> O Lord, (thought I then)
> what occasion was here
> To provide for learning
> and make poverty clear.
>
> The lands and the jewels
> that hereby were had
> Would have found godly preachers
> which might well have led
>
> The people aright
> that now go astray
> And have fed the poor
> that famish every day.

Haunting words. 'He is a wonderful man and has wonderful people around him', a French ambassador in England once wrote of Henry, 'but he is an old fox'. 'Junker Heintz will be God and does whatever he lusts,' said Luther. Maybe Henry was no more unaware and irresponsible than many kings have been; but rarely, if ever, have the unawareness and irresponsibility of a king proved more costly of material benefit to his people. All the same, it was the grief of a stricken man that overtook the lord chancellor on Monday, 31 January 1547, when he announced to the lords that the monarch whom he and they had both feared and revered was dead.

Bibliography

PATRICK COLLINSON, *Archbishop Grindal 1519–1583* (1979).

CLAIRE CROSS, *Church and People, 1450–1660: The Triumph of the Laity in the English Church* (1976).

A. G. DICKENS, *The English Reformation* (1964).

G. R. ELTON, *Reform and Reformation: England 1509–1558* (1977).

CHRISTOPHER HAIGH, *Reformation and Resistance in Tudor Lancashire* (1975).

FELICITY HEAL, *Of Prelates and Princes: A Study of the Economic and Social Position of the Tudor Episcopate* (1980).

RICHARD MARIUS, *Thomas More* (1984).

Women and the Reformation

JANE DEMPSEY DOUGLASS

The Reformation modified contemporary views of women and marriage. Declaring an egalitarian "priesthood of all believers" among Christians, it rejected separate codes of behavior for the clergy and the laity. Not only did Protestants deem marriage and sexual union good and godly, but married life gained superiority over asceticism and virginity in Protestant theology and practice. The family, not the cloister, became the proper "school of faith." Wives continued to be subject to their husbands, but mutual love and sharing gained priority in marriage. And the domestic responsibility of running a household won new respect and praise.

New educational opportunities for both women and children opened up through the Reformation. The new emphasis on family life made parental consent more important in marriage. The most striking change in marriage law was the recognition of a mutual right to divorce and remarry, something never permitted by the medieval church.

Catholic reaction to the Protestant closing of cloisters confirms the Reformation's impact on contemporary views of women, sex, and marriage. The Reformation spurred some women to a new level of political activism and created new worldly responsibilities for many more. On the domestic front, it was a limited but real "liberation movement" in the minds of many who joined it.

The Reformation brought some fundamental changes in the Church's way of looking at women and marriage which greatly influenced society both in the short-and the long-run perspectives. Roland Bainton has written, "The reform, in my judgment, had greater influence on the family than on the political and economic spheres."

From "Women and the Continental Reformation," by Jane Dempsey Douglass, in *Religion and Sexism: Images of Woman in the Jewish and Christian Traditions*. Rosemary Radford Reuther, ed. Copyright © 1974 by Rosemary Radford Reuther. Reprinted by permission of Simon & Schuster, Inc.

Luther found in his biblical studies much evidence to persuade him that marriage had been seriously depreciated by the Roman Church. Even since the Fall, marriage is intended by God to be the normal—rather the ideal—life for human beings, a life that must not be considered ethically inferior to celibacy, as medieval theology had taught. Women and sex came to be seen as fundamentally good. The ensuing attack on monastic institutions had profound consequences, socially and economically. And the home became the new center of women's religious vocation.

This study will begin by sketching briefly the new theology: the Protestant rejection of the distinction between life according to the precepts and life according to the counsels of perfection; the teaching of the sinner's justification in God's eyes by grace through faith in Christ and the active life of service that flows from it; the doctrine of Christian vocation in the world; and the priesthood of all believers. Then it will focus directly on the Reformation view of marriage, women and the home, using materials drawn primarily from Luther of Wittenberg, Bucer of Strasbourg, and Calvin of Geneva.

The second section will deal with a few of the practical consequences of these ideas in the realms of marriage law, education, and Church life. Within the familiar structures of home and Church presided over by men as they had been before, women nevertheless were seeing their old tasks differently and discovering new roles.

In the third section we will look at the role of women in the Reformation as seen through the eyes of a contemporary nun in Geneva, Sister Jeanne de Jussie, who was writing a journal of the city's troubled years from 1526 to 1535.

A New Theology of Marriage

Rejection of the "counsels of perfection": Medieval theology had distinguished between Christian life according to the precepts and life according to the counsels of perfection. The first, obedience to the law of God, was binding on all Christians, and the ordinary Christian found it difficult enough to meet this requirement. The second was a higher calling, possible for a few, which demanded virginity—among many other disciplines—and merited greater reward in heaven. Luther, quite early in his reforming career, ruled out this distinction as untenable. There cannot be two classes of Christians among the baptized. All law given by God is binding on all men, Luther thought, including such hard commandments as "Love your enemies" (Matt. 5:44), which had previously been considered among the "counsels of perfection."

Justification by grace through faith: But however binding the law may be on all, it is also impossible for any person, however saintly, to fulfill the law, Luther believed. Without the gift of God's grace, no one wants to obey

God's will at all. But even the Christian person, justified in God's eyes on the grounds of Christ's righteousness claimed by faith, remains at the same time a sinner. He is unable to claim any reward from God as though he had earned it, however much "religious" activity he may engage in.

Rather, the Christian person, trusting God's promise to him of eternal life, is freed from all preoccupation with merit and reward. In thanksgiving for Christ's gifts he pours out his love joyfully and freely in service to his fellowmen. As he remembers Christ's becoming a servant and dying for sinners like himself, he thinks, "... why shall I not do freely, joyfully, with my whole heart and spontaneously everything which I know will be pleasing and agreeable to Him? I shall give myself therefore as a kind of Christ to my neighbor." And since he is free from the need to be occupied with meritorious religious duties, he resolves to do what is rather necessary, useful, and salutary for his neighbor.

The family as a school of faith: Thus the Christian who can receive only as a gift his faith in Christ and His promise of salvation turns to the world actively in loving service, pouring out the love he has received, doing whatever needs to be done for the meeting of human needs. This is the life of the saint. And the family is the most immediate context for this service. One of the constantly recurring themes in Luther's commentary on Genesis is that

> The legends or stories of the saints which we have in the papacy are not written according to the norm of Holy Scripture. For it is nothing to wear a hood, fast, or undertake other hard works of that sort in comparison with those troubles which family life brings, and the saints [i.e., the patriarchs] bore them and lived in patience.

Moses in describing the life of "the most holy patriarch Abraham" does not create a monastic image with miracles but makes him "a very plebeian man who is occupied with household affairs, for he has a wife and has children." The papists do not understand this sort of sanctity because they do not see his faith. Rebecca is a good example because she was a holy and good mother, flesh and blood, not other than we are, one who suffered and was tempted too. Luther saw marriage as a school of faith where the saints learn to live by faith while struggling with the "worldly" problems of affection and alienation, birth, washing diapers, feeding and educating a family, and death—sometimes of the aged but often of children.

Christian vocation: "Vocation" is no longer reserved for the religious life, that of clergy or monks. Luther believed that just as a secular magistrate by faith can exercise a Christian vocation in the world, so can the housewife. A wife should realize that her many tasks, caring for children and helping or being obedient to her husband, are "golden, noble works." A wife in childbirth should not be encouraged by "foolish" legends of the saints but rather by this: "Think, dear Greta, that you are a wife, and God gives you this work. Take comfort cheerfully in His will." Do your very best to bring forth the child, but if you die, you die in a noble work and obedient to God. Luther clearly contrasts her God-given vocation with "religious" activities.

> If a mother of a family wishes to please and serve God, let her not do what the papists are accustomed to doing: running to churches, fasting, counting prayers, etc. But let her care for the family, let her educate and teach her children, let her do her task in the kitchen ... if she does these things in faith in the Son of God, and hopes that she pleases God on account of Christ, she is holy and blessed.

Superiority of married life: Luther in his enthusiasm for marriage goes beyond merely affirming it as a good gift of God. "The married state is not only equal to all other states but preeminent over them all, be they Kaiser, princes, bishops ... For it is not a special, but the commonest, noblest state." He takes Jesus' words, "Have you never read that the Creator made them from the beginning male and female? ... For this reason a man shall leave his father and mother, and be made one with his wife; and the two shall become one flesh" (Matt. 19:4-5), as a commandment as strong as the ones against killing and adultery. "You should be married, you should have a wife, you should have a husband."

Possibility of voluntary celibacy: Yet at other moments Luther acknowledges that in addition to the physically incapable, there are others who have the gift to live in celibacy and are free to do so—but let them not damn the home! He assumes that this gift is a rare one. Calvin, too, grants that God bestows the grace for celibacy

> on certain men, in order to hold them more ready for his work ... Let no man rashly despise marriage as something unprofitable or superfluous to him; let no man long for celibacy unless he can live without a wife. Also, let him not provide in this state for the repose and convenience of the flesh, but only that, freed of this marriage bond, he may be more prompt and ready for all the duties of piety. And since this blessing is conferred on many persons only for a time, let every man abstain from marriage only so long as he is fit to observe celibacy. If his power to tame lust fails him, let him recognize that the Lord has now imposed the necessity of marriage upon him.

The possibility of celibacy here is clearly a gift of God, a grace, rather than a state that can be achieved by human discipline; it has a practical function in circumstances in which marriage would hinder a person exercising a particular vocation, rather than any ethical superiority; and it should be practiced with the expectation that its need may be temporary, rather than on the basis of a life-long vow.

Marriage and the clergy: The Protestant tradition saw no reason why the clergy should be bound to practice celibacy. In fact, it saw the ancient tradition of clerical marriage in the whole Church and the continuing practice of marriage at least for the lower clergy in the Eastern churches as excellent precedent for married pastors. And it rejected on principle the requirement of a vow of celibacy from anyone. In the early years of the Reformation, in fact, priests felt considerable pressure to marry in order to witness to their new theological view of marriage.

Priesthood of all believers: One reason why the clergy were not expected to live according to a different moral standard than the laity was the new Protestant understanding of the Church. By faith in Christ's work and by baptism, Luther understood that for all Christians,

> just as we are co-brothers, co-heirs, and co-kings, so we are also co-priests with Him, daring with trust through the spirit of faith to appear before God and cry "Abba, father," and to pray one for the other, and to do all those things which we see performed and figured by the visible and corporal office of priests.

He even specifically includes the task of teaching each other the things that are of God. Calvin, too, taught that "every member of the church is charged with the responsibility of public edification according to the measure of his grace, provided he perform it decently and in order."

Note that the priesthood of all believers was not seen primarily in terms of a Christian's intercession on his own behalf before God, but rather in the context of community, the intercession of one for another, the announcing of the Word to one another. But this doctrine did not preclude in the mainstream of the Reformation the necessity for ordained ministers. For the sake of order, educated men were selected to serve on behalf of the community in the public functions of the conduct of worship, the sacraments, and preaching. Yet a theological basis for equality of responsibility between the clergy and the laity—including laywomen—had been established.

Against the despisers of women: Since the state of marriage was now viewed as the noblest way of life for clergy and laity alike, it is not surprising that Luther was eager to refute the "papists ... and all who despise the female sex. And at the same time they produce examples of fathers and saints who were married. By them is adorned the marriage which the whole world depreciates and disparages, just as can be seen in the poets Juvenal and Martial." Luther acknowledges the sins often recounted of historical women, particularly of Eve, but feels they should be remembered "without insult of the sex," for vice is common to both men and women. Though there is no scorn in his observation, he thinks that the female sex is "weaker, carrying about in mind and body several vices. But that one good, however, covers and conceals all of them: the womb and birth."

For Luther, Eve's name reveals her glory—the mother of all men. "God placed his creation of all men in woman, and the use of creation, that is, to conceive, give birth, nurse, educate children, serve the husband and administer the home. Thus among the worst vices and evils this unspeakable good shines forth." Even after the Fall her punishment, the bearing of children in pain, should be rightly seen as a "cheerful and joyful punishment." Eve was not abandoned by God. "She saw that she retained her own sex and was a woman. She saw that she was not separated from Adam to live alone and isolated from a man. She saw that the glory of motherhood was left to her," and was doubtless much encouraged, Luther thinks. Though Luther sees a woman's role closely tied to her capacity to bear children, this is for him a happy and fortunate destiny rather than the curse it so often seemed for writers of earlier centuries. In his thought it is barrenness that is cursed. He has been deeply influenced by the Old Testament texts upon which he commented so often.

Sexual union in itself is good: Luther believed that all of the shame associated with sexual intercourse is the result of sin. There was no shame in Paradise, since God established and blessed sexual union. Adam and Eve then had an "honorable pleasure" in sex such as they had in food and drink. But today, because of the Fall of Adam and Eve, man cannot know woman without a "dreadful madness of lust." The work of conception is linked with "such a shameful and dreadful pleasure that it is compared by the doctors with epilepsy."

The contrast between purity of sex as practiced in Paradise and the shame associated with it because of sin can of course be found in various forms in the whole previous Christian tradition. For Christianity generally opposed dualistic positions that made the body inherently evil. But in the context of Reformation thought, the emphasis fell on the positive acceptance and use of creation, damaged as it is by sin. For it can still be seen as good through the eyes of faith.

If a man burns at the sight of a girl, Luther explains, the sin is not of the eyes but of an impure heart, for eyes, feet, hands are gifts of God. The proper remedy for sexual desire is not to hide as a monk in a monastery to avoid the sight of women but to learn how to use the gifts of God; for vice is not cured by abstaining from things given by God but by proper use and governance of them. When a man is himself without vices, "he uses things piously and in a holy manner and faithfully. May you do the same also, whether in marriage or the magistracy... and you will use things well: wife... things which are good in themselves."

If the modern reader is offended by Luther's including a wife among "things" to be "used," it can be pointed out that elsewhere Luther carefully distinguishes a wife from the household possessions that are subject to a husband's disposition. For only God alone, through the Word and the Gospel, can rule the human soul.

Calvin, too, is eager to repudiate what he considers a depreciation of marriage by the Roman doctrine. He finds it absurd that Roman theologians should on the one hand call marriage a sacrament and on the other hand call it "uncleanness and pollution and carnal filth," from which priests must be barred, even denying that the Holy Spirit is ever present in copulation. He shares generally Luther's conviction about the goodness of marriage. Yet in commenting on the seventh commandment, he can warn married couples not to pollute their marriage with "uncontrolled and dissolute lust. For even if the honorableness of matrimony covers the baseness of incontinence, it ought not for that reason to be a provocation thereto."

Wives subject to their husbands: All the reformers presume in biblical fashion that the husband is the head of the household, and that the wife should be obedient to him. Bucer, following the imagery of Ephesians 5:23–24, indicates that the husband should teach his wife in order that she may have all sanctity and piety of life, should call her away from sin, feed her, cherish her like his own flesh. The wife in turn should offer her body and aid wherever possible for the worship of God and for all other things useful in this life.

Calvin in commenting on Ephesians 5:22–33 clearly does not mitigate the requirement for wives to subject themselves humbly to their husbands. Yet he emphasizes here as elsewhere that Christians are to be subject one to another, men as well as women. The husband's authority is "more that of a society than of a kingdom." He is not to oppress his wife.

Evidence of the seriousness with which the wife's duty of obedience is taken can be found in the *Register* of the Company of Pastors of Geneva. In 1552 an unsigned letter was received from a noble lady who had become persuaded of the evangelical faith since her marriage to a militantly Catholic husband. She explains the unpleasantness with which she is treated because of her faith, the pressure exerted on her to conform to Catholic practices, the way in which she is spied upon and confined, assaulted in spirit and body, unable to confess her faith openly, sing the psalms in French, or possess books about Jesus Christ. The she inquires whether the law of marriage requires her to remain with her husband, or whether she would be free in the Gospel to go to a place where she could worship God in liberty, and whether Geneva would give her up to her husband if she were to flee to Geneva and be pursued by him there. A Christian husband will love, not despise, his wife and cherish her companionship and aid. The reply, probably written by Calvin, expresses pity and compassion for her anguish and perplexity. But it makes clear that scripture does not permit believers to leave an unbelieving partner voluntarily merely because of hostility or suffering. Rather, Christian wives are to strive to fulfill their duties to their husbands in such a way as to win them to the faith. Flight, if a way is provided, is justifiable only in persecution where extreme danger exists. And since the wife is presently complying with her husband's demands of "idolatry" in silence, she is far from such extreme danger. She may pray for courage and constancy to resist demands that would be sin against God and to show her faith with sweetness and humility. If her husband then persecutes her almost to the point of death, she is permitted to escape. And the gentleman carrying the letter will reply further orally concerning her personal security. One fundamental point made here, of course, is that marriage with an "unbeliever" is nonetheless valid; and this point would be applicable equally to the case of a man married to an unbelieving wife. But the husband's legal right to rule over the wife seems to be accepted even to the point of physical abuse, with two exceptions: the wife may escape if she is in danger of death, and she should refuse to obey commands causing her to sin against God.

A briefer reply by Calvin to another unidentified woman suffering similarly dates from 1559, and essentially the same advice is given. But he is more explicit about abuse:

> We have a special sympathy for poor women who are evilly and roughly treated by their husbands, because of the roughness and cruelty of the tyranny and captivity which is their lot. We do not find ourselves permitted by the Word of God, however, to advise a woman to leave her husband, except by force of necessity; and we do not understand this force to be operative when a husband behaves roughly and uses threats to his wife, nor even when he beats her, but when there is imminent peril to her life, whether from persecution by the husband or by his conspiring with the enemies of the truth, or from some other source ... we exhort her ... to bear with patience the cross which God has seen fit to place upon her; and meanwhile not to deviate from the duty which she has before God to please her husband, but to be faithful whatever happens.

Submission applied to politics: At least one of the Reformers, the Scot John Knox, who worked for a time in Geneva, could see nothing but evil in the fact that women, contrary to nature and Scripture, as he believed, were usurping men's authority in his day by ruling nations. Though God has occasionally raised up remarkable women to commanding positions, women by nature are "weake, fraile, impacient, feble, and foolishe; and experience hath declared them to be unconstant, variable, cruell, and lacking the spirit of counsel and regiment." Even without the help of scripture, Aristotle rightly understood that even a man too much dominated by his wife is a poor ruler. Eve's malediction after the Fall to be subject to her husband's will (Gen. 3:16) and the New Testament injunctions to silence in the congregation (I Tim. 2:9-15 and I Cor. 14:34-35), together with the Fathers' writings in the same tone, gave Knox confidence that Mary, "Jesabel of England," would soon be put down from her tyranny by God. And in fact she died a few months later.

Mutual love of the spouses: In Protestant thought about marriage one can discern a gradual shift away from the older emphasis on procreation as justification for sexual intercourse, and even away from an emphasis on marriage as the remedy of incontinence. Luther himself had defined marriage as a "divine and legitimate union of a husband and wife in the hope of offspring, or at least for the sake of avoiding fornication and sin for the glory of God." But he can also say, "What is more desirable... than a happy and tranquil marriage, where there is mutual love and the most delightful union of souls?"

It is true that the Augsburg Confession of Lutheranism, 1530, focuses on marriage as commanded by God to avoid fornication. The Second Helvetic Confession, however, of the Reformed tradition, in 1566, in the section on marriage mentions the remedy of incontinence only parenthetically. God wishes man and woman to cleave inseparably to each other and to live in one highest love and concord. No mention is here made of procreation. The Westminster Confession of Faith, 1647, also Reformed, declares that "Marriage was ordained for the mutual help of husband and wife; for the increase of mankind with a legitimate issue, and of the Church with a holy seed; and for preventing of uncleanness." The order in which the three traditional purposes appear seems significant. In general, without losing sight of the traditional discussions of the role of marriage to remedy incontinence and provide offspring, Protestant thought tended to increase the importance of the mutual cherishing of husband and wife, which had earlier been subservient to the purpose of procreation.

This emphasis can be seen particularly in Bucer in the early years of the Reformation. For him, "The true and entire purpose of marriage is that the spouses serve one another in all love and fidelity, that the woman be the aid and the flesh of the man and the man the head and saviour of the woman." In his later definition of marriage, in *On the Kingdom of Christ*, he retains the same elements: the fellowship and union of a man and woman for the mutual participation in the whole of life with the greatest benevolence and love, after the imagery of Ephesians 5:23–24. He adds explicit reference to the duty to exhibit the communication of divine and human law and to offer the use of the body for sexual intercourse if required. But he makes no mention here of procreation.

The priority of the spouses' mutual love seems also to be present in the treatise of the Spanish humanist Juan Luis Vives, *The Education of the Christian Woman*, dedicated to England's Queen Catherine of Aragon. But the context in which it appears seems to give it a very different function. Vives advises a wife that "the union was not instituted for progeny, but for the communion of life and indissoluble fellowship." But in another context it seems that his point of view is more monastic than Protestant. In discussing the possibility that no children are born to a marriage, he reminds the woman of the perils of pregnancy and birth which should hardly be desired. The ancient curse of barrenness is past; today virginity is better than marriage. A woman can choose children to adopt and love as her own. She should receive as a gift of God that she does not bear children or lose them.

Visible Changes in the Status of Women

It is difficult to find evidence that any conscious effort was made by the Reformation to change the social status of women. Yet the new theology did contribute to greater freedom and equality for women, though certainly not immediately. In marriage law, in education, and in Church life changes were made that immediately benefited men and women alike but provided motivation for more sweeping changes in women's role in later centuries.

Marriage Law: The Reformers in general no longer saw marriage as a sacrament. They urged that laws concerning marriage should be revised, often by the secular authorities, to reform many abuses. One example would be the elaborate system of prohibited relationships, including "spiritual relationships," which limited a person's choice of marriage partners.

Among the actual changes brought about was the increased effort to make all marriages publicly recognized. The banns were conscientiously published, the marital status of strangers desiring to marry investigated, and in Geneva provision was made for marriages to be celebrated in the framework of the normal public-worship services. Considerably more emphasis than in the past was placed on parental consent to marriage.

But the most striking change was the permission given, however seldom, for divorce and remarriage of the injured party. Until the Reformation, separation of bed and board had in some cases been possible, but the marriage bond remained and prevented remarriage so long as both spouses lived. The Reformation as a whole continued to be extremely reluctant to grant divorce. Luther is well known to have declared that he preferred bigamy to divorce, but he is talking of grave pastoral problems, and his statement seems to convey more his horror of divorce than his approval of bigamy. Bucer is the exception to this rule. He tried, though unsuccessfully, to persuade Strasbourg and then England to permit divorce and remarriage whenever the fundamental conditions for marriage, according to his definition, including love, were lacking.

In some cases an effort was made in the legislation to treat women equally with men; in other cases clear discrepancies exist. For example, the point is made in the Geneva Marriage Ordinances adopted in 1561 that, "Although in ancient times the right of the wife was not equal with that of the husband where divorce was concerned... If a man is convicted of adultery and his wife demands to be separated from him this shall be granted to her also, provided it proves impossible by good counsel to reconcile them to each other." Yet in the case where one of an engaged couple disappears before the marriage and the other wishes to be released from the promise, it appears that under certain circumstances a girl would be required to wait a year for her freedom, whereas a man would not.

Public education: Reformation teaching of the "priesthood of all believers" made it very important that all Christians should be capable of reading the Bible and other religious literature. Some public education had existed prior to the Reformation, as early as 1428 for boys—but not girls—in Geneva, part of a general improvement in education of the laity in the later Middle Ages. But the Reformation provided the impetus to expand and develop these small beginnings.

Luther as early as 1524 called on the civil authorities to establish schools to educate the children. After 1536, the official beginning of the Reformation in Geneva, all Genevese children were required to attend school. Those families that could pay for tuition were expected to do so, but the schoolmaster was to be paid by the city so that he could feed and teach the poor children without fees. Girls and boys learned reading, arithmetic, catechism, and writing. After 1541, girls seem to have had their own school for primary instruction, but there were complaints for many years that no public secondary school for girls existed in the city.

Another impetus to the development of women's education must certainly have been the contemporary example of learned noblewomen of the Renaissance who patronized the arts and letters and sheltered religious refugees, as Renée of Ferrara did for Calvin. When one adds to the educated noblewomen of the Renaissance the list of those who actually ruled in the sixteenth century, such as Elizabeth of England and Marguerite of Austria, it is easy to understand why a Renaissance enthusiast can call it the "century of illustrious women."

A number of humanists of the late fifteenth and early sixteenth centuries urged that women, too, should be taught the classics and share more fully the intellectual life of the day: Leonardo Bruni was followed by Agrippa's *De nobilitate et praecellentia feminei sexus* of 1529, Domenichi's *Nobilita della Donna* of 1544, Thomas Elyot's *The Defense of Good Women* of 1534, Bercher's *Nobylytye of Wymen* of 1552, Juan Vives' *De institutione feminae christianae* of 1523, and even Erasmus. Some, like Vives, propose a very modest program of education thoroughly oriented toward protection of women's chastity and humility. But in Bercher's *Nobylytye of Wymen,* around 1552, appears a statement of the equality of women's gifts with men's. "I have noted in some [women] learning, in some temperance, in some liberality . . . and I have compared them with men that have been endowed with like gifts and I have found them equal or superior."

> The bringing up and training of women's life is so strait and kept as in a prison, that all good inclination which they have of nature is utterly quenched. We see that by practice men of small hope come to good proficiency so that I may affirm the cause of women's weakness in handling of matters to proceed of the custom that men hath appointed in the manner of their life, for if they have any weak spirit, if they have any mutability or any such thing, it cometh of the diverse unkindnesses that they find of men.

This interest in improving the education of women flourished in humanist circles, always restricted, where women's social equality with men came to be accepted. A new education was needed to prepare women for new roles. But even at a time when such social equality existed in the governing classes of Florence or Ferrara, for example, it did not exist in the lower or even the middle classes of those cities, and it was seldom to be found in northern Europe. In German, French, and English society down to the Reformation, if women received any education at all, it was geared to the domestic duties that were considered theirs by nature: reading, writing, calculation, elementary nature study (as preparation for nursing the sick), needlework, spinning, music, astrology, religion.

It may well be true that humanism took the lead in transforming the image of women's place in society in the fifteenth and sixteenth centuries. But it must not be forgotten that this was a period of enormous social and economic change, which produced greater social mobility in the lower classes of society as well. The general improvement of educational standards among the laity in this period would work to the advantage of women to some degree. And, on the other hand, one can hardly forget the Renaissance delight in criticizing and satirizing women's foibles.

Church life: With the disappearance of the nuns in Protestantism, women lost one visible, official role in the Church that was not immediately replaced, even by the revival of the deaconesses later in the century. Women were not ordained to the ministry in mainstream Continental Protestantism for centuries, nor were they permitted to be elected as laymen to the official boards that governed the churches.

Yet the Protestant encouragement of a married clergy gave rise to the new role of the pastor's wife, who has been called the "pilot model of the new woman" created by Reformation influence. Luther's former nun Katherine von Bora has acquired a familiar place in histories of the Reformation for her firm though simple faith, her eagerness to help Luther experience the goodness of marriage of which he had been writing, and her valiant skill in managing the enormous household domiciled in the old monastery: the Luther family with their children, theological students, visiting relatives and distinguished theologians, religious refugees—all with a painfully limited budget. No one can read Luther at any length without being deeply impressed by the influence of his experience of marriage on his pastoral theology. The story of Calvin's search for a properly virtuous wife and his marriage to Idelette de Bure is far less generally known, partly because Calvin is far less free than Luther with personal references in his writing. But evidence of his warm affection for his wife can be gleaned particularly from his correspondence.

But genuinely heroic is the story of Wibrandis Rosenblatt. Already widow of the humanist Ludwig Keller, with a child, she was married to the reformer Oecolampadius and bore three children before his death. In the same month the reformer Capito's wife died, and several months later

Wibrandis was married to Capito, bearing five more children before the plague took Capito and three children. Bucer's wife perished in the same outbreak of the plague, but on her deathbed urged her husband to marry their friend Wibrandis and be father to her children. Of Bucer's thirteen children only one still survived at the time of his marriage to Wibrandis, but two more children were born and a niece adopted. Like Katie Luther, Wibrandis, in addition to the burdensome tasks of managing a large household, with a husband deeply immersed in his work, shared the anxieties of the early years when the Reformation had not yet been established officially and when persecution, exile, and death for the new faith were close at hand. In fact she shared Bucer's exile in England, and was left to care for the family after his death.

Not all of the new breed of pastors' wives limited their activities to the household. Katherine Zell, wife of the Strasbourg reformer, began her more public career immediately after her marriage when the bishop excommunicated her husband for marrying and scurrilous tales of his morals were circulating. She published her denial of the tales and a strong defense of clerical marriage, adding:

> You remind me that the Apostle Paul told women to be silent in church. I would remind you of the word of this same apostle that in Christ there is no longer male nor female and of the prophecy of Joel: "I will pour forth my spirit upon all flesh and your sons and your *daughters* will prophesy." I do not pretend to be John the Baptist rebuking the Pharisees. I do not claim to be Nathan upbraiding David. I aspire only to be Balaam's ass, castigating his master.

There soon followed her letter of protest to the bishop, and a published tract about which the bishop protested to the council. She also published a small treatise of consolation for a magistrate of the city suffering from leprosy, and four pamphlets of hymns written by others, to which she added a preface. Katherine made a public address at her husband's death, arousing criticism for her action. She replied, "I am not usurping the office of preacher or apostle. I am like the dear Mary Magdalene, who with no thought of being an apostle, came to tell the disciples that she had encountered the risen Lord." Freed of much domestic responsibility by the death of her only two infants, she cared for the floods of refugees and did extensive visiting of the sick and prisoners; after living for a time in the hospital for syphilitics with a sick nephew, she complained to the town council about conditions and saw her recommendations largely adopted. Just before her death she conducted an interment service quietly at 6 A.M. for a dead Schwenckfeldian woman—and was duly criticized by the town council. The woman's husband had requested a pastor to conduct the funeral, but the pastor had insisted on announcing her apostasy from the true faith, a condition that the husband refused to accept. Katherine's outspokenness caused her to be called a "disturber of the peace of the Church" by one pastor whose sermon she criticized, and Bucer called her "a trifle imperious."

Other Protestant women, too, entered into the controversies of the day. Argula von Grumbach, a Bavarian noblewoman of the house of Hohenstaufen, in 1523 wrote a bold letter to the faculty of the University of Ingolstadt protesting their requiring a recantation of Lutheran theology from a young teacher. Concerning her role in the affair, she says,

> I am not unacquainted with the word of Paul that women should be silent in church (I Tim. 1:2) but, when no man will or can speak, I am driven by the word of the Lord when he said, "He who confesses me on earth, him will I confess and he who denies me, him will I deny" (Matt. 10, Luke 9), and I take comfort in the words of the prophet Isaiah (3:12, *but not exact*), "I will send you children to be your princes and women to be your rulers."

She sent the duke of the region a copy of her protest, but she also wrote to him and the magistrates in general a broader tract against the conduct of the clergy, reminding them of their responsibility not to encroach on God's authority. The authorities left her to her husband's discipline, and he maltreated her in his anger at losing his position. She consulted with nobles in hopes of persuading them to the Reformation, visited Luther, and was twice imprisoned for her subversive activities: circulating non-Catholic books, conducting private services in her home, and conducting funerals at cemeteries without authorization. Elisabeth of Braunschweig, for five years ruler of her land, was deeply influential in the politics of the Reformation and wrote a tract on government for her son, one on marriage for her daughter as well as one on consolation for widows.

Despite their lack of public office in the Church, these—and many other—spirited and courageous women did have theological justification for their involvement in the Protestant doctrine of the priesthood of all believers. This understanding of the nature of the Christian community gave a powerful impetus to the teaching of the laity so that they could carry out their responsibilities. Not only did laymen need to learn to read the Bible, but parents were expected to teach the faith to their children and servants. Catechisms were prepared for teaching the basic elements of theology to all the laity; and in most of the Reformed cities there were regular lectures on the Bible which laymen as well as pastors frequented.

This new way of understanding the Church also required revision of the liturgy so that the laity could become full and active participants—singing, confessing the faith, praying, and hearing the Word in their own language. Laywomen as well as laymen found a new understanding of their ministry in the Church, both in public worship and in their Christian service to the world through their secular vocations.

The Image of Women in Sister Jeanne de Jussie

Having now seen something of the image of women through Protestant eyes of the period, we can check our impressions against those of a nun of the Order of St. Claire, Jeanne de Jussie, who was living in a convent in Geneva during the years just before the Reformation, when Protestant adherents were increasing. A young nun who had learned to write in a Geneva school before entering the convent,[84] she chronicles the events of the years 1526 to 1535 in her volume *The Leaven of Calvinism, Or the Beginning of the Heresy of Geneva*. It is a spirited account, if not a very elegant one in style, with far more references to women than one is accustomed to find in sixteenth-century documents! Sister Jeanne ends her work with the sisters filing out of the city of Geneva, which they now found so hostile to their vocation, and re-establishing themselves at Annecy in France, where she eventually became the abbess.[85]

Sister Jeanne has the strong conviction that the women were more loyal to the Catholic faith than the men. Though many monks and priests disgracefully married, she reports, only one of all the sisters of St. Claire was perverted, and she had not come with good intentions. The others were all strongly persuaded of the heresy of the new faith. There were often torn loyalties in divided families, but Sister Jeanne tells enthusiastically of the firmness in faith of many "good Catholic women" whose husbands were heretics. There was the woman who suddenly died of sadness when her husband had the new baby baptized by the Protestant pastor, Farel. Many others were "more than martyrs," beaten and tormented for their unwillingness to desert the true faith. Three, locked in a room because they would not attend the Protestant Easter communion, escaped by a window to attend Mass. Two "notable bourgeois Catholic women" came, in 1535, at some risk to the convent to console the sisters when Protestant men were ransacking it, destroying pieces of art, and trying to persuade the nuns to give up their vocation.

On Good Friday of 1533 the population of the city was lining up in two armed camps. The Catholics were eager to root out the "infection" that was troubling the city.

> The wives of the Christians assembled, saying, that if it happens that our husbands fight against those infidels, let us also make war and kill their heretic wives, so that the race may be exterminated. In this assembly of women there were a good seven hundred children of twelve to fifteen years, firmly decided to do a good deed with their mothers: the women carried stones in their laps, and most of the children carried little rapiers... others stones in their breast, hat and bonnet.

The same day, after a Catholic man had been fatally wounded by a blow on the head, the "Christian women" let out a great cry and turned on the wife of a Lutheran shouting, "As the beginning of our war, let's throw this bitch in the Rhone!" She escaped into a house, but the women in their anger threw everything in the shop on the ground. Meanwhile the nuns of St. Claire in tears and great devotion prayed for the victory of the Christians and the return of the erring to the path of salvation. Some "good Christian women" came to warn the sisters that if the heretics won, they planned to force all the sisters, young and old, to marry. But the day passed without bloodshed, and a truce was eventually arranged.

The Protestant women are never portrayed as violent. Nonetheless by 1534 two sorts of aggravation are attributed to them: they ostentatiously work on feast days, and they try to persuade the nuns to leave the convent.

While the Catholics were in festival procession in the streets, the Lutheran women sat in their windows for everyone to see them spinning and doing needlework. There were reprisals. After some of them did laundry on the day after Easter and Pentecost, their clothing was thrown in the Rhone. A big Lutheran woman was hit in the head with the distaff someone had snatched from her, then she was trampled in the mud.

As early as 1534 a Lutheran woman, a relative of one of the nuns, came to visit the convent and used the opportunity to pour out her "venom" on the "poor nuns." She claimed that the world had been in error and idolatry till now, that the commandments of God had not been truly taught, that their predecessors had lived wrongly, and finally added "detestable words" on the Sacrament. When the nuns did not succeed in quieting her by their objections, they finally barred the door in her face while she continued to talk.

Twice when city officials came with Protestants to ascertain whether the nuns were being constrained in any way to remain in the convent against their will, they brought Protestant women with them. One, Marie d'Entière, of Picardy, had been an abbess, but now was married and "meddled with preaching, and perverting people of devotion." In spite of the nuns' scorn for her defection, she persevered in her attempt to persuade them to her new view. Sister Jeanne reports that she said,

> O poor creatures! If only you knew that it is good to be with a handsome husband, and how agreeable it is to God. I lived for a long time in that darkness and hypocrisy where you are, but God alone made me understand the abuse of my pitiful life, and I came to the true light of truth.

Regretting her life in "mental corruption and idleness," she took five hundred ducats from the abbey treasury and left that "unhappiness." "Thanks to God alone, I already have five handsome children, and I live salutarily." The sisters replied by spitting on her in detestation.

Another time Lady Claude, wife of Levet, an apothecary, was brought to the sisters, for she also "meddled in preaching." When the Protestants asked "that diabolical tongue" to "do her duty," she began to preach, disparaging the Virgin Mary, the saints, and the state of virginity, praising marriage, and claiming that all the apostles had been married, quoting Paul's approval of being two in one flesh, and "perverting Holy Scripture." When the nuns vigorously protested and asked her to be taken away, they were told by the Protestant men that she was a holy creature, illuminated by God, who had won many souls to the truth by her holy preaching and divine teaching.

It is interesting that Lutheranism for Sister Jeanne is primarily identified with contempt for the Sacrament, iconoclasm, and this new lauding of marriage. A new form of marriage service is reported in 1534 as performed by Farel, consisting in no solemnity or devotion but "only their commandment to join together and multiply the world," and "some dissolute words that I do not write at all, for it is shameful to a chaste heart to think them."

Apart from the "false" sister who became Protestant and married, publicly maligning the sisters' way of life, they believed, only one nun emerges from the journal as a personality. That is the Mother Vicar, who first assists the frail and elderly abbess in dealing with the Protestants and city officials who come to disturb their way of life and then is asked by the nuns to take charge of them. When ordered to attend a public disputation on religion, she and the abbess decline respectfully on the grounds that they have vowed to live the cloistered life. Furthermore, "it is not the task of women to dispute, it is not ordained for women... since it is forbidden to uneducated people to meddle in interpreting Holy Scripture, and a woman has never been called to dispute or witness." But she proves to be a very aggressive and vocal advocate of her own way of life, brashly telling off the Protestant men with as much irreverence as they show her. When she was asked why the nuns wear such garments, she replied that they like them, then in turn asked the questioner why he was dressed so pompously. When Farel and Viret came to preach to the nuns, she put up such a racket of protest that she was removed from the room. But she continued to beat on the wall and cry warnings to the sisters not to listen, telling the preacher he was wasting his effort, till Farel forgot what he was talking about. After this experience he decided not to return to preach there again.

Our glance at the Reformation as seen by Sister Jeanne gives evidence that Protestant teaching in praise of marriage seemed to unsympathetic contemporaries to be of considerable importance in the new faith and a radical departure from the tradition. Furthermore, her journal helps to confirm our impression that women played a more active role in bringing about the Reformation—and opposing it—than has usually been assumed. However colored by her limited experiences and personal preferences the journal may be, it is nonetheless a useful and fascinating complement to other sorts of sources for the period.

The only "women's liberation" of interest to the sixteenth-century Reformation was the elimination of the monastic view of women, sex, and marriage which had flourished both in the monastery and among the laymen. Protestants wanted to give monks and nuns as well as laymen the freedom to take up their Christian vocation *in the world* by providing a new theological understanding of life as well as an opportunity to leave the convent. But we see in Sister Jeanne's account that though the Protestants talked of "freedom," to the nuns they seemed to bring a new sort of constraint, a constraint to marry and be subject to husbands. For to Protestantism the patriarchal structures of society of the day were biblically sanctioned and needed only to be humanized by Christian love.

Yet the Protestant doctrines of Christian vocation and the priesthood of all believers, along with a new view of marriage, did in fact tend to change the image and role of women in the direction of greater personal freedom and responsibility, both immediately and over the centuries.

Bibliography

ROLAND BAINTON, *Women of the Reformation in Germany and Italy* (1971).
MIRIAM CHRISMAN, "Women and the Reformation in Strasbourg 1490–1530," *Archiv für Reformationsgeschch te* 63 (1972): 143–168.
CLAIRE CROSS, "'Great Reasoners in Scripture': The Activities of Women Lollards 1380–1530," in *Medieval Women,* ed. Derek Baker (1978), pp. 359–380.
NATALIE ZEMON DAVIS, "City Women and Religious Change in Sixteenth Century France," in *A Sampler of Women's Studies,* ed. Dorothy G. McGuigan (1973), pp. 18–45.
JOYCE L. IRWIN, ed., *Womanhood in Radical Protestantism* (1979).
IAN MACLEAN, *The Renaissance Notion of Woman* (1980).
STEVEN OZMENT, *When Fathers Ruled: Family Life in Reformation Europe* (1984).
F. ELLEN WEAVER, "Women and Religion in Early Modern France: A Bibliographical Essay," *Catholic Historical Review* 67 (1981): 50–59.

The Massacre of St. Bartholemew's Day, August 24, 1572.   *(detail)*   *Museum of Lausanne*

PART FIVE

Early Modern Europe

During the late sixteenth and seventeenth centuries the religious differences between Protestants and Catholics created ideological and political divisions that kept much of Europe in turmoil. To the fanatic religious mind, the success of "the cause" rendered everything else in life secondary. In France, thirty years of religious warfare, marked by assassinations and massacres, created a general devastation so massive that it was compared to plague. Huguenots or French Protestants, long taught by their leaders that political revolt against legitimate rulers was a sin, began at this time to champion the right of lower magistrates to overthrow royal tyrants, declaring such action a godly duty. By the end of the sixteenth century, Catholics espoused the same doctrine in regard to perceived Protestant tyrants. Donald R. Kelley explains how this intolerable situation came about in France and why, in the end, politics gained priority over religion in the affairs of the French. Subsequent decades would see the French example of putting a country's political welfare first become the model for western Europe as a whole.

Early modern Europe also witnessed the birth of the scientific revolution. The inclination to rely on purely intellectual explanations of reality, especially those that accorded well with reigning theological beliefs, had been a common trait of intellectuals in the Middle Ages.

Copernicus, however, believed that even explanations that conformed to direct observation could be quite false. The earth's diurnal rotation and annual orbit around the sun were scientific facts that contradicted both theology and daily experience. How Copernicus came to defend them is the subject of Edward Grant's essay.

If political realism and a new scientific approach to reality are features of early modern Europe, so are witch hunts. Between 1550 and 1650, witch panics occurred on a scale greater than in previous centuries. Belief in the Devil and witches, together with the willingness of people to blame their personal misfortunes on them, had created an elaborate ideology of witchcraft in the later Middle Ages. Enshrined in law during the fifteenth and sixteenth centuries, such belief thereafter became a political tool of both secular and ecclesiastic rulers. Women, particularly, were singled out and persecuted as witches. How witch trials served the political interests of early modern rulers, and why women became so predominantly the victims, have been subjects of much recent historical speculation. Christina Larner addresses these problems from the vantage point of the rich records of seventeenth-century Scottish witch trials.

Some historians associate the witch hunts with a general hatred of women and a pervasive failure of family life in early modern Europe. They maintain that loving couples and companionable family life were virtually nonexistent before the late seventeenth century, possible only after women gained sufficient social stature to protect themselves from abuse and persecution. Other historians argue that belief in and persecution of witches were in fact concerns of only a small minority of people, exaggerated by historians because of their sensational character. They maintain that freedom and romance characterized the relationship between the sexes as early as the fifteenth century; male tyranny over and abuse of women were the exception, not the rule, of family life. Keith Wrightson weighs this debate on the basis of the evidence available for early modern England.

Religious Warfare in France

DONALD R. KELLEY

Prior to the St. Bartholomew's Day massacre of Protestants in 1572, French Protestant political philosophy, following conservative Protestant tradition, had endorsed the patient suffering of tyrants rather than their violent overthrow. After 1572, Huguenot religious propaganda evolved into a coherent political philosophy. Political authority, following the model of Roman law, was said to lie with the people. Huguenot spokesmen espoused a doctrine of popular sovereignty, that is, the right of the people to raise up rulers and to depose tyrants through their elected lower officials. Religious persecution was no longer sheepishly suffered.

Going beyond conventional Protestant reliance on Scripture, Huguenot spokesmen added rational and historical proofs to traditional arguments based on authority. They invoked the ancient French corporate, feudal, and urban liberties as a legal basis for resisting political tyranny. Especially popular among Huguenots was the conciliarist argument that raised ecumenical church councils above popes—by analogy a subordination of the king of France to the body politic as represented in the assembly of the French secular estates. Huguenot pamphleteers also played on general discontent by waving Luther's banner of Christian freedom before the masses.

Toward the end of the century, with the ascent to power of the Protestant Henry of Navarre, the political fortunes of France turned dramatically. Catholics now espoused the philosophy of political resistance and Protestants opposed it. At this point a watershed was reached in French history. Political considerations clearly became more important than religion in the formulation of political thought. Political realism henceforth gained the upper hand over religious ideology, not only in France, but elsewhere as well.

Reprinted from *The Beginning of Ideology: Consciousness and Society in the French Reformation* by Donald R. Kelley, by permission of Cambridge University Press. Copyright © Cambridge University Press 1981.

The Shape of Ideology

The sixteenth century was in many ways the seed-time of modern ideology, producing... more than 200 heresies along with attendant visions of secular life. This is not, of course, to make any large claims for the originality of this ideologically creative age; and indeed in conceptual terms it might be better to reverse the metaphor—to regard it, that is, rather as the harvest time of western political and social thought. For in a long perspective what is remarkable about this century is less its philosophical innovativeness than its eclecticism and conservatism. Ideologists showed their virtuosity not by divising new formulas but by adapting and rearranging old ones. Yet for all this, the implications of political (if not social) radicalism were profound. It may be suggested, indeed, that mastery over the western political heritage made possible more fundamental departures and insights than neglect or avoidance could have done. As in other areas of the history of thought the most effective and durable changes of orientation and perspective are made possible by taking off from and transforming, rather than affecting to forget, prevailing ideas. Promoting change under the guise of preserving tradition or returning to an earlier and better state has in any case been a frequent device of ideologists, and never more so than in this period of backward-looking (whether fundamentalist or traditionalist) re-evaluations.

The Huguenot party line was many years in the making, but it was not until after 1572 that it took definite ideological shape. Before that time it had normally been hedged in qualifications and claims to political, if not religious, orthodoxy.... St Bartholomew changed all that, at least for a time. In its wake the Huguenot 'cause' was clearly and even philosophically defined; and all the second thoughts and back-tracking of later years could not dull the initial impact nor impede the long-range influence of its ideological offspring. The party line itself continued to be publicized in familiar terms. ... The deeper conclusions were drawn by private persons like [François] Hotman and [Theodor] Beza, and it was through their relatively unfettered investigations and speculations that the shape of ideology was transformed from propaganda to something approaching political philosophy.

Within the space of less than a decade there appeared, in fact, a series of fundamental works which have some claims to be numbered among the classics of the western political tradition. Besides various distinguished historiographical works and the *Reveille-Matin* [*Alarm Bell*], there were Hotman's *Francogallia* (1573), his friend Beza's *Right of Magistrates* (1574), the anonymous *Political Discourse* (1574), La Boétie's posthumous *Voluntary Servitude* (1574), Gentillet's *Contre-Machiavel* [*Against Machiavell:*] (1576), Jean Bodin's monumental *Republic* (1576) and the *Defense of Liberty against Tyrants* (1579), usually attributed to Philippe du Plessis Mornay. Although these works touch upon many other matters and carry us beyond the embattled terrain of sixteenth-century ideology, they are the product of the same dilemma, belong to the same world of discourse, and deserve to be read in part in this same context.

The most influential of these works, those of Hotman, Beza, Bodin and Mornay, were engaged in the same set of debates, but they differed in a number of important respects. Hotman's *Francogallia*, largely a product of the first decade of the civil wars, represents a scholar's search for the causes of the national predicament—historical and antiquarian in substance though legalistic in style and argument. Emotionally as well as conceptually, it was analogous to the Protestant search for a pure and undefiled religion. Although some of its more radical themes were later justified by Hotman as being historical and descriptive and not legal and prescriptive in character, most readers...thought differently; and Hotman himself privately expressed satisfaction at striking a blow against tyranny. Beza's *Right of Magistrates* not only reinforced but often overlapped with Hotman's book, especially in terms of legal and institutional history. Taking off as it did from Calvin's view of resistance as well as [that of the Lutheran] Magdeburg Confession, it had a more religious orientation.... The *Defense of Liberty*, which seemed to pertain to the Dutch as much as to the French scene, represents a further radicalization because it was more abstract, more Biblical (and less institutional) and because it countenanced resistance on an international basis. The *Political Discourse*, combining Biblical and legal arguments, was even more insistent on notions of popular sovereignty and tyrannicide. As for Bodin's *Republic*, though designed as a systematic vision of society, it can also be read as a counterattack on 'monarchomach' ['king killer'] conceptions like those of Beza and Hotman.

In France the concept of sovereignty, or majesty, was the center of attention in the 1570s, and it was no accident that Bodin's classic formulation of the idea appeared at this time. On many levels of thought and action sovereignty was being challenged. Privately, Hotman suggested his own doubts in a rhetorical question: 'How can there be any majesty in such a monster [as Charles IX], and how can one accept as a king a man who has spilled the blood of 30,000 persons in eight days?' Publicly, he seemed to express a similar view that was hardly less inflammatory for all its scholarly and conceptual embroidery. To many, Hotman's defense of 'mixed government' was a flagrant violation of 'majesty'; and few, friends or enemies, put much faith in his disclaimers that he was writing history not political theory.... And Bodin's famous definition of sovereignty...as both 'indivisible and perpetual' can be seen as an explicit contradiction of this thesis. In this polarity we can see the issue dividing the parties formulated on the highest theoretical level.

In agreement with less celebrated Huguenots of the time, 'monarchomachs' like Beza and Hotman inclined more or less consciously toward the principle of popular sovereignty. Behind his scholarly cover Hotman seemed to advocate the idea of elective kingship and the right of people to condemn and depose kings for cause, and in the second edition of the *Francogallia* (1576) he inserted several times, in capital letters, the famous Roman formula, *SALUS POPULI SUPREMA LEX ESTO,* 'The Welfare of the People should be the Supreme Law', which was virtually a code phrase for lese-majesty. Beza was in general agreement with this view, while making more extensive use of Biblical illustrations before applying to legal and historical sources. He also introduced the old conciliarist argument which had survived in France as well as Germany, that the oecumenical council was above the pope, and by analogy he suggested that the secular estates were likewise above the king. So did the Defender of liberty, but characteristically this author was much more dogmatic about the issue. He argued not only that 'kings are made by the people' but 'the people are above kings' and 'kings receive laws from the people'. Nor could time or prescription run contrary to popular sovereignty so conceived. These opinions rested upon an even more fundamentalist and Biblical view of society than those of Beza or Hotman.

Contractualism was of course a common mode of thought and argument among lawyers; and it affected propaganda in several ways—in the form not only of the feudal contract but also of private law, which demanded good faith in any social relationship, and above all of the famous Roman regal law, the *lex regia*. Pierre Fabre introduced this formula, by which the Roman people had bestowed their 'majesty' on the prince,... in 1575. 'When first a people created a king', he wrote, 'they wanted to choose a father who would be a wise governor of faith and of the affairs which they committed to him, and so they also ordered certain and good laws in which they restrained and limited his power; and if the king transgressed them, he was no longer a true king but a usurper and a tyrant.' Hotman introduced the concept into the second (1576) edition of the *Francogallia* and indeed used the term to refer to all the 'fundamental laws' which circumscribed the king. The Roman idea that majesty was vested originally in the people is also discussed by Beza and by the Defender of liberty. 'Has the king made the people?', asked one spokesman in Barnaud's *French Mirror*. 'By no means', answered the Politique, 'but the people have made the king.'

Much more complex was the question of legal and institutional restraints on royal power, and here we return to the eristic and casuistic world of lawyers, in which were lodged precedents and arguments for almost every conceivable position. Seyssel's old notion of three 'bridles' was revived, by Hotman among others, and each played a certain role in opposition propaganda. First, religion was taken as a limit to the king's will in the sense not only that he was supposed to live up to its commandments but also, a more ominous suggestion, that a subject's duty was always to God first and only then to the king. Second, justice implied that the king was bound by certain fundamental laws, such as the Salic law, the principle of the inalienability of the domain, and the need to rule with some sort of conciliar 'consent', which at least tacitly qualified his 'absolute power'.... Finally, the 'police' of the kingdom required that specific laws, agreements, customs and privileges of other groups and institutions be respected. Huguenot propagandists drew heavily upon this medieval view of an organic society with a rich tradition of liberties and corporate privileges and in the process contributed to various kinds of institutional mythology—'constitutional antiquarianism' it has been called—celebrating the antiquity and national superiority of the Estates, the legal system, the peerage, the communes and other products of French society.

The two themes most emphasized in the propaganda of the 1570s were the so-called 'inferior magistrates' and the assembly of Estates, both of which had been part of the Huguenot party program from the beginning. The first involved the highest stratum of the feudal aristocracy, though it could be rationalized in terms of civil as well as feudal law. This concept, made famous in Calvin's *Institutes*, was employed by both Beza and the Defender of liberty, though specific evidence in its support could be adduced also from Hotman's book. The Estates General were celebrated extensively in all three works and indeed in many other contemporary tracts. For Hotman this meant the whole glorious tradition of the 'great Council' continuous from Merovingian if not (*pace* Tacitus) prehistorical times, and the structure of 'mixed government' it implied. Beza followed the same line of argument, using many of the same examples and precedents, and seemed to grant to the Estates an even greater share in sovereignty. So, with less interest in institutional arrangements, did the *Defense of Liberty*.

The ultimate Question, however, was the legitimacy of resistance or rather the conditions under which resistance was legitimate. Beza and the Defender posed it in the crassest manner—asking 'Whether tyranny can be lawfully checked by armed force', in Beza's words; or as the other put it, 'Whether it be lawful to resist a Prince which doth oppress or ruin a public State, and how far such resistance may be extended. By whom, how and by what right it is permitted.'

For Beza, the Defender, and the Political Discourser the answer was a qualified 'yes'. The latter displayed a radical willingness to celebrate the right of a community to 'exterminate a tyrant', adding aphoristically that 'the surest remedy for a tyrant is defiance'. Beza would not recognize armed resistance by a private person, except against violence, but did acknowledge the authority of the 'inferior magistrate', such presumably as Coligny and William of Orange. In any case, argued Beza with reference to the old notion of the 'king's two bodies', a subject's allegiance was to the office not to the person of the supreme magistrate. The principal source of resistance, however, was the assembly of Estates, and indeed a major function of this body was to seek redress for tyranny. Upon it Hotman bestowed all the 'marks of sovereignty' which Bodin and orthodox apologists normally reserved for the king, and later the Defender of liberty was even more assertive about this point. He had no doubt that it was the Estates' business 'to drive out a tyrant, or other unworthy king, or to establish a good one in his place'. And of course the emphasis was always on the word 'king', for none of these three authors could accept the notion of a female ruler, all questions of tyranny aside.

The correlative version of this fundamental question was how to react to religious persecution. It was in the nature of Hotman's book that he avoided the religious issue, although in the preface, composed in the heat of the excitement over the massacres, he did suggest that the corruption of true religion was the principal cause of the corruption of society and the 'Francogallic' constitution. Beza, on the other hand, did not scruple to denounce 'the unjust and sinful submissiveness with which kings have bound themselves by oath to the Roman Antichrist'. In general his answer to the question was that resistance to religious persecution could be undertaken in good conscience if 'true religion' had been guaranteed by law.... And the Defender of liberty responded by a rhetorical question: 'Briefly, if God calls us on the one side to enroll us in His service, and the king on the other, is any man so void of reason that he will not say we must leave the king, and apply ourselves to God's service?'

There is little doubt that such attitudes were common among members of the Huguenot community, especially those in exile or in arms, although specific forms of argument may well have differed. In fact what is striking about the idea of resistance in this period is the great variety of grounds on which it was justified. Partly this was a result of the eclecticism of the age and the attitude of many ideologists that any argument in a good cause was valuable. But it reflected, too, the great range of beliefs and emotions as well as ideas and theories. The means of legitimizing may be arranged on a sort of scale ranging from the most conventional authority to the most free-floating rationalizing: Biblical and literary texts, historical example and legal rules, analogies from private and feudal law, arguments from morality and natural law, and appeals to common sense and pure reason. Far from Luther's principle of 'scripture alone', Huguenot secular ideologists more closely approximated the view taken at the Council of Trent, that demonstration could be achieved in terms of tradition and custom as well as scriptures. In this sense, too, Huguenot propaganda appeared to be 'total' and to touch on every level of experience.

Yet in terms of political thought a certain drift can be detected from an empirical and authoritarian mode of persuasion to more rational methods of proof. Common to all four authors is a tendency to draw illustrations in a comparative way from the experience and institutions of disparate societies —that is, from the field that corresponded to the old law of nations, the *jus gentium*—and then to infer, by a sort of inductive process, patterns that seemed to be universal and, arguably, in conformity with the 'natural law'. In this spirit appeal was made to the oaths of English kings and the Aragonese nobility,... to fundamental laws, and to various kinds of representative assemblies. So there emerged a kind of argument from 'natural law' in a modern, empirical and comparative, as well as a medieval and *a priori* sense which would reach maturity in the more sophisticated formulations of the next century. This can be seen above all in the *Defense of Liberty*, in which an almost pure theory of social contract is put forward and in which the absolutist moral tone is so dominant that, in the face of rampant nationalism, even the notion of foreign assistance for the 'cause' is given rational defense.

It is well known that the arguments of the so-called 'monarchomachs' were adopted and applied not only by Catholics of the next generation, when Henry of Navarre's candidacy for the throne cast them into opposition, but also seventeenth-century English and eighteenth-century American revolutionaries. To some extent these adaptations represent a specific transmission of arguments in a continuum of intellectual history; but it must also be admitted that resistance arguments, as they became more abstract, rationalized and grounded in philosophy and natural law rather than legal precedent or historical tradition, also become universalized and applicable to many predicaments. Notions of tyranny, natural rights, social compact, and the right of revolution were elaborated in other contexts, American as well as English and European, and represent at least an indirect legacy of the sixteenth-century wars, as John Adams and many seventeenth- and eighteenth-century men of affairs believed. But these represent other cycles of ideology with their own 'beginnings' and go beyond the present inquiry.

The Elements of Ideology

How analyze the ideological upsurge of the international Protestant community in the 1570s? How evaluate this epiphenomenal creation that represents perhaps the most intense and coherent expression of a 'total' ideology, at least in public terms and on a world-wide scale, in early modern history? Certainly the visible propaganda involved drew strength from a great variety of social discontents as well as long-standing political division, but no less certainly religious enthusiasm constituted its vital force. This was the view taken not only by partisans of all sorts (despite earlier expressions of doubt about the sincerity of religious motivation on the part of leaders) but also by disinterested observers and professional social critics like the Venetian ambassador to France, Marc' Antonio Barbaro. The turmoil of the age was unheard of, Barbaro wrote in a report of 1564, 'and this great mutation proceeds from no other cause than from religion'. He than went on to list five means by which society was being subverted: the growing inclination of the nobility toward heretical ideas, the popularity of disputations, the intrusion of churchmen into law offices, the failure to punish 'crime' in Huguenot cities, and the favor shown by the great (presumably men of political consequence like Condé and Coligny) toward heresy. These were at least the most perceptible conditions for the generation of ideology in the sixteenth century.

Where Barbaro saw heresy and anti-social behavior we may, on closer scrutiny, detect a more general pattern of opposition signifying more than political inconvenience. Among French, Swiss, German and Dutch Calvinists, or Calvinist sympathizers, an integrated and militant view of the world was formed, if only temporarily, by the convergence of intellectual conviction and social necessity; and the result was a general vision of human nature that went beyond particular confessional formulations. Although this vision was nowhere expressed in anything like systematic form, partial views are apparent in the enormous range of propaganda.... What follows is an attempt to draw together some of the main elements of the Protestant ideological creation....

Most basic is the psychological element, the taproot of discontent and of social and generational upheaval. There does not seem to be any satisfactory way to isolate and to trace the effects of ego-energy on a social level, and certainly an appeal to a generalized 'individualism' is inadequate. Yet some patterns with anti-social implications are undeniably the product of particular acts of will, especially the emergence of heroic models — the 'magisterial' reformers — which came to replace social norms. The wider repercussions of this can be seen in various kinds of unconventional behavior, including the flight from parental control and monastic institutions, the pursuit of martyrdom and more active and militant kinds of resistance. It may be presumptuous in terms of existing evidence to speculate about psychohistorical causes, but the results are indisputable. So is the general inclination to justify actions on the basis of non-conventional standards of conscience and transcendent values, which in practice often meant values of an outlawed or alien community. It is of course true that within a generation this behavior and these values tended themselves to become socialized and conventionalized, just as the magisterial reformers were followed by that less charismatic replacement that has been called 'the Second' — Bullinger following Zwingli, for example, and Beza following Calvin. But this is precisely the process which, according to the various channels we have followed, transforms ideals into ideology.

Secondly, and considerably more accessible to observation, is the evangelical element. In some ways this was the most active ingredient of ideology, just as the major vehicle of propaganda and of the legitimation of unorthodox behavior was the Bible. The theme of 'Christian liberty' sounded by Luther, Pupper van Goch, Farel and many others was not political at first, but it was unmistakably anti-authoritarian and easily accommodated to political causes, as Luther soon found in his contacts with the 'protesting' German princes. Most essentially, according to Erich Fromm's famous formulation of the 'negative freedom' of post-medieval society, the evangelical idea of liberty promised release from the tyranny of materialism and idolatry, from an ignominious 'human' conception of divinity and of course from foreign domination. The implication was that the standard of judgment and action came not from human authority, tradition or institutions but from a transcendent 'word' to be derived from scriptures without any ecclesiastical 'interpretation'. Projected into the secular sphere, the notion of a free and purified faith also provided a means of criticizing and perhaps rejecting human authority. The analogy is with the metaphor of 'the king's two bodies': just as the mass was purged of idolatrous 'real presence', so secular power was separated from its human agency; and the argument was that allegiance, like faith, was due only to the transcendent aspect. With regard to the monarch, in other words, respect was due to his 'majesty' but perhaps not to 'his majesty'. In various ways the 'reformed' religion furnished a model and emotional source of secular ideology. In historical terms Hotman's *Francogallia* was a secular projection of the primitive church; in political terms the *Defense of Liberty* was a secular projection of the Biblical covenant; and both represented analogues to the notion of Christian liberty.

It is also possible to recognize a corporate element, including a variety of group or institutional privileges, which involved in some sense an allegiance separate from that owed to church or state. Guilds, professions, offices and other institutions all had their specially defined and jealously guarded 'liberties' which even the government could not violate with impunity. The Gallican church, the University of Paris, the lawyers' *barreau* [bench] and the Parlement, the guild of printers and even the family, as there has been reason to notice, had all of them their time-honored privileges which the crown periodically confirmed and sometimes added to or subtracted from. It will not do to follow older historians in associating too closely such accumulations of corporate privilege with modern liberal attitudes, in identifying the defiance of sixteenth-century printers and professors with modern 'freedom of the press'... or the 'liberty of speech' enjoyed by sixteenth-century *parlementaires* with more recent conceptions. Certainly there were inequities and authoritarian patterns in earlier notions of 'liberty' at odds with those of the nineteenth and twentieth centuries. Yet recognizing differences does not mean denying historical connections. Earlier social and professional groups were indeed sources of resistance to uniformitarian and oppressive political forces; and in terms at least of ideology the habits, traditions and formulations of protests for corporate 'liberties' contributed to attitudes of heterodoxy, resistance and eventually revolution.

Fourthly, there is the feudal element, which has been and would continue to be a permanent obstacle to royal authority and to national consolidation.... The notion of feudal contract, with its attendant rights and duties for both parties, was implicit in the position taken by the 'conspirators' of Amboise and explicit in that taken by Condé in his 'treaty of association'. It was evident in various complaints by spokesmen for the nobility in particular, which was forced to fight for its 'honor', which is to say its landed property, as well as for religious and political principle. Arguments from and analogies with feudal 'liberty' permeated the propaganda of the civil wars and after the massacres found a prominent place in such more systematic statements as the *Reveille-Matin* and the *Francogallia*. Even the idea of popular sovereignty depended in a sense on this neo-feudal ideal, since the assumption tended to be that 'the people' could act directly through the agency of the 'inferior magistrates', which is to say the grandest of the 'grandes familles'.

It would probably be an exaggeration and historically premature to emphasize a classical element in the political and social consciousness of the civil wars. There is some evidence of republican hyperbole and the precedent of Brutus was occasionally invoked, but even with regard to the issues of tyrannicide and assassination this sort of remote antiquarianism was of secondary importance. In most respects, sixteenth-century ideology did not attempt to extricate itself from the framework and assumptions of feudal society. This was evident even in those most forceful expressions of resistance to 'sovereign' claims, such as those of Philip of Hesse in Germany, Condé and Coligny in France, and especially William of Orange in the Netherlands. Like the defense of Hesse, the 'Apology' of Orange of 1582 was based in large part on his feudal objections (as Duke of Brabant) to treatment at the hand of his suzerain Philip II of Spain. The neo-feudal basis of resistance arguments is apparent also in the continuous calls for assemblies of the Estates both in France and in the Netherlands, where the Estates in 1581 finally 'abjured' the sovereignty of Philip II on the grounds that their relationship was basically contractual—unlike that between Philip and his colonies in the New World....

Related to feudal ideas and even more disturbing to royalist orthodoxy was the civic element of sixteenth-century ideology. Here classical antiquity had more to offer, and in intellectual terms the independence of 'reformed' cities of the sixteenth century, or at least their pretensions thereto, represented a continuation of attitudes associated with the 'civic humanism' of Italian city-states of the previous century. Yet once again medieval patterns seemed predominant. Urban freedoms, while they might be nourished by classical republicanism, had their own indigenous roots and peculiar character. The old proverb 'City air makes free', was given new life when joined to notions of Germanic and Christian 'liberty'; and of course free cities like Strasbourg and Magdeburg had given practical application to such attitudes by taking their place in the front ranks of resistance to the Emperor Charles V. Similar examples can be found in the claims of Dutch cities resisting the Emperor's son, Philip II. The convergence of religious and civic liberties is apparent in the case of the city of Brabant, which supported 'those of the religion' on the basis of certain 'ancient liberties' which forbade the Duke (that is, Philip) to 'pursue' his subjects except by due process of law, to impose taxes without calling the estates and to appoint foreigners to office. According to the published manifesto, the arrangement was like the feudal contract: 'And if the Duke violates or derogates from these liberties, the citizens are absolved from their oath and can do freely what seems best to them'. These manifestos issued by insurgent cities contributed directly to more formal resistance theory, most notably through Beza's *Right of Magistrates*, which purported to be a commentary on the famous 'Magdeburg Confession' of 1550, and through the *Defense of Liberty against Tyrants*, which had recourse to Dutch precedents.

Most significant were the precedents furnished by the cities of Switzerland, which were held up as ideals in particular by Dutch propagandists. The libertarian traditions of Geneva, enhanced by the interrelated process of 'reformation' and the struggle for independence from Savoy, were consolidated by two generations of conflict with that power. Nowhere is the union of religious commitment and political independence—the spiritual and material components of ideology—so clearly illustrated as in the Genevan oath of allegiance: the old civic requirements are maintained (owning property in the city, asking permission to leave or to import foreign goods, giving military service when necessary, and others), but to this was added from the 1540s the prerequisite that citizens 'live according to the reformation of the gospel'. This was, of course, in the name of civic as well as Christian liberty, and not the liberty of Genevans only. 'We are convinced', Beza wrote after the first war of religion in France, 'that if the city falls, it will affect its neighbors and be a disaster even for those who know nothing of it. It would be the end of liberty.'... For ultramontane Catholicism Geneva seemed a fearful 'grotto' of heresy and subversion, for the disillusioned Antoine Fromment (in a sermon which sent him into exile) a second Sodom, for Protestants a 'new Jerusalem' and a 'new republic'; but for all it was a dominating symbol of Reformation ideology.

For France the classic case of civic defiance was La Rochelle, a city which traced its liberties back at least to the twelfth century and indeed claimed descent from a fortification of Caesar. Before 1200 the city had the privilege of establishing a 'senate', which (like the Parlement of Paris) followed the Roman precedent of 100 members. In the sixteenth century the civic liberties of La Rochelle became menacing as the people allegedly began arming themselves against the king's 'majesty' in 1534. La Rochelle's 'rebellion' against the *gabelle* [salt tax] was apparently settled in 1542, but already the religious question was looming. 'I have been warned', wrote Francis I two years later, 'that in La Rochelle and environs there are several persons, greatly tainted with these accursed and damned Lutheran errors, who have joined themselves together in flocks and who go about the country causing endless scandal, sowing among the people their unfortunate and damned doctrine, a thing which displeases me'. But royal displeasure did not prevent the advance of heresy, especially as it gathered support among the nobility. In 1558 it was reported that a band of comedians ridiculed Roman rites in the presence of the visiting King and Queen of Navarre. Four years later the massacre of Vassy provoked 'a mania for pulling down idols', and this soon escalated into armed conflict. During the 1560s La Rochelle began to demand respect for its 'ancient liberties' but also for the more modern 'liberty of conscience'. By 1572 the city was virtually an independent republic, creating a 'myth' to rival that of Geneva and contributing directly to the civic element of the propaganda of the 1570s.

In the ideological movements of the sixteenth century the national element was undeniably visible, but its function was in some ways ambivalent and deceptive, even divisive for some adherents of the evangelical —political 'cause'. This was especially the case in the Empire, in which Luther raised the flag of nationalism in his address of 1521 against the ecclesiastical establishment and inadvertently against the Emperor. In the Netherlands nationalism was based largely on anti-Spanish sentiment and a sort of popular front of feudal, civic and evangelical interests which in many ways was powerless to overcome deeply rooted particularist tendencies. In France the situation was also complicated. The rhetoric and arguments of both Gallicans and Huguenots could be intensely nationalistic, and yet both parties had increasingly entangling alliances with foreign powers—Italian and Spanish on the one hand and German, Swiss, Dutch and, to a lesser extent, English on the other. The paradoxical conclusion seems to be that nationalism was a powerful ideological force, but its effect even within particular states was more divisive than unifying, at least in the short run. Indeed it is a measure of the strength of sixteenth-century ideological movements that they could resist as well as make use of national sentiment.

In general, ideological movements of the sixteenth century were extraordinarily concrete in provenance and in formulation: they reflected immediate human dilemmas and interests and they appealed to particular precedents and traditions. Yet attempts were made to go beyond the authority of history, law and even scriptures and to elevate protests and programs to a philosophic level. In this connection natural law and rational theology reappear as devices of legitimation, reason and universal values replacing human custom and convention. As monarchy seemed to be founded on reason, so might ideas of social contract and popular sovereignty. Ultimately, whatever the claims of positive law, 'God chooses and the people establish a king' (*Eligit Deus et constituit Regem populus*), and parties could choose either or both parts of this proposition to justify a course of action. This was the case also with active resistance, for it was a formula in agreement with reason as well as civil law that force may be used to repel force (*vim vi repellere licet*). In the works of Bodin and the monarchomachs in particular, all the elements discussed here, and more, are combined into synthetic views of the human condition as it essentially is or ought to be in social and political terms.... In ... sublimated form... sixteenth-century views of resistance and revolution have been passed on to a series of posterities, each with its own set of dilemmas—ours as well as Rousseau's and John Adams's among them.

The End of Ideology

By the end of the 1570s the most fundamental expressions of Huguenot ideology had been published and had made their impact, but in quantitative terms the high tide of propaganda was yet to come. So were some of the worst horrors of civil war and private criminality. For political controversy the noise-level at least continued to rise until ... 1588, which saw the failure of the Spanish Armada, the day of the barricades in Paris and the assassination of the younger Duke of Guise (followed the next year by that of Henry III, last of the Valois). In 1580 Henry of Navarre published his own 'declaration', following the pattern established by Coligny and Condé before him. Four years later, however, with the death of the Duke of Anjou and the obvious fact that Henry III would die without issue, Navarre became the presumptive heir; and the Huguenot party line took a legitimist and conservative turn. Hotman, for example, deleted references to the principle of elective monarchy in the third edition of his *Francogallia*. On the other hand the anti-Romanist line became even more intense, especially in 1585, when the papal bull of excommunication against Navarre and Condé once more sharpened exchanges.

From this time on, it was the Catholic party that was forced into an opposition posture in France; but while the predicament had changed and the party roles were reversed, the patterns of ideological conflict remained much the same. Now the Catholic 'princes, lords and cities' issued declarations against those trying 'by all means to subvert the Catholic Religion and State' and demonstrated in their turn 'the causes which have constrained Catholics to take up arms, and to charge King Henry III with "tyranny".' Ideologically, however, their weapons had already been forged for them. 'The Huguenots', according to a pamphlet of 1589, 'have shown the way to the Catholics...' As for the arguments for resistance, the author added, 'It is certain that if they have any color and plausibility for the assumption of arms and war against the king, they are so much the stronger in support of the Catholics, who have taken up arms to destroy the heretics.' And so Catholic propagandists did not hesitate to appeal to the principle of elective kingship popularized by Beza, Hotman and Barnaud, and some even to the idea of tyrannicide....

One opinion shared by both parties helped keep the ideological fires burning, and this was the old assumption that religious indifference was even worse than error. Not long after St Bartholomew one royalist lawyer declared that 'the scorner of religion is the true subverter of the republic', and of course partisans could not agree more. So [Louis] Dorléans was horrified by 'those indifferent folk who have held that everyone can be saved in their own faith'. Even worse was the attempt to hide or to disguise the difference—to 'dissemble' or 'dissimulate'—as did certain 'tacit Huguenots'. Du Laurier was especially incensed at those perverse and unnatural 'hermaphrodites' ... who dissembled their opinions in order to preserve their properties and offices, pretending to accept both religions. This was 'to reason à la Machiavel', and the name of this old Florentine dissimulator— 'doctor of tyranny', in the words of one 'good Catholic'—pervaded the polemic of the last wars of religion.

Once again, then, the issue came to center on the familiar term and concept of the political man, 'le Politique', which increasingly was associated with libertinism and atheism as well as 'Machiavellism'. 'The name "politique" was once a name of honor', wrote one orthodox pamphleteer in 1588, 'of a just governor and prudent magistrate who knew how to rule a city through civil reason and create concord out of the divergent interests of different citizens... Today this fine name, associated with a thousand vices, is a name of horror and destructive of order, a name of filth and contempt because of those who have abused it.' And he added, 'The honor of a "politique" is that of a fox, his eye always on the prince's face and agreeing with him in everything, even against God.' What so many people believed about the lawyer, in short, could be charged against the Politique: he was, from the standpoint of any faith, a 'bad Christian'. Another author presented an exhaustive 'catalogue of errors' characteristic of the politique mentality—among them the proposition that 'he gives first priority to the civil and political affairs of the state'; that 'these political affairs are placed in particular above religion'; that 'nature is the only guide to and mirror of the conservation of man'; and that 'in order to maintain a civil state in peace it is necessary to preserve all religions that have arisen'. And the conclusion: 'Here is the purpose of all Huguenots and Politiques associated with that of the Libertines, Epicureans and Atheists.' It was altogether worthy of 'that atheist Machiavelli, evangelist of today's Politiques'. One author even suggested that it was 'machiavellian' to be unwilling to carry on war against religious aggression.

At the same time, however, there were signs of a changing mood. Even before the massacres of St Bartholomew, disillusionment was settling over some persons who had lost their taste for combat. Even the belligerent *Political Discourses* identified as one cause of the civil war the presence of men who simply had no other métier than that of war. Jacques Cujas, though he had defended the government's position, had contempt for the way in which scholarship had been inundated by controversy. 'I have never read or heard of a century', he wrote, 'more fertile in spirits devoted to calumny than ours.'... The militant spirit... carried over into every sphere of life; and some reflective types, Montaigne most notable among them, began to think that the most serious problem was not in theological disagreement but in human nature itself. As one versifier observed,

> The elephant's big, the lion strong,
> The tiger fierce, but all in vain:
> By hand of Man—or hands of men—
> The beasts are, all of them, often slain.

It was to counteract such instinctive urges to violence disguised as religious fervor that some 'Politiques' presented a counsel of moderation. 'They are called "politiques"', wrote one of the most prominent of their number, Pierre Belloy, 'who do not want to dip their hands in the blood of Christians.' This, too, could be a matter of conscience.

Among Huguenots attitudes of realism emerged with the destructive effects of war.... Less than a decade after the *Reveille-Matin*, Barnaud had launched into his extensive projects to estimate the social and economic costs of the wars, and his results were staggering. Still arguing the 'Francogallican' case and still speaking through the persona of 'le Politique', Barnaud acknowledged in his *French Mirror* that, to reverse the old Gallican formula, there was in France 'neither God, nor faith nor law'....

So we return to the old pre-war themes of religious toleration and 'conciliation', or rather to the complex devices of legal recognition, coexistence and legislative settlement. Before the massacres of St Bartholomew one 'exhortation to peace' suggested the conditions of such a settlement. 'We have two forms of religion in France', this pamphlet acknowledged. 'It remains only to prescribe certain rules for each ... [to ensure] that one does not have too great advantage over the other and that we should enjoy equal liberty and favor in our religions.' The internationalization of controversy in the last quarter of the century complicated this solution, but there did not seem to be alternatives. A pamphlet of 1586 reported the arguments of ambassadors from Germany pleading for 'pity' toward the French evangelicals and for some such political resolution of religious differences. As a family needed a stable structure, a 'bonne police' to regulate the relationships between husband and wife, so a society required a reasonable and mutually accommodating arrangement for its ideological groupings. Bipartisan political agreements might seem as paradoxical and 'duplicitous' as religious hermaphrod[ism], but in the wake of St Bartholomew the compromising Politiques did emerge as an identifiable 'party' and acquired a power base with the candidacy of Henry of Navarre to the French throne. Despite its national claims, however, this 'political party' had, except for opposition to Romanism, only the most attenuated ideology.

There is no question here of reviewing the complex ideological patterns of the last quarter of the sixteenth century. In quantitative terms the outpouring of propaganda reached new heights, and so did the international character of the polemics. The new intelligentsia made possible by printing was creating all kinds of specialisms, one of them the propaganda trade itself. Extremism and verbal abuse became professionalized as well as habitual, especially when reinforced by violence and a variety of social turmoils which had little in common with the confessional conflicts of an earlier generation except for the emotional momentum derived from them. Ideological patterns persisted despite the confusion of political and religious interests.... Tyrannicide, beyond *ad hoc* political assassination, emerged as an explicit issue, as did ideas of popular sovereignty. There were even published appeals on behalf of orphans and the poor, victims of civil conflict without a power base or a 'cause'. But in rhetorical, behavioral and institutional terms the publicity of these years represents variations on established themes and an extension of the same ideological process. What is striking from the perspective chosen here is the growing futility of centrifugal partisanship and the hollow repetitiousness of most propaganda, and what seems significant is the growing tendency to end party strife and to achieve a national settlement and solidarity on political grounds....

So Henry IV returned to 'the religion of Machiavelli', as Beza put it. After his reception (specifically at the hands of his own Gallican clergy) back into Catholicism, his coronation in Chartres and his return to Paris, the king began the work of restoration; and once again published propaganda was the most visible vehicle for the reaffirmation of monarchy and national unity. A series of acts and edicts set forth the program of restoration for every part of French society. The reduction of rebellious cities, the restoration of the Parlement and the University of Paris, the reinstatement of corporate liberties and particular offices and other legislative actions began the long effort to re-establish order. Religious pacification took several years more but followed the guidelines of earlier edicts. By such 'political' means the structure of French monarchy and society—religion, justice and police—was stabilized, and the excesses of controversy were curbed. Discontents and tensions remained; but in political terms this Bourbon restoration represented, at least for that age, 'the end of ideology'.

Yet this was but the political expression of a mood that had been increasingly apparent in the late sixteenth century—apparent at least if we do not restrict ourselves to the drums and trumpets and mounting waves of pamphlets. Nowhere is that mood more evident than in the work of that disillusioned magistrate, Michel de Montaigne, who secluded himself even before the massacres of St Bartholomew and began to reflect not only on the state of his own consciousness but also on levels of social life below the noises of religious and political controversy. Though he celebrated the ego, he denounced egoism and that 'natural and original disease' of intellectual presumption. He deplored disputation and other inflations and abuses of the arts of discourse. 'Grammar is that which creates most disturbance in the world', he declared, and the notorious litigiousness of his age was simply an extension of this. 'Our suits', he continued, 'only spring from disputations as to the interpretation of laws.' What suffered most, of course, was faith. 'When has this been seen better than in France in our day?', he remarked about the variation in religion. 'Those who have taken it to the right, those who have taken it to the left, those who call it black, those who call it white, use it so similarly for their violent and ambitious enterprises ...' Montaigne dismissed contemporary religious enthusiasms as nothing more than insolent egoism. 'See the horrible impudence with which we bandy reasons about and how irreligiously we have both rejected them and taken them again, according as fortune has changed our places in these public storms.'

Unmistakably, Montaigne is referring here to what has been called the 'politicization' of religious movements; but beyond that he also laments the virtuosity with which parties employ religion. The justice of particular causes has been merely alleged, he charged, 'as in the mouth of an advocate, not as in the heart and affection of the party'. This duplicity was most evident in the reversal of party positions that occurred during the mid 1580s, and the revolutionary hypocrisy of this shift Montaigne found most distasteful. 'This proposition, so solemn, whether it is lawful for a subject to rebel and to take arms against his prince in defense of religion', he quoted: 'remember in whose mouth, this year past, the affirmative of this was the buttress of one party, the negative was the buttress of what other party; and hear ... whether the weapons make less din for this cause than for that.' Here indeed was the 'end of ideology'.

Bibliography

FREDERICK J. BAUMGARTNER, *Radical Reactionaries: The Political Thought of the French Catholic League* (1976).

PHILIP BENEDICT, *Rouen During the Wars of Religion* (1981).

ELIZABETH L. EISENSTEIN, *The Printing Press as an Agent of Change* (1979).

CARLOS M. N. EIRE, *War Against the Idols: The Reformation of Worship from Erasmus to Calvin* (1986).

JULIAN H. FRANKLIN, ed. *Constitutionalism and Resistance in the Sixteenth Century: Three Treatises by Hotman, Beza, & Mornay* (1969).

ROBERT M. KINGDON, *Geneva and the Coming of the Wars of Religion in France, 1555–1563* (*1956*).

QUENTIN SKINNER, *The Foundations of Modern Political Thought*, vol. 2: *The Age of Reformation* (1978).

ALFRED SOMAN, ed., *The Massacre of St. Bartholomew's Day: Reappraisals and Documents* (1974).

Copernicus and the Scientific Revolution

EDWARD GRANT

A new attitude toward scientific hypotheses played an important role in the scientific revolution of the seventeenth century. It first appears in the work of Copernicus. Although medieval scholastics used hypotheses in a variety of ways, two are of particular significance. One of the most important was "to save the phenomena," a concept derived from the ancient Greeks. In this approach, an hypothesis was merely a convenient assumption to explain phenomena without regard to its physical truth or falsity. A second way concerned hypotheses, or assumptions, about the world that were naturally impossible—that is, contrary to nature. The purpose of the latter type of hypothesis (described in Latin as *secundum imaginationem*, "according to the imagination") was to conjure up conditions that were contrary to natural operations as understood by Aristotle and to see if the consequences of such hypotheses were plausible or possible. Much, though by no means all, of medieval physics and cosmology involved one or both of these conceptions of hypotheses.

Copernicus, by contrast, no longer worried about saving the phenomena with imaginative hypotheses, the truth or falsity of which were uncertain. For him, as for his famous scientific successors, an hypothesis had to state something real and true about the nature of the universe, even if what the hypothesis asserted was not directly observable. In the mind of Copernicus, the hypotheses that the sun was located at the center of the universe *and* that the earth rotated around it like any other planet were hypotheses that not only saved the phenomena better than the traditional geocentric hypothesis but had of necessity to be true. Only if the hypotheses were true could the consequences derived from them also be true.

Although Copernicus was mistaken to believe that only true premises (or hypotheses) could yield true consequences, his passionate

---

Reprinted with the permission of the author and the editors of the *Journal of the History of Ideas* from "Late Medieval Thought, Copernicus, and the Scientific Revolution" by Edward Grant, in *Journal of the History of Ideas*, vol. 23, no. 2, pp. 197–220. Copyright © 1962, Journal of the History of Ideas, Inc.

conviction of the soundness of this idea gave him the courage to proclaim the truth of the heliocentric system and thereby launch the scientific revolution.

As is well known, the possibility of the earth's diurnal rotation was discussed in the Middle Ages prior to the revolutionary pronouncements made by Copernicus in his *Commentariolus* and *De revolutionibus*. The medieval discussions did not—as far as is known—produce a single adherent for the doctrine of a rotating earth. Hence Copernicus, by insisting on a real physical daily and annual motion of the earth made a momentous break with his medieval predecessors.

In quite properly devoting attention to the main achievements of Copernicus, scholars have slighted another dramatic break which seems indissolubly linked with his new system. His conception of the function and rôle of an hypothesis is so radically different from that of his predecessors that it serves to symbolize his drastic departure from the scholastic tradition almost as much as his new cosmological system.

The aim of this paper is to outline some of the factors which came to shape the medieval conception of a scientific hypothesis and to illustrate them in the actual discussions of the rotation of the earth. Following upon this, the attitude of Copernicus will be set out to reveal the gulf which separates his outlook from that prevalent in the Middle Ages. Indeed, it will be shown that Corpernicus is really the initiator of a very basic attitude which came to be held in some form or other by most of the great figures of the Scientific Revolution—namely, that fundamental principles in the form of hypotheses or assumptions about the universe must be physically true, and incapable of being otherwise.

The medieval scholastic conception of the function and rôle of hypotheses in science was a very sophisticated one.... Scholastic views were the outcome of two currents which probably fused, or at any rate reinforced each other. On the one hand, there was a general adherence to the ancient Greek astronomical principle of "saving the phenomena," and on the other, a number of intellectual currents generated from special problems arising within the scholastic tradition itself....

The sophisticated notion of "saving the phenomena" was widely known and accepted in the Middle Ages. In its medieval form it may have derived from Simplicius' commentary on Aristotle's *De caelo*, which was translated from Greek into Latin ... in 1271. Commenting on Bk. III, ch. I, Simplicius says: "But perhaps Plato and the Pythagoreans did not admit that corporeal substance was truly and absolutely a combination of these triangles; perhaps they did as the *astronomers*, some of whom admit certain hypotheses and others other hypotheses without categorically affirming that these different mechanisms actually exist in the heavens. If they assumed any such principles it was only to make possible the saving of appearances by assigning to all celestial bodies circular and uniform motions: ... these authors took it as an hypothesis that the principles of bodies belonged to those figures which were considered adequate to account for the cause of the facts." The attitude described by ... Simplicius was subscribed to by such eminent medieval figures as St. Thomas Aquinas, Jean Buridan, Nicole Oresme, Albert of Saxony, Pierre d'Ailly, and many others....

This widely accepted doctrine was strongly reinforced by certain significant currents which came to constitute the intellectual milieu of the later Middle Ages. The struggle between philosophy and theology commencing in the thirteenth century and culminating in the fourteenth created an atmosphere of uncertainty and even scepticism toward many seemingly self-evident propositions and metaphysically demonstrated truths. "Hypothetical," "possible," and "probable" arguments became the vogue—especially in theology as well as in philosophical and scientific arguments which touched upon theology. Let us briefly outline some of the significant factors which produced these currents.

Subsequent to the introduction and absorption of the Aristotelian corpus of philosophical and scientific treatises in the thirteenth century, a general deterministic interpretation of nature and God's power became instrumental in the production of a scholastic literature in which reasoning about theological and philosophical matters was done in accordance with Aristotelian metaphysical principles. One of the significant aspects which emerged from this development was Latin Averroism and its associated doctrine of the "double truth." The truths of philosophy, which were about the natural order, might conflict with the truths of theology, which dealt with the supernatural order. In this event it was understood that God had altered the natural order supernaturally. Hence, what was naturally true could be supernaturally false, and conversely. The doctrine of the double truth was a deterrent to any hoped for reconciliation between philosophy and theology as envisioned, for example, by St. Thomas Aquinas.

The theological reaction to the doctrine of the double truth and to determinism generally came in the years 1270 and 1277 when a great many such theses—more or less widely held and including the doctrine of the double truth—were condemned by ecclesiastical authorities. Fearing deterministic arguments restricting the freedom of action of God, ecclesiastical authorities set limits on the absolute validity of many propositions which had been metaphysically demonstrated. These then acquired the status of "possible" truths, and alternatives became tenable propositions—under penalty of excommunication.

Pierre Duhem has insisted that the condemnation of 1277 had a salutary effect on scientific discussions for it set medieval science free from bondage to Aristotelian cosmological and metaphysical prejudices. Propositions to the effect that God could not move the universe with a rectilinear motion, or create a plurality of worlds were condemned with the consequence that discussions on the possibility of a void and the existence of other worlds were forthcoming and served to stimulate scientific imagination.

Despite Duhem's appraisal, ... the overall effect of the condemnations was to weaken confidence in metaphysical demonstration of philosophical and scientific propositions which, in some manner, encroached, or touched upon the theological domain. As for the doctrine of the double truth, it no longer constituted a problem since the "truths" of metaphysics and natural philosophy were clearly subordinated to the truths of faith. Metaphysical principles—in the strict sense—could only acquire a status of probability (*probabilitas*) for they were held to be derived solely from experience, memory, or induction. The truths of natural philosophy were only probable because true according to natural reason, while the truths of theological dogma were absolute and indubitable in virtue of their sacred origin. In the fourteenth century, as we shall see, the truths of faith were held to be indemonstrable.

Emphasis on probability and possibility was strengthened from yet another source. The *Summulae Logicales* of Peter of Spain, a famous and enormously influential logical treatise of the thirteenth century, appears to have been a potent factor in the development of fourteenth century scepticism. [As one scholar has observed:] "At the very beginning of the *Summulae*, Peter of Spain asserted that his entire work would have only the character of probability. For him, dialectic was the science which held the key to the principles of all methods. Knowledge of it was acquired prior to the knowledge of any of the other sciences, for dialectic discussed with probability the principles of all the sciences. Consequently, any development which resulted from a discussion of the principles proper to these sciences had only the character of probability." Furthermore, since the *Summulae* "had to be committed to memory by impressionable youthful students who were then plunged into the dialectical life of the university, one sees that a tendency towards scepticism is a logical outcome...."

In addition to the *Summulae*, and perhaps connected with it, were discussions beginning in the thirteenth century and continuing through the sixteenth century concerning ... theses which had two alternate views either of which could be held with equal probability. One might also conclude that neither of the alternatives was capable of demonstration.

The severest blow to metaphysical confidence, however, came in the fourteenth century as theology continued to free itself from "philosophical presumption." William Ockham (ca. 1280—ca. 1349) and the nominalists who followed him used philosophical argument—not ecclesiastical decree —to confound philosophy and show the futility of many traditional metaphysical demonstrations in the domain of theology. The logical and epistemological critiques formulated by Ockham led to a repudiation by many scholastics of traditional proofs "demonstrating" the existence of God, His unicity, infinity, and other "necessary" attributes.

Rooting his fundamental position in a radical empiricism, Ockham challenged the notion that causal relations could be obtained by inference and insisted that only observation could provide such knowledge. Nor, indeed, was it logically tenable to infer from experience to what transcends experience and thus it became hopeless to prove the existence of God from the order of existence of the world of nature known to us through our senses. Indeed, theology was, for Ockham, not even a science. Theological dogmas were true in virtue of faith and revelation alone.

Ockham's empiricism ... was grounded in his insistence that all knowledge is gained from experience through "intuitive cognition." By this he meant that the immediate apprehension of a singular thing leads one naturally to say it exists. No demonstration can be produced—or is required—to show the existence of a thing apprehended in this manner. It is simply apprehended and its apprehension enables us to form a contingent proposition concerning its existence.

Knowledge of one existent thing gained through "intuitive cognition" does not permit us, Ockham further argued, to infer the existence of any other thing, since there is no necessary connection between contingent things.... Hence causal relations are not inferable, or known, by *a priori* reasoning. They are, however, detectable through experience in terms of temporal and spatial relations, as, for example, when we detect that fire is the cause of heat in a heatable object. Such connections, however, provide no knowledge of any underlying and "real" cause—these are hidden from us. Without a temporal and spatial nexus, no causal sequence is determinable. Indeed, in many cases we cannot even know if there is a cause.

Thus Ockham splits the world into absolutely distinct things between which there are no necessary connections. He then applies his famed razor, or principle of economy, and repudiates the tendency among many of his predecessors and contemporaries to assume the existence of "real relations" between things and unnecessarily to multiply entities of all kinds. These were unjustifiable inferences from experience. For example, Ockham, applying his razor to a physical concept, insisted that motion is not, as many held, a separate entity or form apart from the moving body. Motion is simply a term which stands for a body occupying successive positions or places. As Ockham puts it, one may "say: 'this body is now at A and not at B' and later it will be true to say: 'this body is now at B and not at A,' so that contradictories are successively made true." ...

By treating contingent physical phenomena in hypothetical form, Ockham may possibly have influenced an important scientific current amongst nominalists at Oxford and Paris during the fourteenth century. Ockham, in emphasizing logical rigor and not insisting upon existential implication, may have encouraged others to go further and imagine all sorts of possibilities—and even impossibilities—without regard for physical reality or application. Only one restriction was operative—there must be no formal logical contradictions. The characteristic sign of this approach is the phrase *secundum imaginationem* ["according to imagination"] which appears with great frequency in fourteenth-century scientific treatises....

The cumulative impact on medieval thought of all the currents already enumerated was formidable indeed. The Condemnations of 1277 initiated the demise of metaphysics as well as philosophical demonstration in the realm of theology. The process was, in effect, completed by Ockham.... Stress was laid by Ockham and others on God's *potentia absoluta* [that is, on God in himself, according to his absolute power to do anything he chooses, barring a logical contradiction], which unleashed a theological scepticism that "allowed speculation and uncertainty to reign where knowledge and proof were lacking."...

In the course of the fourteenth and fifteenth centuries, the nominalist movement spread to many universities and became solidly entrenched. The nominalist emphasis on empiricism and the concomitant decline of metaphysics turned philosophy away from theology to the positive sciences and to the mathematical disciplines. But the shadow of the ever-present condemnations hovered over many of the scientific discussions in the later Middle Ages. Where the application of physical concepts encroached upon the theological domain special deference to the theologians and the spirit of 1277 was in order. Thus Jean Buridan, in trying to account for the uniform and unceasing motion of celestial bodies, conjectured that intelligences might not be required to move the planets because God impressed impetus into each of them. "And these impetuses which He impressed in the celestial bodies were not decreased nor corrupted afterwards, because there was no inclination of the celestial bodies for other movements. Nor was there resistance which would be corruptive or repressive of that impetus. But this I do not say assertively, but [rather tentatively] so that I might seek from the theological masters what they might teach me in these matters as to how these things take place...."

In general, nominalist empiricism was confined to that which was directly experienced and sought no underlying realities. Its adherents usually refrained from making bold inferences from experience to fundamental principles. Directly experienced phenomena could often be explained only by possible or probable causal connections between contingent things and it was usually impermissible to infer causal connections not directly observed. The function of many theories and causal explanations was simply to "save the phenomena" by hypothetical propositions. We have already seen that many discussions in fourteenth-century physics were exercises in logic accompanied by explicit disavowals that the results or assumptions had application to physical reality.

The preceding summary of medieval thought patterns in science, theology, and philosophy in the late Middle Ages will serve to bring into bold relief the extent to which Copernicus departed from medieval ideas and ideals regarding both hypothetical explanations and "saving the phenomena."

Three different relevant viewpoints concerning the earth's rotation were held during the Middle Ages and the supporters of each position rejected the earth's motion as a physical reality.... The first position was upheld by François de Mayronnes, Albert of Saxony, and Pierre d'Ailly. The basis for repudiation was the same for each: the earth's diurnal motion could not save the appearances of oppositions and conjunctions of the planets, nor could it account for the eclipses of sun and moon....

The second position is a very significant one and is represented by two of the foremost scientific minds of the Middle Ages [Jean Buridan and Nicole Oresme].... Buridan rejected the first position by arguing that relativity of motion would not enable us to determine the question. The apparent motion of the stellar sphere and the planets could be accounted for either by supposing the earth at rest and the heavens in motion or conversely....

Buridan then moves to arguments from experience. He mentions a number of experiences, each of which is easily accounted for by the rotation of the earth. But finally he arrives at a particular phenomenon which a rotating earth cannot account for. If the earth rotated, an arrow shot directly upwards should be left behind and not fall back to the same spot. But this is contrary to experience and he concludes the earth is immobile. Thus, in typical nominalist fashion, Buridan appeals to an experiential physical—not astronomical—consequence of the earth's motion which is not observed in nature. It was the most powerful argument he could muster.

Nicole Oresme also discussed the question and, like Buridan, rejected the motion of the earth. But Oresme's repudiation of a diurnally rotating earth was not, like Buridan's, founded on scientific argument. Accepting, in large measure, Buridan's reasoning, Oresme, however, refutes Buridan's "arrow experience" even while acknowledging it as the most significant argument for an immobile earth. He offers another hypothesis to explain it.... Buridan anticipated the argument which might be offered in favor of a rotating earth—namely that the air is moved with the earth and carries the arrow along thus explaining why the arrow falls back to the same spot. Oresme undertakes to defend this very position by analogy and example:

> This appears possible by analogy: If a person were on a ship moving toward the east very swiftly without his being aware of the movement, and he drew his hand downward, describing a straight line against the mast of the ship, it would seem to him that his hand was moved with rectilinear movement only. According to this opinion [of the diurnal rotation of the earth], it seems to us in the same way that the arrow descends or ascends in a straight line.... In support of this [position, consider the following]: If a man in that ship were going westward less swiftly than the ship was going eastward, it would seem to him that he was approaching the east, when actually he would be moving toward the west. Similarly, in the case put forth above, all the movements would seem to be as if the earth were at rest.... I conclude then that one could

not by any experience whatsoever demonstrate that the heavens and not the earth are moved with diurnal movement.

... Oresme, with obvious delight and sense of purpose, has reduced the entire question to a stalemate. The alternative hypotheses are equally probable when argued in terms of reason and experience. Reason is impotent to strictly demonstrate a question of science, just as it is impotent to demonstrate articles of faith. Thus Oresme has used reason to confound reason and clearly reveals that he is the heir of the tradition which emerged from the struggle between philosophy and theology when philosophy in the hands of the theologians confounded the philosophy of the philosophers. Oresme, himself a theologian—and this is of some importance—has merely transferred this attitude to the domain of science. It was not possible to *really* know which of the alternatives is physically true.

The third position—that the diurnal rotation of the earth saves the astronomical phenomena better than an immobile earth—is also of great interest in contrast to the attitude of Copernicus. Unfortunately, not a single name can be linked with this viewpoint. Indeed, it is only through a brief remark by François de Mayronnes that we can be confident that such a position was even maintained. He relates that "a certain doctor says that if the earth were moved and the heaven quiescent this would be a better argument."

It is almost certain that this unnamed doctor did not maintain the actual physical motion of the earth, for if he had this would have been worthy of comment by Mayronnes. Presumably, it was for him a better hypothesis for "saving the phenomena" but this would tell us nothing about the true physical situation. Indeed, it is overwhelmingly likely that this person would have insisted that the earth has no rotatory motion. That the earth's rotation would better save the phenomena was for him, presumably, a false hypothesis which yielded better results than the truth.

Coming now to Copernicus we find a radically different attitude that clearly reveals how far he diverged from the medieval philosophical and scientific tradition and its conception of the rôle of hypotheses and "saving the phenomena." The remarkable break with the medieval tradition is not to be found in the arguments Copernicus gave in support of a diurnally rotating earth. Indeed, many of these were commonplace in scholastic discussions. It is found, rather, in the insistence by Copernicus that the earth really and truly has a physical motion and in the methodological rationale which emerged from this profound belief. In the mind of Copernicus these two aspects are intimately connected. In his preface to the *De revolutionibus*, Copernicus remarks that since others have been permitted to "assume certain circles to explain the motions of the stars, I believed it would readily be permitted me to try whether, on the assumption of some motion of the earth, better explanations of the revolutions of the heavenly spheres might be found." When Copernicus became convinced that not only did the "phenomena necessarily follow therefrom, but the order and magnitude of the stars and all their orbs and the heaven itself are so connected that in no part can anything be transposed without confusion to the rest and to the whole universe," he did not suppose that his initial assumption was only a convenient conjecture or probable hypothesis. On the contrary, the simpler universal order resulting from an initial assumption of the earth's motion moved Copernicus to proclaim boldly that he was "not ashamed to maintain that all that is beneath the moon, with the centre of the earth, describe among the planets a great orbit round the sun which is the centre of the world; and what appears to be a motion of the sun is in truth a motion of the earth. . . ."

Asserting the reality of the earth's motions—diurnal and annual—sets Copernicus apart from his medieval predecessors who refused to ascribe even a single diurnal motion to the earth. The break is even more significant, however, when it is realized that *hypothesis* was one of the terms he applied to his basic and fundamental propositions about the motion of the earth. But he did not mean by this a mere convenience to save the phenomena, nor was it simply more probable than other alternatives. It was a fundamental truth of the physical universe. This is made clear by his criticism of the procedures of earlier astronomers: "Therefore in the process of demonstration, which is called 'method,' they are found either to have omitted something essential, or to have admitted something extraneous and wholly irrelevant. This would not have happened to them had they followed sure principles. For if the hypotheses assumed by them were not false everything which follows from their hypotheses would be verified beyond any doubt." Thus *only if hypotheses are true* can the appearances really be saved. The motion of the earth—diurnal and annual—is an hypothesis which Copernicus believed to be indubitably true.

The two-fold motion attributed to the earth produced a symmetry in the universe which was clearly superior to the older scheme. Retrogradations and progressions of the planets were rendered physically intelligible. These consequences of the earth's motion appear to have been instrumental in convincing Copernicus that the earth really moved and that his hypotheses were a true reflection of cosmological reality. But in order to understand where Copernicus departs from the medieval tradition, we must focus attention on these particular words: "For if the hypotheses assumed by them were not false, everything which follows from their hypotheses would be verified beyond any doubt." In "saving the *astronomical* phenomena" it is not a matter of convenience—but truth. For Buridan and Oresme it is not a matter of truth but convenience. They both believed that either hypothesis could equally well save the *astronomical* phenomena. The decision in favor of the earth's immobility was made on non-astronomical grounds. Indeed, adherents of the third position mentioned above would, perhaps, go even further and maintain that the earth is immobile but that if it did rotate, its motion would better save the phenomena. For these medieval speculative cosmologists it was by no means necessary that astronomical hypotheses reflect cosmological truth. Indeed, any number of different hypotheses could theoretically save physical appearances. But Copernicus brings a wholly different outlook and temperament to astronomy. To say that two hypotheses could equally well save the astronomical phenomena would have been, for him, tantamount to confessing ignorance and confusion. Two such conflicting hypotheses for the earth's status could not, upon genuine reflection, truly save the phenomena. Further criteria must be sought and, when found, will enable one to separate the false from the true.

Thus Copernicus' conception of "saving the phenomena" differs radically from the ancient and medieval tradition. In the latter tradition truth and falsity are not at issue—only accounting for the phenomena. For Copernicus to "save the phenomena" in astronomy means to frame true hypotheses.

But Copernicus' insistence on the reality of his new system cuts even deeper. It stands against the entire nominalist position which dominated late medieval science and philosophy. To a nominalist, the Copernican system would be an inference transcending experience. Its greater simplicity and explanatory power would not have justified the momentous step of conferring reality upon the system. God could have made this contingent world complex rather than simple. God's absolute power forces man to restrict his knowledge to what is immediately knowable and perceived. But for Copernicus God's world is essentially simple and its cosmological structure knowable.

Copernicus makes one more important innovation. He seems to subordinate physics to astronomy, thus reversing an ancient and medieval tradition. Convinced that the hypotheses of his new cosmology represented astronomical truths, Copernicus had to devise a suitable physics which, in large measure, consisted in accounting for the motion of the earth.... Time honored physical notions about the earth had now to be drastically altered. Thus physics must follow the basic requirements of a true astronomy. This was a momentous break with an almost sanctified tradition.

The quest for reality conditioned Copernicus' understanding of the rôle of an hypothesis in a scientific theory. Science and its hypotheses must treat of realities—not fictions. In this sense—if in no other—Copernicus may be considered the first great figure of the Scientific Revolution. It was essentially his attitude which came to prevail with Kepler, Galileo, Descartes, and Newton.

Kepler ... aligned himself with Copernicus unequivocally when he wrote: "It is a most absurd fiction, I admit, that the phenomena of nature can be demonstrated by false causes. But this fiction is not in Copernicus. He thought that his hypotheses were true.... And he did not merely think so but he proves that they were true."

Galileo also accepted the earth's motion as a physical reality and in a significant passage reveals the new state of mind which sought not merely to save appearances but to discover "the true constitution of the universe." Declaring that mathematical astronomers merely assume eccentrics, epicycles, equants, and the like "in order to facilitate their calculations." Galileo asserts that these geometrical devices "are not retained by philosophical astronomers who ... seek to investigate the true constitution of the universe —the most important and admirable problem that there is. For such a constitution exists; *it is unique, true, real, and could not possibly be otherwise*; and the greatness and nobility of this problem entitles it to be placed foremost among all questions capable of theoretical solution."

And, referring with obvious approval to that very passage in which Copernicus asserted that hypotheses should be true, Salviati, Galileo's spokesman... states: "Thus, however well the astronomer might be satisfied merely as a calculator, there was no satisfaction and peace for the astronomer as a scientist. And since he [i.e. Copernicus] very well understood that although the celestial appearances might be saved by means of assumptions essentially false in nature, it would be very much better if he could derive them from true suppositions ..." Adopting his revolutionary hypotheses, "and seeing that the whole then corresponded to its parts with wonderful simplicity, [Galileo] embraced this new arrangement, and in it he found peace of mind."

The quest for reality and indubitable first principles is found in Descartes in much more extreme fashion than in any of his predecessors and contemporaries. Seeking true principles in clear and distinct ideas his aim was to reduce the physical universe to mathematical law. He wrote to Mersenne (March 16, 1640): "As to physics, I should think I knew nothing about it if I could only say how things may be without demonstrating that they cannot be otherwise; for having reduced physics to the laws of mathematics, I know it possible, and I believe I can do it for all the little knowledge I believe I have..."...

Newton also appears to have believed that indubitable general principles were attainable about the universe. In his ... *Principia* (1713), Newton asserts that, although he had not yet discovered the cause of the properties of gravity, "to us it is enough that gravity does really exist, and act according to the laws which we have explained...." Now Newton's gravity is not a property of bodies and hence not an observable entity, but rather an inference from the mathematical laws which describe their behavior. Therefore, to assert its real existence is to go beyond the phenomena to an underlying reality. This is clearly in the tradition of Copernicus. Many of the late medieval scholastics would, presumably, have construed Newton's gravity as only a plausible or probable hypothesis, since the phenomena could quite conceivably be explained otherwise.

There is in Query 31 of Newton's *Opticks* a passage which reveals his understanding of the aim and goal of science. Newton insists that the Aristotelians gave the name of "occult qualities, not to manifest qualities, but to such qualities only as they supposed to lie hid in bodies, and to be the unknown causes of manifest effects: such as would be the causes of gravity, and of magnetick and electrick attractions, and of fermentations, if we should suppose that these forces or actions arose from qualities unknown to us, and uncapable of being discovered and made manifest. Such occult qualities put a stop to the improvement of natural philosophy, and therefore of late years have been rejected." Newton, therefore, condemns those who despair and abandon every attempt to make the underlying causes manifest and who take refuge in thinking such causes completely hidden from us. Newton's aim was to make such causes manifest, thus revealing the underlying causes of phenomena. His ideal was "to derive two or three general principles of motion from phaenomena, and afterwards to tell us how the properties and actions of all corporeal things follow from those manifest principles," and this "would be a very great step in philosophy, though the causes of those principles were not yet discover'd...." These principles are described by Newton as "general laws of nature, by which the things themselves are formed...."

Though Newton would start from the phenomena, his ultimate aim was to arrive at true laws which underlie the phenomena and by means of which "the things themselves are formed." Newton was searching for fundamental truths about the ultimate structure of matter from which its properties could be deduced. This is in keeping with the great quest for reality initiated by Copernicus. Newton's world is an intelligible one with some of its laws and fundamental principles already discovered, while others await discovery.

The passages offered here as evidence for a sharp break with the medieval scientific outlook once reflected a new conviction and a new faith. But this seems no longer to constitute part of the present conception of the scientific enterprise and in this connection modern science has shown a greater affinity with the fourteenth century than with the century of Galileo and Newton. In the judgment of Pierre Duhem medieval scholastics had a truer conception of science than did most of the great scientists of the Scientific Revolution.... He could not hide his scorn for the naïveté of some of the greatest figures of seventeenth-century science who confidently believed they could—and should—grasp and lay bare reality itself. Most of their basic errors, Duhem insisted, derived from their delusive search for reality which served only to corrupt the theoretical structure of science.

Duhem is, in general, quite right. Scholastics were most sophisticated and mature in their understanding of the rôle which an hypothesis must play in the fabric of science. They were not, as we have seen, deluded into believing that they could acquire indubitable truths about physical reality. But it is an historical fact that the Scientific Revolution occurred in the seventeenth century—not in the Middle Ages under nominalist auspices. Despite the significant achievements of medieval science—which Duhem himself did so much to reveal—it is doubtful that a scientific revolution could have occurred within a tradition which came to emphasize uncertainty, probability, and possibility, rather than certainty, exactness, and faith that fundamental physical truths—which could not be otherwise—were attainable. It was Copernicus who, by an illogical move, first mapped the new path and inspired the Scientific Revolution by bequeathing to it his own ardent desire for knowledge of physical realities.

Bibliography

ERIC COCHRANE, "Science and Humanism in the Italian Renaissance," *American Historical Review* 81 (1976): 1039–1057.
FREDERICK COPLESTON, *A History of Phiolosophy*, III: *Late Medieval and Renaissance Philosophy* (1963).
A. C. CROMBIE, *Medieval and Early Modern Science*, 2 vols. (1959).
PIERRE DUHEM, *The Aim and Structure of Physical Theory* (1954).
OWEN GINGERICH, ed., *The Nature of Scientific Discovery* (1975).
A. R. HALL, *The Scientific Revolution 1500–1800: The Formation of the Modern Scientific Attitude* (1966).
OWEN HANNAWAY, *The Chemists and the Word: The Didactic Origins of Chemistry* (1975).
REIJER HOOYKASS, *Religion and the Rise of Modern Science* (1972).
ALEXANDER KOYRÉ, *From the Closed World to the Infinite Universe* (1957).
THOMAS S. KUHN, *The Copernican Revolution* (1957).
E. A. MOODY, *The Logic of William of Ockham* (1935).
FRANCES YATES, *Giordano Bruno and the Hermetic Tradition* (1964).

Who Were the Witches? The Scottish Witch Hunt

CHRISTINA LARNER

Between 1400 and 1700 perhaps as many as 100,000 people were legally executed for demonic witchcraft in England and Europe. The witch trials absorbed the interest of ordinary people, intellectuals, and politicians alike. The hunts seem to have been closely connected with the religious revolutions of the period and the self-aggrandizement of new clerical and political elites.

Everywhere the witches were predominantly women. In Scotland, where the witch hunts occurred later than in most of Europe, four-fifths of the accused were middle-aged or elderly women. The "average witch" was the wife or widow of a tenant farmer at or near the bottom of the social order. Why women? Women were both susceptible and vulnerable, both volunteers and victims. Witchcraft could elevate a woman to a position of power and influence within a community, a factor that made it attractive to some of the very poor. Witchcraft was also an acceptable way for women to act aggressively within a patriarchal society that cast them in a passive, supporting role. Both pagan and Judeo-Christian authorities deemed women to be physically and morally weaker than men, hence more easily enticed by the Devil. In Scotland, the women accused of witchcraft had traits that a male-dominated society resented. Accused witches were especially known to be quarrelsome, aggressive, sharp-tongued, and noncooperative, women who refused to stay in their place.

The witches of Scotland were typical of the witches of rural Europe. They were predominantly poor, middle-aged or elderly women. The sources are not often directly helpful in establishing social detail. It is unusual for the occupation or age of a suspect to be recorded. Marital status is given in about a third of the cases. Quite often we have nothing but a name and

Reprinted with the permission of The Johns Hopkins University Press from *Enemies of God: The Witchhunt in Scotland* by Christina Larner. Copyright © 1981 by Christina Larner.

sometimes not even that. Of the 3,000 or so accused collected in the *Source Book* only 192 have their occupation or status or that of their husbands recorded. They can be classified as follows:

Nobility	16
Burgess	14
Craftsmen	46
Indweller	1
Sailors	10
Lairds	2
Ministers/teachers	14
Prosperous tenants	10
Midwife/healers	12
Wage labourers	16
Innkeepers	3
Musicians	3
Servants	23
Beggars and vagabonds	21

These figures are in fact extremely misleading. Fortunately there is internal evidence in a fairly substantial run of documents which shows that it would be absurd if one were to project from the figures given above to the mass of other witches. Indeed the status of the accused seems to have been mentioned in the documents only when it was slightly unusual. The average witch was the wife or widow of a tenant farmer, probably fairly near the bottom of the social structure. If she was categorized in the records at all it was as spouse, for example, to John Graham in Kirkton. It is evident from the accusations that the quarrels which generated them were about the exchange of goods and services in a tenant and sub-tenant economy.

It is hard to speak with great certainty in the absence of more detailed local research on one of the major witchcraft areas such as Fife or East Lothian, but the impression given is slightly different from the English scene, where it is clear that the witches were ninety-three per cent women, and that they were absolutely at the bottom of the social heap. They were the wives or widows of wage labourers; they were on the poor law; they were beggars. The Scottish ones appear on average to be slightly further up the stratification scale. Those really at the bottom of the Scottish scale were the large but unknown number of people who were in a sense outside the system. They were the criminals, paupers, gypsies, entertainers, and wandering wage labourers, all generally summed up under the title of vagabond. Some of the witches whose status is specifically named do fall into this class. A few are identified in the records as being downwardly socially mobile. Jean Hadron, tried in Glasgow in May 1700, was mentioned as being poor and seeking alms and was a baker's widow; Margaret Duncan, who was tried along with her, was a merchant's widow. Catherin Mac-Taiged, who was tried in Dunbar in May 1688 was the wife of a weaver who become a beggar. John Shand of Moray tried in 1643 was described as a fugitive; Marion Purdie, tried in Edinburgh in 1684, was once a midwife. But these glimpses in the records are fleeting. What detailed research on one area might establish is to what extent accused witches belonged to a class which was being dispossessed from small-scale collective farming and was having to make a living from inadequate land supplemented by wage labouring. In the present state of knowledge it looks as though, while a few belonged to the class of outsiders—wage labourers, servants, and the dispossessed—many of the accused witches had a more or less stable domicile and might be related to people in the neighbourhood who had a formal stake in the feudal structure. The majority, however, appear to have been at the bottom of the formal feudal structure itself; they had at least a house with a kailyard, some were part wage-earner, part tenant-farmer; others were sub-tenants and tenants in a farm-town. In other words they had a position in society, albeit a lowly and often semi-dependent one, and they did not mean to drop out. Unless someone had a fixed position in the community their reputation was not likely to have a chance to grow. Exceptions of course were those who were banished for witchcraft and who had to move for that reason, or whose reputation travelled with them....

An indication of the importance of being within the system before being in danger of witch accusation is given in the Kirk session records of Rothesay. This was a burgh on the island of Bute in the Clyde which had a few cases of witchcraft although it never had an epidemic. A woman called Bessie Nicol, daughter to Duncan Nicol, a weaver, was called up by the Kirk session in 1706 for

> imploying Elspeth NcTaylor, spouse to James Stewart, thatcher, by charmeing to find out and recover a gown that was lost and for that end to have given the said Elspeth a fourtie pennie piece with a litle salt in a clout (cloth) to performe the charme.

It might perhaps be thought that Elspeth NcTaylor, the charmer, and therefore potentially the witch, might have been the worse offender but in this distant outpost of the Kirk the local session lacked courage:

> In regard the forsaid Elspeth NcTaylor alledged to be imployed to perform the charme is notourlie known to be most intractable, incapable and infamous and irreclaimable the Session waves troubling themselves with her.

Suspects were then from the settled rather than the vagabond or outcast poor, and they were predominantly women. Witchcraft was, as elsewhere in Europe, overwhelmingly a woman's crime. It was also in Scotland almost the only woman's crime in this period. If one looks impressionistically at those unanalysed central criminal records it appears that apart from a little adultery, a little incest, a surprisingly small amount of infanticide, and (as Covenanters) a bit of rebellion, women were not reaching the Court of

Justiciary. At a lower level, however, they were being constantly subjected to the variety of degradation rituals which comprised the lesser punishments of the Kirk sessions, town councils, or baron courts.

The relative figures for men and women at least are firm apart from the 300 or so witches whose names (unless they are duplicates) we do not know. The number of male witches fluctuated, but overall amounted to about one fifth of the whole.

Percentage of Male Suspects by Decade

Decade	Female	Male	Male Percentage
1560–9	10	2	16.7
1570–9	4	1	20.0
1580–9	10	3	23.1
1590–9	144	36	20.0
1600–9	24	9	27.3
1610–9	62	19	23.5
1620–9	347	49	12.4
1630–9	133	38	22.2
1640–9	396	57	12.6
1650–9	308	55	15.2
1660–9	577	77	11.8
1670–9	162	29	15.2
1680–9	32	3	8.6
1690–9	36	11	23.4
1700–9	63	13	17.1

If one leaves aside those decades in which the numbers are too low for percentages to have much significance it becomes clear that the proportion of men dropped fairly sharply during the major panics. In the quieter periods the proportion of male suspects was from twenty per cent to twenty-seven per cent; during the epidemics it dropped to eleven per cent to twelve per cent. When demand rose, the supply was more definitely female. The trend, which is the opposite of what Midelfort found for south-western Germany, is quite marked but it is not clear how it should be interpreted. It looks as though male witches needed time to build up a reputation, and that during a crisis, when an instant supply of witches was required, accusers were more likely to resort to classic stereotypes. It looks also as though convicted witches, under pressure to name accomplices, felt they were more likely to convince if they named other women.

Whatever one may make of this fluctuation, however, it is clear that overall the figure for men is higher than Macfarlane found for Essex. But

Soman, working on appeals to the Parlement of Paris, has found that half the appellants were men. Midelfort for south-western Germany and Monter for Switzerland found the overall proportions similar to those of Scotland. The very low proportion of male witch suspects found in England seems rather unusual. The substantial proportion of male witches in most parts of Europe means that a witch was not defined exclusively in female terms. If she were, the problem would be simpler, but the two principal characteristics of the witch, malice and alleged supernatural power, are human rather than female characteristics, yet at least four out of five persons to whom they are ascribed are women. Witchcraft was not sex-specific but it was sex-related.

There are two distinct problems about this. The first is that of why witchcraft in Europe was so strongly sex-related. The second is what bearing this sex-relatedness had on outbreaks of witch-hunting. It is argued here that the relationship between women and the stereotype of witchcraft is quite direct: witches are women; all women are potential witches. The relationship between witch-hunting and woman hunting, however, is less direct. Witches were hunted in the first place as witches. The total evil which they represented was not actually sex-specific. Indeed the Devil himself was male. Witch-hunting was directed for ideological reasons against the enemies of God, and the fact that eighty per cent or more of these were women was, though not accidental, one degree removed from an attack on women as such.

So far as the woman stereotype is concerned witches were seen to be women long before there was a witch-hunt. The stereotype rests on the twin pillars of the Aristotelean view of women as imperfectly human—a failure of the process of conception—and the Judaeo-Christian view of women as the source of sin and the Fall of Man. Since witchcraft involved a rejection of what are regarded as the noblest human attributes women were the first suspects. Women were intrinsically and innately more prone to malice, sensuality, and evil in general, and were less capable of reasoning than men were, but were nevertheless to be feared by men. There are a number of ingredients in this fear: through their life-bearing and menstruating capacities they are potential owners of strange and dangerous powers. Shuttle and Redgrove quoted Pliny's description of the menstruating woman:

> If they touch any standing corn in the field, it will wither and come to no good ... Look they upon a sword, knife, or any edged tools, be it never so bright, it waxeth duskish, so doth also the lively hue of ivorie. The very bees in the hive die. Iron and steel presently take rust, yea and brasse likewise, with a filthy, strong and poysoned stynke, if they but lay hand thereupon.

They make the point that this presentation of the harmful attributes of the menstruating woman tallies with descriptions of the characteristics of the witch. These characteristics fit all mature women some of the time. The theory is, however, more historically specific than Shuttle and Redgrove suggest. Pliny himself refers throughout the passage not to the effects of contact with the menstruating woman but of contact with the menstrual blood itself (*mulierum efflurio*). The translation quoted is stylistically sixteenth- or seventeenth-century, though its source is not given, and it is this free adaptation which shifts the evil effects of the menstrual fluid to the woman herself. It is not too fanciful to suggest that this shift reflects an intensified misogyny in this period.

Women are feared as a source of disorder in patriarchal society. Not only are menstruating women to be feared. So too are women as child bearers. It is only by exhibiting total control over the lives and bodies of their women that men can know that their children are their own. They are feared too in the sexual act. The fact that they are receptive, not potent, and can receive indefinitely, whether pleasurably or not, has generated the myth of insatiability. Because it was thought that women through these insatiable lusts might either lead men astray or hold them to ridicule for their incapacity, witches were alleged to cause impotence and to satisfy their own lusts at orgies with demons, animals, and such human males as could also be seduced. James VI was giving a version of the prevailing view when he argued as to why women were more disposed to witchcraft than men:

> The reason is easie: for as that sexe is frailer then men is, so is it easier to be intrapped in these grosse snares of the Devill, as was well proved to be true, by the Serpents deceiving of Eve at the beginning, which makes him the homelier with that sex ever since.

It is perhaps worth noting that the stereotype of the witch is the mirror-opposite of the stereotype of the saint. The witch, through a special relationship with the Devil, performs impious miracles; the saint, through a special relationship with God, performs pious miracles. In the peak period for saints (thirteenth to fourteenth centuries) sanctity was sex-related to males in much the same proportion as witchcraft was later to females. The female stereotype is in fact so strong that in some periods the words woman and witch were almost interchangeable. In twelfth-century Russia when the authorities were looking for witches they simply rounded up the female population. In Langedorf in 1492 they charged all but two of the adult female population.

The presence of up to twenty per cent of males in the European witch-hunt has a variety of explanations. Monter found that male witches in his survey tended to predominate in areas which had a history of confusing witchcraft and heresy. Midelfort found that male suspects tended to be accused of other crimes as well. Urban male suspects could be a source of income to the authorities. This has some parallels with Scotland. The agnatic system of marriage prevailing in Scotland in which the wife retained her father's surname makes it difficult to tell when suspects are related by marriage. The Scottish male suspects whose identity has been pursued have so far all turned out to be either husband or brother of a female suspect, a notorious villain as on the continent, or, in a few cases, a solitary cunning man. The difference between Scotland and England in the proportion of males accused can be accounted for by the fact that the English had very few multiple trials in which male relatives might be embroiled, and the fact that in England cunning folk normally escaped being accused of witchcraft.

Although it can be argued that all women were potential witches, in practice certain types of women were selected or selected themselves. In Scotland those accused of witchcraft can be described, though not with precision, under four heads: those that accepted their own reputation and even found ego-enhancement in the description of a 'rank witch' and the power that this gave them in the community; those that had fantasies of the Devil; those who became convinced of their guilt during their inquisition or trial; and those who were quite clear that they were innocent, and who either maintained their innocence to the end or confessed only because of torture or threat of torture. They are all equally interesting in relation to the image of the witch in the community, but those who embraced the role of witch are also interesting in relation to the actual attraction of witchcraft for women.

This attraction of witchcraft is clear when we ask why the witches were drawn from the ranks of the poor. Apart from the obvious fact that it was socially easier to accuse those who were least able to defend themselves witchcraft had a particular attraction for the very poor. It has been pointed out by Thomas that the English witches, who were more clearly than the Scottish ones at the bottom of the stratification ladder, were people who felt themselves to be totally impotent. The normal channels of expression were denied to them, and they could not better their condition. Witchcraft, Thomas suggests, was believed to be a means of bettering one's condition when all else had failed. The fear of witchcraft bestowed power on those believed to be witches. A reputation for witchcraft was one possible way of modifying the behaviour of those more advantageously positioned. More than that, it was a direct way of providing benefits for themselves. Although the Demonic Pact does not loom very large in English witchcraft it is made something of a centrepiece by Thomas in the psychology of the self-conscious witch. Those who committed what is well described as the 'mental crime' of the Demonic Pact (that is those who not only consciously believed that they were committing effective acts of malefice, the social crime, but also that they were able to do this because of their relationship with the Devil in the Demonic Pact) also revealed in their confessions the exact nature of the promises which the Devil had made to them. We have moved a long way in rural pre-industrial England and Scotland from the classic aristocratic pacts of the Dr. Faustus type where great creative gifts are on offer in return for the individual immortal soul of the human concerned. The economic value to the Devil of the soul of a seventeenth-century peasant was not so great. With these people, in whom hope is expressed in the most circumspect of terms, we are in the world of relative deprivation. Seventeenth-century English women at the margins of society did not expect that their soul would qualify them for silk and riches. Instead they said that the Devil promised them mere freedom from the extremes of poverty and starvation. He told them, typically, 'that they should never want'.

The witches of Scotland used exactly the same terminology as those of England, but since the Pact loomed much larger they used it more habitually and more extensively. The Devil's promises were much the same from the time when the pact is first mentioned in Scottish cases until it faded from the collective imagination. John Feane in 1591 related that the Devil had promised him 'that he should never want'. In 1661 it was the same. The Devil promised Margaret Brysone 'That she should never want', Elspeth Blackie, 'that she should want nothing', and likewise Agnes Pegavie and Janet Gibson. Bessie Wilson was told by the Devil, 'thee art a poor puddled (overworked) body. Will thee be my servant and I will give thee abundance and thee sall never want', and Margaret Porteous was told even more enticingly, that 'she should have all the pleasure of the earth'. Thomas also noted that English witches in their exchanges with the Devil were sometimes offered small sums of money which sometimes then turned out to be worthless. One of the witches in this particular group from Dalkeith in 1661, Agnes Pegavie, also mentioned that the Devil, after making these rather limited promises, gave her 12d in silver which she found afterwards to be only a 'sklait stane' [slate stone].

Equally good indicators of their expectations and sense of the economically possible are the more elaborate confessions which include descriptions of witches' meetings. The food and drink said to have been available at these meetings varied a bit; very occasionally it was said to have been unpalatable, usually in circumstances in which the Devil was also perceived as being generally unkind to his servants and beating them up for failures in wickedness. More often it fell within the range of normal peasant fare: oatcakes and ale. Sometimes it was the fare of the landed class: red wine, wheaten cake, and meat.

There are other suggestions than hope of alleviating poverty as to why women might be attracted to witchcraft. The explanation of the Gonja woman in West Africa interviewed by Goody echoes that of the seventeenth-century European manuals. Although some women gave specific motives one answered 'because we are evil'. Goody suggests that while there are a number of contexts in which men may kill there are few in which women may legitimately use aggression even if they are able to. In situations of domestic stress and tension in which men resort to violence, women use witchcraft. The female witches in the seventeenth-century Scottish courts may be the equivalent of the males accused of slaughter and murder. This is to assume what is sometimes forgotten in analyses which involve oppressor and oppressed, that women are not more virtuous than dominate males any more than the poor are more virtuous than dominant landlords. They are merely less powerful. Another angle on the theme of psychological motivation is suggested by Warner in her novel *Lolly Willowes*. Here witchcraft represents adventure and excitement which are normally excluded from the lives of women. Women may turn to cursing to give vent to aggression or exercise power. They may fantasize about the Devil to bring colour to their lives.

The women who sought or involuntarily received the accolade of witch were poor but they were not in Scotland always solitary. The women who were the classic focus of witch accusations were frequently, it turns out, impoverished not because they were widows or single women with no supporters or independent means of livelihood, but were simply married to impoverished men. The figures which we have obtained for marital status are again not very good, but they are better than those for social status. About half of those whose status is recorded were in fact married at the time of their arrest. Some were solitaries, but solitariness as such does not appear to have been an important element in the composition of a Scottish witch. Nor does ugliness appear to have been of very much importance. Macfarlane has drawn attention to the stereotype of the ill-favoured witch, though Thomas discounts its significance. The presence of a popular literature on witchcraft in England which was almost absent in Scotland may have made the factor of personal appearance a more significant one there. The stereotype of the ugly, old woman certainly existed in Scotland, but there is little evidence connecting this stereotype with actual accused witches.

So far as personal as opposed to social characteristics go we are left with the variable of character. This is a notoriously difficult concept to deal with historically. One can sometimes identify character traits in particular individuals. But it is usually hard to say whether these are deviant in terms of standard behaviours of the period. It has been observed by Heine that 'character has lost its narrow psychological significance and has increasingly been endowed with social content and meaning'. It has become associated in role theory with the acting out of socially prescribed roles. We may observe some of the personal characteristics of the witch; we do not know whether they are characteristic of all seventeenth-century Scottish women near the bottom of the socio-economic hierarchy. This problem was recognized at the time, and much exploited by defence lawyers. The successful defender of Elizabeth Bathgate of Eyemouth argued in respect of a witness who claimed to have been bewitched after being shouted at by the accused, that nothing has been 'libelled to procure his distress but a sort of Railing and Flyting (quarrelling) which is common to women when stirred up by their neighbours and especially by websters as common objects to women's spleen'.

When all this is said, however, the essential individual personality trait does seem to have been that of a ready, sharp and angry tongue. The witch had the Scottish female quality of smeddum: spirit, a refusal to be put down, quarrelsomeness. No cursing: no malefice; no witch. The richness of language attributed to witches is considerable. Helen Thomas of Dumfries was accused by Agnes Forsyth in August 1657 of having said, 'Ane ill sight to you all, and ane ill sight to them that is foremost, that is Agnes Forsyth.' In similar vein Elspeth Cursetter of Orkney in May 1629 hoped that 'ill might they all thryve and ill might they speid.' More aggressively, Issobel Grierson was alleged in 1667 to have said 'The faggotis of hell lycht on the, and hellis caldrane may thow seith in.' Agnes Finnie of the Potterrow in Edinburgh, who was accused in 1642, was alleged to have said that 'she should gar the Devil take a bite of the said Bessie Currie', and to John Buchanan at Lambarr, 'John, go away, for as you have begun with witches so you shall end with them.' And her daughter Margaret Robertson, not to be outdone when called by one Andrew Wilson 'ane witches get' (offspring), replied, 'if I be a witches get the Devil rive the Soul out of you before I come again.' Less dramatically, but packed with economic menace, Elizabeth Bathgate told George Sprot, 'for work what you can your teeth shall overgang your hands and ye shall never get your Sundays meat to the fore.'

The witch may have been socially and economically in a dependent position, but the factor which often precipitated accusations was the refusal to bring to this situation the deference and subservience which was deemed appropriate to the role. In her dealings with relative equals too she was likely to be just as aggressive.

It is one thing, however, to produce a static ideal-type of the commonest features of the witch. She is a married middle-aged woman of the lower peasant class and she has a sharp tongue and a filthy temper. The problem as with so many stereotypes is that its explanatory force is limited in that not only did a considerable number of Scottish witches not fit the stereotype; an even larger number of people who did, and who lived in the danger zones for witch accusation and prosecution, were never accused or identified in this way. It is at this point that the labelling theory of sociology may have something to contribute, for labelling theory stresses the dynamic elements in the process of identifying and thereby creating a socially deviant person. There is a continuous interaction between the individual and society. 'At the heart of the labelling approach is an emphasis on *process*; deviance is viewed not as a static entity but rather as a continuously shaped and reshaped *outcome* of dynamic processes of social interaction.' These, it is argued, occur on three levels of social action; collective rule making, interpersonal reactions, and organizational processes.

Without the collective rule making by which witchcraft was reconstructed as an offence against society in 1563 and the nature of it redefined during the 1590–91 treason trials, there could have been no Scottish witch-hunt. It is possible to develop this argument further and say there would have been no demonic witches. There were, essentially, no demonic witches in the Highlands and Islands during the period of the hunt, and none in the rest of Scotland before the late sixteenth century. There were plenty of specialists. There were charmers, healers, sooth-sayers, poisoners, owners of the evil eye, and there were cursers. Many of these, particularly the successful cursers, would have been called witches. The difference between them and the seventeenth-century east-coast and lowland witch was two-fold: in the first place, the meaning of the label changed to something at once more precise and more universally anti-social: the new witch was not only the enemy of the individual or even of the locality; she was the enemy of the total society, of the state, and of God; in the second place the existence of the third level of social action, the new organizational processes, both created a demand for the production of witches and at the same time made the production more rewarding to the community. It was these factors that generated activity on the second level; that of interpersonal relations.

In the process of building up a reputation in a community there was one important element which provides a link between the static description of the social and personality types which were most likely to attract accusations of witchcraft, and the identification of those individuals who actually ended up in the courts. This was the accused's friends, relatives, and associates. There was nothing like a link with someone already suspected to set the labelling process going. We have already mentioned the daughter of Agnes Finnie. The label of 'witches get' was often the first stage. Evil powers were believed to be transmitted from parent to child (a belief which sits uneasily with the demonic pact). Those cases that have come to light tend to be the ones where mother and daughter were executed together (partly because it is otherwise difficult to identify the relationship when the mother retained her own name while passing her husband's on to the daughter). In 1673 in Scalloway in the Shetland Isles, Margaret Byland and her daughter, Suna Voe, were both commissioned for trial. Two years later, also in Shetland, an unnamed old woman and her daughter, Helen Stewart, were executed together. There must have been many more cases where the label was passed on, and the daughter either lived with the label for ever, or was accused formally at a later date. The term 'witch's get' was part of the normal currency of rural life.

Other relationships had their effect as well. In 1629, the sheriff of Haddington was given a commission to try John Carfra, Alison Borthwick, his wife, and Thomas Carfra, his brother. They were also charged with having consulted with Margaret Hamilton and Bernie Carfra, who was, no doubt, another relative, and who had already been burnt for witchcraft. Husband and wife teams were quite common. In West Lothian, in February, 1624, Elspet Paris was tried along with her husband, David Langlandis, and the following month William Falconner, his sister Isobell Falconner, and his wife Marioun Symsoun were tried with a group of other witches. In the same area, in Kirkliston, near Edinburgh, in 1655, William Barton and his wife were strangled and burnt. Mere acquaintanceship however would do perfectly well. When Elspeth Maxwell was tried at Dumfries in 1650 it was alleged that she had been an associate of a woman who had been burnt three years before, and this was a very common item in the depositions. Yet these links and associations are still only an occasional factor in the making of witches. The build up of reputation seems normally to have taken some time, and to have been a dynamic process of social interaction between witch and neighbours with steady mutual reinforcement. When Agnes Finnie, whose cursing powers have already been mentioned, said, 'if I be a witch, you or yours shall have better cause to call me so,' she was giving a classical demonstration of the move from primary to secondary labelling (acceptance of the label and the accompanying role).

Unfortunately we can tell very little about the crucial initial stage in the process of becoming of ill repute, since the depositions usually bring together a set of accusations allegedly made over a period, but certainly gathered together at one point in time. Sometimes the dates of the malefices are identified, but even some of these may have been recalled, or seen in a new light after the reputation had been established. This is another of the areas where an intensive local study, matching early complaints against witches in the Kirk session with cases which later came to the courts, might be particularly illuminating.

The length of time over which a reputation could be built up varied greatly, a factor which lends support to the suggestion that many reputed witches could live with the reputation for a lifetime and die in their beds, even during the seventeenth century. Some witches who were eventually accused had lived with the label long enough to have acquired a title. In Inverkeithing, in 1631, Walker the Witch was active. Janet Taylor, who was banished from Stirling in 1634 was known as the Witch of Monza. Others had names which simply identified a peculiarity which could make them socially marginal. 'Deiff Meg', whose deafness clearly contributed to her reputation, was tried with four others in Berwick in 1629. More mysterious was Archibald Watt in Lanarkshire, who was known as 'Sole the Paitlet, a warlock'.

Others had a long term reputation without acquiring any special title, and with or without such a title many lived with the reputation for years before they were eventually brought to trial. Janet Wright of Niddry, near Edinburgh, was said in 1628 to have been by her own confession for the last eighteen or nineteen years 'a consulter with the devil has resaved his marks, renunced her baptism and givin herselfe over to the devill's service'; and William Crichtoun of Dunfermline in 1648 'being straitlie posed and dealt with by the ministers and watchers, he came to a confession of sundrie things, and that he hade made a paction with the Devill to be his servand 24 yeirs and more since'.

Labelling theory takes us only so far in suggesting why particular individuals who shared the classic characteristics with many others were selected from them for accusation. It explains the build-up of social reinforcement, but, apart from the selection of daughters of witches, not the beginning of the process. In the last resort it can only be said that these individuals were in the wrong place at the wrong time.

When we turn from the selection of the individual back to the classic characteristics, however, there still remains a problem. What is the relationship between the type of person accused of witchcraft and the growth of witchcraft prosecutions? There is some evidence to suggest that the relationship is a direct one. Witch-hunting *is* woman-hunting or at least it is the hunting of women who do not fulfil the male view of how women ought to conduct themselves. An example from anthropology is that of the Nupe in the nineteen twenties. Nadel describes how the women were money lenders and traders and the men of the Nupe were very often in their debt. These women lived independent lives, took lovers, and rarely had children. They challenged the conventional ideal of women as servicing men and children, and it was they who were accused of witchcraft.

We do not at present have enough evidence to say whether the status of women was radically changing in Europe in the fifteenth, sixteenth, and seventeenth centuries in a manner analagous to the more limited and specific case cited by Nadel. It has been argued that the witch-hunt was an attack by the emergent male medical profession on the female healer. There is a certain amount of evidence for this. In Scotland in 1641 in the ratification of the privileges of the Edinburgh chirurgeons it was noted that unqualified females had been practising chirurgy illegitimately in the city, and a number of witchcraft suspects were identified as midwives. The connection, however, is not direct enough. The main usurpation of midwifery by males took place in the eighteenth century after the witch-hunt was over. The objection to female healers was concentrated in the towns where the emergent male professionals had their strength. While witchcraft prosecutions may sometimes have married conveniently with the suppression of female healing, male professionalization of healing really cannot account for the mass of the prosecutions.

A different argument is that capitalizing agriculture reduced the role of women to that of a mere producer of children rather than a participant in peasant production. Anyone pursuing this argument however is likely to get into difficulties. Not enough is known to support or, what is worse, to make suspect, any large scale theory on the economic history of women. In particular the timing of that major change seems to have varied greatly in different parts of Europe, and in most areas took place after the end of the witch-hunt. The suggestion that this period saw an increase in the number of unsupported women is, again, difficult to substantiate, and the witch-hunt was not primarily directed against them.

If we turn to the sphere of ideology the case for witch-hunting being seen as a woman-hunt is more convincing. The stereotype of the witch was not that of the child-woman; it was that of the adult, independent woman. The religion of the Reformation and the Counter Reformation demanded that women for the first time became fully responsible for their own souls. Indeed preachers went out of their way to refer to 'men and women' in their sermons. The popularization of religion, however, took away from women with one hand what it gave to them with the other, for the particular form of religion was strongly patriarchal. The ritual and moral inferiority of women was preached along with their new personal responsibility. The status of women became ambiguous under the terms of the new ideology.

Witchcraft as a choice was only possible for women who had free will and personal responsibility attributed to them. This represented a considerable change in the status of women in Scotland at least. Up to the time of the secularization of the crime of witchcraft their misdemeanours had been the responsibility of husbands and fathers and their punishments the whippings thought appropriate to children. As witches they became adult criminals acting in a manner for which their husbands could not be deemed responsible. The pursuit of witches could therefore be seen as a rearguard action against the emergence of women as independent adults. The women who were accused were those who challenged the patriarchal view of the ideal woman. They were accused not only by men but also by other women because women who conformed to the male image of them felt threatened by any identification with those who did not.

This explanation is the most plausible of those which identify witch-hunting as woman-hunting because unlike the other explanations the timing seems right. Nevertheless while witch-hunting and woman-hunting are closely connected they cannot be completely identified as one and the same phenomenon. The relationship is at one degree removed. The demand for ideological conformity was simply a much wider one than that aspect of it that concerned the status of women. The present discussion over the direct connection between the alleged uniqueness of English witchcraft and the allegedly unique status of women in England is therefore misconceived. The pursuit of witches was an end in itself and was directly related to the necessity of enforcing moral and theological conformity. The fact that a high proportion of those selected in this context as deviants were women was indirectly related to this central purpose.

Bibliography

NORMAN COHN, *Europe's Inner Demons: An Enquiry Inspired by the Great Witch-Hunt* (1975).

GUSTAV HENNINGSEN, *The Witch's Advocate: Basque Witchcraft and the Spanish Inquisition (1609–1614)* (1980).

RICHARD KIECKHEFER, *European Witch Trials: Their Foundation in Popular and Learned Culture, 1300–1500* (1976).

ALAN C. KORS and EDWARD PETERS, *Witchcraft in Europe 1100–1700: A Documentary History* (1979).

A. D. J. MACFARLANE, *Witchcraft in Tudor and Stuart England* (1970).

H. C. ERIK MIDELFORT, *Witchhunting in Southwestern Germany* (1972).

E. WILLIAM MONTER, *European Witchcraft* (1969).

KEITH THOMAS, *Religion and the Decline of Magic* (1971).

English Family Life

KEITH WRIGHTSON

In sixteenth- and seventeenth-century England men married in their late twenties, women in their mid-twenties. This late marriage pattern, common to much of Europe since the fifteenth century reflected the fact that the English considered marriage a privilege, not a right. It was to be undertaken at an age when a couple could support themselves as a new, independent nuclear family.

It has been argued that the English family evolved through three distinct affective stages: from the emotionally cold and paternalistic family of the fifteenth and sixteenth centuries, to the emotionally warmer and less authoritarian family of the late sixteenth and seventeenth centuries, to the "modern" loving, companionable family of the late seventeenth and eighteenth centuries. In each successive stage greater freedom is said to have been accorded wives and children, as wives came to share greater power and authority with their husbands and children gained the right not merely to veto a distasteful arranged marriage, but even to take the initiative in choosing a life mate.

According to Wrightson, this is a false picture of the English family. It is true that parental influence could be very strong among families of the urban elite and the leading gentry, where financial empires were at stake in marriage, although even here children still could take the initiative in choosing a mate. There are no discernible stages of increasingly loving marriages or of decreasing control over wives and children. Children of the lower classes had the greatest degree of freedom because they left home early in search of employment and had far less contact with their parents and kin. Children of the "middling sort" had freedom too, although they valued parental consent and consultation in matters of the heart. In English society as a whole, freedom of choice and even romance played key roles in marriage.

Reprinted with the permission of Rutgers University Press from *English Society 1580–1680* by Keith Wrightson. Copyright © 1982 by Keith Wrightson.

Marriage and Marital Opportunity

Marriage, according to William Perkins, was 'the lawful conjunction of two married persons; that is one man and one woman into one flesh'. It was an honourable condition, 'ordained of God in paradise' for four principal ends: the procreation of children, the perpetuation of the church, the containment of sexual desire and finally for the mutual assistance and comfort afforded one another by the married couple. For all these reasons, marriage might be considered 'the foundation and seminary of all other sorts and kinds of life in the commonwealth and in the church'.

In ecclesiastical law three forms of 'lawful conjunction' were recognized. The first and only fully satisfactory form of marriage was an ecclesiastically solemnized union, performed in the face of the church after the calling of the banns, or after the procurement of a licence exempting the parties concerned from this formality. Unlike the continental churches, however, the church of England continued to recognize as legally binding two other forms of valid, though irregular marriage. A promise to marry expressed in words of the present tense in the presence of witnesses constituted a binding marriage, as also did a promise made in words of the future tense, provided that it was followed by sexual union. Consent to a marriage could be given by any person over the age of 7, while marriage could be sexually consummated by boys at 14 and girls at 12 years of age. Persons already married, or parties to binding contracts, could not, of course, contract a valid marriage, while marriages between people falling within specified degrees of consanguinity and affinity were prohibited. For the rest, as Perkins put it, marriage was 'free to all orders and sorts of men without exception'.

All this seems clear enough. Yet marriage in England was in reality far more complex and far less homogeneous than was allowed for by the conventional definitions of the moralists or the neat prescriptions of the law. Marriage was indeed a fundamental institution, but marital behaviour was far from uniform. In the relative ability of English people to marry, in the age at which they did so, in the manner in which spouses were chosen and in the criteria upon which choice was based, English marital practice reflected less a uniform code of behaviour than the varying needs and opportunities of people of different social position.

Marriage was 'free to all', yet not everyone married. Perhaps 10 per cent or more of women who achieved adulthood passed their lives unwed. Marriage could be contracted and consummated by any boy or girl who had attained the age of consent. Yet the English married late. The average age of first marriage for men in the period 1600–49 was 29.1 at Aldenham in Hertfordshire, 29.2 at Bottesford in Leicestershire, 27.4 at Colyton in Devon, 27.8 at Hawkshead in Lancashire and 26.7 at Willingham in

Cambridgeshire, while the average ages for women in the same parishes over the same period were respectively 25.3, 25.9, 27.3, 24.8 and 24.8. Within this pattern of comparatively late marriage, variations were observable between the age at first marriage of people of different occupation and social status. Though this issue demands much more thorough investigation than it has received hitherto, it seems clear that in general members of the aristocracy and upper gentry married younger than their social inferiors, while among the common people, wage-earning artisans and labourers married somewhat earlier than landholding yeomen and husbandmen.

In the broad characteristics of their marital behaviour, the English were firmly within what has been dubbed the 'European marriage pattern', the combination of relatively high age at first marriage for women together with the celibacy of a substantial proportion of women which has been historically confined to those parts of Europe west of a line extending from the eastern Baltic to the Adriatic. The origins of this pattern remain obscure. Its demographic implications, however, are plain enough, for such behaviour clearly placed a considerable degree of restraint upon the reproductive capacity of the population. Given an age of menarche in the mid to late teens, women spent much of their potentially fertile lives unwed, while a sizeable minority never enjoyed the opportunity to bear legitimate children. It is doubtful, however, that contemporaries considered the matter in quite this way. As E. A. Wrigley has argued, the demographic rationality of the system was largely unconscious. It was maintained less by a calculating awareness of its demographic effects than by adherence to 'unconsciously rational' social conventions surrounding the question of the qualifications deemed necessary for marriage. These factors underpinned the marital and familial system of the period and shaped the everyday reality of marital opportunity. By far the most significant of them was the fact that young people, and in particular young men, were considered ready for marriage only at the point when they were capable of establishing and maintaining an independent nuclear family.

As we have seen, the vast majority of the households which constituted the basic units of England's local communities consisted of a simple nuclear family, with or without resident servants. A minority of extended family households, including co-resident kin, existed, usually as the product of special circumstances, but only rarely did newly married couples share the same roof as the parents of one of the partners. Such a situation existed in some aristocratic families in which children had married very young. It might also be found lower in the social scale as a temporary expedient or as the outcome of parental retirement and inheritance. But unlike some European peasant societies, arrangements of this kind were not the norm in England. Indeed a strong cultural prejudice existed to discourage such living arrangements. 'When thou art married,' William Whately advised prospective bridegrooms, 'if it may be, live of thyself with thy wife, in a family of thine own.' Two masters and two dames under one roof led in his opinion to 'unquietness of all parties', especially among the common people, and was a situation to be avoided whenever possible. Young couples should start married life under their own roof and standing on their own feet; and usually they did.

Given these circumstances, marriage needed to be deferred well past the legal or physiological minimum age until the point at which a sufficient degree of independence could be secured. This might sometimes involve waiting for parental death and inheritance, though this would not usually appear to have been the case. More often the prospective couple seem to have reached the necessary stage by a mixture of personal saving, perhaps putting aside their wages as servants, and parental assistance. Among property-owning families, ranging from prosperous husbandmen and craftsmen to the aristocracy, parents assisted the couple by providing their marriage portions of goods or money, though among the common people these were rarely large enough to do more than contribute to the setting up of the new family. Where no such assistance could be expected, couples had to provide for themselves and among the labouring poor the chance of regular employment and a cottage for rent may have been the prime consideration, rather than the wherewithal to obtain land or stock a shop, though even so they would need some savings to provide their basic household goods. Such preparations took time and they also involved both partners, except in those cases where a substantial dowry was available for a girl at an early age. The extent to which these realities pervaded popular expectations is revealed in many instances, ranging from paternal advice, such as that given by James Bankes to his son not to marry until he was 'sofecant of abelete to manetane yor estaitt', to the answers given by humbler people questioned by the church courts about their marital intentions. Thus in 1584 Edward Thornton of St Nicholas's parish, Oxford, told the Archdeacon that he had promised to marry Bridget Fayreberne 'uppon condicon that she wold stay untill he cold provide him of an howse', while John King of Dunstow declared his intention of marrying Ursula Saule 'at Michaelmas next, when he hath provided a living for her'. Providing that house and that living might come sooner or later for differently placed individuals, and it is for this reason that variations in average marriage age can be observed between different social groups and areas with different economic structures and differentials in economic, and therefore marital, opportunities. Whatever the particular case, the general situation was that marriage and family formation in this society was a privilege rather than a right. It was something to which all might aspire, yet which some would never achieve, while those who succeeded would do so at a relatively high age—indeed a very high age when we consider the comparatively short life expectation of the period. Economic independence, then, was the principal prerequisite for marriage, and differentials in attaining that independence deeply affected the marital opportunities of both individuals and social

The Selection of Marriage Partners

The selection of marriage partners is an issue of central importance, in part because it might affect the age of marriage and marital opportunity, but much more because the manner in which spouses were chosen might establish the whole character of marriage in this period and deeply influence the quality of relationships within each newly formed nuclear family. Indeed, for Lawrence Stone it is in this matter that the shifts in familial behaviour which he discerns in the later sixteenth and seventeenth centuries can be most clearly perceived. In the 'low-keyed, unemotional, authoritarian' 'Open Lineage Family' of the sixteenth century, Stone argues, 'marriages were arranged by parents and kin for economic and social reasons, with minimal consultation of the children'. In the last decades of the sixteenth century and the early seventeenth century, however, a new form of family emerged which was both more closed to the influence of the extended kin and emotionally warmer in its internal relations. In this 'Restricted, Patriarchal, Nuclear Family', parental power over the choice of marriage partners remained absolute, but a right of veto was conceded to the young parties to a match. This situation persisted until the later seventeenth and eighteenth centuries, when a double shift took place. Parental choice moderated by the child's veto gave place to choice by the child subject to parental consent. Economic and social interest gave way to personal affection and companionship as the principal criteria of choice. These changes heralded the emergence of a third form of family, the 'Closed Domesticated Nuclear Family', in which greater autonomy was allowed to wives and children and in which strong affective ties developed. These successive developments in affective relations within the English family amounted in Stone's view to 'the most important change in *mentalité* to have occurred in the Early Modern period, indeed possibly in the last thousand years of western history' for they laid the foundations of the family as we now know it. In that momentous process the pace was set by the upper and middling ranks of English society, from which change spread downwards by a process of 'stratified diffusion' and the seventeenth century saw the most critical breakthrough from distance, deference and patriarchy in family relations to the rise of 'affective individualism'.

Stone's powerful arguments and adventurous hypotheses constitute the most ambitious attempt yet undertaken to interpret the development of the English family over time. Nevertheless they are seriously open to question in both their characterization of family life in later sixteenth and seventeenth-century England and in their account of change within this period.

Although he is undoubtedly aware of the major distinctions which may have existed between social groups in England, Stone has devoted insufficient care to the exploration of the experience of the mass of the population. As a result his interpretation has been elaborated on the basis of the historical experience of the aristocracy, upper gentry and urban plutocracy with which he is primarily concerned and retains at its heart the tacit assumption that analytical categories derived from their experience can somehow be extended to encapsulate phases in the history of the English family. This is a mistaken assumption. For whatever their historical prominence, the familial behaviour of the English élite was very far from representative of that of their countrymen. Nor can shifts in their behaviour be asserted to have been significant advances in familial development when set in the full context of the already established and persisting characteristics of the family life of their social inferiors. Both points can be well illustrated by considering in turn the issues so central to Stone's argument: control of the choice of marriage partner and the criteria upon which selection was based.

Matchmaking

There can be no doubt that in the opinion of the moralistic authors of the 'conduct books' it was one of the chief duties of parents to 'bestow' their children in marriage. This is not necessarily to say, however, that they advocated parentally arranged marriages. Indeed, the frequent employment of the term 'arranged' by historians, with its implication of unilateral parental choice, may be said to have blunted our perception of this problem. Perkins, for example, was much more subtle. He maintained that the parental duty might be discharged *either* by providing matches for children *or* by advising children on the suitability of prospective spouses. Elsewhere, he made it clear that even where parents took the initiative in proposing a match, they should never force the marriage of a child. Bishop Barnes of Durham was prepared to go so far in his injunctions of 1577 as to lay down that 'yonge folkes by the lawes of God may not marry without consent of their parents', but he did not say that parents should initiate or dominate matchmaking. There was a degree of flexibility, even of ambivalence in the prescriptions of these churchmen which has sometimes been overlooked by historians. To neglect it is to do them less than justice, for as J. L. Flandrin has shown, it was their allowance of a greater degree of freedom in this matter to the young which most distinguished English moralists of the period from their French counterparts.

When we turn to the evidence of actual behaviour, it rapidly becomes clear that the initiative in the making of a match might come from either parent or child, much as Perkins suggested. What mattered was less the identity of the initiating party than the securing of the consent or 'goodwill' of all those concerned. Within this broad framework, however, the degree of parental restraint placed upon children could vary, and where such variation is observable it sprang most commonly from the differences which existed in the needs and interests of families of different rank.

Among the aristocracy, the urban élite and leading gentry families, as Stone has demonstrated, marriage was a matter of too great a significance, both in the property transactions which it involved and in the system of familial alliances which it cemented, to be left to the discretion of the young people concerned. By the later sixteenth and early seventeenth centuries both child marriages and crudely arranged matches which took no account of the opinions of the prospective spouses were largely things of the past. Nonetheless, parents commonly initiated matches and parental influence on the choice of a spouse frequently remained decisive, even though the formal consent of the parties to the match was sought. In some cases such consent was willingly given, as when John Bruen of Bruen Stapleford in Cheshire returned home from Oxford in 1579 to find that his father proposed matching him with the daughter of the Mayor of Chester. John 'did entertain the motion with such respect and reverence as became an obedient son' and gave his assent once he was assured of the affection and willingness of the young woman herself. At other times the consent of the child might be a mere formality, exacted under pressure. Margaret Russell assented to a marriage with the Earl of Cumberland more 'on the ground of common good than any particular liking' and commenced a married life which brought her little happiness. The Yorkshire heiress Margaret Dakins, who was far more fortunate in her husbands, was nonetheless essentially a passive participant in the matchmaking of her elders. Between 1589, when she was 18 years old, and 1596 she was married three times. On each occasion the match to which she assented was proposed and forwarded by others, notably her former guardian the Earl of Huntingdon, though Lord Burghley and Lady Russell took a hand in her third and final marriage to Sir Thomas Hoby.

Such circumstances may well have been the norm in the highest ranks of English society. It is, nonetheless, important to appreciate that even for the children of the social élite, marital initiative did not lie solely in the hands of parents. Among the aristocracy, parental domination of matchmaking may have been stronger in the marriages of daughters than was the case in the matching of sons, while younger children were generally accorded greater freedom of choice than was the case in the marriages of heirs and heiresses. Again there is evidence that in the lower ranks of the gentry where less depended upon a particular match, courtship could become a more personal affair. Anthony Fletcher finds that among the leading families of the Sussex gentry the marriages of heirs and heiresses were usually 'arranged', subject to the assent of the young couple to the match. Courtship among the lesser gentry, however, was a more personal, intimate and romantic process, with the initiative in proposing a match often lying with the couple concerned. G. E. Mingay takes the view that 'among the propertied classes generally the individual's interest in marriage was subordinated to the interest of the family'. Yet he too allows that the child might well initiate matters and subsequently seek formal parental consent and backing in the furtherance of a match. Thus in 1649 Bridget Oglander sought to marry a young gentleman of whom her father Sir John initially disapproved. Yet upon 'her importunity' and her declared resolve 'to have him whatsoever became of her', he gave way and consented to the match.

The question of the frequency with which children took the initiative at this level of society may have depended very much upon the relative freedom accorded to the young in their contacts with other young eligibles and the consequent opportunities afforded them to initiate their own courtships. In this regard it is perhaps of some significance that foreign visitors to England were often struck by what they saw as the surprising degree of freedom allowed to English women. Even among the social élite, women were not cloistered and a fair degree of unsupervised contact was permitted between young people of both sexes. The round of gentry social life in the countryside afforded opportunities enough for the formation of marital preferences among the young which might later form the basis of formal parental overtures. Again, among gentry families participating in the developing London 'season', young people did a good deal of visiting without adult supervision, though girls were commonly accompanied by a chaperone of their own age. As a result, courtships were often initiated well before parental involvement was sought and the making of 'secret vows' was not uncommon. Of course the situation must have varied a good deal from family to family and young men certainly had greater scope for independent action in courtship than was the case with their sisters. Nevertheless, it is clear that even in the higher social ranks where families had most to lose by an imprudent match, the situation was far from monolithic when it came to the selection of future spouses. The 'arranged' match, initiated by parents, which left the child with nothing more than a right of veto was undoubtedly a reality throughout our period. But even among the social élite it presents a picture which is too stark unless accompanied by considerable qualification. The key to the situation may well have been less parental 'arrangement', with or without subsequent consultation of the child, than the seizing of the initiative by one of the parties concerned and the subsequent securing of the consent of the other.

If the choice of marriage partners among the aristocracy, gentry and urban élite was a considerably more complex matter than has been alleged, there is no doubt whatever that lower in the social scale the initiative in selecting a spouse already lay with the young people concerned. However ambivalent the behaviour of their betters, the vast majority of the English people awaited no fundamental transition of their marital norms. Adolescents of both sexes enjoyed considerably more freedom from parental tutelage than was usual even in the most generous of gentry families by virtue of the simple fact that they usually left home to enter service in their early teens. Moreover, if, as was common enough, they had already lost one or both parents, they were very rarely subject to the constraints of wardship. Among fellow servants, at hiring fairs, in the alehouses, at village dancings and at church, they were free to make their own moves in courtship. Such inhibitions as they experienced in the matter were the outcome not of their parents' marital strategies but of their common recognition of the desirability of gaining consent to, or at least approval of, their matches from a variety of interested parties. Even so, the significance of such endorsement varied a good deal between social groups, and between the sexes.

Among the propertied 'middling sort' parental consent could be a matter of considerable practical importance to the future well-being of a couple, if only by virtue of its bearing on parental willingness to transfer property to children at their marriages in the form of dowries and marriage portions. That such arrangements were the norm among small property holders is clear from the evidence of their wills, some of them specifying that married children had already received their 'portion' from the testator, while most allocated goods and cash to be given to unmarried children at the time of their weddings. Indeed, consent to their children's marriages was sufficiently important to some testators for them to attach strings to bequests made to unmarried children. William Ingleby, a yeoman of Great Haswell in County Durham, for example, made a will in 1632 leaving each of his daughters a substantial portion of both land and money if they married with the consent of their mother and two uncles. If they did not marry with such consent, however, they were still to receive the money, and in some cases even more money, but they were not to receive land.

As this example indicates, the right of parents to approve their children's matches was valued, but not insisted upon. Sons in particular were relatively free to go their own way as is made clear by the testimony of three well-known clerical diarists or autobiographers of the period. Adam Martindale, son of a yeoman, described how in the 1630s two of his three brothers not only chose for themselves but braved and faced down parental disapproval of their choices, while a generation later Martindale's son made his own match in London. Ralph Josselin's courtship began when his 'eye fixed with love' upon Jane Constable in church in October 1639. By January 1640 he had proposed to her and they had given one another a 'mutual promise'. They then sought consent to the match before proceeding to a formal contract in September 1640. Such niceties, however, were ignored by their son John, who in due course married without his parents' knowledge. Henry Newcome, whose parents were dead, chose his own bride in the 1640s, though he later admitted that he had 'sinned in that I took not that advice I should have took of my friends in it'. His sons Daniel and Harry both married without either their father's consent or even his knowledge and though this grieved him, he accepted it.

The relative freedom with which young men pursued prospective brides is amply illustrated by the diary of Roger Lowe, an apprentice mercer.

Lowe's remarkable diary provides us with the viewpoint of a young man on the lookout for a bride for some five years from the time in 1663 when he recorded 'this was the first night that ever I stayed up a wooing ere in my life' until his eventual marriage to Emm Potter in 1668. Lowe's courtships generally revolved around such activities as walking in the fields, visiting nearby towns, drinking in the alehouses, or attending weddings and funerals with other young people of Ashton, while he formally courted one of his sweethearts by 'sitting up' with her in her father's parlour. He first approached his future wife Emm Potter in an alehouse during Ashton wakes, though he had spotted her before. They courted on and off for four years, falling out on numerous occasions and once needing a mediator to effect a reconciliation, until in 1668 they 'consummated [their] grande designe of marriage'. In all of this there is no reference to formal seeking of parental consent, though Roger often drank with men of the Potter family and may well have had their tacit approval.

There is little in Roger Lowe's account of his courtships which would be unfamiliar to a modern youth. It does, however, represent a male viewpoint and that of a young man whose parents appear to have been dead. Other examples suggest that while young men were free enough to make their approaches to a girl, young women were rather more constrained by the need to secure the advice and consent of parents and 'friends' (who might or might not include kin). To this extent their independence of action might be considerably more circumscribed. Henry Newcome, for example, recorded the case of a Manchester girl thrown into deep depression when initially crossed in her desire to marry a suitor turned away by her family. Adam Martindale went so far as to remove his daughter Elizabeth from service when she fell for a fellow servant who was 'an unsuitable match for her'. He feared that the girl was being used and tried to compensate by providing 'a farre more lovely match', though understandably the girl refused this parental initiative and Martindale, to his credit, did not press the matter. The marital hopes of daughters could thus be effectively thwarted by failure to gain parental approval for their matches. Nevertheless some young women could show considerable independence in their matchmaking. Katherine Marshall, a Newcastle girl, forced the issue of her marriage to Christopher Robson, a tanner's son, by herself approaching his father, stating her intention, and proceeding to settle the terms of the match. Or again Mary Cooling, daughter of a London linen draper, went so far as to get contracted to a young man of her father's trade and then won her father over, though he was 'much discontented that they had proceeded so far without his consent and blamed his daughter muche'.

It is perhaps significant that Francis Cooling's discontent was not with his daughter's taking of the initiative in finding a suitor but rather with the fact that she had gone so far before informing him and winning his approval. This provides a clue to the probable norm for young women. Ralph Josselin was a father who was prepared to defend the theoretical right of the patriarchal father to choose his children's spouses, but in fact it is clear that in the courtships of his daughters, the initiative usually belonged to the young couple. Suitors presented themselves and sought his approval to woo formally, while once matters were under way the girls themselves were allowed the final and absolute say over the completion of the match. The implication is that the girl concerned had already given the young man sufficient encouragement to make his formal approach but that matters would not proceed further without parental approval. This situation is clearly exemplified by one Somerset case, which may well represent the normal circumstances of a match at this social level. The girl in question informed her father that one Walter Woodrow wished to marry her and requested permission for him to call at the house. Her father replied 'that if she liked the man and was disposed to bestow herself in marriage he should be welcome to his house'. The next Sunday Walter appeared, together with his sister and in the course of a meal asked the father for his goodwill, receiving the reply 'that they should have his goodwill if he and the maid were so agreed'. That accomplished, they settled down to some hard bargaining over the dowry, with the father cannily using Walter's declared affection for his daughter as a lever to reduce his demands in the matter of the marriage portion!

Parental consent, then, was desirable if the match was to be amicably concluded and a satisfactory dowry negotiated. The role of 'friends' is more obscure. It might often have been the case that close relatives such as uncles, or else family friends, acted in the place of a dead parent, perhaps in accordance with the guardianship provisions sometimes to be found in paternal wills. Certainly church court records provide many instances of the influence of friends at work, as when John Stacie of Sandon in Oxfordshire reported to an inquisitive Archdeacon in 1584 'that theare hath beene good will and motion of marriage betweene this respondent and Jane Banister but noe perfett contract because the frendes of this respondent and the same Jane have not yet concluded'. In matches between individuals for whom lack of property rendered the question of settling dowries and portions irrelevant, the advice of personal friends among their peers may also have been of some importance, the more so if they were servants living at some distance from their parishes of origin. At this social level, however, it would appear that in the final analysis agreement to marry was very much a matter for the couple themselves, for the match had little direct bearing on anyone else. Parents, who as likely as not were geographically distant, seem to have been informed largely as a courtesy, and indeed were often presented with a *fait accompli*. Thus, husbandmen's daughters living as servants in London and marrying by licence rarely expected a portion from their parents and many stated explicitly that they had none and that they were therefore at their own disposition. One Hertfordshire girl might speak for many. She asserted 'that her said father doth not as yet knowe of this intended marriage but when he shall understand thereof he will be verie glad of it because it is for her preferment (her father being but a poore man and having more children is not able to give mutch at marriage with her)'.

It seems reasonable to conclude that among the greater part of the common people marriage partners were freely chosen, subject to the advice of friends and a sense of obligation to consult or subsequently inform parents if they were alive and within reach. Among the very poor, however, a further form of consent might be required in the form of the willingness or otherwise of the parish authorities to countenance a marriage which might threaten a future charge on the poor rates. They had no legal right to do this, but they could make their opposition effective by informal means such as withholding rights to settlement, housing or employment. In 1618 Anthony Addames of Stockton in Worcestershire 'fortuned to marry with an honest young woman', but the parishioners were 'not willing he should bring her into the parish saying they would breed up a charge among them'. He had to find a cottage elsewhere while continuing to earn his living in Stockton. Or again the case of the Rector of North Ockendon in Essex could be cited, who, when asked to read the banns for the marriage of a poor cripple, departed from the set form and 'signified to the parishe that they would marry and goe a begging together and asked if any knewe lawfull cause why they might not doe so'. Such instances are far from rare and merely illustrate a practice described by Carew Reynel in 1674 as 'an ill custom in many country parishes'. They serve as a sombre reminder that if the marriages of the labouring poor in some respects appeared free, that freedom could be severely qualified. It was at best a freedom accompanied by a marked insecurity in the actual completion of proposed marriages, as will be further illustrated when we come to consider the problem of illegitimacy.

Having reviewed the evidence relating to the selection of marriage partners at different social levels, it would appear that interpretations based upon the conventional dichotomies of arranged as against free matches, and parental choice as against self-determination by the child, do less than justice to the complexities of reality. There is little evidence of cold-bloodedly 'arranged' matches outside the very highest ranks of society. The likelihood of parents initiating or proposing a match was not uniform even at the highest social levels, while even when they did so, children usually seem to have enjoyed a right of refusal. Below the level of the aristocracy, upper gentry and urban plutocracy, the actual initiative usually seems to have lain with the young people, subject to the advice and consent of parents, friends and even principal neighbours. The significance of that advice and consent would appear to have varied according to both sex and wealth, but on the whole it seems rare for it to have been withheld when a couple were determined to marry.

Finally, it can be observed that the period does not appear to have witnessed significant changes in these matters, except possibly among the aristocracy, upper gentry and leaders of urban society. Professor Stone's interpretation of change may well be sound for the highest social groups, with which he is primarily concerned and of which his knowledge is unrivalled. But neither his characterization of conventional practice, nor his account of change seem adequate as descriptions of the experience of the greater part of the English people. There was no single 'English' norm in this matter, but rather a persisting variety of coexisting practices, a range of experience broad enough to call into question the validity of any single evolutionary schema. The position as regards the selection of marriage partners, then, seems established. It remains to explore the question of the criteria upon which that selection was based.

The Criteria of a Match

Marriage in the sixteenth and seventeenth centuries was usually for life. Given that fact, great care needed to be exercised in the choosing of a partner and this was a matter to which the writers of the conduct books devoted considerable attention. William Perkins distinguished the criteria of selection into two basic categories. First, there were what he called 'essential' qualities: that the couple be of different sex; that there be no impediment of consanguinity according to the forbidden degrees recognized by the Anglican church and displayed in most parish churches; that neither partner be already married; that both be free from contagious diseases and of 'ability and fitness for procreation'. Matches which contravened these requirements were in Perkins's view prohibited. All other matches were, by the same token, permitted, but this was not to say that they were to be preferred. On the contrary, Perkins also offered a second guide to the criteria for the optimum match, with a list of what he called 'accidental' qualities. Like most other writers on this subject he recommended the seeking of a degree of 'parity or equality' between partners in age, condition (by which he clearly meant social status and wealth), 'public honesty and credit' and, of course, 'Christian religion'. Some, though not many, moralists also added that personal compatibility was desirable.

Parity of age, status, wealth, reputation and religion, together with personal attraction, made the perfect match. All this seems straightforward enough. Yet in reality the relative significance given to these various considerations might vary considerably. Among the aristocracy, for example, Stone argues that although other factors were given some consideration, 'marriage was not a personal union for the satisfaction of psychological and physiological needs; it was an institutional device to ensure the perpetuation of the family and its property'. Consequently the greatest attention was ...paid to the financial benefits of marriage' and 'wealth was the most important single consideration' even in the early seventeenth century when children were being accorded greater consideration in matchmaking—indeed it may have actually grown in importance at a time of financial stringency for many aristocratic families.

The aristocracy may not have been alone in this, for historians of the gentry seem largely agreed that throughout the landed class as a whole considerations of property and the status which it conferred weighed very heavily as compared with other criteria of a good match. In Sussex in the later sixteenth and seventeenth centuries 'continuity in the estate and advancement of the family were the gentry's prime considerations in marrying their children'. In Yorkshire the gentry sought above all partners of comparable wealth and status. For the upper gentry Verney family, marriage was 'a relationship characterised by social and economic rather than romantic considerations' and 'the emotional and physical needs of the couple were peripheral considerations'. All in all, as Mingay has argued, the safeguarding of property, the assertion and advancement of status and the forging of alliances between families figured most prominently in the preferred matches of England's landlords.

This situation must not, however, be exaggerated into assertions that the gentry and aristocracy showed a monomaniacal concern with questions of property, for this is demonstrably untrue. The ideal match was rarely conceived of solely in terms of economic gain, but comprehended a range of desirable traits and was not uninfluenced by romantic expectations fuelled by the romantic literature of the day. Nevertheless financial considerations were inevitably of major significance to those whose maintenance of their élite position depended above all upon the consolidation of their landed wealth, and this fact gave to their matchmaking a strongly commercial flavour. Moreover, among families in which the initial proposal of a match often came from the parents, their recognized duty to make the best bargain they could for their children weighed heavily, and even children free to choose for themselves had commonly been brought up to share their parents' attitudes. To judge by his letters, Thomas Hoby was genuinely delighted with his bride's personal qualities, but he had commenced his suit before he had even met her at the instigation of a mother anxious to secure him the hand of a well-connected heiress. When James Bankes advised his children on the choice of wives, he hoped that they would choose girls 'that feareth God and are obedeant to the prince's lawes and of good parentage borne', but his most specific recommendation was that they seek out heiresses, for this was 'the sonist way to increas yor howsus, as mane wyes men have done'. His preferences were clear enough.

Lower in the social scale, among the propertied 'middling sort' of town and country, with whom the initiative in proposing a match more often lay with the couple themselves, property remained an important consideration. Naturally enough a realistic attitude had to be taken to the question of how the new couple would live and both they and their families could bargain with a will to secure an equitable or advantageous property settlement.

Sometimes this could weigh very heavily indeed, as is suggested by the fact that, in a sample of first marriages by London craftsmen and tradesmen, Dr Elliott found that no fewer than 25 per cent married widows, thereby ensuring a good start for themselves. Or again, such cases as that of a Cumbrian husbandman who broke off an otherwise acceptable match when he 'did demaund in mariadg hir fathers farmehold, which he refusyd to graunt' are not unusual. Among small property holders, however, it would appear that a rough parity of wealth was more a necessary than a sufficient condition of a good match and that other considerations were at least equally important, if not more so.

Personal or family reputation could be significant, as when the mother of Ralph Wilson of Durham expressed her dislike of his courtship of Isobel Thompson on the grounds that Isobel's father had been accused of theft and that Thompson's 'evill gotten good' should not be conjoined to the Wilsons' 'well gotten good'. Roger Lowe discovered that Emm Potter's unwonted coldness towards him at one stage of their courtship was the result of her having heard a false rumour that his mother had borne him out of wedlock. Religion could also play its part. The puritan Martindale family were horrified when Hugh Martindale 'growing wild and unmanageable, did to all our griefes marrie a papist'. Hugh's action showed that it could be done, but he had to remove to Ireland and had few further dealings with his family. They were much happier when his younger brother Henry chose 'an holy young woman of pious parentage'.

Such qualities of good reputation, religious conformity and an acceptable portion might, of course, be found in many prospective partners, for the pool of eligibles for people of this rank was considerably larger than among their social superiors. What often seems to have clinched the matter and determined the particular choice of where to woo was personal attraction, even full-blown romantic love. A degree of personal and physical compatibility might be implied by the fact that marriage partners were so often close in age, but yet stronger evidence exists in some abundance. Richard Gough's account of the families of Myddle, for example, frequently alleges love as the basis of good marriages, while for explicit demonstration of its influence we can do no better than to point to Roger Lowe's own account of his courtships. Lowe's breast undoubtedly swelled with romantic impulses of just the kind so evident in contemporary love lyrics and romantic ballads. His courtship of Mary Naylor reached a high pitch of drama when the two vowed 'to live privately and love firmly' and 'ingaged to be faithfull till death' and it is hardly surprising that Lowe was somewhat nonplussed when Mary's affection gradually cooled. Mary's friends did not approve and although Roger had some hopes of winning her father's support, it seems likely that the apprentice mercer was considered beneath her. He did better with Emm Potter, whom he approached after conceiving 'a most ardent affection' and tortured by jealousy at seeing her in company with a rival at the alehouse. She turned out to be an excellent match for him in every way.

Love, or at least personal attraction, could be the keystone in the structure of a good match in the eyes of the young people concerned, if not in those of their parents and friends. Nonetheless it is clear that it was not regarded as something which should sweep aside other considerations. The force of physical and personal attraction was recognized, but in conjunction with, rather than in opposition to, other aspects of parity in a good match. There was more to marriage, as the contemporary proverb put it, than 'four bare legs in a bed'. Henry Newcome clearly married for love, but admitted that he had gone about it in a 'rash and inconsiderate' way and thought 'God might have made it sad to me and done me no wrong; but he very mercifully turned it into good for me'. The selfsame attitude, together with a splendid review of the qualities expected in a match, can be found in Adam Martindale's account of his eldest brother's marriage. Martindale's father, a prosperous yeoman—craftsman, was not 'so severe' as to expect a fully equal fortune from his son's bride, but hoped for a prudent settlement and was well pleased when a match got under way to a young woman 'of suitable years' and good character who had a portion of £140. To the grief of the family, the son suddenly threw over the match when he fell in love with 'a young, wild, airy girle betweene fifteen and sixteen yeares of age; an huge lover and frequenter of wakes, greenes and merrie-nights where musick and dancing abounded. And as for her portion it was onely forty pounds'. The family urgently tried to dissuade him, but 'say and do what we could, he was uncounsellable, have her he would' and at last he won his father's grudging consent and married her in 1632. "Tis true,' Martindale crustily admitted, 'she proved above all just expectation not onely civill, but religious and an exceeding good wife... but that was the effect of God's great and undeserved goodnesse, not any prudent choice of his, and the smallnesse of her portion was a great prejudice to our family.' Love, in short, was a good thing in its place, but one should love prudently.

One of the most significant elements in Martindale's rendering of this story is his comment that, although only 10 years of age at the time, even he was conscious of 'the difference of these two matches'. Children learned early to share the values underlying the complexities of matchmaking and to judge accordingly, of their own volition. Thus Ralph Josselin had nothing to fear when his daughter Jane was courted by Jonathan Woodthorp, 'a sober hopefull man his estate about £500', Jane liked him too, it was an excellent match and matters proceeded swiftly. Josselin was grieved when his daughter Mary decided against Mr Rhea, a neighbouring clergyman, but had to recognize the force of her list of 'exceptions' to the match: 'his age being 14 years older shee might bee left a widow with children'; 'his estate being not suitable to her porcon'; and finally, 'he seemed to her not loving'. This was hard-headed judgement, balancing practical and emotional considerations, with perhaps a final sway towards the latter, as is suggested by Josselin's reflection, 'I could not desire it when shee said it would make both their lives miserable.'

Among the landed élite, a variety of criteria governed matchmaking, but considerations of rank and estate necessarily took first place in determining eligibles. For the 'middling sort' parity of wealth and status was an important matter, but their less elevated social position, together with the greater freedom allowed young people in seeking prospective partners, gave enhanced significance to the element of personal attraction, which could, in the final analysis, prove decisive. Of the propertyless we know much less. For many of them, as was recognized by Richard Baxter and others, the decision to leave service and marry, might mean a marked deterioration in their standards of living. It is to be expected, then, that a girl might favour a man who looked likely to be a good provider, while men would look for girls who could run a careful household and contribute to family income. Friends, as we know, would advise on the reputation and likeliness of prospective partners, but they had little occasion to worry about wealth. 'They value not portions,' wrote Carew Reynel of the poor, 'so [long as] they are able to serve, work, or any way earn their living.' Instead, it seems probable that more attention was paid to personal qualities and individual attraction. Given the material disincentives to marriage, it seems likely that its principal attractions were the desire for independence and for the companionship and emotional and physical gratification which spouses could find in one another, together with the satisfaction of raising their own families.

This situation is borne out by the evidence of illegitimacy cases which provide one of our few opportunities to investigate the courtships of the poor. Illegitimacy was comparatively infrequent in this period as compared with its incidence in the early nineteenth century, though it was more common in England than in seventeenth-century France. For a brief period at the turn of the sixteenth and seventeenth centuries, the illegitimacy ratio calculated by demographers (the proportion illegitimate of all known births) reached a temporary peak. In the main, however, the average parish saw an irregular trickle of illegitimate births. The circumstances underlying these births cannot always be explored, but where additional evidence is available, in the form of court proceedings, the results are highly revealing.

To the religious moralists of the period, illegitimacy was merely a sub-category of the general and perennial problem of 'whoredom', a sexual laxity allegedly produced by a population which regarded sexual transgressions as merely the 'tricke of youth'. In fact the problem was far more complex. English villages did indeed have individuals who regularly bore or fathered bastard children, and even illegitimacy-prone families, though whether they represented a deviant sub-culture or simply a vulnerable, exploited, even demoralized, element among the rural poor, is a matter open to debate. Again, a number of illegitimate births resulted from the classical circumstances of the sexual exploitation by masters or gentlemen of servants or social infferiors. For the most part, however, illegitimate children appear to have been conceived by couples of similar social position, very commonly servants in husbandry, who intended to marry, yet whose marital plans were dislocated.

The association of illegitimacy with marital opportunity is strongly suggested by the fact that close studies of particular parishes have revealed that the age of women bearing their first illegitimate child was almost identical to the average age at which more fortunate women bore their first child in wedlock. It is confirmed by the evidence of depositions and examinations in the courts. In 1602, for example, Grace Burles of Terling in Essex bore a child to Edward Shipman. It was declared in court that Shipman 'mindeth shortlye to marye her' but that he had been 'prest for a soldier'. In this case, as in quite a number of others, the intended wedding did eventually take place. Other girls were less fortunate. Mary Foster and Edward Alexander were fellow servants in the Essex town of Witham and planned to marry. However, they broke up. He had moved on to service elsewhere by the time she discovered her pregnancy. Or again, Alice Jackson was a Worcestershire servant girl who had 'behaved herself very honestly' until in 1617 she was courted by a fellow servant who 'did make great protestations of love ... promising by many great vows to marry her'. When she was pregnant he proved less ardent and fled the county.

In cases such as that of Alice Jackson the girl was doubtless deliberately deceived by her suitor. But many others show clearly that a genuine 'motion of marriage' was underway: friends had been consulted, parents informed, even banns called, before circumstances frustrated wedding. Whatever the particular case, these tragic stories reveal a great deal about courtship in the lower reaches of the social scale. They confirm the relative freedom of choice of the young people concerned—and the dangers which that freedom entailed. They further make clear the significance of personal and sexual attraction in courtship. Again, they reveal how the restraints upon sexual activity imposed by the realities of a precontraceptive age in which sexual activity led almost inevitably to conception, crumbled once marriage was in sight. In this, the parents of illegitimate children were not unusual. Demographers tracing brides to the birth of their first child in parish registers have revealed that English brides were very commonly pregnant in this period—generally between 10 per cent and 30 per cent in different parishes. In some areas this may have been the result of a formally recognized right to commence sexual intercourse after betrothal—for in canon law a public promise to marry followed by sexual intercourse constituted a valid, though irregular marriage. The church, however, frowned upon this practice and the ecclesiastical courts punished it with public penance. What seems most likely is that popular attitudes, though far from loose, were simply more flexible than those of society's professional moralists. When marriage was, or seemed, assured, couples whose attraction for one another was a prime reason for their courtship, commenced sexual relations. Indeed, it may even be possible that for those in service, whose marriage plans were well advanced, but who had good reason to stay under their masters' roofs where they were better housed and fed and could save money, pregnancy was the signal to actually leave service, get married and set up together. Whatever the case, it is clear that bridal pregnancy was widely tolerated.

Some girls, however, became not pregnant brides, but the mothers of bastards. There tolerance ended. They were likely to be brought before the church courts, questioned and ordered to do penance in public. If there was a danger that their children would fall upon the parish poor rates, they might be brought before the Justices of the Peace, and perhaps committed to a house of correction. Dismissal of pregnant girls from service and callous hustling from parish to parish of those whose place of settlement was questionable were not uncommon. Finally, in childbed they found themselves surrounded by midwives charged to refuse to assist them until they declared, often with the accompaniment of bloodcurdling oaths—'that the childe should sticke to me as the barke to the tree' being but one example—the name of the father of the child. It is scarcely surprising that some girls faced with these terrors concealed their pregnancies, bore their children alone and then exposed, abandoned or deliberately killed them.

Such harrying of these wretched girls—for it was they who suffered, the father rarely receiving worse punishment than penance and a maintenance order if he could be found—might be seen as a necessary defence of the implicit principle of England's marriage pattern: that children should not be born save within economically independent nuclear families. Be that as it may, the whole question of illegitimacy reveals something of the human cost of that system. For illegitimacy may provide a fair indication of the disjunction which could exist between marital hopes and marital opportunities. Marriage and family formation might be free to all, as Perkins opined, but they were not easily attainable by all. For the poor, and in particular for poor women, marriage was not secure until it was accomplished. Accordingly many, perhaps most, were cautious, like the Somerset servant who told her eager lover, 'No, truly you shall not lye with me till we be married, for you see how many do falsify their promises . . . . I am but a servant and if your friends should not consent to our marriage we are undone.' Others gambled: some won, some lost.

Conclusion

To draw to a conclusion, it is evident that in the selection of marriage partners the notion of parity in a match, so much stressed by contemporary moralists, did indeed deeply influence choice, whether that choice lay entirely with the individuals concerned, or was subject to the direction or consent of others. Of the various criteria in which parity was sought, however, there were variations in the relative weight placed upon particular factors. At the top of the social scale, personal attraction might be outweighed—*if* the conflict arose—by material and social considerations. As the social scale was descended, personal preference became subject to less severe constraints. It would be unwise, however, to argue too rigid a distinction between material, social and emotional factors in matchmaking, or to rush too readily to conclusions about shifts from one principal criterion to another over time. They ran together. It is clear that a degree of economic calculation was always necessary and its prominence in the marriages of the propertied, highlighted as it is in the surviving documentation, for they had most reason to set it down carefully, should not be too bluntly interpreted. Much may have gone unrecorded. Again, an apparently greater emphasis on emotional considerations towards the end of our period might be in part an illusion created by better documentation in the form of diaries and letters. In any case, it must be remembered that emotions are not generated in a social vacuum. They could be aroused where an individual had, as it were, *learned* to love, in accordance with the values of his or her day and station in life. However analytically distinguishable they might appear material, social and emotional elements in marriage were in practice hopelessly intermingled.

The result, as might be expected, was a great deal of demonstrable 'homogamy' in marriage: like married like. All of the principal social groups were essentially endogamous, marrying within their own ranks. Where they made exogamous marriages, often in the case of younger children, they rarely strayed far in terms of social and economic parity, forming instead what might be called clusters of intermarrying social groups. The peerage might intermarry to some degree with the upper gentry, with wealthy merchants and lawyers, the gentry with mercantile, legal and clerical families, and sometimes with wealthy yeomen. So we might continue down the social scale. As in social distance, so also in physical distance, for the geography of marriage partner selection reflected the spatial dimensions of the world within which families of different rank moved. For the aristocrats and greater gentry who visited court or took part in the London season, marriage alliances might be national in scope. The gentry married for the most part within the gentle society of their counties, though the proportion of gentry marriages thus circumscribed could vary with the size and geographical location of a county, from the 82 per cent of large, peninsular Kent, to the 37 per cent of small, easily accessible Hertfordshire. Humbler people married within the social area in which they moved for various purposes—generally within their parishes of residence (as distinct from their parishes of birth) and neighbouring settlements.

In marriage, as in other respects, social groups frayed and became blurred at the edges and marriage might promote a degree of both social and physical mobility. This should not be exaggerated however. In general marriage confirmed social distinctions, and the process of family formation both faithfully reflected, and served to perpetuate the social order: its privileges, its obligations, its opportunities, its constraints and its injustices.

Bibliography

LUTZ K. BERKNER, "Recent Research on the History of the Family in Western Europe," *Journal of Marriage and the Family* 35 (1973): 395–405.

CHRISTIANE KLAPISCH-ZUBER, *Women, Family, and Ritual in Renaissance Italy* (1985).

JEAN-LOUIS FLANDRIN, *Families in Former Times: Kinship, Household and Sexuality* (1979).

DAVID HUNT, *Parents and Children in History: The Psychology of Family Life in Early Modern France* (1970).

ALAN MACFARLANE, *The Family Life of Ralph Josselin* (1970).

MICHAEL MITTERAUER and REINHARD SIEDER, *The European Family: Patriarchy to Partnership from the Middle Ages to the Present* (1982).

GERALD SOLIDAY, et. al., eds., *History of Family and Kinship: An International Bibliography* (1980).

LAWRENCE STONE, *The Family, Sex and Marriage in England 1500–1800* (1979).